BEIRUT RULES

BEIRUT RULES

THE MURDER OF A CIA STATION
CHIEF AND HEZBOLLAH'S WAR AGAINST
AMERICA AND THE WEST

FRED BURTON
and SAMUEL M. KATZ

BERKLEY
New York

BERKLEY
An imprint of Penguin Random House LLC
375 Hudson Street, New York, New York 10014

Copyright © 2018 by Fred Burton and Samuel M. Katz
Penguin Random House supports copyright. Copyright fuels creativity, encourages
diverse voices, promotes free speech, and creates a vibrant culture. Thank you for buying
an authorized edition of this book and for complying with copyright laws by not
reproducing, scanning, or distributing any part of it in any form without permission.
You are supporting writers and allowing Penguin Random House to continue to
publish books for every reader.

BERKLEY is a registered trademark and the B colophon
is a trademark of Penguin Random House LLC.

Library of Congress Cataloging-in-Publication Data

Names: Burton, Fred, 1958– author. | Katz, Samuel M., 1963–
Title: Beirut rules: the murder of a CIA station chief and Hezbollah's war
against America and the West / Fred Burton and Samuel M. Katz.
Description: First edition. | New York, New York: BERKLEY,
an imprint of Penguin Random House, 2018.
Identifiers: LCCN 2018010839 | ISBN 9781101987469 (hardcover) |
ISBN 9781101987483 (ebook)
Subjects: LCSH: Terrorism—Lebanon. | Buckley, William Francis,
1928–1985—Kidnapping, 1984. | Buckley, William Francis, 1928–1985—Death
and burial. | United States. Central Intelligence Agency. | Hizballah (Lebanon)
Classification: LCC HV6433.L4 B87 2018 | DDC 956.05—dc23
LC record available at https://lccn.loc.gov/2018010839

First Edition: October 2018

Printed in the United States of America
1   3   5   7   9   10   8   6   4   2

Jacket photo: U.S. Embassy in Beirut after bombing: Bettmann/Getty Images
Jacket design by Alana Colucci

While the authors have made every effort to provide accurate telephone numbers,
Internet addresses and other contact information at the time of publication,
neither the publisher nor the authors assume any responsibility for errors, or for changes
that occur after publication. Further, publisher does not have any control over and
does not assume any responsibility for author or third-party websites or their content.

GLOSSARY

A'man Israel Defense Forces intelligence branch

Black September Organization A covert arm of Yasir Arafat's Fatah group responsible for spectacular attacks. The group was formed in 1970 following the Jordanian Civil War and targeted Jordanian, Israeli, and Jewish interests. The group was responsible for the Munich Olympics Massacre in 1972 and the murder of two US diplomats in the Sudan in 1973.

CIA Central Intelligence Agency

DCM Deputy Chief of Mission

DIA Defense Intelligence Agency

DSS Diplomatic Security Service (agency re-created to meet the new global terrorist threat following the bombings of the US embassies in Beirut and Kuwait)

FBI Federal Bureau of Investigation

Force 17 Yasir Arafat's Praetorian Guard and the Fatah's special operations commando group

GDGS General Directorate of General Security

HLTF Hostage Location Task Force, a joint US intelligence and law enforcement working group to investigate the American and Western hostages seized by Hezbollah

IDF Israel Defense Forces

IED improvised explosive device

KGB Soviet intelligence service

LAF Lebanese Armed Forces

Lebanese Forces The Maronite Christian militia of the Phalange (Kata'eb) Party

MI5 Great Britain's domestic counterintelligence and counterterrorist agency

MI6 Great Britain's foreign espionage service, also known as the Secret Intelligence Service

MNF The Multinational Force assigned to Lebanon to supervise the withdrawal of Palestinian fighters first from Beirut and then back to the city following the Sabra and Shatila massacres. The force consisted of French Foreign Legionnaires and paratroopers, US marines, and Italian and British troops.

Mossad Israel's foreign intelligence and espionage service

NSA National Security Agency

PFLP Popular Front for the Liberation of Palestine

PFLP-GC Popular Front for the Liberation of Palestine–General Command

PLO Palestine Liberation Organization

Quds Force The special operations terrorist branch of the Iranian Islamic Revolutionary Guard Corps

RSO regional security officer, the head State Department security officer at an overseas embassy or consulate

Shin Bet Hebrew abbreviation for the Sherut Ha'Bitachon Ha'Klali, or General Security Service

SIDE Argentina's Secretaría de Inteligencia de Estado (intelligence service)

SY The US State Department security arm until 1985, originally created in 1916

Tevel The Mossad division responsible for liaisons with friendly intelligence services

TDY temporary duty assignment

BEIRUT RULES

PROLOGUE

LOCALS REFERRED TO it as "thunder and lightning": thuds of distant artillery, followed by explosive flashes of fire and destruction. Most nights were like this. An orchestra of serenading car horns would be punctuated by the chatter of heavy machine guns, and sporadically interrupted by the sonic booms of fighter jets. But tonight had been quiet. The ambulance crews, who normally shuffled from one kill zone to another, passed the hours playing backgammon while sipping from cups of bitter Turkish coffee. The all-night falafel stands did brisk business on nights when people didn't die.[1]

The American was up long before dawn, his alarm clock ringing at 5:30 sharp. He showered and ate a breakfast of fruit and cereal, then dressed as a light breeze rolled into his one-bedroom flat. Every night he picked out his clothes for the next day and hung them on a closet door—an old habit from his many years of military service. He always chose a dark suit and a conservative tie. In a country of rolled-up sleeves and safari jackets, he would never permit himself to display such casual abandon.

At 6:45 he walked out of his apartment for the final time. A dim forty-watt bulb illuminated the corridor. When it flickered, the light created menacing shadows. He turned the dead bolt key twice to the right to lock the steel door and then headed toward the elevator and stairs. He had been warned against the lift; he took the stairs.

The stairwell smelled of yesterday's garbage and the morning's cooking. He clutched the banister as he negotiated the narrow stairway toward the ground floor. Arabic music blared from kitchen radios. The sounds of children crying and pots and pans banging together assaulted his ears. As he passed the second floor, he could hear a couple arguing. They always were.

His building was a white concrete concoction that combined the regal thumbprint of the French colonial presence with modern expediency. The neighborhood was one of the upper-crust sections of the war-torn city, but few people wore a suit and tie in the morning. When he walked out the door, dressed like an insurance salesman, he looked very much like a European baron stepping into a Byzantine world.

Across the street, the old man who lived on the second floor watched as the American left for work. A pensioner, the old man was always at his window at that hour, tending to the plants he kept in clay window boxes. He didn't know the American by name; the two had never spoken to each other. But surviving in Beirut meant that you knew as much as you could about your neighbors.

The pensioner knew that the American worked ████████. The American's vehicle, a gray 1983 Renault Turbo, was parked in an outdoor lot adjacent to his apartment building. He looked around, making sure he wasn't being followed, before opening the car's driver's-side door. Satisfied that the landscape was safe, he tossed his black attaché case onto the passenger seat. Inside, along with a newspaper, a cassette recorder, and some index cards, was a ██████████ nine-millimeter semiautomatic pistol. He knew there was little such a weapon could do in Beirut. Compared to the ordnance that the militiamen carried openly, a pistol was like a Swiss Army knife. Still, in a city ruled by the AK-47, it was good to be armed.

He checked the rearview mirror before placing the key in the ignition. The first beads of sweat had already appeared on his brow. His drive to work would take about two minutes, even in the frenetic traffic. He could have walked to work, of course, but it was too dangerous— assassins were everywhere. He signaled a left turn.

Close by, two black Mercedes sedans waited, engines running. Inside were four bearded men dressed in army field jackets. When the American turned onto the street, two of the men pulled masks down over their faces and readied the AK-47 assault rifles resting on their laps.

The first Mercedes overtook the Renault on the driver's side, speeding past and then blocking it off at an angle. The second Mercedes swung in from behind and blocked off any chance of escape; the American lived in a cul-de-sac and was now completely closed in. He glanced at his attaché case. With AK-47s held at the ready, the masked men approached the car fast and determined, barking orders in Arabic. They had rehearsed this before.

It took all of a handful of seconds. In the blink of an eye, and with the barrel end of a Kalashnikov to the temple, the American vanished into a Mercedes, which made a right turn at the intersection and sped off to the south, toward the labyrinth of the Shiite slums. From his second-story window, the old pensioner had witnessed the entire abduction. The Renault was still in the street, engine running, driver's door open wide. In his living room he picked up the phone, checked for a dial tone, and called the operator, demanding to be connected to the American Embassy.

The old man was eventually patched through by a Marine gunnery sergeant and reached Jeremy Zeikel, the State Department deputy regional security officer, who took the call at 7:15.[2] Zeikel's heart sank when he heard the old man's story. William Francis Buckley, the CIA Chief of Station in Beirut, one of the most important and dangerous American intelligence postings in the world, had been abducted.

BOOK ONE

THUNDER AND LIGHTNING

1

THE PREAMBLE TO DISASTER

The shahada [martyrs] are the candles of society.
They burn themselves out and illuminate society.

If they do not shed their light, no organization can
shine.

—Iranian Ayatollah Morteza Mutaharri[1]

THE ISRAELI MILITARY headquarters in Tyre was a seven-story high-rise situated inland from the sea, and the site from which most of Israel's security and intelligence operations in southern Lebanon were controlled. The building was the administrative nerve center for Israel Defense Forces units operating in the area, and it housed two companies of Border Guard policemen as well. The Border Guards, Israel's paramilitary police arm, were in Lebanon to maintain law and order in the towns and villages of southern Lebanon. The policemen represented the mosaic of Israeli society and included Jews, Druzes, Bedouins, and Circassians. Many of the Border Guard personnel spoke Arabic, and many had spent careers policing a hostile population in the West Bank and the Gaza Strip. The building was more than just a military garrison. The Tyre facility was the Israeli intelligence hub in southern Lebanon. A'man, Israeli military intelligence, ran many of its human intelligence (HUMINT) operations. Handlers from the ultra-secretive Unit 504, the military intelligence unit that ran agents behind enemy lines, used the regional headquarters as a safe and comfortable location where assets could be debriefed and espionage endeavors coordinated.

The Shin Bet, Israel's domestic counterintelligence and counterterrorist agency, was also based inside the building. The Shin Bet was responsible for all counterterrorist investigations in southern Lebanon and for rounding up the last vestiges of Arafat's legions in southern Lebanon.

Business was booming for the Shin Bet. The basement holding cells were full of Lebanese and Palestinian men suspected of belonging to one popular front or another. The detained were often a remarkable source of information.

Many of the men serving inside the headquarters building were reservists—from Israel's citizen army, doing their annual thirty-day stint of call-up service. The reservists were a mixture of middle-aged men happy to have a few weeks away from wives and kids, and men young enough still to be in school, still trying to save enough to get married, and still holding on to dreams of lives out of uniform. Captain Dubi Eichnold, the commander of the Military Police investigative unit at the base, was preparing a small party for some of the officers that evening, November 11, 1982; it was to be a celebration to mark the halfway point of the reservist stint for him and his team.[2] A small feast, including snacks and soft drinks, was being readied for the party. Everyone was itching to go home.

Captain Eichnold was already sitting with a few of his fellow officers in the mess hall at 7:00 that Thursday morning. The officers were in full kit, battle rattle at their sides. An electric space heater failed to mitigate the bone-numbing cold and the officers wore their olive green winter parkas as they guzzled cup after cup of army-issue rocket-fuel-grade coffee. Upstairs, the Border Guard's morning garrison was getting ready for morning roll call. Downstairs, the prisoners in the holding cell had already eaten. Some were in the middle of morning prayers.

The military policeman standing guard outside next to a small embankment of sand bags could hear the clanking of metal forks scraping plastic plates and he smelled the eggs cooking. He hoped that someone would bring him a cup of coffee soon. A white Peugeot 504 appeared from the west, speeding toward the headquarters building. The rain had intensified. The sky darkened.

AT 7:15 ON the morning of November 11, 1982, the Israeli military headquarters in Tyre collapsed in a blinding flash of light, the seven stories reduced to rubble beneath a rising plume of black smoke.[3] At the time, more than a hundred Israeli soldiers, policemen, and spies had been inside the building; many of those not killed instantly became trapped inside tiny air pockets, their bodies bloodied by the explosion and debris. The Israel Defense Forces had little experience in pulling survivors out of a building hit by a catastrophic blast—there had never been a need; a terrorist might throw a hand grenade into a crowded cinema, but he didn't demolish a building. Rescues were done painstakingly by hand. Combat engineers were flown in, and helicopters shuttled the wounded to awaiting trauma care thirty-five miles away at the Rambam Medical Center in Haifa. The dead were removed, the shattered bodies covered with coarse, olive-colored blankets. Rain created puddles that formed cement-like patches of caked-together blood and dust. By nightfall, the magnitude of the calamity was apparent: sixty-seven IDF and Border Guard personnel were dead, along with nine Shin Bet agents and fifteen local detainees. November 11, 1982, was one of the deadliest days in Israeli military history.

Few understood it yet, but the attack represented a new struggle for Lebanon's soul—and one that would be pursued with a new tactic, suicide bombing. The man responsible for the destruction wasn't even a man yet. Ahmed Qasir was a fifteen-year-old boy when he drove the explosive-laden Peugeot 504 that destroyed the Israeli military head-quarters. He had lived an unexceptional existence in the Shiite village of Dir Qanoun an-Nahr, located in the foothills ten miles north of Tyre—a setting more akin to the last century but beset by the horrors of twentieth-century destruction. He attended the local mosque, but left school after the fifth grade to work at his father's vegetable stall in the village market.[4] According to reports, Ahmed was never a shooter— someone who took up arms against the Palestinians or the Israelis—but he did associate with local young men who carried their AK-47s openly, and he began to embrace the Khomeini-brand fanaticism-laced Shiite Islam.

Young and impressionable, Ahmed Qasir was obviously infatuated by the powerful and indomitable men in camouflage fatigues and Ray-Ban sunglasses. He felt a sense of pride and privilege being in their company, and a sense of duty when they asked him to carry out small-scale reconnaissance sorties in and around Beirut, smuggling arma-ments and monitoring the movements of Israeli patrols. Qasir soon began to borrow his father's truck for daylong assignments. He never had a driver's license and his feet barely reached the pedals. His father never knew where he was going, or what he was doing. On the morning of November 11, Qasir disappeared—never to be heard from again. His parents were certain that he had been kidnapped—possibly killed—by Christian militiamen.[5]

Qasir's martyrdom should have been celebrated in Dir Qanoun an-Nahr. The old women of the village would have brought pots of food; the men, including village elders and the local imam, would have been huddled in the living room, drinking sweet tea with mint leaves and chain-smoking cigarettes while proudly gazing at a framed portrait of Ahmed Qasir displayed on a chair with red velvet cushions. But the notion of the boy's martyrdom had yet to be publicly revealed. The men who sent Ahmed Qasir on his mission, the men who purchased the Peugeot and wired it with explosives—including several members of Syrian intelligence and a few senior men who spoke Farsi—were able to convince the teenager that by blowing himself up, he would be re-enacting the sacrifice of Imam Hussein, the core of the Shiite faith, and that as a result he would secure his spot in paradise.[6] Yet the facilitators of this new brand of terror wanted to keep the Tyre operation a secret. Ahmed's parents wouldn't learn of their son's fate until two and a half years later, when a shrine to the martyr was built in Ba'albek.[7] They did not know what would have motivated the youngster to perpetrate such an act.

Tehran's emissaries tasked with introducing to Lebanon the cult of the suicide bomber, a tactic that had become a common weapon in the Iran-Iraq War, were determined to redraw the map of the Middle East, a region engulfed in the flames of fundamentalist Islamic fervor. Ahmed Qasir would be the first of what was to be a legion of martyrs fighting both Israel and the United States. November 11, 1982, would be known as the Day of Martyrs.[8]

THERE WEREN'T SUPPOSED to be any martyrs, of course. Israel had never intended to be at war with Lebanon's Shiites. On the morning of June 6, 1982, five months before the attack on the HQ in Tyre, sixty thousand Israeli troops crossed into Lebanon in a three-pronged invasion to remove the Palestinian terrorist infrastructure that threatened the residents of northern Israel. The objective of the incursion, claimed Israeli defense minister Ariel Sharon, was to push Palestinian forces twenty-five miles to the north of the Israeli frontier. The Israeli operation was dubbed "Peace for Galilee."

The war had erupted like many Middle Eastern bloodbaths—with a spark: pro-Iraqi terrorists from the Abu Nidal faction shot and almost killed Shlomo Argov, the Israeli ambassador to London. In retaliation, Israeli warplanes attacked Palestinian terror targets throughout Lebanon; the Palestinians then launched rocket barrages against the towns and cities of Israel's north. The war to secure Galilee commenced.

The assassination attempt on the ambassador in London was nothing more than a pretext. For years Israeli intelligence had been working with Lebanon's Maronite Christians to initiate a new regime in Beirut that would rid the country of the Palestinian terrorist presence and launch a new Jewish-Christian alliance to reshape the Middle East for generations. And now, with bullets fired by an Abu Nidal gunman, Israel had the instigation it needed to invade Lebanon.

Full-scale wars in the Middle East never ended the way the politicians and generals intended. Syria's president Hafez al-Assad considered Lebanon to be a province of Greater Syria, and had permanently garrisoned thirty thousand of his troops inside the country. During Lebanon's civil war, the Syrians had protected their interests with brutal and cunning force, intervening to help the Palestinians and the Christians when Syrian concerns were threatened. Now war in Lebanon meant that Israel and Syria would engage in open conflict.

The campaign was hard fought and bloody, yet the Israel Defense Forces advanced quickly and decisively. Palestinian forces that stood to fight were overwhelmed by the mechanized might of the Israeli military; Syrian forces—even with the latest and greatest armor, missile systems, and aircraft that the Soviet Union could provide—proved no match for Israel's technological superiority. The Syrians were humbled in open warfare, and the Israelis reached the outskirts of Beirut in a matter of weeks. In the attempt to rid the country once and for all of the armed Palestinian presence, the IDF laid siege to Beirut, trapping some fourteen thousand of Arafat's men in the western—Muslim—half of the city. American-led international diplomacy worked out a deal wherein international peacekeepers—Italian naval infantrymen, French paratroopers, and US marines—secured the evacuation of Palestinian forces from Beirut. The heavily armed Palestinians were forced to board ships destined for Algeria, Tunisia, Iraq, Yemen, and the Sudan. Israeli officers looked on from the hills above the city.

On August 23, 1982, Bashir Gemayel, the military commander and political leader of the Lebanese Phalange Party, was elected the country's new president. Even though he was the only candidate, Gemayel's election gave many in the West high hopes for Lebanon. Perhaps, American and European diplomats wished, the Lebanese people would be offered a brief respite from the endless cycle of violence. The international peacekeepers withdrew from Beirut on September 10, having completed their mission efficiently, and without incident or casualty.

Hope can be a fleeting currency in the Middle East—especially in a nation repeatedly torn apart by religious enmity and outside manipulation. No plan, no matter how cunning or virtuous, ever works in the Middle East without an insurmountable toll of bodies and generations' worth of misery that would have to be avenged. Israel's grand scheme for its troubled northern neighbor soon imploded with extensive—and unstoppable—collateral damage.

ON SEPTEMBER 14, the Lebanese president-elect was in the middle of an address to followers in his Beirut headquarters when the room—along with much of the building—was decimated by nearly a quarter ton of high explosives. Three weeks after his election, Bashir Gemayel was dead. A Christian operative working at the behest of Syrian intelligence agents had placed the bomb in an apartment directly above the central meeting hall where Gemayel was speaking. The blast, as one Christian woman would later state, did not kill a man but murdered a country.[9]

Rumors soon spread that the Palestinians had been responsible for Gemayel's murder, and rumors were enough to sound calls for vengeance. Retribution came fast and with untold carnage. Christian militiamen from Beirut and southern Lebanon converged on the Sabra and Shatila Palestinian refugee camps and in two days of butchery killed between 760 and 3,500 men, women, and children in cold blood. The international peacekeepers, still on ships off the Lebanese coast, were forced to return to Beirut, this time to protect the Palestinian and Muslim residents and to try—impossibly—to initiate law and order in a city that had seen neither since civil war had erupted seven years earlier. US marines were responsible for the southern tip of Beirut, including the international airport and the Shiite slums; the French and Italians patrolled West Beirut. Israeli forces, faced with the onset of an inescapable quagmire, withdrew to the hills outside the city.

For several years the United States had feared that the situation in Lebanon could easily escalate into a full-scale Arab-Israeli war. War had nearly broken out in April 1981 when the Syrian military introduced Soviet-made surface-to-air batteries into Lebanon's Beka'a Valley; only tense shuttle diplomacy, spearheaded by US special envoy Philip Habib, stopped Israel from responding militarily. When Israel invaded Lebanon in June 1982, the Reagan administration was divided on the war. Some, such as Secretary of State Alexander Haig, the former commander of NATO, understood that the conflict in Lebanon was an extension of the Cold War—Israel was a client of the West, while both Syria and Palestine were allies of the Warsaw Pact—and he supported Israel's push to eradicate the Palestinian terrorist base in Lebanon, as well as to rid the area of the Syrian military. Others, like Vice President George H. W. Bush and Secretary of Defense Caspar Weinberger, pressed President Reagan to force the Israelis to halt their offensive and to impose sanctions if they didn't withdraw immediately.[10]

Israeli forces did halt their advance at the outskirts of West Beirut, but ultimately they entered the city in the wake of Bashir Gemayel's assassination. Following the murder, President Reagan issued this statement: "The news of the cowardly assassination of Bashir Gemayel, President-elect of Lebanon, is a shock to the American people and to civilized men and women everywhere. This promising young leader had brought the light of hope to Lebanon. We condemn the perpetrators of this heinous crime against Lebanon and against the cause of peace in the Middle East." Reagan went on to add, "The tragedy will be all the greater if men of good will in Lebanon and in countries friendly to Lebanon permit disorder to continue in this war-torn country. This must not happen. The United States Government stands by Lebanon with its full support in this hour of need."[11]

Gemyael wasn't just another high-ranking casualty in Lebanon's bloody war of competing beliefs. And his death wasn't just a loss to stability in Lebanon. In fact, Bashir Gemayel was a highly placed—and highly paid—asset for the Central Intelligence Agency.[12] The CIA had countless assets in Lebanon, ranging from Palestinian terror chieftain Ali Hassan Salameh,[13] the head of Black September and the architect of the Munich Olympics Massacre (his crypt, or code name, was MJ/TRUST2), to lower-level Lebanese Christians, Sunnis, Druzes, and Palestinians, as well as Armenians, Kurds, and members of every other tribe and religious faction that made up the fractured glass that was Lebanese society. But with Gemayel's election, the president of Lebanon was to be Langley's man in the country.

Some men had altruistic motivations for working with the CIA; some had in mind a ticket to the States and an escape from the hell of post–civil war Lebanon. Men such as Gemayel and Salameh, however, were in it for the money—millions of dollars, according to reports. The money flowed from CIA Station ███████, America's eyes and ears inside a colonial-style building in West Beirut that had taken shell and sniper fire during the civil war.

The man in charge was thirty-eight-year-old CIA Chief of Station Kenneth Eugene Haas—the top-ranking American spy in Lebanon. A native of Akron, Ohio, Haas had earned his PhD at Syracuse University before enlisting in the ranks of the CIA, where he became a distinguished operative, serving tours in Bangladesh, Iran, and Oman, among many other places.[14] Bespectacled, with a neatly trimmed mustache and rugged Midwestern looks, Haas landed in Beirut as the capital, already reduced to rubble by civil war, was under relentless Israeli siege, hammered around the clock by artillery, air, and naval bombardment. It wasn't a normal tour by any stretch, and Haas' top asset, an invaluable source of intelligence for his CIA handlers and an intrinsic pillar of policy decisions, was now dead.

A fount of intelligence and influence ████████, Gemayel had also been the heart and soul of Israeli intentions for Lebanon. Now both the United States and Israel were unsure how to fill such a gaping void. The United States, determinedly, seized the initiative to steer the country in a new and more stable direction. The Reagan administration pledged its unwavering backing—diplomatic, military, and intelligence—for the new Lebanese president, who just happened to be Bashir's younger brother, Amine. Rather than stepping back from the spiraling horror, the United States joined a long list of powers that had tried to fix the ethnic divides that plagued the country.

Under the accords of the 1943 Lebanese National Covenant, the office of the president was reserved for a Christian, the prime minister's office was the province of the Sunnis, and the position of speaker of the house was earmarked for a Shiite. The Shiites, constituting half of the Muslim majority in Lebanon, were traditionally the poorest and, as a result, the powerless bottom of Lebanese society. The balance of power—especially the numbers of men under arms—usually handicapped the Shiites in the jigsaw puzzle of Lebanese life. The Shiites—especially in the southern portion of the country—were hardworking but clannish, and they had suffered mightily under the yoke of the Palestinian guerrilla factions that controlled the area; the Lebanese Army, Christian-run and largely ineffectual, had little to do with the fortunes or freedoms of the Shiites living in the south. When Israeli forces invaded on June 6, many Shiite villagers greeted the IDF columns of advancing troops as liberators. A Christian-led local militia, the South Lebanon Army, or SLA, recruited Druze and Shiite villagers into its ranks to fight the Palestinians.[15] But this was before the Syrian Military Intelligence Directorate, and the all-powerful Air Force Intelligence Directorate answerable only to President Hafez al-Assad, allowed the Iranian emissaries into the country to create a Shiite underground to battle the Israelis. The narrative that Israeli forces had liberated the Shiites of southern Lebanon would soon be forgotten.

The politicians and generals who planned and executed the invasion were already dealing with the domestic—and international—blowback of the most controversial decision in Israel's history. Many pundits feared that Operation Peace for Galilee would soon become a quagmire, spiraling into an endless cycle of casualties and eventually becoming Israel's Vietnam.[16] High-ranking officers openly questioned the morality of Israel's offensive actions in the Palestinian refugee camps and Lebanese population centers. In a move unheard-of in the egalitarian citizen-soldier world of the Israel Defense Forces, Colonel Eli Geva, an armored-brigade commander, was relieved of duty after asking to be demoted to a simple soldier rather than having to give orders to enter Beirut.[17] Some three hundred thousand Israelis—twenty percent of the national population—protested in Kings of Israel Square in Tel Aviv to express outrage that the Sabra and Shatila killings had been committed under the nose of Israeli forces. Israel did not need more bad news. Already there were commissions formed to reveal Israeli complicity in the carnage, and the political fate and perhaps legacy of Israeli prime minister Menachem Begin had been sealed. Begin was a man known as an unflinching warrior; his reputation as commander of the Irgun underground force during Israel's struggle for independence was forged in resolve and in blood. As prime minister he had made peace with Egypt and ordered warplanes to bomb Osirak, the Iraqi nuclear site. Yet Israel's invasion of Lebanon, and its deterioration into an inescapable military muddle, had humbled Begin. When, three days following the Tyre bombing, Begin's wife of forty-three years died, the Israeli prime minister retreated from public view.

The Tyre bombing highlighted just how little Israel's intelligence services controlled the Lebanese battlefield. So even though it was impossible for Israeli investigators sifting through the debris of the destroyed headquarters not to notice the mangled chassis of the Peugeot 504, and not to have found remnants of Ahmed Qasir, it was better to make no mention of any terrorist involvement. Investigators must have detected the residue from Czech-made Semtex, but admitting that a suicide bomber, one of the human cruise missiles that had come to personify the fanaticism of the Iranian Revolution, had come to the Israeli front lines would have been devastating for the

Israeli public, already perplexed by the foreboding reality of a presence in Lebanon that appeared impossible to depart from. To this day the Israelis claim that the First Tyre Disaster* was not a terrorist attack. The Shin Bet website even claims that the "reason for the explosion was probably a gas leakage and inadequate planning and construction of the building. A probe was set up inquiring and deciding that the explosion had nothing to do with a terror attack since no explosives were found at the building or nearby."[18] The Shin Bet did not want it known that nine of its best and brightest were killed by a new terror presence that had flown so blatantly below Israel's radar.

In targeting the Israeli military and intelligence nerve center in southern Lebanon, the new Shiite entity had temporarily weakened Israel's ability to recover, react, and rebuild networks and files destroyed in the blast. ███████████████████████████ ████████████████████████████████████ ████████████████████████████████████ ████████████████████████████████████ ████████████████████████████████████ ███████████████████ The CIA Station in Beirut already had its hands full. There were explosions every day in the city and throughout the countryside; the blast in Tyre, with the exception of the death toll, was viewed as nothing out of the ordinary where massacres were commonplace. The new Station Chief was already overwhelmed by the aftermath of war and the presence of US marines as peacekeepers and US Army Special Forces teams advising the ineffective Lebanese Armed Forces.

---

* A second Israeli headquarters would be destroyed by a Hezbollah suicide bomber a year later.

* * *

RECEIVING SCANT NOTICE as the war in Lebanon progressed was the fact that five thousand Iranian Revolutionary Guardsmen had been flown into Damascus[19] and then deployed across the border into eastern Lebanon, along the smugglers' routes usually reserved for arms merchants and poppy traffickers. While the Syrian president had no inclination to allow the Iranians, fresh off their zealous execution of an Islamic revolution, to start a full-scale war with the Israelis in his backyard (especially as his military was still reeling from the defeat it had been handed months earlier), Assad knew the value of presenting Israel with a proxy war of attrition. What's more, nine million tons of free Iranian oil every year sweetened the deal for Damascus.[20] Of those five thousand Revolutionary Guardsmen—all combat veterans of the Iran-Iraq War eager to ply their suicidal skills in a holy crusade against Israel—fifteen hundred were operatives from the Office of Islamic Liberation Movements who set up shop on the Syrian-Lebanese frontier. They possessed ample stores of cash, weapons, explosives, and vehicles. The first November rains signaled winter's arrival to the Beka'a Valley and southern Lebanon. Temperatures dropped, and the Iranian emissaries covertly covered the back roads where they knew the Israelis didn't patrol.

On November 21, 1982, inspired and controlled by Iran, the emboldened vanguard of the armed Shiite movement in Lebanon established its immovable foothold in the country. At just after dawn that morning, a small force of Shiite militiamen, led by members of the Iranian Revolutionary Guard Corps, marched into the Sheikh Abdullah Barracks, a sprawling Lebanese army base overlooking Ba'albek, and raised the flag of the Iranian Revolution in the blustering wind.[21] Alongside it, militiamen raised a new flag, a yellow banner with green Arabic writing. The logo proclaimed Hezbollah, the Party of God, along with the image of a fist raising an AK-47 over the globe.

There was too much going on in Lebanon for the Americans—or the Israelis for that matter—to pay attention to the sudden appearance in the slums of southern Beirut of banners pledging allegiance to the Ayatollah Khomeini. The men speaking Farsi were invisible to the Western intelligence services.

Once again the Shiites had gone unnoticed.

2

THE GHOST

ISRAELI FORCES THAT swept through Lebanon on the road to Beirut captured an astounding amount of weapons and ammunition from the Palestinian terrorist camps they overran. A portion of the spoils of war included 420 armored combat vehicles, 636 soft vehicles (noncombat), 34,321 assault rifles and pistols, 1,193 antitank weapons and mortars, 334 rocket launchers, 150 antiaircraft weapons, and 7,507 Katyusha rockets. The captured matériel, worth billions of dollars and consisting of Soviet Bloc weapons, was ferried to Israel in what appeared to be an endless convoy of one-way traffic.

The PLO, and the other Palestinian groups, had built a heavily armed mini-state in Lebanon. They had also hosted a network of terrorist universities throughout Lebanon that attracted wanted men and women—revolutionaries and KGB-financed freedom fighters—from around the world to the Spartan camps where volunteers learned how to shoot, build bombs, evade the police, and hijack airliners. The who's who of international terror had, at one time or another, trained in Lebanon—the best and brightest from the Provisional Irish Republican Army, Germany's Baader-Meinhof Gang, the Japanese Red Army, and groups in Armenia, Africa, and South America had all ventured to the notorious Spartan camps to hone their skills. The Palestinians kept records of the comings and goings of all these foreign brothers and sisters; the names of their Iraqi, Syrian, Libyan, Soviet, East German, and Romanian instructors were also jotted down. Photos of some of these underground fighters were kept on index cards with Latin and Arabic scribble; some of the files even included fingerprints. The Palestinian groups also maintained records of their own personnel, including operatives dispatched overseas for missions of the highest importance.

The amount of paperwork that Israeli forces seized was enormous—enough to fill several warehouses.[1]

Sifting through this terrorist treasure trove was no small feat for Israeli intelligence specialists. Reservists, some with myriad language skills, spent countless hours deciphering the gold mine of material. The Israelis shared this windfall with their allies in the intelligence world. Britain's MI5 and MI6 all received a chance to glance at some files, as did West Germany's Bundesnachrichtendienst, the country's foreign intelligence service known inside the CIA as CASCOPE.[2]

HUNDREDS OF MEMBERS of the Mughniyeh clan gathered in the small farming village of Tayr Dibba, situated four and a half miles due east of downtown Tyre, on December 7, 1962, to celebrate the birth of Imad Fayez Mughniyeh. The Mughniyeh clan dominated the small, dusty village that was a pit stop on the road heading east, along inhospitable, mountainous terrain, pushing toward the Syrian frontier. Like most of the members of the Mughniyeh clan, he was born in a dusty home in Tayr Dibba without the benefit of a doctor. He was the first of four children; he had two brothers and one sister. His parents—Mahmoud Jawad and Amina—had married a year earlier in a large but humble ceremony at which the entire village, as well as elders and distinguished guests who had traveled by foot for miles from other hilltop villages, had celebrated. Life in the village the day Imad Mughniyeh was born and blessed by the local imam was pretty much the same as it was a hundred years earlier.

The Mughniyeh family was poor, and like so many other Shiite clans who lived in the south between the Litani River and the boundaries of the Jewish State, they squeezed out a meager existence by farming lemons and olives, and by smuggling—everything from hijacked cigarettes to stolen submachine guns. The Mughniyeh family was typical of Shiites from Lebanon's south—stoic and impoverished survivors of the unfair balance of power and privilege in the Lebanese state that constitutionally favored Sunnis and Christians.

The Mughniyeh family's world of tribal safety evaporated in September 1970 when civil war hit Jordan, and King Hussein's bedouin army forced fighters from the Palestinian resistance movements to flee their state within a state in the Hashemite Kingdom. The stateless fighters set up shop in southern Lebanon and in Beirut, joining the approximately hundred thousand refugees who had fled the fighting in northern Israel during the 1948 war for Israel's independence and ended up as hopeless refugees in the cesspools of the sixteen camps that had sprouted up throughout the country. The Sunni Palestinians who clawed their way into the country in 1948 severely disrupted the status quo of Lebanon's ethnic and religious mosaic—a delicate balance of Sunnis, Christians, Shiites, Druzes, Alawites, and Armenians who had coexisted, albeit uncomfortably and unfairly, for centuries. For hundreds of years, the ethnic factions had been forced to respect the religious and political divides under the Ottoman bayonet. When Lebanon's fractured landscape was shattered by the arrival of twenty-five thousand armed Palestinian guerrillas from Jordan, the balance of power and the fabric of Lebanon's identity forever and irreversibly changed.

Every Palestinian attack launched from bases in southern Lebanon against northern Israel produced a decisively harsh Israeli response—artillery barrages, commando strikes, and air raids. Innocent civilians were always caught in the cross fire, and tens of thousands fled the fighting. The Mughniyeh clan, reluctant and bitter, headed north toward an impoverished future of uncertainty in the Shiite slums of south Beirut. Scores of Shiites escaped the fighting in the south for temporary shelter and, ultimately, permanent poverty.[3]

In his native Tayr Dibba, the cherubic Imad was remembered as a happy child, content in his surroundings. In the south Beirut slums, however, the chubby Imad was targeted by neighborhood bullies who taunted and beat him regularly. He developed a fascination with and an appreciation of the only symbol of self-respect that existed in Lebanon—the AK-47.

In 1976, a year into Lebanon's civil war, the fourteen-year-old Mughniyeh volunteered to fight for Yasir Arafat's Fatah guerrilla army. The man who recruited him, according to Kai Bird's book *The Good Spy*, was none other than Ali Hassan Salameh. The son of a respected sheikh killed in the 1948 war of Israeli independence, Salameh was a masterful politician, a wheeler-dealer worthy of a stall in any Middle Eastern suq—or market—and a cold-blooded tactician willing to perpetrate mass murder as a means of publicity and promotion. Known by his nom de guerre, "the Red Prince," Salameh had clawed his way up the ranks of the Fatah to become one of Arafat's top security chiefs and special operations commanders, becoming one of the heads of the Black September Organization—a deniable and spectacular mission element within Fatah—in the aftermath of the Jordanian civil war in September 1970. His reign of terror included the 1972 Munich Olympics Massacre.

Salameh was also known to have a falcon's intuition when it came to selecting talent. The men and women Salameh had selected for Black September's operations around the Middle East and beyond were highly motivated components of a terror machine that wanted to prove to the world its ruthlessness and bloodthirst. Salameh's men did not smoke hashish the night before an operation and wake up too stoned to get to the airport on time; Salameh's men didn't miss train connections and they didn't lose the street number of a safe house; and, most importantly, they never hesitated when pulling a trigger.

Salameh saw promise in Mughniyeh—the fourteen-year-old Shiite boy with the slight belly and the wickedly beguiling smile had raw talent and drive.[4] Shiites were not welcome in the ranks of the PLO, though; the Palestinians looked at their religious cousins with hatred and absolute contempt, yet there was something about the young Mughniyeh's untapped reservoir of rage that caught the eye of the Fatah recruiter. The fourteen-year-old soldier swore his allegiance to Abu Ammar, the nom de guerre of Yasir Arafat, and swore to help liberate Jerusalem. He received a quick and rudimentary basic training course and was remembered as standing out from the other trainees.[5] The course curriculum included marksmanship, explosives, cold killing, and intelligence tradecraft. The camps were dirty and Spartan, the food was basic, and the sleeping quarters were harsh. The terrorist-training camps were an odd place for a young Shiite boy from the south. There was little—if any—praying going on in them. The Palestinians training in the camps were Sunnis; those who weren't Muslims were Christians: Roman Catholic or Greek Orthodox. Men and women trained together. Some of the women in the camps were European or Asian—underground diehards determined to learn the A to Z of guerrilla warfare and revolution and have a good time in the process. Drugs and alcohol were everywhere. Women trainees, according to reports, were sexually assaulted to stiffen their resolve. Women in tank tops who smoked hash were something new to the young Shiite recruit from Tayr Dibba.

Becoming a member of Fatah was a game-changing experience for Imad. The bullies could no longer pick on the young, chubby boy from the south: anyone who attempted to pick on Mughniyeh or any member of his family would have a new clan—the fifteen thousand heavily armed Palestinian gunmen in Beirut—to contend with. Mughniyeh wore lizard-pattern camouflage fatigues and black leather combat boots shined to an impressive glow. The AK-47 and the Fatah paycheck enabled the Mughniyeh family to move out of their crowded slum flat into a more spacious home. Even though the Palestinians and the Shiites were often at one another's throats, Mughniyeh was regarded as less of a traitor and more of a practical opportunist. Survival in time of warfare required pragmatism and a cutthroat, live-for-the-day strategy.

Mughniyeh was a model gunman, and he displayed enormous courage under fire in the street-to-street and house-to-house bloodletting of civil-war Beirut. His doggedness and brutality impressed even the most veteran of Palestinian trench warriors, and, reportedly, Mughniyeh was personally decorated by Arafat, in particular for his skill as a sniper along Beirut's dividing Green Line, where the young Shiite marksman excelled at picking off Christian housewives as they tried to return home from the market weighed down by baskets full of fruits and vegetables.

*   *   *

PICKING OFF HOUSEWIVES fending for their families required a special sort of sadistic talent, and Fatah commanders saw great promise in Mughniyeh. The young Shiite shooter was soon welcomed into the ranks of Force 17, Arafat's elite Praetorian Guard. Only the most ruthless operatives—and only the most loyal—were permitted close to Arafat and it was unheard-of for a Shiite ever to serve inside this select, inner-circle force. Force 17 was more than Arafat's elite bodyguard—it was the Fatah's special operations commando unit responsible for executing the most audacious and horrific attacks against targets in Israel.

On the evening of March 11, 1978, in a bold strike to interrupt the Camp David Accords being worked on between Egypt and Israel, Palestinian terrorists from Lebanon launched a seaborne raid landing on the Israeli coast south of Haifa. They seized two buses full of hostages with the intention of flying their captives to Libya. But at the entrance to Tel Aviv at a junction on the coastal highway, a standoff ensued with Israeli forces. In the melee that followed, thirty-eight Israelis—including thirteen children—were killed along with all but two of the terrorists; those two had slipped away in the confusion, only to be killed hours later on nearby sand dunes. The Country Club Junction Massacre, as the incident became known, was the worst terrorist attack ever perpetrated in Israel. The Israeli response was swift and immediate. On March 14, 1978, the IDF launched a mini-invasion of southern Lebanon to root out Fatah and other Palestinian terrorist bases near the Israeli frontier. The incursion became known as Operation Litani, as Israeli forces halted their push into Lebanon on the southern banks of the Litani River. Some twenty-five thousand Israeli soldiers crossed the border into Lebanon; most of the Palestinian forces simply raced north toward Sidon and Beirut, while others shed their uniforms in the hope of mixing in invisibly with the local population of the south.

During the Israeli operation, the imam of a mosque in one of the villages near the Litani River had asked to meet the local Israeli commander to extend his wishes for peace and to promise that his village supported the Israeli presence. The thirty-three-year-old officer responsible for the sector gladly accepted the invitation; a meeting was hastily arranged. The imam, from one of the prominent clans in the area, provided the Israeli officer and his entourage with sweets and endless cups of sweet tea. "An older man met me to talk about not wanting any trouble in the area," the officer recalled. "He had even brought his sixteen-year-old nephew, a chubby young teenager wearing lizard-pattern camouflage fatigues to the meeting. The boy was unimpressive, nothing really. The imam brought him to the meeting because his nephew was a member of Fatah and the doting uncle wanted to make sure that nothing happened to him. I even gestured to the boy in an offering of peace."[6] The local imam was a respected and elderly member of the Mughniyeh clan. The nephew was Imad. The Israeli officer, as fate would have it, was Lieutenant Colonel Meir Dagan, a deputy brigade commander who would, years later, become the director of the Mossad.

THE ISRAELIS HAD hoped that the Operation Litani mini-invasion of southern Lebanon would cement close ties to the local Shiite population. But Imad Mughniyeh ventured deeper into the ranks of the PLO. Force 17 sent Mughniyeh to a KGB-taught dignitary-protection course and ultimately assigned him to protect Abu Iyad, Arafat's second-in-command, the head of Fatah's intelligence services and

Salameh's boss in Black September. Imad Mughniyeh even received his own Force 17 nom de guerre. His call sign was al-Fahad: "the Leopard."

Abu Iyad was reported to have taken great interest in Mughniyeh. The young Shiite bodyguard accompanied his principal on many of his covert trips to Libya, Syria, Saudi Arabia, the Persian Gulf states, and the Warsaw Pact. Mughniyeh was able to see, firsthand, the inner workings of state-sponsored terror and the laborious minutiae and exhaustive networking that went behind the day-to-day running of a war of national liberation. Abu Iyad was quite the mentor for the young and impressionable Shiite in Arafat's service. Iyad, whose real name was Salah Khalaf, was behind many of Black September's most notorious attacks—including the Munich Olympics Massacre.

By his twentieth birthday, Imad Mughniyeh had assembled an impressive CV full of combat experience and operational counterintelligence fieldwork. Had Israel not invaded Lebanon, Mughniyeh would have been a true corporate climber in the ranks of Arafat's Fatah. He had bloodthirst and ambition.

When Israeli tanks closed in on Beirut and tightened the noose around Palestinian forces in the city, Mughniyeh destroyed his Fatah documents and shed his fatigues. Under cover of darkness, he abandoned his post and rushed home past the bombed-out craters of the city. Israeli forces already controlled most of southern Beirut. IDF tanks and armored personnel carriers stood guard on the tarmac at Beirut International Airport, minutes from his home, where it would be easy for him to disappear into the nameless backstreets. Mughniyeh somehow remained anonymous, and was able to flee south to the village of his birth.

POSTERS OF IMAM Musa al-Sadr could be found everywhere in Imad Mughniyeh's south Beirut neighborhood. The images, some as large as billboards, showed the bearded Shiite cleric in various poses; he smiled charismatically in most of the photographs, and was always seen in religious robes. The self-proclaimed leader of Lebanon's Shiite community, Musa al-Sadr was born in 1928 in the Iranian holy city of Qom and pursued a life of religious scholarly study. In 1960 he accepted an invitation to become the religious leader of the Shiite community in Tyre and soon went on to become a vibrant and determined political force dedicated to steering the most poorly represented of Lebanon's minorities to economic equality and political strength. Imam Sadr helped forge the creation of the Battalions of Lebanese Resistance, which would ultimately become known by its acronym Amal.[7] Amal received assistance from Syrian intelligence in establishing its armed militia—weapons were acquired on the black market. Amal's peak order of battle is believed to have been fourteen thousand militiamen. They often engaged Palestinian factions in open warfare.

The Shiites of Lebanon revered Imam Musa al-Sadr as a savior—a man who possessed the piety of a holy man as well as the knuckle-scraping grit of a street fighter. He turned old religious rituals into practical politics in Shiite Lebanon,[8] but he vanished—never to return and presumed dead—during a trip to Libya in the summer of 1978; it is believed that he was killed by the Libyan intelligence service working in collusion with Arafat. The disappearance of the imam created a power vacuum in the ranks of Lebanon's Shiites. The more moderate Amal movement continued its war for representation while an emerging force led by some, including a Beirut cleric named Sheikh Muhammad Hussein Fadlallah, sought to re-create Lebanon in the image of a Khomeini-like fundamentalist Iran. Another figure in the Khomeini-inspired group was Sheikh Hussein Abbas Musawi, who broke away from Amal and headed to the Beka'a Valley to lead the armed struggle of the Iranian-backed revolutionary Shiite movement;

Musawi's zeal, and Iranian money, attracted fundamentalists from around the country and the Middle East, including scholars and men itching to fight a holy war from as far away as Najaf, Iraq.[9]

The face of the Ayatollah Khomeini soon joined images of Imam Musa al-Sadr throughout the neighborhoods of south Beirut and in the markets and villages around Tyre and elsewhere in southern Lebanon. Toward the end of August 1982, young Shiite men flocked to the Imam Rida Mosque in the Beirut slum of Bir al-Abd to hear one of Sheikh Mohammed Hussein Fadlallah's sermons. Fadlallah's heavy Najaf accent did not hide a flowing classical Arabic oratory that both inspired and enraged. But Imad Mughniyeh was not one of the men in the growing sea of bearded men shouting, "God is great." Mughniyeh was just another unemployed young Shiite man lost in the labyrinth of a smoldering city looking to retain the status he had earned so despicably in the ranks of Arafat's special operations protection unit. He walked the decimated streets of Ayn al-Dilbah looking at Israeli soldiers, arrogant in their victory, patrolling the alleys and avenues as conquerors who appeared to be in no hurry to pull back and head south to the border. From this same vantage point, Mughniyeh could see hundreds of US marines setting up their peacekeeping perimeter around the airport.

The Iranian Revolutionary Guard officers in Lebanon already had a file on Mughniyeh. Arafat's Shiite bodyguard was something of a mysterious—almost legendary—figure in the slums of south Beirut; the Mughniyeh clan was well known, with no history of collaboration with the Israelis or any other enemy factions in the country. Lebanon's clerics, wary because of Imam al-Sadr's fate, were always looking for the services of experienced and skilled gunmen to act as bodyguards.

Sheikh Fadlallah's inner circle was very interested in this twenty-year-old trained to protect a leader targeted by so many. Sheikh Fadlallah's followers were increasingly concerned that someone would try to kill the religious leader. On July 4, 1982, three Iranian diplomats and a journalist were abducted at a checkpoint in northern Lebanon by a squad of Christian Lebanese Forces militiamen headed by Samir Geagea, a man who would later be implicated in the Sabra and Shatila massacres. The kidnapping outraged the Iranians and caused worry among the nascent underground forces taking shape in Beirut and in the Beka'a. Fadlallah needed a bodyguard.

There are discrepancies in the accounts of just how religious Mughniyeh was. Some believe him not to have been religious at all, while others, including Lebanese journalist Ghadi Francis, with unique access to Hezbollah, claim that Mughniyeh grew up in a very religious Shiite household and that he was fascinated with Shiite clerics who traveled to Iraq and Iran; he was spellbound by the teachings of the Ayatollah Khomeini, and, according to Francis, Mughniyeh taught himself how to speak Farsi so that he could listen to the Ayatollah's sermons, bootlegged on audiocassette.[10]

Fadlallah was undeterred by the fact that Mughniyeh was not a pious Shiite. The Hezbollah leader understood that pragmatism and blind ambition were as important as Islamic fervor when creating a new force on the scarred Lebanese political landscape. The Iranians, of course, weren't looking for saints when it came time to select a chief bodyguard for Fadlallah; they were looking for a ruthless—and experienced—trigger finger to safeguard their investment. Heading Sheikh Fadlallah's security detail was a dream assignment for Mughniyeh and it was a perfect fit for his shameless ambitions. Mughniyeh understood the explosive pressure of his battlefield, and the Iranians liked what they saw in Mughniyeh—ambition, rage, intelligence, and boundless tactical creativity. Mughniyeh reveled in Iranian audacity and spirit; to the young man from the south, who saw the Palestinians destroy themselves—and Lebanon in the process—through their arrogance, cowardice, corruption, and pure stupidity, the unyielding Iranian religious fervor was captivating. Mughniyeh not only wanted to be part of this new phenomenon—he demanded a central role.

Some accounts have credited Imad Mughniyeh with introducing martyrdom to the Lebanese battlefield. The tactic—based less on the postrevolution Iranian version of the Shiite notion of self-sacrifice and paradise and more on Mughniyeh's own personal ambitions—was a diabolical rewiring of the battle for Lebanon's existence. Mughniyeh is said even to have openly talked about the use of suicide bombers during the Israeli siege of Beirut, and to have secured an ample supply of explosives from Khalil al-Wazir—Arafat's military commander also known by his nom de guerre, Abu Jihad ("Father Holy War")*—to be used for such attacks.[11] According to some accounts, it was Mughniyeh, believed to have been a childhood friend of Ahmed Qasir, who reportedly persuaded his teenage friend to drive the Peugeot 504 straight into the Israeli military headquarters in Tyre on November 11, 1982, on the condition that his identity remain a secret until Israeli forces left the area of his village so that there would be no retribution against his parents and siblings.[12]

Word of Mughniyeh's Tyre operation quickly spread to the contingent of Iranian Revolutionary Guardsmen entrenching themselves in the Beka'a. Mughniyeh's operation showed initiative and great skill; a native of the southern approaches in and around Tyre, Mughniyeh

---

* Israeli commandos from the Sayeret Mat'kal General Staff Reconnaissance Unit, along with a Mossad task force, assassinated Abu Jihad in Tunis, Tunisia, on the night of April 14, 1988.

was said to have personally reconnoitered the Israeli headquarters for weeks prior to the bombing.

Shortly after the bombing, Mughniyeh left Beirut—or Tayr Dibba—for Ba'albek. Traveling on side roads that only locals knew, he evaded Israeli patrols until he reached terrain where even the IDF refused to enter. He was eager to meet with the Iranian emissaries and to offer his services. He needed a job.

A meeting had been arranged—through word of mouth and personal messengers—between himself and Ali Reza Asgari, the thirty-year-old Revolutionary Guard head of intelligence in Lebanon. Asgari was square jawed and no-nonsense. Young revolutionaries like Asgari had witnessed firsthand how the shah's intelligence service, the SAVAK, terrorized dissidents; many in the Revolutionary Guard were the sons or brothers of torture victims. Growing up in Isfahan, Asgari had learned firsthand that the only way to outfight an opponent was to be more ruthless and cunning. Lebanon, to Asgari and his legion, was a jigsaw puzzle that had fallen off a table and was in a million pieces. The country was ripe for pure cunning.

Ali Reza Asgari's office was a spacious but Spartan room, the kind usually reserved for a battalion commander or higher, inside a nondescript row of French-built military buildings that sat to the rear of the Sheikh Abdullah Barracks. The Lebanese army had neglected the offices; paint peeled off the walls, and the floors of cheap marble tile were chipped and heavily scuffed. The base itself was in horrible disrepair, the victim of underfunding, the fractured and corrupt Lebanese government never investing in its ineffectual military. The drainage system was in such a poor state that whenever it rained the parade ground turned into a lake of mud and overflowing sewage. But the horrible conditions mattered little to the Iranians. A space heater kept the bone-biting chill out of Asgari's office. A local boy, eager to earn a few pounds a month, eagerly made mint tea with shovelfuls of sugar for Asgari and anyone who sat in his office behind closed doors.

Mughniyeh and Asgari were similar men of unique capabilities with uncontainable ambition. Mughniyeh was young and, so, eager to impress. He was a spymaster's dream come true. Asgari was utterly confident and cold, yet also beguilingly charismatic. The Iranian commander was so different from the Arafat sycophants Mughniyeh had seen come and go while in Force 17. Asgari became Mughniyeh's mentor and lavish benefactor.

The two men sat in Asgari's office for hours on end in November and December 1982. They spoke at length about what could be done in Lebanon against Israel and, as far as the Revolutionary Guard was concerned, especially the United States. The two men engaged in lengthy discussions about the profession of undermining a Western power, and they drank endless kettles of tea. There was a lot of work to be done.

3

FLASH AND FIREBALL

IT WAS ALWAYS advised to get to the United States Embassy early. The lines, the embassy switchboard operators said, tended to get long by the time the consular section opened for business. The first intrepid souls usually arrived before dawn to stake their spots and hopefully be among the first to be seen by a consular officer; sometimes it was a young woman who wanted to study in the United States, and sometimes it was a family of four, who were wired money and Air France tickets from a relative in Brooklyn for a break from the madness of Lebanon for a few weeks or for the rest of their lives. There were long lines of those hoping to find safety and freedom during the bloody civil war, and there were long lines of desperate families seeking to leave during the Israeli invasion. Young couples, hoping to leave the country, clutched passports and notarized statements from state security that they were neither criminals nor terrorists. People desperately waved airline tickets in sweat-soaked hands, while some held copies of their land deeds to show that they came from families with means. Lebanese policemen and local security guardsmen did all they could to maintain order, but there was always pushing and shoving. There was desperation in the lines. The desperation in the country, and the undefeatable Lebanese spirit, was inescapable.

Staffers at the United States Embassy tried to convince themselves that they weren't in the most dangerous country in the world. Junior diplomats, some fresh and eager faces in the Foreign Service, still saw fit to put on their alma mater T-shirts and jog on the Corniche. Some went to the famed Saint-George Yacht Club and Marina to lie out on beach chairs next to almond-eyed beauties, who splashed suntan lotion on their olive flesh while sipping cocktails and trying to ignore the shelling in the Druze mountains nearby. Other Foreign Service staffers, those with friends at the nearby American University of Beirut, enjoyed access at the AUB Beach at Corniche el-Manara where students and professors enjoyed the surf and soft drinks. Lebanon—the Lebanon of the 1960s when Omar Sharif and the Saudi princes used the country as a playground—was one of those places where you could surf in the morning and ski in the afternoon. There were romantic seaside cafés north of Beirut and awe-inspiring Roman ruins in the Beka'a Valley. The blasé attitude drove the RSO, the regional security officer in charge of embassy security, crazy. Rich Gannon was the RSO.

SY, the US Department of State's Office of Security, was a small and little-known law enforcement entity at Foggy Bottom, the neighborhood in Washington, DC, where the State Department is located, and was responsible for security at US diplomatic facilities around the world. SY was woefully neglected when compared to other federal law enforcement agencies. It was negligently understaffed, and agents were poorly equipped—a .357 Magnum revolver and a shield—overwhelmed, and outnumbered in the field. Even as terrorism changed in the 1970s, when attacks were no longer specific to diplomats but now included full-scale destructive assaults against diplomatic posts,[1] little changed in how SY conducted its business. The 1979 takeover of the US Embassy in Tehran should have changed the paradigm in embassy security, but it didn't. The November 1979 assault on the US Embassy in Islamabad, Pakistan, when mobs set fire to the chancery and a Marine Corps security guard was killed by a sniper, did little to prompt the State Department—and the elected officials who controlled its purse strings—to do anything dramatic to change the philosophy of embassy security. Rich Gannon was a one-man shop in Lebanon. Security at the US Embassy in Beirut, one of the most sensitive, strategic—and besieged—American diplomatic posts in the Middle East, was handled by only one man.

Gannon* was a young SY agent, Beirut was his first post, and he knew the stakes in Lebanon were high. The US Embassy in Beirut was routinely rocketed and mortared by various factions fighting for neighborhood control during the height of the Lebanese Civil War. The embassy was a tempting target: Palestinian groups in particular liked to launch rocket-propelled grenade and sniper fire at the sprawling seven-story complex on Rue de Paris along the Corniche. Windows, hit by sniper fire and collateral shrapnel, were replaced frequently. Chunks of the building's façade were routinely blown off by ricochets and rockets. Security personnel who requested to evacuate the embassy because of the incessant attacks were denied by the State Department.

---

* Gannon's brother Matthew was a CIA officer ███████████████████
██████████. He was returning home to the United States when he was killed, along with 269 others, on board Pan Am Flight 103 on the night of December 21, 1988.

The American presence in Lebanon, according to Henry Kissinger's Department of State, served a higher purpose.[2]

On June 16, 1976, Francis E. Meloy Jr., the incoming US ambassador to Lebanon, and Robert O. Waring, the economic counselor assigned to the embassy, were kidnapped in West Beirut, the abduction carried out as the two were en route to the Lebanese presidential palace to present their credentials to Suleiman Frangieh. Their bullet-riddled bodies were found later that afternoon, abandoned along the surf of the beach at Ramlet al-Baida. The Popular Front for the Liberation of Palestine was linked to the crime.

There were threats—ballistic realities of imminent danger—in Beirut that Gannon understood but headquarters simply couldn't comprehend. On December 15, 1981, a van packed with explosives rammed through a barrier wall protecting the Iraqi Embassy in West Beirut. The van, driven by a Shiite suicide bomber, continued fifty feet into the complex before erupting into a fireball and spreading death and destruction. Chunks of the building, and shredded body parts, were thrown hundreds of yards away. The attack, the first suicide bombing of its kind, killed sixty-one people and wounded more than one hundred.

Gannon knew that the US Embassy was vulnerable to a similar strike. The seven-story structure was built with three wings—left, center, and right—in a giant horseshoe shape; a circular driveway brought visitors to the main entrance. Post One, the fortified US Marine Corps Security Guard position, was situated right behind the main doors and controlled access inside the facility; the Marine Security Guard assignment at overseas embassies was the safeguarding of classified material inside the embassies proper. Consular services were conducted through a separate side entrance. Gannon had worked with the Lebanese police to prevent parking directly in front of the embassy. Plainclothes agents from Lebanese intelligence, the al-Amn al-'Aam, monitored vehicular traffic and possible lookouts who might be considering targeting the embassy; agents from the Christian-dominated Deuxième Bureau, Lebanese military intelligence, also monitored Palestinian groups and Iranian intelligence assets that could target the embassy.

The State Department procured for the embassy physical security barriers and fencing designed to impede a vehicle-borne improvised explosive device, or VBIED. Yet they were never installed, remaining in their original crates in the embassy's basement. US Ambassador Robert Dillon did not want barriers. "This is what we do," he reportedly told Gannon, explaining that risk was part of the business. The ambassador didn't find the barriers to be aesthetically pleasing.[3] The RSO may have been responsible for the security programs at an embassy, but the ambassador was always king.[4]

Robert Sherwood Dillon had a pedigree that should have made him appreciate security. The Chicago-born diplomat started his career in the CIA and worked at posts, some hazardous, throughout the world before joining the Foreign Service. A veteran of the Korean War, Dillon was sharp, square jawed, and a career diplomat who knew how to talk to undersecretaries of state with the same candor as to warlords and dictators. Lebanon was a make-or-break post for a diplomat with higher aspirations—it either made you a star or ruined your career. Ambassador Dillon had been in Lebanon six months when the Iraqi Embassy disappeared into a crater of fire and debris. He had been in the country a year when the Israelis invaded and laid siege to Beirut; he was Ronald Reagan's point man in the aftermath of the Gemayel assassination and the Sabra and Shatila massacres. Ambassador Dillon hoped that the situation wouldn't get worse before it got better.

Lebanon had become the centerpiece of America's Middle East policy. The political, economic, military, and intelligence might of the United States was pledged to bolster Lebanon's fragile standing and shore up its shaky foundation. There were endless visits of high-ranking Department of Defense officials shuttling back and forth from Washington in feverish attempts to turn the Pentagon's promises into pragmatic policy; much of this work fell upon the shoulders of Special Forces training teams coming into the country to work with the fledgling Lebanese Armed Forces, the LAF. USAID managers facilitated economic aid, while the political section worked diligently to maintain the very threads of the country's fractious political system ███████████████████████████████████████ ██ ██ ██ ██ █████████████

There were high-level visitors coming and going as well—underscoring Lebanon's importance to Ronald Reagan's foreign policy. Special envoy Philip Habib, a tough-talking, Brooklyn-born veteran Foggy Bottom troubleshooter of Lebanese descent, was shuttling back and forth between Washington, DC, the US Embassy, and the presidential palace in Baabda in attempts to solidify the presidency of Amine Gemayel and convince both Israeli and Syrian forces to leave the country. Habib's efforts were noble. Bloodshed was always the end result of such altruistic intentions.

Everything was run out of the embassy. It was impossible to keep track of all the comings and goings of men in uniform and those who lurked in the shadows.

*   *   *

THE VISA LINES began to form before dawn outside the US Embassy on the morning of Monday, April 18, 1983. The first beams of orange light emerged over the horizon, offering hints of the fierce blue skies and refreshing breezes to come. The mist of the sea could be tasted by those walking in the sunshine along the Corniche. From his penthouse perch Ambassador Dillon could see the sand and surf, and he determined to go jogging at the running track at American University of Beirut a few blocks away. Due to the city's inherent dangers, each three-mile regimen required his security detail to close down the facility and scan the nearby rooftops for snipers.

Rich Gannon was busy at his desk that day. He was hosting the SY Regional Security Supervisor, or RSS, who was touring embassies in the region and reviewing security protocols at the embassy and sifting through reams of intelligence—self-cultivated and assembled elsewhere—concerning the threats in Lebanon. Across the hall, past the framed photos of the president and vice president, Kenneth Haas was preparing the talking points for a high-level lunchtime meeting at the station with staffers, along with in-country assets. Robert Ames, the CIA's Near East Division's chief analyst, had arrived in Lebanon the day before; the Near East Division was responsible for intelligence operations and analysis, as well as stations, for the entire Middle East—stretching from North Africa all the way to Iran, Afghanistan, and Pakistan. Ames was something of a legend in the CIA, having cultivated a ten-year relationship with Munich Olympics Massacre mastermind Ali Hassan Salameh.[5] He had traveled to Lebanon on business unassociated with the Beirut Station and didn't have plans to visit the embassy or his CIA colleagues during his brief visit to Lebanon. The heads of the Near East Division would have none of it. Not visiting the station would have been a slight, an insult. His visit coincided with the station holding an all-hands meeting in the embassy. His timing was pure coincidence.[6]

The meeting was going to be an important one. A hot lunch was going to be served. ████████████████████████████████████ ████████████████████████████████ and was held in the secure Acoustic Conference Room, known simply as the ACR; in Agency talk, the room was known as "the Bubble."

IN A GARAGE deep inside the Shiite labyrinth of south Beirut, an anonymous young man turned a key that ignited the V-8 engine of a black GMC pickup truck. Nearly a ton of explosives and propane tanks had been loaded in the back, so overloading the vehicle's suspension that as it pulled out and moved slowly along the street, its tires appeared to be flat.

Ali Reza Asgari and Imad Mughniyeh were both anxious about an operation they had been planning for months. Master bomb builders had spent weeks designing and constructing a massive two-thousand-pound payload that was blueprinted to produce a lethal yield that could topple a building. A veil of absolute secrecy had blanketed the operation. There was no chatter that any of the intelligence services spying in Lebanon could have picked up, were no informers inside the nascent Shiite organization who peddled secrets on the Byzantine marketplace to the highest bidder. Both spymaster and operational executioner now awaited word that the operation had been a success.

The driver has never officially been identified, yet he is believed to have been Muhammed Hassuna, a young Shiite from Awza'i—a slum near Beirut International Airport[7]—who had frequented Hezbollah-controlled mosques in the previous weeks and had been primed psychologically for the operation. As was the standard order of business, he would have been told how he had been selected personally by one of the clerics for this most important martyrdom operation. The driver might have been briefed personally by Imad Mughniyeh; it cannot be confirmed. Mughniyeh wouldn't have revealed his identity to the eager suicide bomber. Men like Mughniyeh who were commanders were identifiable by swagger.

While Kenneth Haas and the Station convened their meeting, and while Asgari and Mughniyeh fretted, the driver drove carefully to avoid roadblocks and police checkpoints on his circuitous route through the war-torn streets. Most feared of all were French peacekeepers from the Multinational Force. The French, particularly Foreign Legion paratroopers, were no-nonsense; they routinely responded to sniper fire in their sectors by deploying wire-guided antitank missiles to destroy possible firing positions, floor by floor, even on the top floors of residential buildings.[8] The pickup, investigators believed, was trailed by several Mercedes sedans, all packed with armed individuals, who provided route security for the laden-down truck. Their orders were to open fire on anyone who tried to interrupt the operation.

The surveillance around the target was intense. Reportedly, a green Mercedes had reconnoitered the US Embassy all morning. At 12:43, the Mercedes drove past the GMC across from the Ayn Muraysah Mosque. The Mercedes driver flashed his headlights three times. That was the predetermined signal that the coast was clear. The green light to launch the attack had been given. Midday traffic was gridlocked. Intersections were blocked and Beirut drivers, as drivers throughout the Arab Middle East do so skillfully, negotiated the slow movement by creating an earsplitting symphony of honking horns. The GMC inched closer and closer to the US Embassy. It was already past 13:00 hours. The occupants of another sedan that was parked within radio range of the embassy watched carefully. The car was far enough from the embassy that it was shielded from the kill zone, yet still close enough to initiate a signal to detonate the GMC's lethal cargo just in case the driver had second thoughts and failed to do what the commanders and the clerics had sanctioned him to do. It is believed that the GMC driver was equipped with a deadman switch, a mechanical apparatus to ignite the payload even after the bomber was dead in case the local guard force killed him before he could crash his truck into the embassy.[9]

Inside the embassy, Rich Gannon was at his desk on the seventh floor. The RSO's office faced the rear of the building; SY personnel rarely had a room with a view at the embassy. Members of the local Lebanese guard force that Gannon supervised monitored security at the embassy from a small office placed just outside the chancery. The office was usually busy around mealtime as the patrol force popped in for a cup of mint tea or mudlike coffee. Ambassador Dillon was in his office putting on his US Marine Corps Security Guard T-shirt for the planned jog.[10]

At precisely 13:04 the driver noticed an opening in the traffic just in front of the embassy. He accelerated and swerved the GMC onto the curb on Avenue de Paris, hit an outbuilding, and positioned himself next to the local guard booth at the building's entrance. The GMC hit the building with such speed that the local guard force had no time to respond with gunfire. By placing the VBIED at the center of the U-shaped circular driveway, where only the ambassador's armor-plated limousine was allowed to enter, the driver ensured that the explosives (believed to have been made up of powerful pentaerythritol tetranitrate, or PETN) and propane tanks created a shaped charge that caused the center wing of the building to collapse.

Even compared with Lebanon's long history of massive explosive devices, this bomb was all-powerful. A US Navy seaman walking toward the embassy when the bomb detonated later described the explosion as a flash and a fireball.[11] Crew members on board the USS

Guadalcanal, an Iwo Jima–class amphibious assault ship anchored five miles off the Lebanese coast, felt the concussive force of the blast.

The afternoon's brilliant sunshine could not penetrate the thick, suffocating plume of black and acrid smoke that hung over the remains of the chancery. Day had turned to night. Fire brigades responded from stations throughout the city, but the fires burned more ferociously than their equipment could contain; dozens of cars parked on nearby streets were destroyed by the explosion, their fuel tanks exploded in a series of blasts that made the rescue effort impossible.

The US Marine Corps Security Guard (MSG) Post One and the main entrance to the embassy had been hit the hardest. Ryan Crocker, then a Foreign Service Officer assigned to the embassy, reflected: "The enormity of what had happened was clear because that [Post One, the main entrance to the embassy] was like walking into hell. It was pitch black. The face of the building had collapsed in on the lobby and fires were burning inside. It was very clear that no one in that area could possibly have survived."[12]

Members of the Marine Security Guard contingent on duty elsewhere in the chancery recovered from the massive explosion. The marines drew their M16s, shotguns, and M60 light machine guns from the armory, and deployed outside the building to fend off a possible second strike. Marines were no longer permitted outside the embassy walls, but many of the actual load-bearing walls had collapsed.

Lebanese soldiers and policemen rushed to the embassy, and were bewildered by the devastation. Body parts were scattered in the rubble; survivors, some terribly hurt, screamed, begging to be rescued from floors that had collapsed all around them. "Some of the Lebanese security personnel stood frozen and helpless inside the chaos," Nora Boustany remembered. Boustany, a young Beirut-born stringer for the *Washington Post*, was having her hair cut at a fashionable West Beirut salon on Clemenceau Street when the embassy was attacked. Boustany remembered rushing to the embassy on foot. "Some of the Lebanese security forces were hitting themselves in the head, like a woman wailing in grief, at the horrific carnage. It was surreal. After civil war and full-scale war, you just knew that this was a moment that would be a turning point for Lebanon."[13]

The evacuation of the wounded and the removal of the dead were attended to with adrenaline-fueled enthusiasm laced with a heavy dose of Middle Eastern confusion. The wounded were brought out of the rubble by stretcher and then rushed by ambulance or pickup truck to nearby hospitals. The dead, the bodies that were visible, were removed from the rubble quickly. It was impossible to track who had been removed. Rescuers wearing many uniforms tried to organize an impactful effort. Men and women, wearing their embassy uniforms of business casual, screamed from gaping openings on the upper floors, pleading for someone to rescue them before the building collapsed. Black, acrid smoke began to flow in the energetic spring winds from the sea as evening neared.

Marines from the Multinational Force were rushed in from the airport and helped to establish a perimeter around the blast zone. The scene was absolute bedlam. The young marines, many of whom were only a year or so out of high school, looked bewildered amid the chaos and death. Some of the marines were ordered to sift through the rubble to look for any classified material that could have been blown about in the blast. Cardboard boxes were brought out to collect the loose papers and file folders. Metal garbage cans had been brought out and fires set so that material could be incinerated on the spot.

A few of the marines assembled a pole from wreckage found strewn about. They attached an American flag to metal sticks wired together and, in Iwo Jima fashion, hoisted the Stars and Stripes for all to see. The destroyed embassy still stood defiantly in the background. French and British forces soon arrived to offer security and support as the rescue effort continued.

As night fell, Ambassador Dillon spoke to the press. "You can imagine how saddened and angry we all are but this does not change anything," he said with the collapsed center of the building smoldering behind him. "The United States will continue to operate in Lebanon. The Habib mission goes on. Just as soon as I can get some office and put my staff in it we're going back to work."[14] Sir David Roberts, Britain's ambassador to Lebanon, immediately offered use of the British Embassy to Ambassador Dillon and his staff, wanting to help out his friend and Great Britain's most important ally.[15] The Foreign Office was not consulted; accordingly, London was not pleased by the benevolent gesture. Still, surviving members of Ambassador Dillon's staff assembled what they could and walked northwest toward the British Embassy, where the political, military, and consular sections set up shop in the building's basement.[16] US marines from the Twenty-second Marine Expeditionary Unit were already manning defensive positions around the British Embassy.

███████████████████████████████████

███████████

Of the sixty-three people killed in the attack, seventeen were Americans. Most were CIA attending the regional meeting on the seventh floor. The dead included Phylis Nancy Faraci, Deborah M. Hixon, Frank J. Johnston, James F. Lewis, and Monique N. Lewis, all listed as State Department employees.[17] Also killed were Kenneth Haas and Robert Ames, one of the Agency's most important Middle East minds, a man who had the ear of President Reagan and was in his security inner circle. According to Robert Baer, a fellow CIA officer, Ames' hand was found a mile offshore, floating in the Mediterranean. The wedding ring was still on his finger.[18]

IT WAS THE deadliest day in the history of the Central Intelligence Agency. There are no accidents in terrorism, though. Ali Reza Asgari and Imad Mughniyeh had planned the operation meticulously, finetuning the date once news of the CIA meeting was discovered. Both Asgari and Mughniyeh employed small armies of spies to surveil the chancery: men and women who could watch, learn, and jot down patterns to provide the operations team with an intricate, multidimensional portrait of the embassy and its many vulnerabilities. Information on the location was easy to obtain. There was no countersurveillance program in place for SY to monitor the many eyes watching the building.

The destruction of the embassy was collateral damage—the target of the suicide truck bombing was the top secret gathering chaired by Kenneth Haas and Robert Ames. In a blinding flash, Asgari and Mughniyeh had ████████████████████ in Lebanon. Iran—and Hezbollah—had fired the first shot in a declaration of war, like a latter-day Pearl Harbor. Iran and Hezbollah had telegraphed their intentions for months. Reports of the growing Shiite movement, which Christian and Sunni newspapers referred to as a new invasion, were signposts for America's spies in the country. It didn't matter. No one read anything unless it was classified top secret. The bombing was a declaration of war against the United States. Few in Washington, DC, understood the depths of the threat. Even fewer could predict the carnage that was to come.

SOME OF THE best print and television journalists in the business were based in Beirut—David Ignatius, Jonathan Randal, and Thomas

L. Friedman, to name a few. The Beirut Press Corps was known as "the Tribe," a stellar group of future stars who earned their stripes—and scars—covering a city that was ground zero in an active war zone. Reporters could have breakfast with an Israeli general in the morning, enjoy tea with a staffer in President Gemayel's cabinet before noon, and meet a Syrian spy for coffee before dusk, and still get a good table at West Beirut's Romano restaurant for pasta and prawns.

There would be no lavish meals on this evening, however. The Tribe had converged on the shell of the US Embassy, the sounds of bulldozers clearing rubble masking the usual nighttime serenade of the surf hitting the beach. By the time David Brinkley interrupted programming with a live feed from Beirut, ABC's man in Beirut, Peter Jennings, already knew who was responsible. "This is the worst attack there has ever been against the United States in the Middle East," Jennings began. "An Islamic group, calling itself Islamic Jihad, which means 'holy war,' claims to have planted the explosives. The group, which says it has attacked the Multinational Force here before, of which little is known or understood, is believed to be pro-Iranian. Its aim today, so it said, was to end American occupation of Lebanon."[19]

Indeed, hours earlier a pro-Iranian group calling itself the Islamic Jihad Organization had taken responsibility for the bombing in a telephone call to a news office. "This is part of the Iranian Revolution's campaign against imperialist targets throughout the world," said the anonymous caller. "We shall keep striking at any crusader presence in Lebanon, including the international forces."[20]

At Langley, Richard L. Holm watched Jennings' report and simmered in frustration and anger.

The clacking of IBM Selectric typewriters made a nerve-gnawing racket as the beat of the teletype engulfed the office. Cigarette smoke hung thick above the desks, and yellow streaks of nicotine stained the walls. Spies, and especially their bosses, were not supposed to be clueless.

Holm ran the Counterterrorist Group, or CTG. The CTG was established in the late 1970s, as an operational arm of the Agency where analysts and clandestine officers worked side by side to combine academic insight and operational expertise in order to track the world's terrorist organizations and the bombings, hijackings, and assassinations they were perpetrating. The CTG analyzed which usual suspects—the Soviet Union and the Warsaw Pact, the Communist Chinese, the North Koreans, Cubans, Libyans, Syrians, and others—supported which terrorist outfits; alliances sometimes changed on a weekly basis, and everything was documented in an analysis titled "The Soviet Role in Revolutionary Violence." The importance of the fledgling CIA focus on terrorism was felt by all in Holm's shop. On the night of December 23, 1975, Richard Skeffington Welch, the CIA Chief of Station in Athens, Greece, was assassinated in front of his family by gunmen from the Revolutionary Organization 17 November as he returned from a Christmas party at the American ambassador's residence. At the time of his death, Welch was the highest-ranking CIA officer killed in the line of duty.[21] Holm was determined that Welch be the last CIA officer killed by terrorists.

The reams of data—both raw, and translated and analyzed by some of the best experts working on the Agency's payroll—were brought to the attention of Holm and his deputy, William F. Buckley. The two men were the most important figures in America's nascent and undefined war against international terror and perhaps the only knowledgeable men who could report on the growing scourge of terror to the policy makers. The CTG also analyzed the counterterrorist needs of allied governments, outposts in the Cold War, who found themselves besieged by the popular fronts and the liberation movements funded by the KGB and staffed by graduates of Patrice Lumumba University in Moscow and the Palestinian training academies of pre-1982 Lebanon.

Holm was a natural to lead the small office that was increasingly growing in importance. He was a paramilitary officer, someone capable of setting up an underground army, and he used his talents to establish cells and armed elements in Laos and Vietnam during President Kennedy's attempt to neutralize a growing sideshow to the Cold War. In September 1964, Holm reported for duty to the Directorate of Operations' Africa Division for service in the Republic of Congo.[22] He suffered horrific injuries in a plane crash, with burns to nearly half his body; his scars, evident and telling, spoke of a man who suffered yet persevered through a hellish rehabilitation to return to active duty. He had worked in Hong Kong before spearheading counterterrorism for the Agency.

Holm was a natural-born manager, someone who could multitask and direct multiple operations being carried out simultaneously in multiple locations around the world. On the other hand, Buckley, Holm's deputy and executive officer, was an expert in the paramilitary side of the office—what Holm referred to as the "block and tackle" aspect of the CTG's tactical responsibilities.[23] A former US Army Special Forces officer and the recipient of two Silver Stars, Buckley had been recruited by Holm for the CTG in the spring of 1982. Buckley was a special operations whiz and he had just come off a successful stint with the Protective Security Branch of the Agency's Special Operations Group. At CTG, Buckley had helped to create the Incident Response Team,[24] or IRT, a rapid-reaction force to provide solutions to fluid terrorist crises where American citizens or American interests were threatened around the world.

Buckley watched the news flashes and reviewed the teletypes and the dispatches from the coded sources that flowed into the CTG. As he read the reports and prepared analysis for CIA director William Casey, the bulldozers were still working under floodlights on Rue de Paris in Beirut. Marines were painstakingly sifting through the twisted steel and smoldering ruins desperate to find survivors; they were determined to honor those who had been killed.

NBC News broke into a feed from the White House Rose Garden. President Reagan and Vice President Bush, himself a former director of the Central Intelligence Agency, had been attending a morning ceremony honoring the Peace Corps when news of the embassy bombing broke. Reagan, a man never at a loss for words, was suddenly caught off guard but remained resolute. "This criminal attack on a diplomatic establishment will not deter us from our goals of peace in the region," Reagan said. "We will do what we know to be right."[25]

Some new CTG staffers watched and were confident that the American response would be massive and decisive. President Reagan would administer the wrath of the mightiest nation on earth on the terrorist scum responsible for this crime. The veterans, though, knew otherwise. They had been around long enough—in Central America, Southeast Asia, and South America—to realize that bad situations turn into nightmares in the blink of an eye. They continued to work the phones and review the streams of data—some plausible, some the chaotic clutter of raw information that flows in after an incident—trying to track down leads and assemble something cohesive enough to resemble fact. The cigarette smoke now began to look like a meandering fog. Ashtrays, some made of cut crystal, souvenirs from previous foreign postings, were already overflowing.

William Buckley was one of those old-timers. He hated cigarette smoking and wouldn't allow anyone to light up in his office. He worked with his door closed to keep the toxic stench out and to be allowed some quiet while reviewing his files on Lebanon ██████

██

███████████████████████████████████████

██

███

███

███.

Another miracle would be needed now. The Agency had never suffered such a calamity before.

4

THE SOLDIER SPY

WILLIAM FRANCIS BUCKLEY was born on May 30, 1928, in Medford, Massachusetts. Only three miles north of downtown Boston, Medford was a picturesque community of colonial homes, tree-lined streets, and Norman Rockwell–like vistas of fireplaces and snowfall. William was the oldest of four children; he had two sisters—Joyce and Maureen—and Bob, his younger brother, would eventually serve in the US Air Force.[1] Buckley's father, William H. Buckley, fought in the First World War; reportedly, he lied about his age in order to join the navy. He went on to be a salesman and then an insurance executive with John Hancock.[2] Buckley's mother was a homemaker. The family lived in a rented home on Riverside Avenue, a short walk from the Mystic River.

In 1941, the family moved to 612 Main Street in Stoneham, a fifteen-minute hop from downtown Boston on the trolley. "He was a good student and an athlete," his sister Maureen Moroney recalled.[3] Young boys dreamed of playing either for the Red Sox or for the Bruins. William Buckley collected metal soldiers and imagined himself in uniform.

"Bill was fascinated by history and dreamed of being a soldier," says Moroney. "It was his ambition." Patriotism ran through the blood of most in the Boston suburb. Memorial Day parades were holy events in Medford. Veterans from the Great War marched in their carefully maintained uniforms, some of which had received extensive tailoring to allow for middle-age spread. Veterans from the campaigns in the Philippines and the Spanish-American War also waved to the flag-waving crowds; the last surviving Civil War veterans waved as they sat in Studebaker convertibles.

Bill Buckley was thirteen years old when the Japanese bombed Pearl Harbor. The older brothers of his friends all signed up to serve; those too young to volunteer waited for their turn to become members of the Greatest Generation. Bill still had six years of school remaining, and like many teenagers who anxiously followed the world at war, he read the papers, watched newsreels, and waited his turn to fight. Bill attended Stoneham High School and was an honors student and an award-winning hockey forward. Bill was also vice president of his senior class and was on the yearbook staff, in the boys' glee club, and on the traffic squad. In 1947 he graduated a standout pupil and a star athlete. He enlisted in the US Army almost immediately after receiving his diploma.

William Buckley's military career commenced with two years as a military policeman. Buckley was commissioned a second lieutenant in an armored unit after attending Officer Candidate School. First Lieutenant Buckley attended the Engineer Officer Course at Fort Belvoir, Virginia, as well as the Advanced Armor Officer Course at Fort Knox, Kentucky. To round out his CV and to prepare him for taking command of a combat formation, Buckley was sent to the US Army's Intelligence School at Oberammergau, West Germany. Buckley was assigned to the First Cavalry Division—one of the oldest formations in the US Army—as a company commander. Buckley did not have to wait long before being immersed in the horrors of combat. The First Cavalry Division was dubbed the "First Team" by General Douglas MacArthur.

Captain William Buckley landed with his division at Pohangdong, crossing the Thirty-Eighth Parallel on October 9, 1950. Buckley saw extensive combat on the Korean peninsula and was the recipient of a Silver Star, the third-highest medal awarded for gallantry in action. Buckley received the Silver Star for single-handedly taking out a North Korean machine-gun emplacement; he was wounded in the assault and was also awarded the Purple Heart. He rarely spoke to colleagues and family about what happened on that ridge in Korea; the experience of charging head-on into a hail of bullets belonged only to him.

Following Korea, William Buckley left the army to earn a college degree under the provisions of the GI Bill. He graduated from Boston University in 1955 with a bachelor of arts degree in government; the CIA had requested his transcripts ten months earlier, in October 1954. William Buckley was a CIA recruiter's dream come true. His college application indicated that Buckley had studied French for three years while at Stoneham High School. At Boston University he studied elementary and intermediate German, as well as two semesters of Russian; other courses he took included Russian Literature, Politics of the Far East, Soviet Foreign Relations, and Governments of Europe.[4] With several years of military experience and foreign language proficiency, Buckley was offered a job with America's foreign espionage service.

The CIA craved men with Buckley's mettle: officers and gentlemen, educated with an analytical approach to history; patriots with a rigid philosophy of God and country. Being Catholic, like Buckley, was a plus as well. The men of New England were especially sought after. This was a period when many of the CIA's future leaders were recruited from the Ivy League: Princeton, Yale, Harvard, and Columbia. Secrecy was a religion among this cadre; members of Skull and Bones, the Yale secret society, were sought after. The Agency even recruited future conservative pundit William F. Buckley Jr., who served as a CIA officer in the early 1950s. The confusion would follow both men for years.*

Buckley's initial stint in the CIA was brief and remains classified. It is known that he was an intelligence officer but the location and details of his activities remain secret and he did not share them with his two sisters or any friends. "Bill was a very private person," his sister Maureen Moroney reflected, still protective of the secret life he chose to lead. "He wouldn't want to have anyone know what he was doing either for the army or for the CIA."[5] It is unknown why he left the CIA.

Buckley's love of history and military books brought him to work as a librarian in his native Massachusetts. He first worked in the Concord Library, and then the Winchester Library, before being hired as the assistant director of the Cary Memorial Library, in Lexington, Massachusetts. The library's location, on the very real estate where the

---

* The Central Intelligence Agency found the fact that they had two men named William F. Buckley on the roster very confusing. The payroll department repeatedly made mistakes and sent William F. Buckley Jr. paychecks belonging to William F. Buckley (of Medford, Massachusetts). The issue, annoying and frustrating, followed the two men throughout their careers; it followed Buckley (of Medford) all the way to Beirut.

American Revolution was trip-wired in an epic battle, made it a popular tourist destination. Many visitors to the center often commented that someone should make a diorama of the Battles of Concord and Lexington so that people could see what really happened. Buckley agreed. He was fascinated by the problem of understanding what America's self-appointed soldiers had done on that first of this new country's battlefields, and he took it upon himself to build a historically accurate depiction of that fateful battle in American history. He lived in a house just above the battle road in Lexington; it was the same path that Paul Revere had used to warn of the impending British advance. An amateur historian, Buckley felt a kinship with the spirits who fought in the Revolutionary War when he looked at the battlefield from his window every day.[6]

Buckley researched the battle with meticulous precision, consulting American and British archives, plus combing through the works of leading contemporary historians.[7] Every detail and aspect of the battlefield reconstruction had to be made from scratch. Lexington Green was a scraggly, muddy waste area with old stumps, rocks, and bushes surrounding the meetinghouse, and with a belfry nearby. Buckley reconstructed the actual number of Minutemen present, with their probable clothing and weapons; the exact dress, insignia, and other equipment of the British; and their probable marching order and personal appearance after a hard night of marching and delay. All this came to light from painstaking research. John F. Scheid, a world-renowned maker of military miniatures and historic dioramas, was called in to transform Buckley's research data into a vivid, three-dimensional model of Lexington Green just after the first shots were exchanged. Every detail—including the houses, shrubs, trees, earth, sky, and weather, along with the 173 soldiers on the battlefield—was re-created to appear as it must have been on April 19, 1775.

Following his work for the library, Buckley took on odd jobs. One of the most telling was a stint as a private investigator for up-and-coming legal superstar F. Lee Bailey. It is not known whether Buckley used any of the skills he had been taught during his brief stint in the CIA to help Bailey's fledgling law practice.

But Buckley was a far cry from Sam Spade. His life was about service, and he wanted to get back in uniform.

CAPTAIN WILLIAM BUCKLEY joined the US Army Reserves in 1960 and was assigned to the 320th Special Forces Detachment. At the age of thirty-two, Buckley underwent basic airborne training and the grueling Special Forces Officers Course. His unit ultimately became the Eleventh Special Forces Group (Airborne), and Buckley was assigned as a Detachment Alpha, or A-Team, commander. Each Special Forces Operational Detachment Alpha consisted of twelve operators, each with a specific mission skill. Later on, Buckley was assigned to command an Operational Detachment Bravo, or B-Detachment, which supported A-Teams at the headquarters level. He ultimately saw combat duty in Vietnam.[8]

The CIA was recruiting out of the Eleventh Special Forces Group (Airborne). Vietnam was heating up, an old colleague of Buckley's remembered, and the CIA was looking for men with special operations capabilities, the right pedigree, and a desire for danger. Several NCOs were recruited through an office in downtown Boston by a mysterious figure known only as "Gurl."[9] It is believed that Buckley was recruited into a little-known CIA program ███████████ ███ which targeted Special Forces veterans due to the growing clandestine war in Vietnam.

Buckley rejoined the Agency in 1965, though he continued as a Special Forces officer, serving in Vietnam with MACV—the Military

Assistance Command Vietnam—and as a senior military adviser to the Army of the Republic of Vietnam.

Still serving in the Special Forces, Buckley was by now also a member of the CIA Special Activities Division ███████████████ ███.

Green Berets like Buckley were perfect for these dangerous duties.

In Southeast Asia, Buckley served with indigenous anti-communist guerrilla forces set up by the CIA to fight the Vietcong, the North Vietnamese Army, and other communist forces involved in the conflict. Buckley served in Luang Prabang Province in Laos from 1971 to 1973 as a paramilitary officer. "Buckley's gift was his ability to take a ragtag force of barefoot tribesmen, sometimes carrying nothing more than a spear and their determination, and to assemble them into a conventional military formation," a former paramilitary colleague from the Agency commented. "Buckley knew how to drill these people, equip them, train them, and lead them on missions against the enemy. He was able to establish a logistics pipeline that turned primitive into potent. He helped these forces establish their own intelligence and operational capabilities. To many of these formations, operating inside the jungles of Asia or the mountain tribal areas, Bill was both George Washington and George Patton rolled into one."[10]

Remarkably, on break from his CIA duties, Buckley served as a capable Special Forces combat commander. As a comrade recalled, some of Buckley's Agency service in Vietnam was in the CIA-run Phoenix Program. The program was an intelligence-driven campaign that was spearheaded by the CIA Special Activities Division, US special operations units, US Army intelligence-collection teams from Military Assistance Command Vietnam (MACV), special operations squads from the Australian Army Training Team Vietnam, and South Vietnamese Special Forces and Provincial Reconnaissance Units, or

PRUs. The PRUs were accused of being hit squads, and the questioning of suspects often involved outright torture. More than twenty-five thousand people were killed in these operations. Buckley's role in the Phoenix Program is believed to have centered on the establishment of PRUs in 1967 and 1968. Buckley didn't like talking about his battlefield exploits, but he did send to a close friend back in Massachusetts a few black-and-white snapshots showing him cradling a World War II–era Thompson .45 caliber submachine gun.

Buckley received a Silver Star, his second such medal for valor, for courage under fire for his role in operations actions on September 2, 1968, while he was serving in Phuoc Tuy Province as an adviser for a Provincial Reconnaissance Unit that targeted a communist headquarters in the Long Hai Mountains. The team that Major Buckley led came under heavy fire while they placed demolition charges inside a network of fortifications and tunnels. Buckley did not let the incessant enemy opposition deter his command of the operation. He lit the fuses before seeking cover. Moving down the mountain, he then discovered an enemy base camp containing many items of equipment and a cache of explosives. While he was setting the charges to destroy the supplies and ordnance, the area came under intense hostile fire and Buckley's men were dangerously exposed. Realizing that the charges he had set would explode in their midst if hit by enemy fire, Buckley ran about the camp moving charges out of the line of enemy fire. Buckley then called in an air strike to silence the enemy fire and cover him while he lit the fuses of the remaining explosive charges; he zig-zagged from point to point to avoid the snipers firing at him. When all the charges were set, Buckley gave the command and the base camp was destroyed in a thunderous explosion.[11]

Buckley was a daring operator and officer, a comrade recounted. On one mission, he led a Vietnamese reconnaissance element into enemy territory. They initiated contact with the North Vietnamese and were being followed, harassed, and attacked as the unit exfiltrated overland. Along the way out, Bill and the team encountered several enemy tunnel systems and ammunition supply depots, which Bill entered, rigged for demolitions, and destroyed, inflicting damage to the enemy supply systems as well as inflicting casualties on the enemy forces in pursuit.[12] Buckley also received commendations from the South Vietnamese military. One such citation indicated Buckley as being an "exemplary intelligence officer."

Buckley would remain in Vietnam, serving both the US Army and the Agency, until 1972.

SOUTHEAST ASIA WAS a magnet for soldiers, spies, opportunists, and rogue souls, and Buckley met about all of them. One of those men was Chip Beck, who soon became one of Buckley's closest friends and colleagues. Beck began his military service as a Navy frogman before going on to work in Naval Intelligence. In 1969 he arrived in Vietnam for a combat tour of duty with the US Marine Corps. A swashbuckling spirit with a gregarious personality, Beck was outgoing and artistic. He sketched much of what he saw in Vietnam, capturing the sights of war and the countryside it ravaged as only a soldier could. He was quickly recruited for service in the CIA.* "Bill and I met in Laos in 1971," Beck recalled. "I was a first-tour SOD Paramilitary Officer assigned to Luang Prabang as an adviser to MR-I Guerrilla Battalions (BGs). A few months into my tour, Bill was sent up from

---

* Beck would eventually see Agency service in wars and conflict zones in Vietnam, Laos, Cambodia, Angola, ███████████████ Beirut, ██████, Honduras ████████████████████ and Operation Desert Storm. As a Reserve Intelligence Officer, he was Commanding Officer of a Navy Criminal Investigative Service unit and a Defense Intelligence Agency unit.

Udorn as the senior PM advisor. We worked together during some exciting events from 1971 to 1973. Bill and I were in several combat situations together and formed a close professional and personal relationship."[13]

One of Buckley's mentors in the CIA's Special Activities Division was Tucker Pierre Edward Gougelmann, an Agency legend. Gougelmann was a Columbia University graduate and maverick US Marine Corps major who saw extensive combat around Guadalcanal and the Solomon Islands. Seriously wounded by a Japanese sniper on New Georgia in 1944, Gougelmann fought the War Department for the right to return to active duty despite his wounds. In 1947, he joined the newly formed Central Intelligence Agency.

Gougelmann had fought in the Pacific with the Marine Raiders, an elite special operations unit that carried out amphibious missions deep behind Japanese lines. In a nascent intelligence service staffed largely by Ivy Leaguers, his commando skills were highly valued. During the Korean War he led CIA special operations; following the war, he ran agents in and out of Eastern Europe. Reportedly, he was knee-deep in the disastrous Bay of Pigs invasion of Fidel Castro's Cuba.[14] In 1962 Gougelmann arrived in South Vietnam to take over covert maritime operations. He directed attacks against North Vietnamese targets before going to work at the CIA station in Saigon, where he met William Buckley. The Marine veteran took an immediate liking to the ex–Green Beret, even though they were two very different types of men: Gougelmann was quick-tempered and hard-charging, foul-mouthed and loud; Buckley was quiet and reserved, soft-spoken and deliberate with each word. Yet the two men formed a unique working relationship. "Bill was very much a 'yes sir, no sir' kind of man. Military protocol and spit-and-polish discipline was in every breath he took, every move he made," a colleague of Buckley's recalled, "and

Tucker appreciated men who were always ready and forever reliable for a journey into danger on a dark and treacherous night."[15]

By the summer of 1976, a year after the end of the war in Vietnam, Gougelmann was a civilian living in Bangkok. Although he enjoyed the comfortable life of an eccentric expat in an exotic paradise, he decided to return to Vietnam to assist women and children in escaping the communist onslaught. He was betrayed and arrested. Agents from the General Directorate of State Security of the Ministry of Interior tortured and interrogated him inside Ho Chi Minh City's notorious maximum-security prison; it is believed that the KGB was hands-on in the brutal questioning he was subjected to. Although the Vietnamese denied holding Gougelmann, his remains were turned over to the US government in 1977. An autopsy revealed the extent of the beatings and cruelty. Over thirty bones had been broken; some had been shattered and then crushed over and over again in what must have been an endless regimen of savage cruelty.

Gougelmann's grisly fate haunted Buckley. His biggest fear, a colleague at Langley recalled, was that he'd be captured by the enemy, beaten to within an inch of his life, and left to rot in captivity, alone and forgotten.

WILLIAM BUCKLEY TRAVELED the world for the CIA as a paramilitary officer with great command-and-logistics skills. "Bill did one thing great," a former Agency colleague reflected, "and that was creating special operations counterterrorist units from scratch,"

██

██████████

When Buckley wasn't in Angola, Cambodia ████████████████

████████████

██, he
was one of the many Brooks Brothers–suit-wearing middle-aged
men walking through the turnstiles at CIA headquarters in Langley.
He dressed conservatively. He rarely rolled up his sleeves or even loos-
ened his tie. He wore only one piece of jewelry, his OCS ring, which
was stolen in the late 1970s during an assignment ████████████. He
never had it replaced.

Buckley was a company man in every sense of the term. He lived a
nondescript and secretive existence, like a man who might need to
disappear at a moment's notice. "Bill kept an apartment in Northwest
Washington, near N and Twenty-Second Street," Chip Beck remembered. "As a bachelor who was frugal with his income, he could afford
to do that. Bill rarely invited people from work to his apartment, preferring to keep his private life separate from his professional one. I was
one of maybe two or three exceptions to that practice. Inside the dwell-
ing, Bill had it tastefully decorated with antiques and memorabilia
from his world travels and early life in historic New England. Bill was
incredibly neat and organized. His desk at work was always squared
away with papers in tidy stacks and never strewn about the desk. His
apartment reflected the same orderliness."

Buckley was low-maintenance and predictable, friends recalled.
He had a dry sense of humor. He liked listening to music from the
1950s. He would often joke with those he felt comfortable talking
to—and their numbers were small—that his politics were "to the right
of Genghis Khan."[16] One passion was antiques. Buckley was a true
American picker and he relished any opportunity to explore history

through artifacts and memorabilia. He even purchased a portrait of George Washington dating to the late 1770s that he had found for a bargain in an estate sale. Chip Beck shared this hobby, and the two friends went into business together, taking over a small antiques shop in Virginia that they named the Eagle's Nest and operated together on weekends.

According to Chip Beck, "Bill and I both enjoyed bartering with customers. One old Jewish guy was really aiming at the lowest price possible, noting that his grandfather always said, 'It's better to make a quick nickel than wait for a slow dime.' Great advice, we thought. Some people would like a piece and offer to pay the asking price. Bill would say something like, 'Well, you're not from New England, are you? You're supposed to bargain the price down, you know.' Bill's humor was so wry and crisp that people often did not realize he was joking or pulling their leg."[17]

Beck and Buckley ran the store for over six months—until Beck had to deploy overseas for an Agency assignment. Both had agreed at the outset that when the time came for one or both to go overseas, they'd sell the place lock, stock, and barrel, just as they had bought it. After accounting for the monthly rent, overhead, and the fact they had worked only on weekends, the profit was three thousand dollars. The bounty was split equally between the two friends.

ANOTHER FRIENDSHIP THAT Buckley forged at the Agency was with Sam Wyman. Wyman was one of the most capable and experienced Middle Eastern hands in the Agency's Near East Division. His father had been an officer in US Army intelligence who was posted to Cairo in 1946 and later served as Defense Attaché in Pakistan. Childhood travels in the Middle East fascinated Wyman: upon his graduation from Georgetown University's School of Foreign Service, he faced a choice—law school or Middle Eastern studies. He opted for the addictive, fascinating, and frustrating world of Middle Eastern studies. Wyman pursued a graduate degree at the School of International Affairs Middle Eastern Studies Institute at Columbia University in New York; the focus of his research was Iraq. The knock on the door from the CIA followed shortly thereafter with an offer he couldn't refuse: "Would you like to ███████████?"[18] It was the launch of a thirty-one-year career.

Wyman went on to serve as a clandestine officer throughout the Middle East, including assignments to ██████████ during ████████ ████████ and stations in the ██████████. He met Buckley in ████████████████████, while Buckley was working as a project leader for a paramilitary project with special operations units. Wyman found him capable and focused. "He was very flexible in how he dealt with situations and indigenous personnel he interacted with," Wyman would explain. "He may not have known the details of the local culture he was dealing with, but he appreciated that there was a local culture."[19]

When Wyman was assigned to the CIA station ████████, he summoned Buckley to lead the project to create an indigenous CIA-trained ██████████████████ counterterrorist force. The friendship between Wyman and Buckley blossomed ████████. Wyman's wife, Laurie, made sure that Buckley was a frequent dinner guest in their home.

The friendship continued in Langley. The two men went out to eat once or twice a month. The conversation never centered on shoptalk. "Bill hated office gossip and office politics. It was beneath him," Wyman recalled. "He talked about history, politics, music, and movies. He never spoke about his wartime exploits. He was humble. He would never toot his own horn. Bill was a man who was comfortable in his own skin."[20]

* * *

BUCKLEY WAS A handsome man, with slight salt-and-pepper shading to a hairline that withstood the ravages of war and middle age. His piercing gray eyes and chiseled features made him a standout, while his athletic past and adherence to military self-discipline shaped his frame to one that men half his age would have relished. With his Hollywood looks, Kennedy accent, and mysterious ways, Buckley could have been like many of his contemporaries at Langley: divorced two or three times and juggling a series of lovers in stash apartments throughout the Beltway and around the world. Buckley, though, didn't fit that profile. He was a bachelor—his life was the job, his existence serving his country. It was cliché to some. It was sacrosanct to him.

Though reticent to share his life with others, Buckley did have a significant other. Beverly Surette, like Buckley, was a Massachusetts native. The two first met in 1961 at the Memorial Day parade held in Lexington. They lived together on and off, dependent on Buckley's military and Agency missions, until 1983. When Buckley was deployed overseas, he corresponded with Surette through letters and audiocassettes that he would record on an old Panasonic tape recorder. When his missions weren't covert, Buckley was able to write a few notes on a postcard and send it to Surette to show her a glimpse of where his travels had taken him.

Beverly Surette's name and telephone number were listed on Buckley's personnel file, the first to call if anything happened. Buckley, though, never wanted to get married. He never wanted children. A man, he believed, whose career could summon him away from home for a week here, or one or two years there, shouldn't assume the role of the absentee head of a family. There was great risk and danger in what Buckley did for a living, and he didn't want to subject a child to the torturous existence of waiting endless nights for Daddy to come.

He had also seen more than his share of widows and orphans standing graveside at Arlington, at the funeral of their husband or father, wincing in tears as the twenty-one-gun salute was fired into the sky.

There was freedom to being a bachelor, and Buckley enjoyed it. But there was also a professional downside. Men who had no dependents were often volunteered for assignments that no one else wanted, to go where few others were willing to go.

5

A RACE TO BEDLAM

*The righteous shall flourish like the palm tree: he shall
grow like a cedar in Lebanon.*

Psalms 92:12

THE UNMISTAKABLE STENCH of decaying flesh was already inescapable around the Corniche where the US Embassy had stood.
Earthmoving equipment chugged slowly over rubble, clearing out
blocks of concrete and eviscerated chunks of automobiles that were
thrown violently by the force of the blast. The explosion had turned
the seven-story structure into a field of debris. The ground was a car-
pet of shattered glass. Those lucky enough to be wearing protective
combat boots made a crushing sound as they walked around the area,
crunching smaller bits of blown-out windows into powder like sand.
Rescue workers wore scarves around their mouths to protect against
inhaling the debris and smelling the dead; some of the lucky ones
worked with surgical masks. Ambulance drivers stood by smoking
cigarettes while waiting to be summoned when a body, or a piece of a
corpse, was found among the twisted rebar. The morgue, especially at
the American University of Beirut Medical Center, was overflowing

with bodies. The families of the dead—and the missing—maintained vigils, waiting for loved ones to be identified, or for pieces of them just to be located. Young marines, their battle rattle on and their weapons at the ready, attempted to maintain a protective perimeter around the devastation. Their tempers—and tolerance—were on short fuses. There was tremendous fear of a second strike.

US State Department SY Special Agent Pete Gallant arrived in Beirut on April 20. He had been on assignment in Bulgaria when he was summoned by headquarters to rush to Beirut to assist in the investigation and the recovery of remains from the blast site. He drove through the night, hightailing it from Sofia to Athens in order to catch a Middle Eastern Airlines flight to Beirut International Airport. The airport, nestled along the Mediterranean coastline and snuggled against the Shiite slums in the southern precincts of the capital, was the only official way in or out of the city from overseas. CIA security specialists were also rushed to Beirut to try to piece together the details as to what had happened and to try to Scotch-tape the remnants into something useful. A lone FBI special agent, a forensic specialist, was also dispatched from Quantico: his job was to take the fingerprints of the dead for identification. In some cases, all he'd be able to find was a loose finger.

Gallant was unarmed when he arrived in Beirut, but the investigators were protected by twenty US Navy SEALs who were flown in by chopper from a US Navy warship in the Mediterranean. The SEALs were ordered to shoot first and ask questions later. The ambassador, the remaining shreds of the embassy, and the crime-scene investigators were to be protected at all costs. There was a lot of work to do.

There were more than physical security concerns to contend with. The collapse of the building's façade had exposed the Acoustic Conference Room, the "bubble" used for sensitive conversations and classified meetings, as well as storage of classified files. What was left of the ACR was now within eyeshot of the Soviet Embassy located approximately 1,500 meters to the south. Under the cover of darkness, the contents of the room were carefully lowered to be concealed from prying KGB eyes. Safes containing highly classified files were blown open by US Navy Seabees.

State Department SEOs, or Security Engineering Officers, were flown in to help secure the embassy's move from the smoldering crater down the Corniche to the British Embassy. "The SEOs cut aluminum sheets and placed them inside car doors to provide temporary light armor, while main operations relocated down the Corniche to the British Embassy," Pete Gallant remembered. "A row of apartments next to the embassy and AUB were mustered into temporary office space. David Pugh, the chargé d'affaires, and his wife, Bonnie, were wonderful, with the missus baking cakes and cookies for the body-recovery crew in the days that followed."*[1] A Marine rifle platoon from "Black Beach" secured the perimeter—along with the Corniche area between the bombed-out embassy and the British chancery—while the rescue effort proceeded.

There was good reason for the security. Well-trained eyes were focused on the marines and the federal investigators. The watchers, some sitting in cars parked far away, observed and photographed.

PRESIDENT RONALD REAGAN ventured to Andrews Air Force Base late on the afternoon of Saturday, April 23, 1983, to preside over the

---

* Bonnie Pugh was killed on September 19, 1989, in the terrorist bombing of UTA Flight 772. The aircraft, a DC-10, was destroyed shortly after taking off from N'Djamena International Airport. The bombing was perpetrated by Libyan intelligence.

return of remains of the Americans killed in the bombing of the Beirut Embassy. The president and first lady solemnly walked past the sixteen* flag-draped coffins in the hangar at the base. President Reagan's voice cracked, overcome as he was by the loss of life, as he told the assembled 150 family members of the dead that their loved ones had not died in vain. "The dastardly deed, the unparalleled act of cowardice that took their lives, was an attack on all of us," Reagan said. "We would indeed fail them if we let that act deter us from carrying on their mission of brotherhood and peace."[2]

The White House did everything it could to keep the deaths of the eight CIA officers and analysts out of the press. The *New York Times* reported, "There have been press reports that most of the Americans killed in the explosion were C.I.A. employees, but the Administration has only confirmed that one of those killed actually worked for the C.I.A."[3] News of so many CIA personnel killed in the strike could have been devastating.

Iranian complicity in the bombing, an unbridled act of war, should have sparked enormous concern in the White House about the onset of a quagmire in Lebanon. Reagan had been elected with an unwritten pledge to lift the United States out of its Vietnam-induced stupor. It was morning in America again, after all, and the United States would no longer be sucked into conflicts that slowly drained the national resolve. But Reagan's foreign policy focus was on Lebanon and the other allies in the Middle East that were threatened by a whole host of Soviet-supported sponsors of terrorism. The most dangerous threat to Lebanon, the Reagan administration understood, was Syria—the Soviet Union's chief client in the Arab world. "Syria is a terrorist state

---

* The body of the seventeenth victim, Albert Votaw, was buried in Lebanon at the request of his family.

and is so classified by the State Department," former Secretary of State Alexander Haig had once said.

Haig's enthusiastic support of Israel's policies in the region as being the same as those of the United States was not shared by President Reagan or Secretary of State George P. Schultz; they were equally opposed to the often anti-Israel sentiments of Defense Secretary Weinberger. Israel's 1982 invasion of its northern neighbor had created an opportunity for a Lebanon rid of Palestinian forces to be the linchpin of a new Middle East that the Reagan administration hoped to forge. America's allies in the region would be armed to the teeth with the latest in US hardware, ready, willing, and able to fight Soviet-sponsored states and terrorist factions.

DURING THE SECOND World War, William Casey was assigned to Army Intelligence and ultimately to the Office of Strategic Services, and headed espionage operations in Nazi-occupied Europe from his headquarters in London. Casey, a native of Queens, New York, was known for his blunt style, sharp wit, and uncannily analytical mind. He was a natural for the covert world of intrigue and danger. Casey was a star in this nascent American espionage service conducted behind enemy lines—many agents were killed or executed; some were even sent to concentration camps. "All we could do was pop a guy into Germany with a radio and hope to hear from them,"[4] Casey was quoted as saying of his service running agents in and out of Europe. He knew many of the agents would never return. The human cost of such service would remain on his conscience for the rest of his life. The lives of agents, Casey knew, were to be protected by all means necessary. Casey was awarded a Bronze Star for meritorious service with the OSS.

Casey became a millionaire following the war—as a packager and processor of legal and economic information for corporate customers, and later mainly as a venture capitalist.[5] Casey was highly respected and admired on both sides of the political divide. During his confirmation hearings, Senator Daniel Patrick Moynihan, a Democrat, introduced his fellow New Yorker by saying, "Were there more men like William Casey in this nation the president would have less difficulty in filling his cabinet." William Casey was a Reagan favorite, a stoic and outspoken counsel, who was nominated to lead the Agency in 1981 after running the president's election campaign. The appointment wasn't just an act of political gratitude to a wily—and successful—campaign manager. There were few other men with his résumé of espionage experience, his direct, shoot-from-the-hip style, and his analytical mind.

Casey was an outspoken proponent of the Agency's support of Third World forces combating communism. Second World War veterans like Casey compared the epic struggle against communism to the all-out fight against Hitler. The CIA director had a special place in his heart for the ███████ officers that led this epic struggle on battlefields around the world. They were direct yet disciplined. ███
██
██
███████████████████████████████[6]

Casey first took notice of Buckley in 1982, shortly after the IRT became operational. International aid workers had been kidnapped in the Sudan and the CIA deployed its special operations assets, including helicopters and other forces, to rescue them. After the mission, Richard Holm instructed Buckley to brief "the Old Man," as Casey was affectionately known. His briefing was well received and "no doubt it raised the profile of our group up on the seventh floor," Holm recalled.

After the bombing of the Beirut Embassy and the loss of so many

CIA personnel, including Station Chief Kenneth Haas, Casey remembered Buckley's performance at the briefing several years before. He had liked what he saw. When it came time to select a replacement for Haas, Buckley's name was on the short list of candidates bandied about at headquarters.

Beirut Station fell inside the organizational flowchart of the Near East and South Asia Division in the Directorate of Operations, and thus Chuck Cogan, the division chief, was responsible for the selection of the new man in Lebanon. Elegant, almost aristocratic, Cogan had joined the Agency in 1954, ███████████████████████████ ████████████████████ before being named division chief.[7] Cogan had been one of those anonymous men at Andrews Air Force Base who received the coffins of so many of the CIA's fallen. They were the remains of Cogan's men and women, heroes like Kenneth Haas and Robert Ames and the others, some still unnamed. Those bodies were his friends. For him, the selection of a new leader for Beirut Station was personal.

Sam Wyman, Cogan's chief adviser, recommended Buckley for the post. Cogan concurred. Buckley's special operations training, his abilities, and his battlefield experience were unrivaled in the Agency. "What do you think about Bill heading our office in Beirut?" Cogan asked Richard Holm, a courtesy from a division chief to the head of the Counterterrorism Group. Holm's response was quick and confident. "Bill would make a fine station chief, especially in that stress-filled environment. What's more," Holm continued, "I'm sure if you ask him he'll say yes."[8] Holm knew that Buckley would never refuse an assignment. Even if the job was unsavory and dangerous, Buckley was one of those men at headquarters who would smile, thank their boss for the opportunity, and pack their bags.

Some in Langley argued that Buckley wasn't the right choice to head to Beirut and rebuild the apparatus constructed by Kenneth Haas and others. He was a paramilitary officer, not a clandestine officer, the type who typically became a Chief of Station. Clandestine officers were experts in establishing intelligence networks, running agents, and manipulating HUMINT sources into cohesive long-term operations. "Bill hadn't had that experience yet," Holm recalled. "I told Cogan that I was confident that Bill would handle the job, a tough one at the time as you know, with his standard professional approach. My vote was a strong yes."[9]

When Wyman spoke to Buckley about the prospect of the Beirut assignment, his initial response was one of resigned disbelief. Sitting silently in Wyman's office, dressed impeccably in a Brooks Brothers suit, he was careful not to express just how much he didn't want the job. In fact, no one in the Agency wanted the assignment. Few understood the complexities of the forces that were propelling Lebanon even deeper into bloodshed and conflict, but few believed that the nation could be saved. Beirut was considered suicide. But Buckley, even at the age of fifty-five, could not refuse a mission. "Make sure you support me," was all he asked. "Make sure you brief me and bring me up to speed."[10]

"Buckley's selection reflected the posture we were in [in Lebanon], a military presence and not necessarily one requiring an intelligence specialist," a former officer with experience in Beirut reflected. "Buckley was the kind of man who could bring discipline and organizational skill set to the task at rebuilding the presence in Lebanon. He had also been at war for much of his adult life."[11] Casey soon summoned Buckley to the seventh floor for a one-on-one. The Old Man had already assembled a dossier on his new Beirut chief, and he liked what he read. Buckley was no stranger to danger, used to living under siege. He was capable of surviving in a city beset by shortages—food, water, electricity—and ruled by the AK-47. The fact that Buckley hadn't served as a clandestine officer was irrelevant given his background. Casey realized that there were never absolutes in the espionage business—only multiple shades of gray accented by trade-offs.

The two men met privately, behind closed doors. It is not known what was said during the meeting, though the sit-down was brief. Casey was personable yet direct; Buckley was pure respect. Even if Casey came out from behind his desk to sit across from Buckley in a less formal setting, Buckley would have been all "Yes, sir! No, sir!" Rank mattered to him. He was formal in everything he did. He addressed everyone above him in the chain of command as sir.[12] This is why he didn't argue the Beirut assignment. Buckley was a soldier. He did what he was told.

The meeting between Casey and Buckley ended with a handshake. It was now official.

BOOK TWO

BEIRUT

6

BRASS BALLS

William Buckley wore a dark gray business suit his first day on the job. His shoes were polished and his dress shirt ironed to sharp angles that would have made any army sergeant major blush with pride. His tie was conservative, worn in a half-Windsor knot. He was clean-shaven, and his salt-and-pepper hair, longer than usual, was parted on the right and neatly slicked back over his ears. Despite the care he had taken in his appearance, he looked tired. It was an exhaustion that went beyond that of a man getting on in years and who had spent far too much time walking about distant lands with a rifle slung over his shoulder. This fatigue was pronounced, longer lasting than the effects of jet lag and the Beirut heat. All it took was that first drive to the office, past heavily armed psychopaths in undershirts smoking cigarettes and aiming their RPGs at oncoming traffic, for Buckley to truly appreciate the magnitude of the job for which he had been volunteered. That weariness became overwhelming when he drove past the bomb site where the old embassy had stood.

US marines manned sandbagged positions that surrounded the British Embassy near the Corniche. Concertina wire was laid all around a perimeter that allowed the Marine M60 light machine guns to decimate any vehicle speeding toward the chancery with a wall of devastating fire. State Department Security Engineering Officers constructed a fortified side door that separated the British side of the building from the portion of the building now allotted to the US Embassy. US Navy Seabees and other engineers from the Department of Defense prepared the phone and telex lines, as well as offices belonging to the Defense Attaché. CIA specialists from the Office of Technical Services built the compartments and offices for the CIA station. ███████████████████████████████████████.
████████████████████████ The station, basically an elongated corridor, faced north. It consisted of a communications section; a "bullpen," where case officers had their desks, typewriters, and telephones; a reports office; a technical office; and the deputy's office. A row of chargers for Motorola field radios was positioned near the technical office. A Xerox machine was positioned near desks. Buckley hated the contraption. Early on, shortly after his arrival in Beirut, he unsuccessfully tried to photocopy a document and banged on the machine in frustration. "This thing doesn't work," he complained, only to be directed to a light blinking the words "add paper," which caused a lighthearted chuckle by his staff.[1]

The Chief of Station had the only private office. It was cramped and claustrophobic. Some of Buckley's personal mementos, photos and books that he had packed before departure, were carefully placed in his office. The room was furnished with odds and ends thrown together ██.

The Chief of Station had a full-time secretary. A sign-out board was posted on the wall near where the secretary sat. It was one of the only ways that the Chief of Station could keep tabs on where the case officers were.

███

███

██ The station smelled like the United States: the rugs were shampooed with the same industrial cleanser that all federal offices used. IBM Selectric typewriters clacked away at a furious pace, filling the mauve-colored walls with a kind of pulsating Muzak that rivaled the white noise back at Langley; there weren't enough electric machines to go around in the station, so some of the officers remembered having to pound out reports on manual typewriters. The ribbon tapes from the typewriters were locked up at night to prevent foreign spies from stealing them and reading the content—tapes left in typewriters and uncovered by ████████████████████ were a security violation. Portraits of President Reagan, Vice President Bush, and Director Casey were strategically placed throughout the office. An American flag was positioned near a row of file cabinets. A ████ guarded the staircase leading up to the third floor. Access to the station was secured with a black-dialed S&G Cipher lock.

Langley had also requisitioned two four-drawer Mosler safes for the new Beirut station. The safes were behemoths, each weighing hundreds of pounds. ███████████████████ had warned, with great worry, that the floors were not strong enough to withstand the weight of the Moslers. ██████████████████ working on the floor below were terrified that the American spies and their safes would collapse in on top of them. ████████████████████████████████

But the bombing of the US Embassy had come without warning or telltale chatter, and MI6 had been caught completely by surprise. It angered him just how little even the best spies in the business knew about what was actually happening in Lebanon. Still, to MI6 the Americans were the competition, rivals fighting for the same golden nuggets of intelligence in an elimination contest of which service could recruit the highest-level source. Both MI6 and Buckley were up against the efforts of the friendly services operating in the Lebanese capital—the Mossad, France's Action Service, Italy's Servizio per le Informazioni e la Sicurezza Militare (Military Intelligence and Security Service), as well as the Arab spy services, wary of what their own citizens might be up to in Lebanon (Algerian military intelligence, the Sécurité Militaire, maintained a particularly bold presence in Beirut). The Soviet KGB and the East Germans had vast resources invested in Beirut—the American and British intelligence stronghold was permanently in their crosshairs. Officers from Syrian military intelligence meddled wherever they could, manipulating whoever pushed an independent agenda that didn't coincide with the grand scheme for Lebanon being orchestrated in Damascus. The Syrians were always scheming.

Spies and traitors were everywhere. The espionage backdrop was surreal. William Buckley was simply the latest arrival to the espionage battlefield.

AS THE HIGHEST-RANKING US intelligence officer in Lebanon, Buckley was responsible not only for running the day-to-day intelligence-gathering operations at the station, but also for executing American foreign policy through covert and overt means to support the central government. The US government did not support the sects, and their corresponding militias were at least as strong, as well armed, and as well trained as the central government. "There is a cost to be paid to support an irrational fiction of a central government when there is no such thing though we insist that there is," a former CIA officer in Beirut reflected.[2]

The Lebanese Armed Forces, or LAF, were in utter disarray following eight years of civil war, Syrian intervention, and Israeli invasion. The army was rife with desertions and poor morale; the best fighters in the country found combat opportunities with their own sects in their indigenous militias. Sunnis deserted from the Christian-led ranks in droves. Still, US plans for Lebanon were dependent on the reestablishment of a strong central government that could field a military backbone. The Army Intelligence Directorate (Muchabarat-al Jaish, in Arabic) was considered the most reliable arm of the LAF

Because the Army Intelligence Directorate was run by Maronite officers, men who spoke French with sentimental pride, the military spy service was known in the country as the Deuxième Bureau, the Second Bureau.

Buckley's status in Lebanon

██████████ Kassis was a mysterious and wily spy chief who worked tirelessly to preserve some semblance of Lebanon's past so that it would have a sliver of hope for its future. Kassis was a Maronite, a French speaker, and someone who tried to place his love for the country over the sectarian divides that had metastasized during the 1970s into full-scale civil war. The Kassis clan was powerful in the Lebanese military. Kassis' relative Louis, a colonel, was in charge of the presidential guard.[3] Kassis was what was known in the business as a juggler—though he juggled hand grenades with their pins already pulled. He knew all of the local warlords, including those who swore to kill him. Gemayel's government was made up of Shiite, Sunni, and Druze gang leaders and Kassis had to meet and placate each one of them. Kassis, like many survivors of the Lebanese battlefield, kept his friends close and his enemies even closer.

Kassis was middle-aged and balding. His salt-and-pepper hair was close-cropped and he was physically fit. When he worked from his office, dealing with his soldiers, Kassis was always in fatigues. His sage green military uniform featured razor-sharp creases; his sleeves were immaculately folded. When an important guest ███████████ ████████████ came calling he made it a point to wear a dress blouse and slacks that had been flown in from Paris. Kassis was soft-spoken. His English was excellent. He was the type of man who chose to listen carefully, eager to dissect the most important words and to weigh their sincerity by the inflection of the speaker's voice. But Kassis also had a spymaster's swagger. He made it a point to show off his car, a 1981 Jaguar XJ-S HE that he had bought for a song from one of

Arafat's top henchmen just before the Palestinians were expelled from Beirut. Kassis parked it in front of his office at the Ministry of Defense in Yarze under the red and white LAF flag bearing the motto "Honor, Sacrifice, Loyalty."

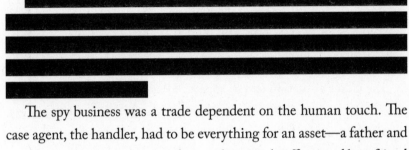

The spy business was a trade dependent on the human touch. The case agent, the handler, had to be everything for an asset—a father and a mother, a priest, banker, warden, pusher, parole officer, and best friend forever. Some assets were walk-ins, locals who simply stood on line outside an embassy and told one of the security guards that they needed to talk to a security agent about matters of the direst importance. Other assets and sources had to be recruited, cajoled, blackmailed, and entrapped. No matter how the source ultimately became a source, trust was an integral element of the relationship between handler and source.

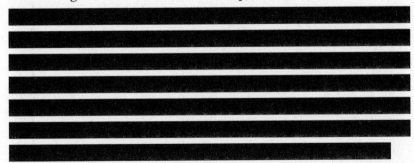

Langley rotated CIA officers in and out of Beirut following the embassy bombing. The men and women were primarily young officers on temporary duty. There were safe houses and apartments to rent throughout Christian East Beirut, considered far safer for American personnel in the country, so that officers and assets could meet under the radar of hostile eyes that might be watching. The accommodations were expensive and the young officers had to be lavished with manila envelopes full of cash to keep the leases flexible. The station car pool also required effort and investment. There were new sedans—vehicles armored in local garages to be able to withstand small-arms fire—and beat-up jalopies, known by American cops as ghetto cars, that could be used for surveillance and insertion.

The Chief of Station had to approve all acquisitions. Buckley managed everything at the station, and he supervised a team of case officers, reports officers, logistics-support officers, communications specialists, and cryptographers. Buckley was responsible for managing the talent and for coordinating their work into reports that would be sent to headquarters via cables and other secure means. Most of the CIA officers sent to Beirut Station were young. "All of the men and women assigned to Beirut were first-tour officers," one of Buckley's officers explained. "It could be understood if Buckley was a little hesitant about just who he was getting on his team."[4]

Bob* was the Deputy Chief of Station, and the only member of Buckley's station with a CV's worth of operational experience. Bob was a Near Eastern Division veteran who had earned his stripes in Arab nations that were both friend and foe to the United States. Bob spoke fluent Arabic and was a highly experienced case agent and handler who could recruit high-level and top-tier human sources. Bob had been recruited to serve as Buckley's number two specifically because of his clandestine experience. Chuck Cogan knew that Buckley didn't have the experience or the time to properly supervise the officers in the sta-

---

* A pseudonym.

tion in their intelligence-gathering responsibilities. Bob would oversee the espionage component of Beirut Station.

Buckley and his deputy clashed from the onset.[5] Like all clandestine officers worth their salt, Bob sought intelligence—raw or refined—from the most reliable sources possible, preferring those possessing inside insight available to few others. ████████████████████████

██

██

██

Buckley's arrival was intended to restore law and order to Beirut Station and reestablish the flow of information from the city's alleyways to the decision-makers in Washington. He was determined to let everyone know that he was, indeed, in command. Things at Beirut Station would be done his way.

CHIEFS OF STATION, according to one veteran clandestine officer, were the "lords of the manor." They were autonomous rulers whose word was final. Buckley ran Beirut Station like a rifle platoon. He looked after his men and women in the field above all else. During the day he never ate lunch unless he was certain that all of his staff had already eaten. In Buckley's station there weren't any of the trappings of rank or privilege that existed at headquarters or at other CIA offices throughout the world. Buckley led by example. He was a field commander in combat and the welfare of his troops was part of a military code of honor he followed religiously.

Like any army officer in the field, Buckley wanted to make sure that his men made it back home alive. Or, at least, he wanted to give them a fighting chance. Beirut was rife with dangers. In the summer of 1983, a mini-war—a sideshow to the larger chaos—erupted in the Chouf Mountains. The first skirmishes were between the Lebanese Forces and the Druze militias; the enmity dated back to 1860 when Christian and Druze forces fought when Lebanon was ruled by the Ottoman Turks. The fighting was blowback to exhausting and ultimately futile negotiations to initiate the evacuation of all foreign armed forces from Lebanon. The Syrians refused to remove their thirty thousand troops; Israeli deployments depended on the Syrians. Lebanese Christians and Muslim forces opposed the arrangement. The fighting in the mountains spilled over onto the streets of the Lebanese capital. Neighborhood warfare exploded at intersections throughout the city and in the hills around the capital.

Checkpoints in Beirut were manned by pill poppers, hashish smokers, and psychopaths. A motorist who answered a question incorrectly, or who belonged to the wrong religion or militia, could be dragged out of his car and shot point-blank in the head. Murder was part of the Beirut landscape; it had long since ceased being a prosecutable crime.

Station officers, along with the SY staffers, were the only ███ personnel permitted on the streets of Beirut. ████████████

██
██
██
██
██
██
██
██
██
███████████████████████████

Buckley drove vehicles with ██████████. At first he was situated in armored cars. The term "bullet and blast resistant" was misleading when describing a vehicle's level of protection. RPGs could slice through the armor of a battle tank, and would have little difficulty turning a sedan with a few plates of AR500 steel into a smoldering pile of twisted chassis and flaming tires. Buckley despised the slow-moving armored vehicles. One day he complained that his vehicle was sluggish and smelled funny. It was brought to a local garage—one that the embassy considered reliable—where a mechanic discovered the remains of a cat that had inserted itself inside the inner workings of the vehicle. The young agents jokingly called the vehicle the "Catmobile."[6]

Station personnel were not authorized by headquarters to carry weapons on the street. Since Langley was six thousand miles away, station officers were autonomous in their decision on whether or not to carry a sidearm. ██████████ One day, a car bomb near the embassy highlighted the dangers that station personnel faced when they ventured outside the barbed wire and sandbag fortifications to do their job. Buckley was furious to have his men so exposed, so he wrote a cable to headquarters; the subject line was "Brass Balls." The cable emphasized that since Beirut had daily occurrences of car bombings and shelling, as well as full-fledged combat at any turn between an assortment of combatants, station personnel had brass balls and little else to defend themselves with.[7] Buckley could sometimes be as subtle as a B-52 air strike, a colleague once commented, and headquarters got the message. The Near East Division soon authorized officers to carry nine-millimeter pistols and submachine guns.

"Still," as one station officer commented, "nine-millimeters weren't going to do much when up against militiamen arrned with AK-47s and RPKs, but that was the kind of commander Bill was. He had your back. He was one of the best Chiefs of Station I have ever had the privilege to work for."[8]

7

MADNESS

IT WAS HARD to tell who was happier—the young Israeli conscripts who had hoped to get out of the country before experiencing their own baptism of fire, or the reservists, the citizen soldiers who had wives and children at home, and businesses to run, who wanted to get back home before the bullets began flying again. Everyone was happy to leave Beirut.

At sunrise on the morning of September 3, 1983, the IDF began Operation Millstone, the phased withdrawal from the southern entrance points approaching Beirut, as well as along key strategic positions over the Beirut–Damascus Highway that connected the Lebanese and Syrian capitals. Israeli generals—and, of course, Prime Minister Menachem Begin—considered Operation Millstone to be not a sign of defeat, but rather a repositioning of forces to more advantageous positions. Within twenty-four hours of the commencement of the

Israeli repositioning, the IDF established new defensive lines south of the Awali River some twenty miles to the south, ever so close to the Israeli frontier.

LAF units were rushed into the vacuum left by the departing Israeli units, especially in and around Khalde, south of Beirut International Airport. Heavy fighting erupted near Aley, the country's fourth largest city, which sat eleven miles uphill from Beirut on the Damascus Highway. The combat in Aley, intense even by Lebanon's standards of butchery, pitted Druze militias against Lebanese government forces. The country was dissolving into a deeper muck of bloodshed and barbarity. Israel had tried to solve Lebanon's woes by focusing on eradicating the Palestinian terrorists from its northern frontier and by backing a Maronite militia to lead the country. It took the Israelis less than ten months in the mess to realize that they didn't comprehend the quagmire that was Lebanon. No one did. Beirut Station was at least trying to figure out what was what and who was who. It was an exercise in frustration.

Beirut Station was so new, its officers so inexperienced, that the men and women assigned to Buckley's shop arrived in Lebanon with their eyes wide open. These first-tour officers hadn't had the time on the job or the academic pedigree to establish an opinion of the country that was skewed by religion, politics, and frustration. Buckley created esprit de corps by leading by example and letting the young officers know that all of them—including him—depended on one another to figure out the puzzle of Lebanon together. He took the time and the effort to mentor the officers, to reassure them that their contributions and insight mattered. Alan Jones,* one of Buckley's officers in Beirut, fondly remembered how the Chief of Station tried to

* A pseudonym.

motivate his staff through the fear and confusion. "He came out of his office one day and told me that he had just read one of my intelligence reports from an asset debriefing," the officer remembered. "Without being at all gushy or false about it, he simply said if he continued to read the material that I was producing from my assets, he might one day understand what was going on in Beirut and Lebanon."[1]

No one really knew what was going on in Lebanon. The spymasters at CIA headquarters in Langley, it appeared, certainly didn't. The Mossad had played it wrong. But hidden in plain sight, right under the noses of everyone, was a growingly arrogant Iranian influence in the embattled nation.

The Iranian effort in Lebanon was not even hidden in plain sight.

THE IRANIANS DIDN'T understand the mess of Lebanon either, but they had money. The official policy of the Khomeini regime was to spread the Shiite Islamic revolution to wherever it could grow and blossom. Even though Iran was fighting a war of survival against Saddam Hussein's Iraq, a conflict that resulted in hundreds of thousands of Iranian dead and the near bankrupting of the country, Tehran poured money, men, and matériel into Lebanon. Some of Iran's capital investment came from the SAVAMA, the Sazman-E Ettela'at Va Aminiyat-E Melli-E Iran, or the National Information and Security Organization of Iran, the intelligence apparatus that replaced the Shah's SAVAK secret police and intelligence service.[2] Most of the money, though, belonged to the Revolutionary Guard Corps and the ultrasecretive Quds Force. The Quds Force was the Revolutionary Guards' tip of the spear, formed at the start of the Iran-Iraq War as a covert special operations force. The Quds Force was staffed by the best and the brightest on the Revolutionary Guards' payroll—only the most fanatic, most capable, most sinister, and most pious were recruited to spearhead the

Ayatollah's revolution. Quds operatives distinguished themselves on the killing grounds of the Iran-Iraq War as zealous flag bearers of Imam Khomeini. The charismatic, and those needing a break from the ankle-deep blood in the trenches, were sent to Lebanon to flip the switch igniting the Shiite revolution in Lebanon.

To the vast majority of Lebanon's Shiites, the Iranian emissaries were an amusing army of benevolent gift givers promising salvation. Only a few of the visitors spoke Arabic, and those spoke with an accent that was so absolutely Farsi that they were unintelligible to many of the locals. The money they carried, however, didn't require an interpreter. The gifts started out small. Handouts of banknotes to local merchants, school kids, and the unemployed were common in the slums of south Beirut and in the Shiite areas of southern Lebanon; bags of vegetables and other staples, including poultry and lamb, were also distributed freely. Local businesses reaped the rewards of the Shiite benevolence. Printshops earned a windfall from the full-color posters and billboards of Imam Khomeini that the Iranians ordered. Teams of men were hired to hang the posters and signs throughout the Shiite areas. Café and catering-hall owners made a nice business serving the Iranian visitors the meals they ordered. Taxi drivers made a fortune ferrying the Iranians from the border crossing points in Syria to Beirut and destinations beyond.

The Iranian ambassadors were also armed. Everyone carried a sidearm; some carried Uzis and AK-47s. The message they wanted to send was one of Shiite power—money and firearms would launch an Iranian-inspired revolution in Lebanon. The Shiite men and women had already survived years of discrimination, Palestinian control, an Israeli invasion, and now the country being dismantled once again would provide an endless march of martyrs. Instilling a sense of piety into the local Shiite population was one of the Iranians' most ambitious and important objectives. Iran was determined to provide a new social order for Lebanon's Shiite population. Many of Lebanon's Shiites, especially those in the cities, had enjoyed a fairly secular and somewhat modern existence. Religion was a factor, but far from the dominant force in day-to-day life. The Iranians were determined to change that and they targeted the women first.

Shiite women in Beirut and other cities, and even some in the Beka'a villages, did not cover themselves in public in significant numbers before or after the civil war. Lebanese women, in fact, enjoyed greater sexual openness than women in other Arab nations. "There were many jokes in Lebanon, especially among the Sunnis and Christians, about the elastic band on the undergarments of Shiite women being loose," an officer said, "because they were constantly being pulled down."[3] The Iranian emissaries launched their campaign by offering young women—those still in school and even those recently married—one hundred dollars a month as a religious donation to wear hijabs and cover their heads and chests in public;[4] the hijab was usually worn by all postpubescent females in the presence of adult males who were outside the realm of their immediate family. The young women were told that the hijab was a symbol of modesty. There were religious provisions, however, that enabled the young women to continue their lifestyles.

The notion of *sigheh*, a Farsi term for the Shiite practice of temporary marriage, was foreign to Lebanon's Shiites before emissaries arrived from Iran. Khomeini's revolution had swept across an Iranian society that was, in urban areas at least, fairly modern, where women enjoyed many liberal Western freedoms, and many religious rules and restrictions were created to accommodate matters of the flesh. The practice of *sigheh* is believed to have existed during the lifetime of Muhammad, and the practice became a moral requirement during the Iran-Iraq War when so many young Iranian men—including husbands—were killed in savage combat. *Sigheh* became both a necessity for allowing widows to fulfill their sexual needs with a religious nod and a wink, and a perk for soldiers heading to the front who needed to serve their basic human desires.

The practice was known in Arabic as *muta'a*. Quds Force volunteers and Lebanese clerics trained in Iran promoted the practice aggressively among the young and impressionable. The visiting Iranians even sponsored the cleric fees involved in arranging the marriages—unions that could last a few minutes or a lifetime. There were even reports that a special military hospital run by the Revolutionary Guard was set up for the consequences of the religiously sanctioned sexual trysts. A small army of Iranian and local Hezbollah operatives, determined to keep all unauthorized intruders out of the area, protected the hospital. There were, after all, religious provisions for any and all contingencies; children born out of these unions are considered legitimate, and are even entitled to a share of the father's estate.[5]

With the sexual needs of the men who would fight and die taken care of, the Iranian emissaries could focus on the war they would launch.

The majority of Iranian cash flowing into Lebanon focused on the hundreds of thousands of young, angry, and unemployed men who could be transformed into a new breed of Shiite warrior who could defeat Israel, the United States, and any other group determined to impose its will on the disciples of Imam Khomeini. Small satellite training centers were set up throughout the Shiite enclaves of the Beka'a and southern Lebanon. Sometimes the facilities consisted of nothing more than a classroom and some open spaces where guerrilla tactics could be learned and mastered. The men were paid for their time and they were issued weapons. The volunteers were indoctrinated into a new mind-set with a new cause—the cause of the Party of God.

Quds Force instructors wanted to mold the nascent cadre of Hezbollah into a force that was both reliable and defiant. There was great emphasis on physical training—the turning of soft bodies into solid muscle. The first legions of this new Shiite army marched and drilled from dawn to well past dusk. They marched like German soldiers on a parade ground and not like the unsynchronized rabble of most Arab armies. Firearms proficiency was instilled into the volunteers with zealous focus. The Iranians disdained the PLO practice of firing wildly into the sky; bullets were destined for the enemy, not foolish celebrations glorifying defeat. There were also advanced courses in intelligence gathering and reconnoitering, explosives, and sniping. There were religious sermons as well: sermons about the Shiite experience, and sermons exhorting the notion of martyrdom. The families of the martyrs, the students were told, were taken care of for eternity.

The young Shiite men in training noticed visitors coming to watch them engage targets on the range. Some were clerics from Ba'albek and Tyre wearing new robes and flanked by bodyguards toting AK-47s; some of the religious men looked as if they came from very far away. Movement in and out of Beirut had become much easier since the Israeli withdrawal.

THE EDITORS OF the major Lebanese newspapers, men from all ethnic and religious persuasions, published extensively on what was called the Iranian invasion.[6] The foreign reporters who would converge on West Beirut's Commodore Hotel to decompress over whiskey like a tribe stuck together by misfortune couldn't help but see the growing number of Farsi banners in the southern slums and the jarring sight of young women wearing the hijab. There were constant communiqués released by shadowy groups in the southern slums of Beirut and sent to the offices of press agencies reporting from Beirut warning the United States and the other Western powers to stop arming Saddam Hussein.

It is unknown whether Langley had been warned that the war in the Persian Gulf had migrated west. Beirut Station cables and reports remain, for the most part, classified. The telltale signs that strong and fanatical undercurrents were pulling the country inside out were impossible to ignore, however. Case officers were finding it harder and harder to infiltrate the southern slums. The checkpoints were fortified by heavily armed men wearing green headbands and standing behind large-scale placards of the Ayatollah Khomeini. Some of the graffiti on the walls of the narrow streets vowed Lebanon's support for the brave warriors on the front lines battling the Iraqi invaders; by the fall of 1983, nearly a hundred thousand Iranian soldiers had already been killed in the war.

As a new sense of piety and militancy spread, south Beirut began to resemble Tehran. Glen Smith,* who had worked with Buckley at the CTG and followed him to Lebanon, encountered the new reality firsthand. "There was a man [an asset] that I was in contact with, [and] he was a Muslim. I was having lunch with him one day and Ramadan was about to start. . . . He said, 'I am going to observe Ramadan this year. This is the first time I am going to observe Ramadan in several years. I am rediscovering my faith. I am recommitting myself to my faith.' And he looked very hard at me and said, 'Do you understand what I'm telling you?' I paused, I said yes, I do, and I asked, will I get out of here alive? He said, 'Yes, but I should not see you again.'"[7]

---

* A pseudonym.

It was becoming ever more dangerous to dispatch case officers and support agents into the southern slums. Checkpoints sprouted up at intersections, and vehicles with official diplomatic plates were turned back by heavily armed gunmen. The more religious the Shiite neighborhoods became, the greater the number of checkpoints seemed to be. Officers venturing toward the southern slums noticed that armed men now patrolled the rooftops. Armed men were always watching.

US Marine patrols from the Multinational Force moving in and around Ouzai, a forgotten pocket of squalor and anger just north of the international airport along the Mediterranean coast, noticed the change as well. There were always eyes watching them.

IT WAS SOMETIMES difficult to tell the warring factions apart in Lebanon. One needed a scorecard to identify all the peacekeepers as well. Dozens of nations contributed fighting formations to the United Nations peacekeepers in southern Lebanon, and four nations contributed peacekeepers to the Multinational Force: Britain, Italy, France, and the United States. The marines represented the largest contingent to the MNF. From the halls of Montezuma to the shores of Tripoli, the United States Marine Corps had earned a reputation as a fighting force second to none—they were not, by pedigree, peacekeepers. The initial Marine mission was crystal clear. It had a beginning, middle, and end, even though supervising the expulsion of Palestinian fighters from Beirut seemed distasteful. In an *Army Times* political cartoon, an exasperated officer tells a young marine, "Look, I'll explain it once more: We're U.S. Marines defending PLO terrorists who are celebrating their victorious expulsion from Beirut. Now what's so hard to understand about that?"[8] Following the Sabra and Shatila massacres, the marines were landed in Lebanon once again, this time to protect elements of the Lebanese people from themselves. But as the US policy in Lebanon shifted from peacekeeping to nation building, the Marine mission became muddled and conflicted. Marine elements assisted in the training of the Lebanese Armed Forces, an act that ensured that they antagonized many of the groups they were ostensibly there to protect. President Reagan stated, in a May 1983 news conference, "The MNF went there to help the new government of Lebanon maintain order until it can organize its military and its police to assume control of its borders and its own internal security."⁹

Marine peacekeeping duties were shared between two Marine Amphibious Units, or MAUs: the Thirty-Second and the Twenty-Fourth. The Thirty-Second had been assigned to oversee the withdrawal of Palestinian fighters from Beirut in September 1982, and returned to the Lebanese capital in the chaotic wake of the Sabra and Shatila massacres. The MAU tours were generally four or five months in length. The Twenty-Fourth MAU returned to Beirut on May 30, 1983, for what was slated to be a five-month deployment.

The marines were based at Beirut International Airport and their zone of operation included the outskirts of the southern neighborhoods, including the Bourj el-Barajneh Palestinian refugee camp, and the Shiite areas of Ouzai, al-Joura, and al-Dachia. The Marine contingent established checkpoints on key roadways around the airport; other positions, such as one near the Shiite village of Hay es Salaam, were established in coordination with LAF units. Artillery batteries were brought in to enhance the presence of the Marine perimeter. The marines were headquartered in a two-story building once used as the firefighting school, while the barracks for the Battalion Landing Team, known as the BLT, was down the road in a dilapidated four-story shell of a building southwest of the MAU headquarters. The barracks became sarcastically known as the "Beirut Hilton."

Amid the shelling, sniping, and constant internecine warfare, Beirut International Airport remained opened for business. The airport accommodated thirty-five daily flights and 2,400 passengers moving in and out of a war zone. The marines were based at the airport, though they could not interfere with day-to-day commercial flight operations.

Following the April 1983 bombing of the embassy, sandbagged positions reinforced the area's defenses. The adjacent Beirut Airport highway that led toward the Marine position was guarded by the LAF. [10] There were incidents to report, occasional problems with the locals. The most serious clashes, interestingly enough, occurred with Israeli patrols who repeatedly tried to test Marine lines. [11]

There were numerous incidents of mortar shells landing inside the Marine compound. Bullets whizzed by all of the time. The primary rules of engagement called for restraint: for the most part marines were not allowed to carry loaded weapons, and they were permitted to shoot only if they could verify that their lives were in danger, and then only if they could identify a specific target as a threat. [12] The MAU headquarters became known as the "Can't Shoot Back Saloon."

Everything changed in the fall of 1983. On August 29, Second Lieutenant George Losey and Staff Sergeant Alexander Ortega were killed when an eighty-two-millimeter mortar round landed on their position. The combat escalated. The marines began to use antitank rockets. When sectarian fighting erupted in the summer, President Reagan dispatched the USS *New Jersey*, a relic of World War II modernized to carry missiles, to the Lebanese coast as a deterrent. On September 25, the battleship fired at Druze and Syrian positions near Suq al-Gharb along the strategic Aley–Beirut Highway. The United States had become a full-fledged combatant in the Lebanese quagmire.

The marines continued to take fire. On the doorframe of one Marine bunker at the airport compound was the prophetic epitaph:

They sent us to Beirut
To be targets who could not shoot
Friends will die into an early grave
Was there any reason for what they gave?[13]

THERE WAS PRECIOUS little coordination between the CIA station and the marines at the airport ███████████████████████
███
████████. Station and military attaché personnel saw one another, and sometimes they ate together, but they didn't share details about what they were doing. Agency and DoD missions competed for the same tax dollars. Rivals were reticent about sharing scuttlebutt, even in a contained universe like Beirut. Still, there was the odd way that the Chief of Station and his military counterparts communicated. Buckley would offer little nonclassified tidbits of information to non-Agency personnel at times. "There might be a little interruption in electricity over the next few days," Buckley was once overheard telling a ██████████████████ member of the embassy staff. "Just get ready." Buckley knew this because a contact, a businessman, had ordered several large containers full of brand-new generators from a distributor ██████████████████. The businessman wouldn't bring the goods into the country until the shelling took out a power plant. People paid top dollar for generators when the lights were out.[14] There were always opportunists in a land void of stability.

███
███
███

████. The message was addressed to the ambassador, Ali Akbar Mohtashamipur, and marked top secret. Mohtashamipur had been trained as a cleric in the Iraqi holy city of Najaf and was a disciple of Ayatollah Khomeini. Ruthlessly loyal, Mohtashamipur looked like a long-shoreman with a leathery punching bag for a face. There was a natural anger to his snarl, part of the overall picture that made him one of the most respected—and feared—members of the Iranian Revolution. He had Khomeini's ear and he espoused the need to export the Shiite revival overseas. Mohtashamipur's target was Lebanon. He was one of the first emissaries to Ba'albek and the training camps in the Beka'a Valley. He was one of the revered figures who visited the Shiite neighborhoods of south Beirut, meeting men in the basements of the bombed-out apartment buildings. He was appointed the Iranian ambassador to Syria specifically to oversee the intelligence effort to raise Hezbollah into Iran's proxy army.

██████████████████████████████████████

██████████████████████████████████████

██ The message directed the Iranian ambassador to contact Hussein Musawi, the leader of the terrorist group Islamic Amal (and prominent Hezbollah commander), and to instruct him to have his group instigate attacks against the multinational coalition in Lebanon, and "to take a spectacular action against the United States Marines." Mohtashamipur was instructed to engineer an attack on the marines based at Beirut International Airport.[15] Imad Mughniyeh had already executed two brilliantly planned and executed suicide bombings. Mohtashamipur ordered Mughniyeh's case officer, Ali Reza Asgari, to make it happen. Asgari was the senior Quds Force commander responsible for Hezbollah. The instructions from Tehran would be carried out to the letter, though both Mughniyeh and Asgari would add certain complexities and additions to the original intent. It took a little less than a month for Mughniyeh and Asgari to deliver. Asgari was considered a diabolically brilliant spymaster. During the Iranian Revolution he had made a name for himself hunting down former high-ranking members of the shah's CIA-backed SAVAK intelligence service.[16]

Present at the subsequent meetings to plan and coordinate the logistics and blueprint of the strike were also Sheikh Abbas Musawi and Sheikh Hassan Nasrallah—two men who would later serve as Hezbollah secretary generals.

███

████████████████████████████████ CIA headquarters wasn't notified of the invaluable intelligence; neither was Beirut Station. Human assets did not report anything peculiar brewing in the Shiite strongholds of south Beirut. There was no chatter, per se, hinting that the marines at the airport had been specifically targeted. William Buckley felt responsible for keeping tabs on any intelligence that involved a threat directed against American diplomats and military personnel in Lebanon.

REGINALD BARTHOLOMEW, THE new US ambassador to Lebanon, arrived in Beirut early in the evening of Saturday, October 22, 1983. Buckley was at his desk in Beirut Station when the wheels of Bartholomew's aircraft touched down at Beirut International Airport. News of the ambassador's arrival had been filtered to the Chief of Station from one of the officers assigned to the office, who received an update either on his Motorola radio or on a landline from the Marine positions. Buckley looked at his calendar to see what time he was scheduled to brief the ambassador the next day. Buckley was eager to meet the new ambassador. Although his paychecks came from Langley, in Lebanon the buck was going to stop with Reginald Bartholomew.

* * *

DAWN BROKE OVER Beirut with a warming orange glow on Sunday, October 23, 1983. William Buckley woke up before dawn, as he did every day. He looked out his window and then washed up. He shaved and put on his suit. He would be briefing the ambassador after breakfast.

Six miles to the south of Buckley's window, the marines of Twenty-Fourth MAU were about to greet a new morning in Lebanon. The day would be a much-needed break from the day-to-day danger of hunkering down for security operations. Reveille was scheduled for 06:30 and chow was slated for 08:00 to 10:00; some of the marines asleep in their barracks twisted and turned in the struggle to wake up, knowing that it was best to be at the chow line early regardless of what day it was.

Sundays were days for services, letters home, and the odd pickup game. There was always a football stored with their gear; some of the marines had baseball gloves and a few balls for a relaxing Sunday catch. With some luck, there would be no shelling. Burgers and hot dogs could be barbecued for a real Sunday lunch.

Lance Corporal Eddie DiFranco manned one of the two posts around the barracks. Traffic was light on the main perimeter road but a yellow Mercedes* stake-bed truck was being driven suspiciously. The laden-down vehicle entered the parking lot south of Corporal DiFranco's post and then disappeared. At 06:22 DiFranco noticed that the truck had returned to the parking lot. Instead of turning around, the vehicle took aim for the barracks and accelerated toward the concer-

---

* According to testimony offered in *Peterson v. Islamic Republic of Iran*, a case brought by the relatives of victims of the bombing of the Marine Corps barracks, the vehicle used was actually a Dodge pickup truck that was painted and disguised to look like the vehicle that sometimes delivered water to the MAU.

tina wire that separated the barracks from the lot and headed straight for the barracks building where over four hundred marines and naval personnel slept.[17] Marines on post were not permitted to man their positions with magazines inserted inside their M16 assault rifles. By the time the marines realized it was happening and inserted the thirty-round magazines into their weapons, it was too late.

Sergeant of the Guard Stephen E. Russell was at the barracks' main entrance. He saw the driver of the Mercedes truck crash through a perimeter fence and rev his engine for the final burst of speed that would propel the vehicle straight into the barracks lobby. The driver was so close, in fact, that Sergeant Russell could see his face. Russell screamed, "Hit the deck! Hit the deck!"[18] His warning was too late. The driver of the yellow Mercedes simply floored the gas pedal until he was in the dead center of the barracks lobby. The peacekeeper status of the Marine MAU at the airport virtually earmarked a path for the suicide bomber. Major General Paul X. Kelley, the Marine Corps commandant, would later testify before a congressional subcommittee on November 1, 1983, "While traveling at a high speed, now estimated to be sixty miles an hour, this truck crashed through the outer defensive barbed wire emplacements, moved at high speed between two sandbag sentry posts, crashed through an iron gate, jumped over a sewer pipe which had been placed as an obstacle to impede the forward movement of the vehicle."[19] In reality, the restrictive security protocols in place could not have stopped any vehicle, let alone a nineteen-ton truck crammed with explosives.

It is likely that none of the three hundred marines and sailors asleep in the barracks heard Sergeant Russell scream his warning. Only a few seconds passed between the yellow Mercedes truck crashing into the barracks and detonation. The bomb, believed to have been fabricated in an underground garage in Biralabin, somewhere in the Beka'a Valley, consisted of a ton of pentaerythritol tetranitrate, PETN, a military-grade high explosive. The explosive yield was enhanced with the insidiously diabolical placement of compressed butane gas canisters in the bed of the truck in an effort to replicate the effects of a fuel-air explosive. The detonation produced one of the largest non-nuclear explosions in history, mimicking the force of twenty thousand pounds of explosives. The barracks disintegrated into rubble and debris. Men and their belongings were thrown three hundred yards away. Seismic sensors indicated an earthquake. The mushroom plume of smoke could be seen miles away. According to one marine whose life was miraculously saved because he slept in one of the tents outside the barracks and opted to return to sleep rather than enter the barracks for morning chow, "I don't think that there are words in the English language to describe the magnitude of the blast."[20] Luke Johnson,* one of the officers assigned to Beirut Station, had been awakened by the earthshaking anger of the suicide truck bomb and looked out the window to see the black plume of smoke and acrid destruction emanating from the airport. He wondered who could have survived such a powerful blast. He wondered how many of his friends at the barracks were still alive.

The blast killed 220 marines, 18 Navy corpsmen, and 3 soldiers. It was the single deadliest day for the US Marine Corps since Iwo Jima.

A second nineteen-ton truck had been fabricated with two thousand pounds of pentaerythritol tetranitrate and compressed-butane gas canisters. This one had been painted red. It had been driven from the Shiite slums of south Beirut toward the heart of Sunni West Bei-

---

* A pseudonym.

rut, toward the beach at Ramlet al-Baida. When the blast at the barracks reverberated throughout Beirut, the driver of the red truck headed straight for the building housing elements of the French MNF, primarily from the third company, the First Parachute Chasseur Regiment (1er RCP), and the Ninth Parachute Chasseur Regiment (9e RCP), one of the oldest and most decorated airborne regiments of the French army.

The truck crashed into the Drakkar building as the soldiers inside slept. The explosion was so massive that it tossed the building off its foundation and caused the nine-story complex to come crashing down into a twisted heap of devastation. Between the Marine barracks attack and the destruction of the French barracks, there wasn't a searchlight or bulldozer left in the city. Fifty-eight French paratroopers were killed in the bombing. Dozens more were seriously wounded. It was the deadliest day for the French military since Algeria.

According to Hezbollah legend, Mughniyeh and some of the Iranians watched the bombing from a hill that overlooked the airport. Hussein Musawi, one of the architects of the two-pronged attack, would later say, "I salute this good act, and I consider it a good deed and a legitimate right, and I bow to the spirits of the martyrs who carried out this operation."[21]

WILLIAM BUCKLEY RUSHED to the station when he heard the first blast, followed moments later by the bombing of the French barracks a short stroll from his apartment. Inside ███████ an ataxic-like state of bewilderment had set in. Men and women used to the bedlam of Beirut were overwhelmed by what they had heard and what they feared would come. Within hours, a military chopper had landed near the Corniche, near the British Embassy, and flown Ambassador Bartholomew toward ground zero. It was impossible to comprehend the devastation. "All I remember was the underwear, T-shirts, and bits and pieces of one's personal kit were hanging on trees three hundred yards away from the destroyed remnants of the barracks," one of the SY agents protecting the ambassador recalled.[22]

Buckley, along with members of the station, also made his way to the airport to survey the destruction. The road to the airport from West Beirut was, for once, clear. Buckley, wearing his characteristic suit and tie, looked out of place amid the bloody confusion even though he was no stranger to war and death. One member of his team simply recalled that the Chief of Station was stunned. Buckley looked to make sure that Colonel Geraghty was all right; Buckley and the commander of the Marine Corps contingent had become friends. Sometimes the only way to mentally process the magnitude of horror is to make sure a brother-in-arms is still alive.

AMBASSADOR BARTHOLOMEW PLEADED with the White House to retaliate for the slaughter at the airport. Bartholomew, who reportedly slept with a pistol next to his pillow in the heavily fortified ambassador's residence,[23] realized that diplomacy in a place like Lebanon mattered only when it was backed by massive force, and the failure to respond dramatically to the bombing at the airport all but sealed the fate of America's interests in Lebanon. The Iranians and their Shiite proxies expected massive retaliation. When none came it became apparent that Tehran could do what it wanted in Lebanon.

The bombing of the Marine and French barracks was the beginning of the end of the multinational effort to save Lebanon from itself. The Reagan White House wanted the Pentagon to launch punitive air strikes against Iranian Revolutionary Guard positions around the Sheikh Abdullah Barracks, but indecision from Defense Secretary

Caspar Weinberger, an opponent of American involvement in Lebanon, scuttled any military retribution.[24]

The French did retaliate. On November 18, 1983, fourteen French Navy Dassault-Breguet Super Étendard fighter jets from the aircraft carrier *Clemenceau*, off the Lebanese coast, flew at least two raids against Iranian and Shiite targets near Ba'albek. Although damage was minimal, one of the two targets was the home of Hussein Musawi.[25]

Lebanon became a test of wills for the United States—a symbol of American resolve. A distinguished roster of political dignitaries visited the besieged Marine encampment at the airport, including Vice President George H. W. Bush and the Marine Corps commandant, Major General Paul X. Kelley. Congressmen and senators flocked to the shores of Beirut in a pilgrimage designed to show the constituents back home that the suicide forces of Shiite terror would not force the United States' resolve to buckle. US military support for the Gemayel presidency increased, as did the shelling from the *New Jersey*.

American aid to the LAF increased. ███████████████████
██

Station case officers pushed their assets for any information on those responsible for the Marine barracks bombing, as well as any word of future plots against the hunkered-down American presence in Lebanon. Money was no issue. America, after all, was at war. Even Bob Hope came to Lebanon—actually to the Sixth Fleet warships moored off the Lebanese coast—for a series of shows to help the beleaguered servicemen celebrate Christmas and the New Year. "I'm sure the US marines will end the fighting in Beirut," Hope told an audience of reporters and servicemen, "once we find out who the enemy is."[26] For Buckley, it must have felt like Vietnam all over again: a few moments of levity, a few Hollywood starlets in revealing costumes, taking the edge off of a war that the policy makers didn't quite get and that the people back home had little patience to stomach.

In the aftermath of the Marine barracks bombing, Buckley authorized his case officers to take more risks in collecting intelligence. It was difficult to work under such conditions. Beirut Station had to manage the chaos of spy work amid the perpetual threat of imminent danger. "One officer did his best to infiltrate Shiite lines," Luke recalled. "███████████████████████████████—something that Bill had said was too dangerous before the bombing."[27] The gloves, in Buckley's eyes, were off.

THE IRANIANS AND their Shiite proxies in Lebanon made extremely difficult the CIA's national mission of providing the policy makers with hard intelligence from which they could make prudent policy decisions that enhanced the security of the United States. The apparatus did not yet exist for the various intelligence agencies of the United States to exchange intelligence expeditiously and efficiently, even though the need for the government entities to work together was enhanced by the intelligence failure of the Marine barracks bombing.[28] Human intelligence was nearly impossible to come by. The Shiite areas of south Beirut, the Beka'a, and southern Lebanon were inaccessible to traditional espionage tradecraft. These were armed enclaves where the residents didn't trust anyone they hadn't known forever. According to one member of Buckley's Beirut Station, "The moment someone recognized a face, a license plate, clothing that was out of place, someone raced to the mosque and then the loudspeaker warned of an intruder. Within seconds the streets were filled with armed men."[29] Beirut Station was denied access to the names, faces, and addresses of an enemy daringly hiding in plain sight.

The policy of the United States—its pragmatic post-Vietnam-era desire—was to contain the madness befalling Lebanon within the boundaries of Lebanon itself. The Reagan White House was determined that American involvement not entail politically unacceptable American casualties. But Iran's path to war against the United States, Israel, and any other Western power foolish enough to intervene in Lebanon had been a rapid march of calculated measures defined by cold-blooded ruthlessness. The ferocity of the warfare—and its cunning execution—caught the United States, as well as Israel and the other Western powers involved in the Middle East, completely off guard. It was impossible to contain the madness in Lebanon.

On December 12, 1983, an ambitious assembly of Hezbollah and Iranian-backed Iraqi Shiite terrorists executed a seven-pronged assault in Kuwait. The terrorists launched a series of coordinated suicide and truck bombings of the US Embassy; the French Embassy; Kuwait International Airport; the Kuwait National Petroleum Company; Raytheon; and a government-run power station. Kuwait, in its support of Saddam Hussein in the Iran-Iraq War, had placed the small Gulf state in Tehran's crosshairs. The day of terror lacked the sophistication of Iran's financed operations in Lebanon. The attacks in Kuwait failed to bring about the same number of body bags as the bombings in Lebanon.

Among the seventeen members of the hodgepodge terror cell apprehended by the National Security Bureau was Hussein al-Sayed Yousef al-Musawi. Musawi, one of the operational lieutenants of the Kuwaiti operation, was also the first cousin of Hussein Musawi, the head of Islamic Amal in Lebanon.[30] Also arrested was a young man with a crooked face and antagonizing grin who entered the country with a Lebanese passport in the name of Elias al-Sa'ab.[31] Sa'ab was an alias.* The suspect's real name was Mustafa Badreddine. Badreddine

---

* Some reports indicate the alias used was Fuad Sa'ab.

was not only Imad Mughniyeh's cousin but also his brother-in-law; Mughniyeh had recently married Mustafa's sister Sa'ada. The two men were now linked by blood and honor. There were rules in Lebanon, and the most powerful was that clan meant everything—it was more important than religion.

Badreddine's trial was slated to begin sometime in early 1984. The sentence he faced, once the three interrogators finished torturing him, was death. Mughniyeh would not be allowed to forget that a member of his clan was awaiting the noose in a Kuwaiti prison.

8

BEIRUT RULES

T HE RULES OF spycraft developed during the Cold War seemed utterly upended by the new, unfamiliar Beirut rules. The spies attempted to make sense of the mess. But there were few sources or assets that could be trusted. The LAF was rife with traitors; the police had been bought ten times over by the Syrians and Iranians, or perhaps by both; and the Christians played the Americans and Israelis against one another in skillful displays of "both sides against the middle." "Anyone in the security services would drop their weapons and put on militia uniforms if the call was issued in their town or village," a former CIA officer who worked in Lebanon admitted.[1] And this treacherous and unstable landscape made Buckley's work ever more dangerous and difficult. With no one else to rely on, the spies in Lebanon simply spied on one another. Despite protocol warranting that all communications between allied services go through headquarters, it was routine for officers of Beirut Station to meet with their ▇▇▇▇▇▇▇▇▇▇ intelligence counterparts in the city. The sit-downs were always informal: a meeting over dinner in a restaurant or coffee and sweets in a café off the beaten path. The meetings were always pillared on suspicion and guile. The spies tried to glean information without revealing too much of what they held close to the vest.

One Beirut Station officer remembered a meeting with the local ▇▇▇▇▇▇▇▇ representative in Lebanon. Each man arrived at the predetermined location with bodyguards in tow, even though both nations were allied and involved jointly in the multinational peace-keeping efforts. The two spies discussed the threats in the city and what their sources were telling them. The ▇▇▇▇▇▇ agent took a sip of his coffee, a drag on his cigarette, and then presented his American counterpart with a piece of onionskin paper with a list of names typed in two columns.

"The names on the left," the spy explained, "belong to those who we need permission to kill. The names on the right belong to people who could simply disappear."[2]

In another meeting, between an officer from Beirut Station and his intelligence service counterparts from a "friendly" Middle Eastern nation, the Americans came to the sit-down at a neutral site in order to share information. The other spies came with a valise full of files of names, places, and photos, which they gave to the Americans in the hope that the Beirut Station officers at the meeting would be equally generous in what they provided. But glancing at the information, including what one officer referred to as a bizarre story of Druze suicide bombers wanting to blow up the USS *New Jersey* with exploding skiffs, the CIA case agents realized that they were being handed fabrications in the hope of acquiring hard information from sources that were denied to this agency.[3]

Intelligence was a commodity like any other in Lebanon. It was bought, sold, and traded. It was one of the most valuable forms of chattel in Lebanon, and it was as easy to peddle as poppies from the Beka'a Valley, guns from Syria, and women from the camps. The Americans were buyers, primarily. The CIA always paid well above the going rate—the Americans always paid top dollar for everything—but the intelligence it received was spotty.

STAFFERS AT THE US Embassy in Beirut still lived in the western half of the city, despite the peril. Assistant RSO Jeremy Zeikel was one of the members of the embassy security detail living in the crosshairs. Zeikel was a young SY special agent assigned to the US Embassy in Beirut. He had joined the State Department's security arm in February 1981 and had paid his dues working in the Washington field office and then globe-trotting when assigned to the protective detail for Secretary of State Haig and later Schultz. Eighteen months of living out of a suitcase and standing guard in hotel stairwells was more than Zeikel could take, so he asked to be assigned overseas. And, as fate had it, a slot had opened up in Beirut shortly after the April 4 bombing of the embassy. It was Zeikel's first overseas assignment for SY. He had a New Yorker's street sense about him and he made Beirut work. The embassy job was different and it put Zeikel in touch daily with the diplomats, the Defense Attaché's office, and even the Chief of Station. "Bill [Buckley] gave the initial impression that he wasn't a people person," Zeikel recalled, "but once he got to know you and he liked you, you could tell that behind the outer armor that he had of being an officer and a member of the CIA, he was a good guy with a very special sense of humor."[4]

Zeikel lived in a high-rise in a large, palatial flat that overlooked the Corniche and the Mediterranean. The Sixth Fleet was offshore and the office a three-minute walk away. If it weren't for the shelling, sniping, and air strikes, it could have been an exotic Miami Beach.

The morning of Sunday, January 8, 1984, was cool and windy—a grayish overcast spread its somber pall over the awakening city. Zeikel was still in bed when he heard the escalating thud of helicopter rotors nearing. A stretch of the Corniche that doubled as a parking lot had been used as an impromptu landing zone for naval choppers ferrying men and matériel back and forth from the Marine encampment at the airport to the British Embassy just across the street. The helicopters had become part of the landscape and soundtrack—a scheduled element of the city's armored tapestry. Zeikel could tell by the noise that the incoming choppers were US Marine Corps Boeing CH-46 Sea Knight medium-lift tandem-rotor transport helicopters powered by twin turboshaft aircraft engines. The CH-46s were all-weather. Day or night, the choppers landed on the Corniche and then quickly took off again for the Marine carrier offshore. Zeikel grabbed his covers and returned to sleep.

The first CH-46 landed and quickly unloaded a force of twelve marines. The marines raced toward a stone wall at the edge of the landing zone to provide cover. Gunfire erupted as the second CH-46 came in for a landing. A truck full of heavily armed masked men screeched to a halt and unleashed a furious fusillade toward the incoming marines. Corporal Edward J. Gargano, a native of Quincy, Massachusetts, was killed in the exchange of gunfire. He was the first American casualty in Lebanon in 1984. The helicopters had brought a twelve-man work detail to fill sandbags in order to reinforce security in a defensive perimeter in front of the British Embassy.[5]

Zeikel jumped out of bed and grabbed his SY-issue Smith & Wesson Model 19 .357 revolver. He rushed to his window but was too high up and too far away to do much. He phoned the gunnery sergeant on duty at Post One but before the marines at the embassy could muster a response the attackers had stopped shooting and disappeared into the side streets, back to their gopher holes in the southern part of town. The bloodshed was commonplace. The dangers gave Al Bigler many sleepless nights. Bigler was the regional security officer, the SY special agent in charge of safeguarding the embassy and its personnel. Bigler wished everyone lived in more secure confines, ███████████ ████████████.

WILLIAM BUCKLEY LIVED in a four-story block of flats in a cul-de-sac off of al-Qala'a Street in a posh West Beirut neighborhood known as Ras Beirut. Before the civil war, Ras Beirut, or "the Head of Beirut," was one of the swankiest parts of town and justified the "Paris of the Middle East" accolades that the Lebanese capital had earned over the years. Ras Beirut was near the beach, near the casinos, and near the ritziest eateries in the city. During its better days, Hollywood stars, Saudi princes, Palestinian revolutionaries, and KGB spies all threw cash on the table, buying lavish meals and a few hours of pleasure. French could still be heard on the streets. The latest fashions from France's top designers were on sale in Ras Beirut. Buckley's alcove was quietly removed from Beirut's bustling, car-honking boulevards. Many of the thoroughfares in the city still had a few palm trees standing to blanket the small shops still in business with a few hours of midday shade, and the corner of al-Qala'a Street and the cul-de-sac had a Parisian feel to it thanks to a cluster of concealing trees that made the neighborhood appear upscale.

Ras Beirut's better times were behind it, however. By 1984 the neighborhood was a shrapnel-scarred patchwork of buildings under repair. The residents were stubborn survivors who still ventured to the corner bakery for steaming hot pitas for afternoon lunch. On Buckley's corner there was a pharmacy that had managed to remain open during the civil war and the Israeli invasion. It did a booming business in aspirin, Valium, and condoms.

Buckley lived on the top floor in a two-bedroom apartment. The living room and terrace faced west, toward the sea. The flat had a tile floor and the kitchen had only the bare essentials. The apartment had very little warmth to it. There was no art on the walls, nothing by way of an attempt to make the place anything more than it was—a CIA stash pad. The only personal touch Buckley managed was an elaborately constructed pyramid of Middle Eastern beer cans that he had assembled on a marble counter separating the kitchen and living room. There were a color television and a VCR in the living room. A battery-operated transistor radio was shuttled between his bedroom and the kitchen. Everything on his dresser, a colleague recalled, was laid out at a right angle.

The rental agreement provided for a bed, a sofa, and a few chairs around a small rectangular kitchen table. He had brought from home a few framed photographs of personal significance and one or two books about Lebanon and the Middle East. One book, *Going All the Way: Christian Warlords, Israeli Adventurers, and the War in Lebanon* by Jonathan C. Randal, was on Buckley's nightstand and considered mandatory nighttime reading.

Buckley's apartment was less than a half mile east of the Mediterranean shoreline and just over a half mile from his office ███████████
███
██.

Every checkpoint was different; each one was an adventure. Some checkpoints were organized, with permanent positions reinforced by heavy machine guns or even recoilless rifles. Others, the precarious ones, were manned by bored and violent teenagers who halted traffic for the hell of it. For Buckley, every morning's drive to work was an exercise in putting the dangers of West Beirut in his rearview mirror.

The militias owned street corners, neighborhoods, and competing criminal enterprises that dabbled in everything from smuggled goods to heroin and arms. Ownership of the street corner could change in the muzzle flash of a close-quarter killing. A checkpoint belonging to a Sunni militia in the morning could have a photo of the Ayatollah in front of the sandbags by evening. A militia that was anti-American one day could change its loyalties and suddenly change its politics— the political winds shifted like the weather. A Druze militia, loyal to Progressive Socialist Party leader Walid Jumblatt, augmented security around the British Embassy. The militiamen, recognizable in their red berets and camouflage fatigues, provided an invaluable and reliable ring of deterrence surrounding the chancery where the British and American diplomats ███████ went to work each morning.

THE TWO MEN who entered the campus of the American University of Beirut on the morning of January 18, 1984, were confident that word of their intentions had not been sold to the spies with the suitcases full of cash. They hadn't been searched even though the sprawling seventy-three-acre campus was protected by the LAF and agents from the Lebanese security service. Many in Lebanon—indeed, the entire Middle East—considered the university to be a regional treasure.

Rain was in the air as Dr. Malcolm Kerr rushed from his parking spot to his office. As American University's president, Kerr was an able ambassador for American values to a new generation of students and future leaders. Though his campus was considered a safe haven even during the darkest days of the civil war, the university had offered Kerr a driver and bodyguard. Thinking it inappropriate for a university president to be shielded by men with guns, he turned the offer down.

At 9:09 a.m., he stepped out of the elevator on the third floor of the administrative building and walked hurriedly to his office. With a head of unkempt hair and large eyeglasses and dressed in a sweater, Kerr looked every bit the college professor. He carried a briefcase in one hand and an umbrella in the other. Two men followed as he quickened his pace. One placed a silenced revolver close to Kerr's head and fired two shots. By the time the local security contingent was alerted, the assailants had disappeared. The head of the university's history department, Kamal Salibi, would later say, "Malcolm Kerr was a friend of Lebanon, a friend of the Arabs, and a friend of Islam."[6]

Later that day, as Kerr's blood was being mopped up from the marble floors, the Islamic Holy War claimed responsibility for Kerr's assassination. A male caller to the Beirut office of Agence France-Presse claimed, "We are responsible for the assassination of the president of the American University of Beirut, who was a victim of the American military presence in Lebanon. We also vow that not a single American or Frenchman will remain on this soil."[7]

The marines would, indeed, be gone in less than a month.

The US position in Lebanon had become untenable. The encampment at the airport—and the marines in the trenches—could not be defended. There was strong disagreement within the Reagan administration about potential US involvement. The Joint Chiefs of Staff, reportedly, unanimously opposed the deployment. The National Security Council and State Department were eager to promote this adventurous and risk-laden component of American diplomacy.[8] Reagan worried about abandoning Beirut because of the message it would send: namely, that the killing of innocents could achieve political gains. But a heavily redacted top secret

CIA report dated January 12, 1984, titled "The Terrorist Threat to US Personnel in Beirut"[9] made it impossible to ignore that the reality on the ground was beyond repair. The report stated:

> The Iranian Government encourages and materially supports the terrorist activities of the radical Shia groups. These Shia and Palestinian groups, as well as their Iranian and Syrian sponsors, almost certainly believe that the bombing at the Marine compound in October has influenced US public opinion and put pressure on US policy makers to withdraw from Lebanon. They are therefore convinced that an intensifying campaign of terrorist violence against the MNF will advance their objective. Shia extremists are increasingly willing to sacrifice their lives in attacks on the MNF. Confident that they are serving the will of Allah . . . [The remainder of the paragraph was redacted.]
>
> The Marine contingent at Beirut Airport will continue to be a tempting target for the radical groups. The exposed military layout of the airport is aggravated by its proximity to the southern slums of Beirut, which are inhabited primarily by Shias and serve as centers of radical activism. Moreover, the Lebanese Army has failed to cut off the infiltration route of men and material from the Beka'a Valley into southern Beirut. It is nearly impossible for the MNF or the Lebanese Army to establish control over these Shia neighborhoods. Beirut is essentially an armed camp in which nearly every household possesses firearms and often larger weapons. Killing has become commonplace after eight years of intermittent civil war. In this environment the terrorist-prone Shia and Palestinian can operate freely.[10]

The analysis for the president had been prepared at Langley, but its content was put together by Beirut Station.

The murder of Malcolm Kerr was further proof that Lebanon had descended into anarchy of disastrous dimensions. On February 7, 1984, President Reagan ordered the six hundred marines at the airport to begin withdrawing to the safety of naval vessels offshore. A small contingent from the Twenty-Fourth MAU would remain behind to bolster security at the British Embassy. Without the marines at the airport, the US Embassy and the diplomats ███████ who worked there were dangerously exposed.

THE IRANIANS WERE pleased that their vast financial investment in Lebanon's Shiites had proved so profitable. The spymasters and Revolutionary Guardsmen posted to the Iranian Embassy in Beirut should have been jubilantly riding a wave of accolades and promotions for their stellar work in the shadows. Nineteen eighty-three had been a banner year for the Shiite revolution in Lebanon, and 1984 had begun with the United States cutting and running from the country. The mood in the Shiite slums of south Beirut was celebratory.

But the victory was far from complete. Tehran had never become reconciled to the fact that the four Iranian diplomats abducted in northern Lebanon on July 4, 1982, were in all likelihood dead. The intelligence indicated that the four were seized by Lebanese Forces gunmen, summarily executed at close range, and then buried underneath a construction site in Karantina, a predominantly Palestinian low-income area in Christian East Beirut, so that their remains would never be found.[11] Yet Iranian intelligence was convinced that the four were alive; after they were captured, Tehran believed, the Phalangist militiamen turned the men over to Israeli intelligence, who incarcerated them at a secret location. Tehran wanted their men back and would settle for nothing else.

Imad Mughniyeh's wife demanded that her husband use his special talents to secure her brother's release. Hussein Musawi would not rest until his nephew was freed from his Kuwaiti jailers. The withdrawal of US marines from areas adjacent to the Shiite neighborhoods freed the operational minds inside Hezbollah and the Revolutionary Guard to think without fear of retaliation or repercussion.

The rains intensified in the Beka'a as February eased toward March. The Beka'a was a terrible place to be in when the precipitation turned the roadways into deep pits of impassable mud. The Sheikh Abdullah Barracks in particular was cold and dreary when winter arrived. The Iranian officers headed to Beirut that February to get out from the bone-numbing chill, and to plan. The Iranians had taught their Shiite brethren well: nothing of importance was ever spoken of on the telephone. If anything of significance had to be exchanged, a Hezbollah commander traveled to Damascus or Tehran.

The Revolutionary Guard commanders who traveled to Beirut in February had already received their instructions from Tehran. The emissaries met with their Lebanese comrades in the tenements of south Beirut. Instructions of importance were exchanged mouth to ear. The planning of the most audacious of kidnappings had to be done in absolute secrecy.

DESPITE THE ESCALATING chaos and bloodshed, life continued for Buckley and the men and women of Beirut Station. Four or five times a week Buckley dined at his favorite restaurant in the city, a restaurant station personnel affectionately nicknamed "Mama Washington's." It served watered-down Chinese- and Asian-style dishes reminiscent of plates found in the Beltway; the place was clean and, most importantly, safe. Buckley sometimes invited friends from the CTG or from the Agency to dinner. He never went out afterward for a cocktail or cigar, instead always returning to his apartment by 7:00 p.m. to watch television and go to bed. Occasionally he recorded an audiocassette to send to Beverly, telling her about how he was faring in such an insane place. Sometimes he just wrote her a postcard.

In January 1984, Buckley finally convinced Langley to send Chip Beck on a sixty-day temporary-duty assignment to serve as his special assistant. Buckley wanted at his side someone he trusted and who would protect his endeavors. The marines were leaving and the Druze and Amal militia had taken over most of West Beirut. Buckley was adamant that the men and women under his command remain stoic in their outpost under fire. Everyone had to look out for one another.

Soon, the Lebanese Forces as well as the Lebanese military began shelling Muslim militias in West Beirut. The artillery barrages were indiscriminate and deadly, some coming dangerously close to the British Embassy where the Americans worked. "It was a miracle," Beck recalled, "that none of the marines or embassy personnel were killed or wounded in the shelling."[12] One night, the shelling was particularly fierce and Buckley lost his temper. He phoned Colonel Kassis and laid down a threat—if the shelling didn't stop, he would have the *New Jersey*'s guns turned on to Kassis' artillery and destroy it. No matter that Buckley didn't have any direct communications with the battleship, or any authority to order a bombardment. Kassis appreciated the man's reputation as a warrior, and he feared the anger that had been hidden from him ███████████████████████████████████. Four hours later, the guns fell silent.

* * *

ON THE MORNING of Tuesday, January 17, 1984, Hussein Farash, a forty-five-year-old Saudi consul working out of the kingdom's embassy in Beirut, was seized by a gang of armed gunmen as his chauffeur negotiated the crowded streets of the Raouché neighborhood of West Beirut near the Corniche. At 10:20 a.m. the consul's vehicle was overtaken by three cars, all without license plates, in front of witnesses and oblivious onlookers. Six men brandishing assault rifles and handguns emerged from the cars and quickly seized Farash. For good measure, the kidnappers then sprayed the diplomatic vehicle with a fusillade of gunfire. According to reports, the Saudi Embassy in Beirut had received a call a few weeks earlier threatening the safety of senior diplomats posted in Lebanon; the caller was speaking on behalf of Hezbollah, one of the first times that the organizational name had been used in a context outside of the Islamic Jihad.[13]

The Iranians and their local proxies were becoming calculatingly audacious. On February 6, masked gunmen seized Frank Regier, an American engineering professor at the AUB. Jerry Levin, a CNN producer, was kidnapped on the morning of March 7 as he walked to work from his West Beirut flat. The threats to Americans, intelligence and security staffers in the embassy realized, had become acute.

Safety and security should have meant everything to Buckley. But remarkably, as one of the CIA agents who would later work the kidnapping case would attest, "Buckley was incredibly cavalier about his own security."[14] The threats to his safety were impossible to ignore.

The threats, Beck believed, were growing day by day. One early morning shortly after Levin's abduction, he was picking Buckley up for work in front of his apartment building. As always, Beck came ready for combat and dressed for a street fight, wearing rugged khakis and an open and untucked shirt that he could use to conceal his ██ ███████████████████ nine-millimeter pistol; Buckley, of course, wore a suit and tie. Once Buckley entered the sedan, a vehicle pulled up in front of it, blocking any way out of the cul-de-sac. Beck jumped out of the car, his pistol aimed straight at the driver's-side window. "Move the car, now!" he ordered, closing ground on his target as his fingers applied a progressively stronger pressure on the trigger. The driver, a Lebanese man in his thirties, gave Beck a cold, fearless stare and pulled away.

Beck believed that this incident was Hezbollah perpetrating a dry-run abduction exercise targeting the CIA Station Chief. The close encounter, combined with a sixth sense of battlefield realities, provided a sobering reality to Buckley. He had always said that he would be the last one out ███████████. He wasn't going to let the cruel threats interfere with his sworn mission. Premonitions of his fate grew stronger. At a CIA Chiefs of Station conference held in Western Europe in February 1984, Buckley made a foreboding remark to a colleague. "My demise or my departure," he said, "whichever comes first?"[15]

Chip Beck and William Buckley met one final time, in Cyprus on the night of March 9, 1984. With ██████ staffers no longer allowed to fly in and out of Beirut on commercial flights, an air bridge of US Navy and Marine Corps helicopters shuttled the diplomats, soldiers, and ████████████████████████████ on the southern tip of the island 150 miles from the Lebanese capital. Crossing paths at the base, the friends embraced and enjoyed a meal together. The dangers of Beirut were hanging over Buckley's mind, like a grim medical diagnosis over a man who accepted, grudgingly, that this was his fate and there wasn't a thing he could do about it. "Bill seemed very concerned," Beck remembered. "He asked me to do whatever I could to help him in the event he was taken hostage, saying that he did not want to die of ill health or execution like Tucker [Gougelmann]. When we met, Bill even gave me a list of names of the Near East and Director-ate of Operations personnel who he felt would not be competent to rescue him if he were taken hostage." Buckley predicted his demise, Beck would later recall. Over drinks and a plate of Greek delicacies, Buckley requested that if he was ever seized by hostile forces, Beck should push the bureaucracy so that he wouldn't die of ill health or execution. He told Beck, "I'd rather die in a botched rescue attempt than waste away."[16]

THE WORKWEEK BEGINNING March 12 was routine for Chief of Station Buckley and the officers he led. There were briefings for Ambassador Bartholomew ███████████████████████. There were agents and assets to meet, sources to cultivate, manipulate, interrogate, and orchestrate. Money always changed hands.

On the afternoon of Thursday, March 15, Buckley asked his secretary to type up a list of the officers in the station along with their telephone numbers and addresses. The request bucked all security protocols, of course. The identities, even radio call signs, of the officers attached to the station were secret. He offered no explanation for the request—Buckley didn't have to explain himself to anybody. The secretary complied, of course, and typed the information onto a white index card.

Buckley said good night to his staff when he left later that evening. Dinner was at 6:00 p.m. at Mama Washington's.

SUNRISE CAME TO Beirut at precisely 5:48 on the morning of March 16, 1984. Even in Beirut—a city where residents could display such a bloodthirst toward one another—sunrise was always peaceful. William F. Buckley was up before the first embers of light introduced the dawn of the new day to the Lebanese capital. The alarm clock rang at 5:30 sharp every morning. Buckley showered and shaved and then walked to the kitchen table to turn on a battery-operated Panasonic transistor radio that was always kept on the kitchen table near an impressive collection of Lebanese beer cans and bottles. The radio was tuned to the BBC World Service. Buckley listened to the news from London every morning as he readied himself for work.

Buckley checked the contents of his Samsonite attaché case one last time before heading out the door. He had a copy of a three-day-old *International Herald Tribune*, a clipping from a *Newsweek* article, a few pens, and a performance review of Bob, his Deputy Chief of Station.[17] As the two men still did not get along, the review was not a favorable one. Buckley checked his ███████████ nine-millimeter semiautomatic pistol, holstered it in its black leather case, and slid it into the briefcase. Buckley ███████████ handheld radio that linked him to the duty officer at the station. ███████████[18]

Buckley liked to be in the office at around 7:00 a.m. ███████ ███████████ was only a few blocks away but protocol required that he drive to work. He walked out of the building into the Beirut sun.

Buckley hated his station-issued gray 1983 Renault 18 Turbo. The Renault was purchased because of its advertised speed and handling capabilities, critical requirements of a car in Beirut. So the vehicle would be fast and light—it wasn't armored; yet even though it didn't carry the extra weight of bullet-resistant steel and glass fastened to its frame, the car was still sluggish. The Renault always stalled negotiating the steep inclines of the Chouf Mountains; it overheated a minute after the air-conditioning was switched on. Buckley had requisitioned a Jaguar XJ-S for himself, just like the one that Colonel Kassis drove, but the car was sitting somewhere in Cyprus waiting to clear the usual hurdles of customs forms and bribes. The Renault was always parked in an open-air lot next to his apartment building. Buckley didn't think anyone was stupid enough to steal it.

The men waiting for Buckley down the block on al-Qala'a Street were expert at overpowering their prey ████████████████████

██

██

██

██

██

A fifty-five-year-old CIA Chief of Station would pose very little challenge. By the time Buckley realized that he was the target of an actual snatch-and-grab operation, the AK-47s were pointed at his head and the hands were yanking him out of the car. He didn't have time to reach for his case and his pistol.

The attaché case was left behind on the passenger seat. Perhaps the kidnappers feared that the case had a tracking device inside. There was none. Buckley's pistol remained holstered.

William Buckley was thrown into the back seat of a Mercedes getaway car and driven, it is believed, on a circuitous route through the streets and avenues of West Beirut. William Buckley disappeared into a landscape of narrow alleys, television antennas, electrical lines, and Khomeini posters, never to be seen again.

THE NEIGHBOR TENDING to his plants did not know William Buckley's name. He might have suspected that the man working ████████ ████████ was a spy. But when he witnessed the abduction he immediately telephoned the US Embassy. The call was panic filled, and when the switchboard operator heard the words "American" and "kidnapped," she immediately contacted the Marine Corps Gunnery Sergeant at Post One, who summoned the RSO's office. Al Bigler was stateside, home on leave, and Jeremy Zeikel took the call. The station was notified at once.

Luke, back at the CIA station, had sensed that something was amiss when Buckley didn't show up at 7:00 a.m., and he called Buckley's home phone. There was no answer. Luke summoned Alan, another CIA officer. They removed weapons from the armory and ventured to the parking lot with the keys for one of the "ghetto cars," the unmarked vehicles in the CIA station motor pool that the officers often used when out in the field. The vehicles had bullet holes in them and more wear and tear than a junkyard jalopy, but they looked genuine and they were remarkably innocuous when going in and out of checkpoints.

Station personnel and the special agents from the RSO's office and the Defense Attaché were the only staffers permitted out on the streets of Beirut. There were no exceptions.

The Americans traveled in separate vehicles toward Ras Beirut. The drive took less than five minutes. The two CIA officers drove together; SY agent Zeikel came in a small convoy assisted by a former Lebanese cop and a team of M16-toting members of the embassy's local guard force. There were no protocols or guidance on what to do for a missing Station Chief, other than to go look for him. The CIA and SY team became the first responders, in a city without law.

The Americans found Buckley's Renault still in the middle of the street. The passenger door was still open. Buckley's attaché case was still on the front seat. Alan opened the case and found Buckley's pistol untouched. No one knows what became of the papers he carried or of the Pearl brand microcassette recorder he used for dictation and for agent meetings. The two CIA officers rushed up to Buckley's apartment. They searched the apartment to empty it of anything that could be of use to hostile entities, such as names of station personnel and phone numbers, a spare ███ radio, and addresses of safe houses. Buckley's clothes were quickly rounded up, as well as a few books, a foreign edition of *Newsweek*, and some of the photos of his days in Vietnam that he always traveled with. An antique rocking chair Buckley had purchased on a day off remained behind.

While the two CIA officers sanitized Buckley's flat, Zeikel dealt with the cops. Zeikel had notified his contact with the Lebanese police to meet him at Buckley's flat. Without providing the gendarmerie with too much information, Zeikel handed the shift commander Buckley's photo and his description. The Lebanese officers cordoned off the area, preventing onlookers or the Iranian post-incident reconnaissance from getting close to the crime scene. One of the Lebanese police commanders began to bark orders into a walkie-talkie. The responding officers looked confused.

A small pocket of Lebanon's internal security apparatus functioned, but that cadre was too minuscule and compromised by clan affiliation to matter much. Zeikel and his Foreign Service National redirected the embassy guards toward the Beirut–Damascus Highway and the Beka'a Valley. The hope was that they'd come across a checkpoint where someone would say something if he saw something. Zeikel was grasping at straws.

JEREMY ZEIKEL'S BEKA'A gateways bore no fruit. The men at the checkpoints, angry and armed, were in no mood to talk to any Americans or the Lebanese in their employ. It was early afternoon. The late winter sun provided a bright glow to the day. As the vehicles entered the secure parking area ████████████████, Zeikel noticed a group of men and women standing outside, looking nervous. Samsonite suitcases were at their feet. As he looked on, he realized that Beirut Station was being evacuated of most of its personnel.

The State Department Chief of Mission, Robert Pugh, had been notified of Buckley's abduction and contacted the station. Alan was in the CIA station bullpen and received the troubling phone call informing him of Buckley's abduction. Alan asked Pugh to put his political and diplomatic contacts to work and to ask the Shiite militias to close the southern exits out of Beirut.[19]

Zeikel returned to his office and began to put together a cable for headquarters at Foggy Bottom. It was the most difficult cable that Zeikel had ever had to write. When he completed it, he turned to Chief of Mission Pugh and asked him how he should send it. "Send it FLASH," Pugh demanded. When Zeikel said, "I always thought that FLASH was to be used only in a nuclear emergency," Pugh responded, "Well, what do you think this is?"[20]

BUCKLEY'S KIDNAPPING WAS, indeed, a twenty-megaton nuclear strike. The duty officer at headquarters had been notified about the FLASH cables coming in from Beirut Station. There were DC notifications that had to be made. The CIA director of the Near Eastern Division was woken out of bed. A senior officer from the CIA Operations Center called Director Casey. The Ops Center looked at Buckley's file and found the name and telephone number for Beverly Surette. The CIA Duty Officer had to make the grim notification.

Chip Beck was in Florida when he learned of his friend's abduction. He was reaching the end of a five-mile run when his girlfriend came chasing after him. "Bill's been kidnapped. We just heard it on the news," she yelled. It was what Beck had feared all along.[21]

Beck raced home and called headquarters. A rush of emotion and anger overpowered him as he spoke on the phone. At first he asked to be sent back to Beirut to look for Buckley, and then he demanded to go back into the lion's den.

DAZED AND CONFUSED

*A blind man who sees is better than a sighted man
who is blind.*

—Persian proverb

ELIEZER TZAFRIR WAS the Mossad's Chief of Station in Beirut. Tzafrir was a veteran of Unit 504, Israeli Military Intelligence's HUMINT force, as well as the Shin Bet secret service, but he eventually found a home in the Mossad, where his fluency in Arabic and his knowledge of the Islamic world made him a natural for covert operations on behalf of Israel's world-renowned espionage organization. He served the Mossad in pretty much the same way that Buckley served the Agency—as a paramilitary officer helping the local Kurd rebels build an indigenous intelligence and special operations force to fight Saddam Hussein and the notorious Iraqi security services that butchered the ethnic minority for sport.

In 1979, as the last Chief of Mossad Station in Tehran, Tzafrir helped to organize the evacuation of all Israeli nationals from a once-friendly nation that was in the throes of the Khomeini revolution. His career had been one of risk and results. In 1983, the fifty-year-old Tzafrir was appointed the head of the Mossad's Beirut station. This was located beyond the northernmost confines of the Lebanese capital, on the Mediterranean coast near the port city of Jounieh. Jounieh, nestled ten miles north of Beirut, was known for its lavish seaside resorts, exciting nightlife, gourmet dining, and old market, or suq, which was a dream for antique hunters. Jounieh was also the epicenter of Maronite power in Lebanon. The Our Lady of Lebanon shrine was a symbol of the Maronite presence in the country; the patriarch of the Maronite Church was based in the mountains above the city. Ironically, Jounieh was also home to Maameltein, considered Lebanon's red-light district. Beirut and other sections of the country consisted of a series of go and no-go areas based on ethnicity, but Arabs of all faiths and sects were allowed to venture to Maameltein to enjoy the company of Palestinian and Shiite girls forced from their homes by war, poverty, and versions of family honor. Women from the Euphrates all the way to the Atlas Mountains worked the clubs and the apartments of Maameltein. It was a location frequented by the many spies who worked the Lebanese theater of operations.

Jounieh was a Lebanese Forces stronghold. LF militiamen and women—wearing their Israeli-style fatigues and Israeli-manufactured ballistic helmets and load-bearing gear—were everywhere. The LF Navy, equipped with Israeli-manufactured patrol boats, prevented infiltration by sea. LF armor, mainly old Lebanese and Israeli military surplus, prevented the Palestinians, the Syrians, or any other militia with armor from punching through and leveling the enclave. Some of the tanks were Soviet-produced T-54s and T-55s, known in Hebrew as Tiran. The IDF captured many of these tanks from the Syrians and Egyptians and then upgraded them and pressed them into service.

Mossad Station was located on the beach, inside a heavily fortified LF facility. The beach was an ideal location to situate so sensitive a location—egress and ingress could be controlled and defended. A contingent of shooters, the very best that Israeli special operations could produce, provided round-the-clock security.[1]

Tzafrir's job in Lebanon, like that of all foreign spy chiefs, was to lead his service's intelligence-gathering effort in the county, along with any aid and liaison programs for local forces. And, like all the other foreign spy chiefs in Lebanon at the time, Tzafrir was pressed by Mossad headquarters to help in any way that he could to locate William Buckley.

Officially, the call for Mossad assistance to help locate any tidbits on Buckley's location would have come in a roundabout way.

But by the time official word of Buckley's kidnapping reached Tzafrir, as well as all the foreign intelligence station chiefs working the murky bogs of Lebanon's espionage middle-earth, the spies were already working the case, trying to find leads and develop some sort of insight into what had happened. The diligent investigative effort was, according to a former French military officer serving in Lebanon at the time, "more a gesture of self-preservation than benevolence."[2] The other intelligence chiefs knew that if the CIA Chief of Station could be nabbed, so could they.

The question remained, though: Who took Buckley? Which group was crazy enough to go to war with the Central Intelligence Agency?

* * *

THERE WAS, OF course, the odd chance that Buckley had been seized by amateurs, thrill seekers, or a criminal gang for a quick ransom. CIA headquarters realized that stranger things had happened before.

But Buckley's kidnapping revealed what had been an open secret inside the halls of Langley for many years: that the CIA was still only a semblance of its once mighty self, like a fighter knocked senseless but not unconscious by a series of merciless blows. Morale at the Agency was already at an all-time low in the post-blast rubble of Vietnam and the United States Senate Select Committee to Study Governmental Operations with Respect to Intelligence Activities chaired by Democratic senator Frank Church of Idaho in 1975. In addition to what became known as the "Church Committee," in 1975 Vice President Nelson Rockefeller chaired the United States President's Commission on CIA Activities within the United States, under the direction of President Gerald Ford, to investigate CIA actions in the country. The public scrutiny of the Agency's role in destabilizing foreign governments, including the assassination of foreign leaders, was akin to slicing the CIA to the bone with a serrated dagger.

Director Casey was particularly paralyzed by the news of Buckley's abduction. Casey had brought an OSS ethos to the Agency, returning a spinal column of heroism and daring to an Agency that had been castrated on Capitol Hill. Casey had been a warrior, a behind-enemy-lines operative who knew very well that men went to their deaths in the spy business but they did so knowing that their commanders back at headquarters would always go above and beyond to secure their release if captured; if killed, the spies knew that their remains had value and that men would move mountains to bring their bones back to the United States for a proper burial. Casey had to break the news to President Reagan. This in itself would be a difficult enough task. But Casey would also have to look into the eyes of the men and women at headquarters who, one day, could find themselves in a foreign city, suddenly overpowered by armed men, only to vanish off the face of the earth. Casey personally let his counterparts at MI6, the German BND, Canada's CSIS, and all the Arab services know that it was a CIA priority to bring Buckley back alive and immediately. Spy chiefs and section heads in a dozen capitals around the world in just as many times zones received the word from their ambassadors or their Agency liaisons. Some even received it from Casey himself.

CHIP BECK RETURNED to Langley expecting that the Agency's Special Activities Division already had top spies and shooters on the ground in Beirut, poised to strike immediately and decisively. He was quickly disappointed. "By the time I got back to headquarters the next day, I was informed that HQ did not want to 'unnecessarily risk' another officer's life by sending [me] back to Beirut. Everything that Bill had feared would happen, and that he expressed during our last meeting in Cyprus, came to being ██████████████████████ ██ ████████████████████."[3]

The Agency had never planned for the kidnapping of a Chief of Station. The Moscow Rules of the Cold War and John le Carré did not allow such visceral statements of declared war. The Agency's first response was damage control.

On March 16, a secret memorandum (partially declassified in May

2003) from the National Security Council addressed to Robert McFarlane, Oliver North, Donald Fortier, and Philip Dur stated (in the portion not redacted) that the most prudent call for action was to assemble a Terrorist Incident Work Group (TIWG) meeting in the White House Situation Room. Requested participants included Eagleburger and Sayre from the Department of State, CIA official McMahon and another redacted name from the CIA, and Admiral Arthur S. Moreau and Major General Rice from the Joint Chiefs of Staff. Also present would be Taft and Richard Armitage. The TIWG wanted to address two pressing issues. Those issues remain classified.[4]

On March 20, 1984, Secretary of State Schultz sent a memo to President Reagan. The title of the memorandum was "U.S. Efforts in Response to the Abduction of William Buckley." Heavily redacted, the memo stated:

CIA Station Chief Bill Buckley was kidnapped in Beirut the morning of March 16. We are using every available diplomatic channel to encourage his safe and rapid return. We are also taking steps to prepare for a rescue operation should it prove necessary. Within a few hours of Buckley's abduction, we had contacted all of the main government officials and militia leaders who could be helpful, both in Beirut and in Lausanne, where the Lebanese reconciliation talks are underway. Reggie Bartholomew also instructed that all US personnel be drawn inside the embassy perimeter and that any personnel leaving the perimeter travel by car with a chauffeur and bodyguard. We also have sought Syrian cooperation. Within a few hours of Buckley's abduction, we approached Foreign Ministry officials in Damascus requesting that all Syrian security checkpoints in

Lebanon be on the lookout for Buckley. Shortly after, we also met with the chief aide to Syrian Vice President Rifaat Assad. The aide said that Syrian units in Beirut and at Damascus airport would be notified immediately and requested a photograph of Buckley which we later delivered.

We do not have any firm evidence as to who is responsible for Buckley's kidnapping or where he is being held. The conflicting intelligence reports we have received suggest either the complicity of Iran or pro-Iranian factions.

THE POWERS THAT be that could have acted decisively and immediately hemmed and hawed about what to do. Each agency, it appeared, pulled in a separate direction. There were parochial interests to protect.

On March 21, John M. Poindexter received from Oliver North a memo concerning the TIWG meeting regarding the Buckley kidnapping. North was very direct. "There is growing concern that this not a team effort and that we could well be doing more. Our objectives for the meeting show me to determine the current level of information and effort; and, to arrive as some consensus regarding what more (if anything can be done)"[5] [errors in original].

North's memo went on to point out that both the Department of State and the Department of Defense concurred that if Buckley was located the US might have to react in a matter of hours. US assets in the area, Lieutenant Colonel North assessed, were inadequate. He wrote:

Our current disposition would preclude action by any forces other than the Marines offshore—who are not trained/equipped for the specialized tasks ███ can perform.

There is resistance at JCS for moving to an Intermediate Staging Base (ISB). They believe that until we have a better fix on Buckley's location (Beirut, Damascus, Tehran, other) we should not degrade our response capability by pre-positioning forces in the wrong locale. JCS does support moving the rest of the Incident Response Team (IRT) ████████████ as soon as possible."[6]

North added one troubling element about the rescue plans and efforts: "No one seems willing to move further on ████████ ████."[7] The redacted element has not been declassified.

The memo concluded with something that everyone at the Agency was already all too aware of:

Privately, you or Bud should take up with ██/McMahon/Casey the counterintelligence aspect of what Buckley knew—and could reveal under torture. This should be second nature to the Agency (it used to be), but may well not have been covered. We had to suggest to them the idea of interview ██████ discern what he might be able to contribute—and this may also have slipped through the cracks. This issue should not be raised at the meeting since it is unlikely that either ███ Cogan would know.[8]

According to Chip Beck, "The Near East Division never formed a task force to retrieve Bill. Not even a single officer was assigned to manage Bill's recovery, although I volunteered to be that person. Instead, a NE case officer was assigned to Bill's case on a part-time basis. I remember a conversation I had with him in which he put his feet on his desk and told me, 'These things take time.' I replied, 'You have to operate like there is no time, that every day will be Bill's last day alive, because some day that will actually be the case.' The cables flowed and the rooms filled up with paper, while little was done effectively on the ground in Beirut, even though I had lined up several willing assets on my own."[9]

The CIA believed that all roads in and out of Lebanon, even those now leading toward the Islamic Revolution in Tehran, crisscrossed through Damascus. The Israelis knew it as well. There was one man in the halls of the Near East Division who had the contacts, the experience, and the sheer tenacity to travel to Damascus to try to see what the Syrian intelligence services knew and how they could be used to locate Buckley and help secure his release. Sam Wyman was summoned by Casey and ordered to the Syrian capital.

Wyman was fluent in Arabic and, among his many Middle Eastern postings, had served as the Chief of Station ████████ from 1979 to the end of June 1982. Damascus was a treacherous no-man's-land for intelligence officers, especially those serving one of Syria's enemies. A visit to Damascus had to be cleared. Langley contacted Ambassador Robert Paganelli. Paganelli had been the US ambassador for nearly three years, having been appointed by President Reagan in 1981, and was considered one of the State Department's most capable Arab specialists. Paganelli began his career in 1958 as an intelligence research specialist and then went on to serve in Beirut, Basra, Baghdad, Damascus, and Amman, as well as in Qatar and Italy. Syria was not an easy posting but Paganelli was not the kind of man to let a police state interfere with his mission as the personal representative of the president of the United States—a New York native, Paganelli was, according to one former member ████████, "a tough-as-nails diplomat who understood the very depths of the Arab world."[10] Paganelli made some phone calls and arranged for Wyman to sit down

███.

███████████████████████████████████████ Sam Wyman knew many of these men. He knew of those he had not personally met. One's reputation in this line of work was often more daunting than one's CV.

With his path cleared, and all the byzantine protocol attended to, Wyman received the green light to fly to Damascus. As he packed his suitcase and awaited the Agency ride to Dulles, his wife, Laurie, looked into her husband's eyes and said, "Bring back my Bill."[11]

WYMAN'S POINT OF contact in Damascus was Rifaat al-Assad, the brother of Syrian president Hafez al-Assad, and the commander of the Sayara al-Difa, or Defense Companies. The Syrian Arab Republic fielded five espionage services to keep enemies—both foreign and domestic—at bay ███████████████████████████████

███

███

███

███

███

███

███

███

███

███

If anyone would know where Buckley was being held, it was ████████████████████████ Wyman had a lot of experience in dealing with men who could charm and garrote an acquaintance with equal ease. Wyman had known █████████████████████████████████, Wyman recalled, "were geopolitical realists who understood the need for back-channel access but also realized the shortcomings of such access."[12]

Sam Wyman ████████ though not well. The sit-down was arranged by Ambassador Paganelli. The meeting between Wyman and ████████ was conducted at night—most rendezvous that mattered in the Syrian capital took place under the cover of darkness. Wyman was picked up from his hotel in an unmarked vehicle, a German sedan, and then driven through a circuitous route of avenues and boulevards of Damascus. ███ AK-47-toting ██ ██ ██ greeted Wyman with a handshake. The office was large and well lit.[13] The two men spoke for two hours in full candor. The pointed conversation was conducted entirely in Arabic. The two men drank sweetened tea from crystal glasses as they discussed William Buckley's whereabouts and the importance to the United States of his prompt and safe return. Wyman remembers ████ as a gracious and outgoing host.[14] Wyman pressed the Syrian ████████ with the urgency involved in locating the missing CIA Chief of Station. The very fact that William Casey would send so high-level a representative indicated to the Syrians that there was political value in helping the CIA bring Buckley back home. These were the types of conversations—late-night talks in a hostile capital—that moved pieces on the chessboard among protagonists in the Middle East. ████████ gave his guest the impression that there could be developments—he told Wyman to remain in Damascus for a few days. But the fires of hope stoked in Langley were soon doused when Wyman was driven back to Damascus Airport and sent home with a few baubles and a "We'll let you know if we uncover anything."

Still, the CIA director placed Wyman on point to help sort out the mess emanating from Buckley's abduction and the vacuum left behind at Beirut Station. Wyman would travel back and forth to Lebanon over the next months. He'd do what he could from his desk at Langley.

The clock was ticking. Buckley's friends knew that the chances of bringing their colleague and comrade back alive diminished with every day that passed without some sort of proof of life. On March 27, 1984, Kuwait's State Security Court sentenced Mustafa Badreddine, also known as Elias al-Sa'ab, to death. Several of his coconspirators received life or lengthy prison sentences. Badreddine's sentence could be carried out only when the emir, Jaber al-Ahmad al-Sabah, signed off on the order of execution.[15]

ACCORDING TO ISRAELI journalist Ronen Bergman, the Israelis had picked up a smoking gun. One of Israeli military intelligence's top human sources inside Hezbollah, code-named "Hypnosis," dispatched an encrypted message of paramount importance to his handlers in southern Lebanon. The intelligence came from Imad Mughniyeh, and indicated that a handpicked squad of operatives had been training for a top secret mission for several months and had been ordered to be ready to carry out their mission in the next few days. The target of the mission was the abduction of a senior American intelligence official.[16] Bergman claims that the Israelis were wringing their hands over what to do with this intelligence; the safety of their source in the Shiite underground in Beirut and the Beka'a was of paramount importance, but so, too, was relaying this vital information to the

Agency. Contents of the encrypted Mughniyeh order, dated March 9, were eventually passed to the CIA.[17] However, none of the CIA officers who worked with Buckley, or worked the Buckley case, and were interviewed for this book remember ever seeing the intelligence from Israel.

There was a very short list of suspects on the CIA's radar concerning who abducted Buckley. There was absolutely no idea as to where he had been taken. One intrepid CIA officer working ▮▮▮▮ ▮▮▮▮▮▮ had a hunch. Bob Baer was a thirty-two-year-old case officer when Buckley was abducted. Baer suspected that the Iranians were involved. The Iranian presence ▮▮▮▮▮▮▮ was large-scale and aggressive. Baer thought that eyes on a possible target were better than any satellite request, so he readied one of the ▮▮▮▮ unmarked vehicles for a road trip east. Baer didn't have a lot of respect for his Chief of Station, so he didn't bother asking for authorization ▮▮▮▮▮ Baer's cover story was that of a Belgian named Remy Martin.[18]

It was evident to Baer that Ba'albek had become the center of Iranian operations in Lebanon and that the Sheikh Abdullah Barracks was a virtually impenetrable fortified forward outpost for the Ayatollah's aspirations in the country. If Buckley was there, Baer assessed, it would be virtually impossible to get him out.

10

ONE OF THE FAMILY JEWELS

There are tigers roaming this world, and we must
recognize them or perish.[1]
—Peer de Silva, former CIA Chief of Station,
Saigon, the Republic of Vietnam

N O ONE KNOWS when exactly William F. Buckley was brought to the Sheikh Abdullah Barracks.*[2] It could have been hours after he was seized or days following the abduction. Hezbollah executed the kidnapping of the CIA Chief of Station but the interrogations and torture were definitely an Iranian endeavor.

---

* There were some reports that suggested that Buckley—along with the other hostages—were also held and interrogated in the basement of the Iranian embassy in southern Beirut. The FBI, declassified files revealed (FBI FOIPA Request No. 1252354, dated February 26, 2014), believed that Buckley had been flown to Tehran.

No one at the barracks was allowed to know the identity of the man being held under such heavy guard at a remote corner of the facility. Even the Revolutionary Guard members who patrolled the base were not supposed to know or talk about the man being held in the Beka'a. The Sheikh Abdullah Barracks was a massive facility—over 2,500 feet across at its main wall, 1,500 feet deep on its sides. The barracks consisted of offices, several armories, parade grounds, quarters for the lower ranks as well as officers, and a dispensary; there were two mosques on the base, as well as a soccer field. It was easy to disappear inside the sprawling base.

The American intelligence community marveled at the tradecraft displayed by the kidnapping squad and the Iranians who protected them. There were no radio interceptions of telephone or radio communications between Lebanon, the Beka'a, Damascus, or Tehran where the fibers of loose chatter could be woven into a single lead. Imad Mughniyeh used an insular group of clan members and locals from the Tyre area whose loyalty was impenetrable. Communications were relayed in conversations; a whisper was the volume generally used between messenger and recipient. The Iranians in the Beka'a did not use the telephone or their encrypted-communications gear. The National Security Agency and US naval eavesdropping stations and ships patrolling the Mediterranean did not register a single syllable of chatter that could help locate William Buckley.

Mughniyeh's handpicked thugs and the Iranian intelligence officers who approved of their actions showed little mercy to Buckley. Based on the testimonies of other hostages seized, Buckley was beaten, isolated, and shackled to a post or radiator without letup. Unlike the hostages who would later be seized, Buckley possessed actionable intelligence that transcended Beirut Station operations in Lebanon. He knew the names and backgrounds—as well as vulnerabilities, shortcomings, and personal capabilities—of many high-ranking CIA officials at Langley and around the world. Buckley knew the names of spouses and children of other Chiefs of Station posted around the Middle East. He knew code names and nicknames. He knew the bitter secrets held closely inside the guarded gates of Langley, and he knew of future plans in the region and beyond. "Buckley should have never been assigned to Beirut," former FBI Assistant Director Oliver "Buck" Revell commented. "He was too well briefed, too knowledgeable, and too important to be over there."[3]

The men who seized Buckley knew precisely how valuable he was. US law enforcement and counterterrorism officials likened his abduction to seizing one of the family jewels. William Buckley, it is believed, was interrogated by street toughs and well-trained professionals. The knuckle-dragging men from the south, boyhood friends of Mughniyeh's who could be trusted, were the muscle that punished Buckley for being an American, for being a spy, for being an enemy of the Islamic Revolution. Buckley's resilience had to be shattered; his resolve required disassembly, one punch to the gut and one kick to the head at a time. ■■■■■■■■■■■■■■■■■■■

■■■■■■■■■■■■■■■■■■■■■■■■■■

The weather warmed in Ba'albek as the weeks passed. Buckley's treatment worsened.

MEANWHILE, THE KIDNAPPINGS of Americans continued. Benjamin Weir, an American Presbyterian minister who had been working in Beirut as a missionary for close to thirty years, left his West Beirut home early on the morning of May 9, 1984. Several armed men emerged from a white Peugeot as Weir walked onto a Beirut street;

they wrestled him to the ground and threw him in the back of the car to disappear into traffic. Weir was sixty years old and a man who had spent his entire life, in Lebanon and in the Sudan, helping others. He was not a legitimate target under any rules of engagement. But Hezbollah was emboldened by the successes they enjoyed in the human bazaar. The Weir abduction complicated efforts to locate and retrieve Buckley; hunting season on Americans became the norm. More hostages would be taken; occupations didn't matter; nobody was safe.

For two months the CIA fretted over Buckley's whereabouts. IOUs were called in all over the Middle East. Veteran Near Eastern Division hands crisscrossed the Atlantic a dozen times following leads, interviewing cutthroats and warlords. An army of counterintelligence specialists interviewed the members of Beirut Station who were forced to flee for their lives once Buckley was abducted in order to ascertain what secrets were being spilled; the files inside Buckley's office were combed through with exhaustive scrutiny. From an operational perspective, Buckley's abduction had been a disaster. Agency operations in Lebanon had already been in disarray since the embassy bombing the previous year, and now everything done during Buckley's tenure, Langley had to assume, was compromised. Intelligence-gathering efforts must now start from scratch. The financial cost of establishing new networks, seducing new sources, and instilling confidence in men and women who would risk their necks for a few dollars would be mind-boggling. The human cost could not be calculated.

During his first year in office, President Reagan had been forced to contend with charges that prior to the 1980 election his campaign had brokered a deal in which Iran would delay the freeing of American hostages until after Election Day, thereby denying President Carter any political windfall from their release. Now Iran's manipulation of hostages once again threatened to redefine

Reagan's presidency. The Reagan White House and the CIA found themselves facing a three-dimensional hostage crisis: Buckley's abduction was a national security emergency; the abduction of noncombatants like Jerry Levin and Benjamin Weir was a domestic political quandary demanding that the government take action— any action—to bring these men back to their families; and the failure of the United States to deal decisively and forcefully with the kidnappers telegraphed a level of impotence to America's allies and enemies and threatened to endanger America's interests in the region for years to come.

In July 1984, the State Department forwarded to the CIA a videotape.[4] The tape, which held only a few seconds of footage, showed a man who looked liked William Buckley. He appeared bewildered and broken: pale, with an expression of someone who's been jostled out of a sound slumber and shoved before bright lights. The two other American hostages, CNN journalist Jerry Levin and Reverend Ben Weir, also appeared in the video proof of life. They seemed to be healthy and well-fed.[5]

CIA and FBI forensic specialists were summoned to review the tape, frame by excruciating frame, and to attempt to assemble some sort of evidence as to where and when the footage was filmed. Images were compared for commonalities such as lighting, shadows, props, and backdrop. Audio enhancements were done in an effort to pick up background noises such as aircraft (civilian or military), children playing on the street, animals, and even car horns honking. The medical staff at the CIA would put together an assessment of Buckley (along with the other hostages) based on their pre-abduction condition; Agency medical specialists would examine the tape to evaluate their medical state and evidence of torture. The tape was also meticulously examined, slowly and frame by frame, to check for any signals that the hostages possibly tried to transmit through blinking, facial gestures, or speech.

The footage of Buckley sent CIA Director Casey into a state of unchecked fury. According to one account, the abduction "drove him almost to the ends of the earth to find ways of getting Buckley back, to deal with anyone in any form, in any shape, in any way, to get Buckley back."[6] The images of a Chief of Station shattered by cruelty and a perverted lust for suffering was a humiliating blow for Casey, as well as the other men and women who worked the top floor in Langley.

But the anger was more bark than bite. The Agency never formed a dedicated task force to retrieve Buckley. Not even a single officer was assigned to manage Buckley's recovery, although some of his paramilitary officer friends, men like Chip Beck, volunteered to do so. Ultimately, a part-time case officer was assigned to the "Buckley Desk." Chip Beck boiled over with anger over the lack of resources and effort applied to retrieving his boss and close friend.[7]

Other agencies, though, saw merit and opportunity in the hubris in Langley. The very elite of the US counterterrorist community was already in Lebanon. Advisers from the US Army's Special Forces Fifth Group (Airborne) routinely trained the LAF, including its special operations components, during FID deployments. FID, or Foreign Internal Defense, missions were one of the pillars of Green Beret operations around the world; the Green Berets, especially those assigned to Fifth Group, all spoke other languages, including Arabic. The US Special Envoys to Lebanon, men like Philip Habib and Morris Draper, all had highly skilled protective details made up of shooters from the tip of the spear of America's covert community who worked side by side with SY agents. "█████████ received the Buckley file roughly four months after his abduction," a former high-ranking officer in the unit remembered. "Planning commenced, no idea regardless of how outside the box was ever ignored, but operationally Lebanon was a nonpermissive environment."[8]

*   *   *

SPECIAL AGENT AL Bigler greeted the sunny September morning in his office at the US Embassy Annex located in Awkar, in Christian East Beirut. Bigler, the SY regional security officer at the US Embassy in Beirut, had been a range instructor and countersniper for the US Secret Service before making a lateral career move to the State Department's security arm in 1976. Rugged and handsome, with a laserlike focus on his work, Bigler worked domestically for SY for a few months before tours in the People's Republic of China, India, and Afghanistan following the Soviet invasion and the February 14, 1979, murder of Adolph Dubs, the US ambassador to Afghanistan. Dubs was killed in an exchange of gunfire between the Islamic extremists who kidnapped him and Afghan security forces. In August 1983, Rich Gannon rotated out of Lebanon, having survived the destruction of the chancery four months earlier. Bigler was the first in line to volunteer to be his replacement.

Bigler had been in Rome, at an RSO conference, when the truck bomb built by Mustafa Badreddine smashed through the Marine barracks on October 23. Bigler was home on leave when William Buckley was kidnapped. Even though the city became more dangerous with each day that passed, the threats of kidnap and assassination didn't stop Bigler from crisscrossing West Beirut on a Honda 450 motorcycle, his issued Smith & Wesson .357 Magnum holstered, traveling from law enforcement contacts to those with other affiliations to those who might be holding Buckley, in order to gather a lead, a clue, that could help secure Buckley's release. Bigler had looked at Buckley as a role model; he was a friend, a comrade-in-arms in the trenches of Beirut.

Beirut was unraveling fast, however. West Beirut had simply become one of the most treacherous confines in the world. Daily firefights between rival militias threatened to spiral the city into unprecedented destruction. Armed groups, each sworn to the others' destruction, battled openly only blocks from the Corniche and the ad hoc American Embassy, firing 106-millimeter recoilless rifles at nearly point-blank range. The US State Department realized that the risk far outweighed any rewards of remaining in West Beirut. Ambassador Reginald Bartholomew recommended moving most of the embassy's operations and personnel to a new office building in East Beirut, while keeping a token presence in the western half of the city. SY fully supported the move, but expressed strong reservations about maintaining even a token presence in West Beirut. The diplomats, however, feared that abandoning the Muslim part of the Lebanese capital would telegraph a message of retreat to moderate Arab forces in the country and throughout the Middle East.

An office complex in East Beirut was selected as the site of what would become known as the US Embassy Annex. The Annex was housed inside the Baaklini Office Building, a six-story concrete structure with porches and perimeter walls and fencing dug into a sloping hillside. SY engineers coordinated, supervised, and installed most of the building's extensive security upgrades, but there was still a lot of work to be done as the summer of 1984 came to an end. Many of the physical security barriers that needed to be installed to provide greater deterrence and protection against the type of vehicle-borne suicide bomber that took out the first embassy and the Marine and French compounds were sitting in crates, waiting to be attended to on the morning of September 20, 1984.

Supervising the installation and assembling a competent local guard force to deal with any possible threats to the Annex or Annex staff had been Bigler's primary concern for months. He had returned from leave only the day before and found his desk at the Annex submerged by paperwork. He had started work just as the first glimmers of sunshine emerged over the Beka'a. It was almost noon, and Bigler was well on the way to clearing the mountain of paper from his desk when he noticed that a good chunk of the day had disappeared already. He was hungry and in need of a coffee. He headed to the cafeteria.

Outside the Annex, in a secured courtyard and vehicle-reception area, several British Royal Military Policemen were standing in front of the heavily armored and armed Land Rover used to augment the armored limousine used by British ambassador David Miers and his protective detail as it traveled throughout the country. Miers, a veteran Near East hand for the Foreign Office, was concluding a strategy meeting with Ambassador Bartholomew. Two MPs noticed an embassy guard arguing with the driver of a van at the main gate. Suddenly a shot rang out and the van accelerated toward the front gate of the Baaklini Office Building. Soon additional members of the embassy guard force opened fire on the van but there was nothing they could do. The MPs, in an ideal position to intercede, opened fire as well. The two policemen took aim with their Heckler & Koch MP5 nine-millimeter submachine guns and killed the driver.[9] The vehicle had penetrated the inside perimeter of the heavily fortified Annex but failed to crash into the structure. The van then smashed into a parked truck on the right side of the road, bounced off of it, and exploded. The blast chewed through the asphalt and left a crater that was nearly eight feet deep.

"I heard shooting, or I thought I did," Bigler recalled, "but my assistant turned to me and said, 'Al, you are not in West Beirut anymore. That was a jackhammer doing construction work. Relax!'"[10] But Bigler rushed out the front door and toward danger as the truck bomb erupted into a fireball. His six-foot frame was thrown more than sixty feet back inside, clear across the cafeteria. He was so gravely injured with blunt head trauma that rescue workers mistook him for a fatality and tossed him onto a pile of corpses awaiting movement to the morgue. A small twitch saved Bigler from being transported in a body bag for identification. Rushed to an emergency room, he was stabilized before being transported to Europe and then home to the States.

The blast killed twenty-four people, including two Americans assigned to the Defense Attaché's staff. Lebanese investigators assessed that the van was packed with close to two hundred kilograms of explosives.[11] It was believed that the payload of the device would have been far more lethal had Mustafa Badreddine, Mughniyeh's architect of destruction, been in Beirut and not languishing behind bars waiting for the emir of Kuwait to sign his death sentence.

According to reports, a full mock-up of the Baaklini Office Building had been built at the Sheikh Abdullah Barracks so that Mughniyeh and his Iranian sponsors could plan the bombing to perfection.[12] The mock-up was expensive, but worth the petrodollars.

The CIA, the ISA, the DIA, the NSA, and all of the other covert forces based in and around the seat of power behind the fortified fences in northern Virginia failed to pick up even the slightest chatter that a suicide truck bombing against the US Embassy Annex had been in the works for months.

NEWS OF THE successful suicide strike against the US Embassy Annex reached the Sheikh Abdullah Barracks shortly after lunch. The Hezbollah commanders and the Iranian Revolutionary Guard officers who sanctioned the daily steps of their brothers from the Beirut slums received the coded word via messenger that the attack had been successful. The green light was given to the men from Beirut to take credit for the attack. Publicity, in this context at least, was deemed productive.

Two hours after Al Bigler was rushed to the hospital, barely clinging to life, a caller representing the Islamic Holy War called the Agence France-Presse claiming responsibility for the Annex attack. The caller spoke with an unmistakable Beirut accent, and said, "The operation goes to prove that we will carry out our previous promise not to allow a single American to remain on Lebanese soil."[13]

Fall quickly became winter. The rains changed the Beka'a Valley palette into a lush assortment of dark browns and greens. The temperatures plummeted and snow capped the peaks of the mountains that stoically stood as a backdrop to the lawless crossroad. The young Shiite men from southern Beirut and southern Lebanon training at the Sheikh Abdullah Barracks wore woolen sweaters and leather jackets to shield them from the harsh winds. On the fifty-meter shooting range, and on the training ground where explosives instruction was given, the young men blew into their hands to keep the cold out. Even the Iranian officers wore their winter parkas and leather gloves when supervising the instruction. Soldiers in any army hated the cold and the mud.

There would be no Thanksgiving leave for William Buckley. There would be no ushering in of the holiday season in Washington, DC, with Beverly Surette or his colleagues at Langley. There would be no ▮▮▮▮▮ Christmas party ▮▮▮▮▮ ▮▮▮▮▮. The harsh reality was that Buckley was in chains, the victim of torture and incessant interrogation, and held in seclusion inside a bone-numbing Beka'a Valley dungeon. There were no glimmers of hope or thoughts of survival.

On the morning of December 3, 1984, Peter Kilburn, an American citizen and the librarian at the American University of Beirut, was abducted from his home. He was seized, it is believed, by thugs hired by Hezbollah to kidnap an American. It is believed he was driven toward the Sheikh Abdullah Barracks. He was the fourth American kidnapped

in Lebanon since the destruction of the US Embassy in April 1983. The
Reagan administration was in the thick of a hostage crisis.

The Shiite plan to eradicate the American presence from Lebanon
had been a brilliant and bloody success. The defeat of America's presence in Lebanon was masterfully played. Lebanon had become a
graveyard—and a prison—for American intentions in the Middle East.
Lebanon was a bewildering mystery even to America's spies who were
supposed to understand it.

11

MELTDOWN AND MURDER

As the cold winds howled, the four men discussed the details of the operation—the hijacking of a Kuwait Airway Airbus A310 jetliner traveling from Bangkok to Kuwait City with stopovers in Karachi and Dubai. The hijacking was to take place several days following the Sheikh Abdullah Barracks gathering, but Iranian intelligence learned that three Kuwaiti diplomats would be on board the flight, as would three American citizens. The mission was delayed. The planning intensified. The four men selected for the operation were issued forged papers and passports. Hezbollah had yet to hijack an aircraft. There were many people in the organization, including Mughniyeh, who were eager to see what the end result of the operation would be.

The Hezbollah hijackers boarded a Middle Eastern Airlines flight from Beirut to Dubai on the afternoon of December 3, 1984. Hezbollah operatives working at the airport secreted the four men inside the tarmac perimeter; the men boarded the aircraft without passing through metal detectors or even airline scrutiny. The three-and-a-half-hour flight to Dubai was uneventful, routine. The men transferred at the airport, years from becoming the intercontinental travel hub that it would morph into, and proceeded toward the departure lounge. The men dispersed among the other travelers; al-Yafi, a terrorist, reportedly headed toward a men's room in order to shave off his beard in an attempt to look more Western. Two members of Iranian intelligence waited for the Kuwait Airways flight in Dubai alongside the hijackers—they were to act as hostages and covertly assist in the aircraft seizure.

Forty minutes out of Dubai, the four men produced hand grenades and .25 caliber pistols that had been smuggled on board at the Dubai airport. They overpowered the security agent on board, and then shot him in the leg. Screaming in Arabic that they were willing to die, they ordered the aircraft to Tehran's Mehrabad International Airport. After landing, the aircraft was diverted to a remote stretch of the airport and negotiators began to work on releasing the 153 passengers on board. The gunmen then hunted one of the Americans—Charles Hegan, a fifty-year-old Agency for International Development worker—

and brought him to the first-class cabin. The hostages remembered hearing a scuffle and then a gunshot. One of the hostages, a British citizen, described al-Yafi's demeanor on board. "The leader was absolutely psycho, a crazy man. They were all crazy men."[1] The next American to be killed was William Stanford, fifty-two years old, who was ordered to beg for his life and then shot in the head. His body was tossed from the aircraft door onto the tarmac below.

The terrorists' demands were simple and pointed: the release of the Kuwait Seventeen in exchange for the lives of the hostages. The Iranians, acting with the skill of bazaar merchants, played the impartial intermediaries. They negotiated with the hijackers, and passed on the urgency of the moment to try to convince the Kuwaitis to commute the sentences of the men languishing on death row and serving life sentences for the terrorist attacks perpetrated a year earlier.

The terrorists rigged themselves—and the aircraft cabin—with explosives. They threatened to blow themselves up should their demands not be met. The theater continued for six brutal days. Many of the hostages, primarily Pakistani and Asian laborers, were freed. The hijackers even added some vaudeville to the event by shooting out the windows in order to terrify the captives. But the Kuwaitis refused to budge. So, to end the ordeal without further loss of life, the Iranians staged an assault of the aircraft themselves. Commandos masquerading as mechanics stormed the aircraft. During the assault they didn't fire a shot in anger. The terrorists, who had made statements in preparation of their martyrdom, surrendered without the slightest hint of resistance.

The hijackers were apprehended but were never tried or incarcerated. The attempt to make some noise in order to secure the release of Badreddine and his subordinates ended with two dead and little more to show for the time and money invested in the operation.

On the morning of Tuesday, January 8, 1985, Reverend Lawrence Martin Jenco, the fifty-year-old head of Catholic Relief Services in Beirut, was grabbed off of a West Beirut street by several armed men. He was thrown into a waiting getaway car to disappear into the labyrinth of alleyways and narrow streets heading toward south Beirut. From there, it was speculated, he was driven to the Beka'a Valley to join the other hostages.

Mughniyeh's collection of American citizens was growing.

MOST RADICAL ORGANIZATIONS based in Lebanon that wanted to communicate indirectly with the rest of the world used the West Beirut office of *An-Nahar*, Lebanon's most prestigious newspaper and one often called the *New York Times* of the Arabic-speaking world, as a convenient—and free—press service for the dissemination of demands, manifestos, and images for a global audience. Groups like the PLO, as well as a myriad of other popular liberation fronts and aggrieved shadowy ethnic militias, all used *An-Nahar* to spread their latest and greatest to a worldwide audience. It was standard operating procedure for Lebanon. The *An-Nahar* staff maintained close but guarded links with many of the men who topped international wanted posters. Hezbollah preferred less conventional lanes of communication. A Lebanese man of no particular distinction of appearance walked into the Beirut office of Visnews, a London-based Middle Eastern news service, and dropped off a videotape wrapped suspiciously in a brown manila envelope. The messenger, faceless and ordinary, disappeared into the traffic of a frenetic city without leaving a calling card. The videotape, capable of holding up to six hours of material, held only fifty-six seconds of footage of a man talking to the camera. He looked fit, but tired. His hair, it was evident, was rapidly turning white; his salt-and-pepper beard was much more salt than pepper. The man was very pale and his eyes seemed unaccustomed to light. He wore large wire-framed glasses and stared straight at the camera, as if begging for help or at least a moment of compassion. The man wore a dark olive tunic, something resembling military fatigues, and he held a January 22, 1985, copy of the Beirut French-language daily newspaper *L'Orient-Le Jour* over his chest. The man was William F. Buckley.

"Today, the twenty-second of January, 1985, I am well, and my friends Benjamin Weir and Jerry Levin are also well," Buckley stated in a slow and deliberate delivery. "We ask that our government take action for our release quickly."[2]

It was the first proof of life of Buckley that Langley had seen in nearly seven months. The tape, the plea for government action to end a tormented ordeal, was reminiscent of other prominent terrorist kidnappings in Europe a few years earlier: the German Red Army Faction filmed a nearly identical scene after it kidnapped West German industrialist Hanns Martin Schleyer in 1977, and Italy's notorious Red Brigades did the same when it seized former premier Aldo Moro. CIA analysts studying Buckley's tape and searching for any hidden messages that his captors might have planted on his dress or the newspaper he held realized that each of those kidnappings in the 1970s ended with the execution of the prominent hostage.

Once again CIA specialists—linguists, photo analysts, videographers, medical doctors, and psycholinguistic analysts—were summoned to prepare an in-depth dossier of Buckley's state of mind and demeanor. Dr. Murray S. Miron pioneered the concept of psycholinguistic analysis at Syracuse University and was used by the Hostage Location Task Force for his expertise. In his book *Hostage*, published in 1978, Dr. Miron stated, "Many acts of terrorism are really acts of expressive suicide. They have as their sole purpose the establishment of the significance and importance of the perpetrator. They are acts designed to establish the perpetrator's importance through media coverage."

The assessment at headquarters was somber. But the terrorists appeared willing to barter. The Agency had dealt with cold-blooded killers, scoundrels, and sociopaths before, after all—many of whom were based in Lebanon. It was critical that the mood remain one of peace and quiet so that back-channel dealings could be attended to.

THE NIGHT OF February 13, 1985, was cold even in comparison with the subzero, frostbitten norms of the Beka'a Valley. The five Syrian soldiers manning a checkpoint on one of the unmarked roads near Ba'albek did all they could to keep warm, but the winds were too strong. The soldiers blew into their hands and hunkered near an emptied petrol drum that was filled with tree limbs set alight. The flames helped, but it was a dark Wednesday night, well after midnight, and the soldiers shivered in the bitter cold. The checkpoint consisted of a U-shaped configuration of green canvas sandbags, a Soviet-built RPK 7.62 light machine gun, a Soviet field radio, and two larger-than-life cardboard posters: one of President Hafez al-Assad and the other of his brother Rifaat. The young lieutenant commanding the checkpoint, an Alawite from a prominent family, sat inside a dilapidated concrete guard booth that offered a measure of protection against the winter's howl. The lieutenant made sure that his men were alert, despite the boredom and the cold. The Syrian soldiers were guarding a deserted stretch of paved road that was rarely used at night, and then crossed only by smugglers and spies.

The night dragged on endlessly; then the cries of a man begging for help punctuated the darkness. The soldiers were startled by the sounds of a man reaching toward a depleted reservoir of energy in order to bellow a cry for help. The young soldiers readied their assault rifles and dropped to a knee in order to meet the mysterious figure approaching in the distance. The man spoke English, had wild hair and a hippie beard, and wore tattered clothing. The man raised his hands in full surrender, determined not to be shot by accident, and begged for help. "I am Jerry Levin," the man exclaimed. "Please help me." As Levin lowered himself to his knees, begging for help, an IAF Phantom flew a reconnaissance sortie overhead.

The Iranians controlled the Sheikh Abdullah Barracks but they did not possess the Beka'a. The Syrian soldiers were disciplined and part of a very rigid and highly political command framework that Soviet advisers had installed years earlier. News of the man found at a checkpoint was relayed immediately to the Syrian intelligence services in Ba'albek. The duty officer at one of the headquarters in Damascus relayed the news to a colonel. Rifaat Assad would have been notified within the hour. Levin was given warm clothing, a bellyful of sweet tea, and a VIP ride to Damascus under armed escort. By the time the Iranian Islamic Revolutionary Guard liaison to Syrian intelligence could react angrily, Levin was on al-Mansour Street, sitting inside the US Embassy in Damascus, enjoying a heart-to-heart with Ambassador William L. Eagleton before being debriefed by the RSO and ▮▮▮▮▮▮▮▮▮▮▮▮▮▮. By the time the Iranian ambassador in Damascus was lodging a formal complaint with President Assad, Levin was on the phone with his wife, Lucille.

According to Levin's account, he escaped from the Sheikh Abdullah Barracks by slipping out of what he described as "carelessly" fastened chains. Using a makeshift rope of blankets, he lowered himself from his second-story balcony onto a darkened landing. He wandered for nearly two hours before happening upon the Syrian soldiers at the checkpoint. Levin told reporters that he had been kept in solitary confinement for most of the year that he was held as a captive; he was chained to a radiator for most of the day and exchanged only the briefest of words with his captors when they brought him food or when they escorted him to the toilet.

Levin's escape from captivity set off a panic alarm in Iran's Beka'a Valley nerve center. Iranian commanders were convinced that the CIA debriefing of Levin, to be followed by the DIA debriefing, would reveal the location where Buckley and the other hostages were being held. There was a fear in Ba'albek, as well as at the Iranian Embassy in Damascus, that the dungeons inside the Sheikh Abdullah Barracks would become a legitimate target and that American commandos would soon be ordered to rescue Buckley and the other captives. Losing Buckley as a prisoner paled in comparison to having a Pentagon spokesman display Revolutionary Guard documents, uniforms, and radios at a celebratory press conference for the international media. In the after blast of the destruction of two US embassies and the massacre of 241 US peacekeepers in Beirut, Iranian involvement in the kidnapping and torture of a CIA Chief of Station would have been a cause for war. It was a war that Iran could not have. By the end of 1984, following four years of savage warfare not seen since the end of the Second World War, some three hundred thousand Iranian soldiers had been killed in brutal combat against Iraqi forces. Thick red goo flowed from the Blood Fountain, a macabre two-story-high monument, in the Beheshte Zahra cemetery in Tehran, to the men killed in the struggle against Saddam Hussein; during the war, some ninety-five thousand children, some as young as ten and twelve, were killed in human-wave suicidal assaults against Iraqi positions.[3]

A full-scale war against the United States had to be avoided at all costs, the Ayatollah and the generals knew. And Iranian revolutionary officials were wary about antagonizing the Americans any further. On

January 23, 1984, Secretary of State George Schultz designated Iran a "state sponsor of terrorism," a response to the Islamic state's support for the Shiite militants in Beirut responsible for the bombing of the US Embassy and the Marine barracks. Following Buckley's kidnapping, the abduction of more Americans, and the bombing of the US Embassy Annex, the State Department sharpened the teeth of that designation. On September 24, 1984, the State Department at the White House's insistence imposed crippling economic sanctions to punish Iran for its support of terrorism. The four main categories of sanctions resulting from designation under these authorities were restrictions on US foreign assistance, a ban on defense exports and sales, certain controls over exports of dual-use items, and miscellaneous financial and other restrictions. The sanctions included a ban on sales of aircraft, spare parts for aircraft, high-powered outboard motors, and other goods and technologies that could be used for military purposes.[4] The Islamic Republic Iranian Air Force, the IRIAF, was almost entirely "Made in the USA." The IRIAF suffered heavy losses repelling Iraqi advances, and by 1984 the aging F-4E and F-4D fighter-bombers, as well as F-5 Tiger and F-14 Tomcat fighters, were deployed in the heavy fighting to defend the ultrastrategic Kharg Island, the hub of Iranian oil exports needed to fund the conflict. Iran could not risk isolating its international position any further by having Mughniyeh's hostages—any formal connection to the embassy and Marine bombings—linked with Iran.

Iranian commanders were confident that Beirut was a pragmatic place to hide the hostages. Revolutionary Guard commanders were confident that Americans would be too wary of trying to locate needles in a highly populated haystack and all the risk that would entail. The Iranians correctly assessed the mood inside the Reagan White House and, indeed, inside the Pentagon. Reagan, in Tehran's view, was cautious and pragmatic; the Iranians knew that Lebanon had been a graveyard for America's best intentions in the Middle East. The Iranians also assessed that the Pentagon, still reeling from the debacle of the April 1980 Iran hostage rescue effort, would be wary about launching another multipronged rescue attempt in a hostile capital.

A Revolutionary Guard messenger would have raced to Beirut to meet with Imad Mughniyeh and members of his operational cells. The Iranians did not use phones or radios. Mughniyeh would have been ordered to make immediate provisions to warehouse the hostages—especially Buckley—inside the Shiite labyrinth of south Beirut. Preparations were made ███████████████████████████████████████ ██████████████████ in a predominantly Sunni precinct ██████████ ██████████████████████████████ A contingent of loyal gunmen would have to be recruited in short order to provide a garrison of eyes and trigger fingers to watch over the hostages. The men had to be disciplined. Mughniyeh needed his human trinkets alive. He didn't want one of the guards to unleash a savage beating unless it was called for and sanctioned by one of the Iranian intelligence specialists known to have interrogated all the hostages—especially Buckley. Mughniyeh would have to locate a building where the hostages could be housed quietly without raising a signature profile that would spark the interest of residents eager to sell a secret for cash or a visa to the United States. Mughniyeh would have to hire a kitchen staff fairly quickly. The hostages were held chained to their beds or radiators all day but they still had to be fed three times a day; in the Sheikh Abdullah Barracks, the meals were served to hostages by Iranian soldiers in uniform.[5] Beds had to be located as well; linens had to be purchased. The transfer of bodies from the Beka'a to Beirut was done in haste but involved an all-hands effort.

Buckley and his fellow hostages were pounced upon late at night. Burlap hoods were forced over their faces and they were handcuffed and shackled with heavy chains. Forty-one miles separated the Sheikh Abdullah Barracks from West Beirut. Mughniyeh dispatched vehicles, mainly vans, toward the barracks in order to transport Buckley and the other hostages to the Lebanese capital. Some of the vehicles were decoys, meant to confuse spies and to thwart any surveillance by the IAF drones that constantly buzzed overhead. The vehicles took a circuitous route to Beirut, some traveling via the back roads of the southern stretches of the country. Countersurveillance measures were strictly followed as per instructions from Tehran.

The Iranian Islamic Revolutionary Guard commander wanted the hostages in Beirut before Levin had a chance to sit down with CIA analysts and operations officers.

The CIA, according to one Near East Division officer working in the area, knew that the hostages would have had to be removed to Beirut or southern Lebanon once Levin escaped. Perhaps, it was believed, the new location of the hostages exposed a sense of vulnerability to Hezbollah's master plan. Perhaps there was room for military action. Perhaps there was even an option for a backdoor contact to negotiate the release of Buckley and the other Americans. There were rumors among those who made it their business to know what went on inside Lebanon that the Algerians were busy behind the scenes working to get the hostages released.[6]

Many in CIA headquarters wondered if Buckley was even still alive.

EVERY FRIDAY, COME rain or shine, hundreds gathered inside a small mosque in the southern Beirut neighborhood of Bir al-Abd to attend morning prayers. Bir al-Abd was a Shiite stronghold a mile and a half from the sprawling Bourj el-Barajneh Palestinian refugee camp, and four miles from ground zero at Beirut International Airport. The mosque was the spiritual nerve center of the Shiite awakening in Lebanon and the headquarters of Sheikh Muhammad Hussein Fadlallah. Born in Najaf, Iraq, in 1936, Fadlallah was known as Lebanon's Grand Ayatollah, and was the spiritual leader of Lebanon's Shiites and considered to be a brilliant and analytical thinker who had preached about creating a Shiite Islamic state in Lebanon. But Fadlallah, like his predecessor Musa al-Sadr, the Lebanese Shiite cleric who disappeared and was believed to have been murdered in Libya in 1978, also preached tolerance and cooperation with Lebanon's Christian, Sunni, and Druze populations. There were many in the CIA and the other intelligence services working the Lebanon desk who believed Fadlallah to be the brains of the Hezbollah movement, though his connection to the group—and to Iran—were murky. There were times when Fadlallah's sermons sounded like a checklist of Hezbollah's platform; at other times, though, he opposed some of their practices. Fadlallah also preached a line quite separate from the Iranian clerics. He reportedly rejected Ayatollah Khomeini's concept of the *wali al-faqih*, or supreme spiritual leader.[7] "Fadlallah wasn't an ally of the Iranians," Robert Baer, a CIA officer ████████ at the time commented. "He opposed the Iranians on many issues."[8]

Fadlallah, still, was recognized by Lebanon's Shiites as a *marja al-taqlid*, a beacon of spiritual authority and religious righteousness to whom the faithful should turn for guidance. They flocked to his sermons—the pious, the poor, and those in need of advice. The morning of Friday, March 8, 1985, was cold in Beirut. The harsh morning winds did not keep the worshippers away. Hezbollah guards ringed the streets and stood watch from rooftop perches. Traffic hurried on the street outside the mosque. Vendors honked as they rushed to and from market. Men sped by on motorbikes and Vespa scooters.

Once morning prayers ended, Fadlallah walked out of the mosque surrounded by a phalanx of bodyguards and neighborhood residents. Fadlallah, in a television interview, recounted what happened next. "I was about to leave the mosque when a woman of our acquaintance came to me to ask that I answer some of her questions or solve some of the problems she was relating to me. I refused because I was extremely tired [after the sermon] but she insisted and I complied. I was talking to her when in the middle of our conversation the big explosion occurred. Had I not answered the woman, I would have been in the exact spot of the explosion where it happened."[9]

The car bomb that detonated just in front of Sheikh Fadlallah's apartment, adjacent to his mosque, was extremely powerful. It is believed that more than two hundred kilograms of military-grade explosives were crammed inside a sedan and triggered to go off forty yards in front of exactly where and when Fadlallah would be in the street walking from the mosque to his building. The VBIED's destruction was absolute. The blast killed eighty-five people, including young children and several pregnant women. More than two hundred people were critically wounded in the bombing; the force of the blast destroyed two seven-story apartment buildings and caused a cinema to buckle and fold. But fate, the ever vigilant hunter, spared Fadlallah from harm that morning. "The perpetrators thought that I had died. Some local Lebanese stations stated that I was underneath the debris and destruction. Being killed to us is an ordinary matter and martyrdom dignifies us before God."[10]

One of those martyred that dark and gloomy Beirut morning was Imad Mughniyeh's younger brother Jihad.[11] Jihad Mughniyeh, like his older sibling years earlier, was one of Fadlallah's most trusted—and capable—bodyguards.

Many blamed the Mossad for the explosion. Others in Lebanon blamed the Christians. But most of the people trying to dig their loved ones from the debris and fire began to call for blood and demanded, "Death to America." Guns fired wildly into the air as relatives of the dead wailed. A banner was hung over the crater that had been carved into the pavement by the force of the blast. It read, "Made in the U.S.A."[12]

There have been many allegations—primarily in Bob Woodward's explosive national bestseller *Veil*—that CIA Director William Casey was behind the failed attempt on the life of Sheikh Fadlallah. The contention centers on the fact that the CIA, prohibited from engaging in assassinations by the Church Commission and the issuing of Executive Order 11905, had to subcontract the operation to foreign players and a foreign intelligence service. President Reagan sharpened the teeth of the CIA restrictions when, in 1981, he issued Executive Order 12333, which decreed, "No person employed by or acting on behalf of the United States Government shall engage in, or conspire to engage in, assassination." The men assembled for the Fadlallah strike included, according to these contentions, a former British SAS (Special Air Service) officer, Christian operatives, and money from Saudi intelligence funneled through Prince Bandar bin Sultan bin Abdul Aziz, the longtime Saudi ambassador to the United States.[13] Reportedly, the operation cost the Saudi General Intelligence Directorate close to three million dollars.

Yet according to Robert Baer, the car-bomb strike against Fadlallah caused a meltdown at CIA headquarters.[14] The furor wasn't because the operation had failed, but because the collateral damage and destruction had, in Langley's opinion, been carried out by the very men that the Agency had trained to protect Lebanon from the destructive wake of indiscriminate terror. The consensus at Langley was the Lebanese Armed Forces Deuxième Bureau and the Moukafaha,[15] ███████████████████████████████ Buckley's expertise, after all, was to create ███████████████████████████████████ ███████████████████████████████████████ ███████████████████████████████████████

CIA Director Casey was a proponent of this preemptive deterrence strategy.[16]

According to a report in the *Washington Post*, Lebanese intelligence took credit for the Fadlallah bombing. "My service did the [March 8] Fadlallah bombing. I believe it was done to show we are strong. . . . You've got to stop terrorism with terrorism."[17] The Deuxième Bureau was virtually entirely Christian and maintained close ties to the Lebanese Forces; the LAF's intelligence arm also maintained close ties with Saudi intelligence, who viewed Iranian attempts to expand their sphere of influence into their onetime summer playground as a clear and present danger to Saudi interests in the Middle East.

One of the names regularly associated with the Fadlallah assassination attempt was Elie Hobeika.[18] Hobeika's name always topped a short list of usual suspects when notables ended up missing or dead in Lebanon. Hobeika liked being called "HK," after the Heckler & Koch submachine gun he carried, and was said to have been permanently affected by the massacre of Christians, including many members of his own family, by Palestinian forces in the town of Damour, south of Beirut, in 1976. Ruthless, charismatic, and politically sharp like few other field commanders, Hobeika curried favor with spies, scoundrels, family godfathers, and enemies. He was believed responsible for the kidnapping and murder of the four Iranian diplomats north of Beirut in 1982, precipitating the hostage crisis. Hobeika was the Lebanese Forces liaison officer to the IDF in 1982 and was one of the leaders behind the Sabra and Shatila massacres[19] in which more than one thousand men, women, and children were murdered in a two-day orgy of homicidal savagery. ████████████████████████████

██

██

██*

These moves mattered little to Mughniyeh. On March 9, he buried his brother in Beirut's Martyrs' Cemetery in the south of the city. The calls for vengeance resonated loudly that sunny Beirut morning amid the graves of men killed by Christian and Israeli forces. The widows and grieving parents of those who died in the Shiite revolution demanded vengeance. The issue of the hostages, for Mughniyeh at least, now transcended the issue of Mustafa Badreddine and the intelligence value gleaned from the torture and interrogation of William Buckley. Tehran would not be able to control Mughniyeh with the same level of restraint and plea for common interests. His brother was dead, his family honor was at stake, and the United States would pay a dear price.

On the morning of March 16, 1985, gunmen kidnapped Terry Anderson, the Associated Press bureau chief in Beirut. Anderson, who had been covering the carnage in Lebanon for two years, had just completed a set of tennis at a posh country club. "I was sloppy with my security," Anderson would later admit angrily. "The terrorists held a minister, a priest, and a journalist. The journalist escaped, so you knew they were going to pick themselves up another journalist."[20]

Anderson would join Buckley and the other hostages to suffer the anguish of beatings, malnutrition, humiliation, and interrogations.

---

* Hobeika was assassinated on January 24, 2002, when a car bomb detonated outside his Beirut home.

The hostages would no longer be treated with even the slightest modicum of decency. Specialists from Tehran were brought in for good measure to make the beatings and the psychological anguish matter. More hostages were seized as the months dragged on. In May 1985, David Jacobsen, an administrator at the American University Hospital of Beirut, had stopped in the hospital parking lot to talk to a doctor when two men brandishing semiautomatic pistols forced him into a station wagon.

12

PROOF OF DEATH

THE MEN FROM the slums in southern Beirut knew how to make news. They blew up embassies, kidnapped spy chiefs and professors, and shelled refugee camps. On May 15, 1985, Imad Mughniyeh's kidnapping enterprise, known by the convenient nom de guerre Islamic Jihad, released six Polaroid photos of the men they held captive: Father Lawrence Jenco, Terry Anderson, Father Benjamin Weir, two French diplomats (Marcel Carton and Marcel Fontaine) kidnapped in the spring of 1985, and William Buckley. The Polaroid photographs were mug shots, instant-flash hostage cards designed to capture the plight of men who were prisoners of a mysterious and violent group demanding a ransom that no one was willing to pay. Each of the hostages was photographed on a different background: a bedsheet, a Byzantine-patterned rug. William Buckley was photographed against a background of what appeared to be a mustard-colored tablecloth with a white lace design. He was clean-shaven. Gold-framed glasses covered his pale and gaunt face. It looked as if his nose had been broken but there was no definitive way to tell. CIA and FBI specialists examined the images for days trying to find any telltale clue or secret messages in the image.

Buckley was wearing a ragged long-sleeved work shirt, indicating that the image was taken during the winter months; there was some speculation that he was wearing a jogging suit.[1] He wasn't perspiring. It was unlikely that the images were recent, from April or May, when the looming summer swelter approaches Beirut.

The Polaroid photos of the hostages that made their way to Reuters and the Associated Press were for international consumption. There was another photo released specifically for internal CIA review.[2] That image made its way to the CIA director sometime in late May 1985. The eight-by-ten color glossy was sent to Langley via a circuitous route; the photo was not meant for the media, and wasn't dropped off at one of the newspapers in the Lebanese capital for global distribution. The photograph was a message, a macabre attempt by Imad Mughniyeh to show Langley that Buckley was still alive. But the image printed on common Agfa stock barely resembled the chiseled Green Beret officer who took enormous care to project himself as a man of style and symbolism. It took forensic specialists days to determine that the man in the photo was, indeed, Buckley. His face was bent and his jaw twisted as if it had been shattered with a sledgehammer. Buckley's nose was broken. He was gaunt and pale; it was clear that he was malnourished. A whitish beard covered most of his face, and his hair, once combed smartly and sealed in place with Brylcreem, was wild and unkempt. He wore a white shirt with a polyester look and a garish blue design; it wasn't something that the impeccably tailored Buckley would ever be caught wearing. Buckley's friends and colleagues in the

CIA, men who served with him in Southeast Asia and in the Middle East, could not recognize him. By the time the photo had been analyzed, scrutinized, and reviewed by specialists in the Near East Division, as well as placed on Director Casey's desk, William Francis Buckley was days from death.

The last months, certainly the last few weeks, of Buckley's life in captivity were harsh. It is known that Buckley, along with the other American hostages, was held in an apartment complex that was under construction in the southern suburbs. The half building looked innocuous enough from the nearby streets. Each hostage was held in a small room in one of the finished flats, chained to a bed and blindfolded all day, former captive Terry Anderson recalled. Exercise and proper nutrition were nonexistent. The guards, many of whom were thugs in their early twenties, relished beating the hostages. Anderson knew that Buckley was on a bed at the edge of the wall in the same room, perhaps six feet away. "One of the guards," Anderson recalled, referred to the man in chains as "Mr. William" in a very typical Lebanese manner.[3]

Buckley was ill, Anderson recalled. He moaned and cried and he was always coughing. He could be heard complaining that his body was giving out on him. Ultimately, the only thing that stopped the abuse, the beatings, and the torture, it was assessed, was the fact that he was so very ill. The Iranian liaison officer to the kidnappers, a man known among the hostages as "Ali the Iranian," often acted as a buffer between the rage of Mughniyeh's men and the larger picture of keeping the hostages alive. Also called "Trust Me Ali" because he always told the hostages "Trust me," Ali was one of the few men involved in imprisoning Buckley who understood that the captives were worth more alive than dead.

Ali was a liaison to the hostage-taking hierarchy. Others involved in Mughniyeh's team included lieutenants and captains in his kidnapping cell who were responsible for the welfare of the Americans and Frenchmen they held. Some were military men, professionals. Others, as Terry Anderson recalled, were pure slime in their demeanor and how they interacted with the men in their charge. Torture was common. Some of the hostages underwent the bastinado, the Turkish art of caning a prisoner's feet.

During the day, four or five armed men guarded Buckley and the hostages; at night, there was always one armed man who was awake and on duty to tend to the hostages and to take them to the bathroom. These armed men weren't the professionals that Mughniyeh had summoned to perpetrate the actual kidnappings—those trigger pullers were trained in the Beka'a, disciplined by the mullahs who had come from seminaries in Iran and Iraq. Some of the horrific treatment was opportunistic. The guards, Terry Anderson recalled, were very young—all in their late teens and early twenties—and it didn't appear as if they had much in the way of military or firearms training. These men were street thugs from south Beirut. They were Shiite, and full of rage, machismo, and boredom. Often, these young men beat the hostages for thrills.[4] There were many instances of the guards playing with their weapons, mainly AK-47s and nine-millimeter pistols. Often, the guards unintentionally discharged rounds into the floor or ceiling. In one instance, a bored guard playing with his sidearm launched a round that landed inches from Terry Anderson's stomach. Another hostage suffered a blow to the midsection for the hell of it. No reason was ever needed. No one dared to protest.

The captains and the lieutenants provided the guards with money to buy food and provisions for the hostages. One guard, it was known, pocketed the money given to him and bought what he felt like for the captives to eat. This went on for quite some time before the lieutenants who occasionally stopped by noticed that the hostages looked mal-nourished and ill.

The interrogations, the torture, the beatings, and the lack of food took their toll on the CIA Chief of Station. Buckley's condition wors-ened. He was no longer fully aware of his surroundings; he was slowly losing his grip on life. One night he coughed and choked and then went still. The guards told Anderson that Buckley had gone to an-other place.

The American war hero, the Green Beret, the CIA paramilitary officer, and the one man in Langley courageous enough to accept the assignment in Beirut, died on June 3, 1985. He died in a south Beirut dungeon alone, tortured, savaged, and neglected. William F. Buckley was a prisoner of war, a captive of state-sponsored terrorists, for 444 days. He died more or less forgotten. His emaciated and brutalized corpse was ferried in the back of a delivery van to a nondescript hole in the ground somewhere in the city. It was a far cry from burial with full military honors in Arlington National Cemetery. There was no bugler playing taps. His brothers-in-arms were not there to salute him and to say one final farewell.

Even if Buckley had survived the beatings, the starvation, and the sleep deprivation, Imad Mughniyeh and the Iranian Islamic Revolu-tionary Guard would never have allowed him to return to the United States. Buckley would have delivered damning proof of Iranian state sponsorship of the group that was behind the destruction of two US embassies and the obliteration of a Marine Corps garrison full of peacekeepers. Buckley's death sentence was signed the moment he was seized.

Buckley, however, was Mughniyeh's sole poker chip worth any-thing. The CIA Chief of Station was without question the commod-ity in captivity that the United States would bargain for if realistic back-channel negotiations for a swap with Badreddine ever materialized. Buckley's death meant that Mughniyeh would have to tone down his demands and place his brother-in-law's fate on the back burner. He would have to develop new tactics as well.

The warm winds introduced another summer to the Lebanese capital. Mughniyeh strategized with his Iranian liaison partners in the bowels of the Iranian Embassy in Beirut—where it was safe to plot and plan far from NSA eavesdropping and away from any possible prying eyes and ears.

ALIA* FLIGHT 402, the shuttle between Amman, the Jordanian capital, and Beirut, took a little over an hour, but the distance separating the two capitals was defined by danger. The pilots chosen for the short hop were all highly experienced, and eight armed sky marshals, all members of the Jordanian Special Forces, flew each leg of the flight. Due to security concerns, Alia crews no longer spent a night in Beirut, which made the stewardesses unhappy and the pilots even unhappier. Flight 402 on Tuesday, June 11, 1985, reminded the veteran crew of the charms of Beirut that were no longer available to them. The afternoon sun was bright and inviting; in the background, the unmistakable rat-a-tat cadence of twenty-three-millimeter cannon fire—the soundtrack of vicious fighting miles away in the Bourj el-Barajneh camp between Palestinian fighters and Shiite forces[5]—was a sobering wake-up call to the crew that everything in Beirut encompassed violence and hatred. Still, Flight 402 was to be routine. The aircrew read-

---

* The airline, named after King Hussein's eldest child, Princess Alia bint Al-Hussein, was established in 1963 and quickly became one of the most far-reaching Arab airlines, with routes throughout the Middle East; routes eventually stretched to the Far East and North America. Renowned for its service and security, the airline changed its name to Royal Jordanian in 1986.

ied the Boeing 727-2D3 for departure. Cans of Pepsi and 7 Up were loaded on board, the aircraft was fueled, and the flight crew checked their instruments and flight plans. They had flown the route so many times before that the pilot and copilot were confident that they could handle the short hop in their sleep. The stewardesses welcomed the passengers off the coach that brought them from the terminal to the aircraft's spot on the tarmac. The passengers, carrying small travel bags, climbed the mobile stairs. Before the mobile stairs could be removed from the aircraft door, a vehicle carrying six men raced toward the Alia jet. The men were armed with AK-47s and explosives and hand grenades. Some wore body armor. Before the Alia crew could react or the sky marshals deploy, the men had raced onto the aircraft and seized all on board. One of the terrorists placed the barrel of his AK-47 sharply against the forehead of the pilot and ordered him to get the aircraft airborne quickly. A caller to a local Lebanese news outlet claimed that the aircraft had been seized by the Imam Musa Sadr Brigades.[6]

For the next forty-eight hours, the aircraft crisscrossed the Mediterranean, flying to Nicosia, Cyprus, and Palermo, Sicily, before returning to Beirut. The hijackers rigged the aircraft with explosives and then hustled the hostages—three pilots, six flight attendants, eight sky marshals, and sixty-five passengers—off the aircraft and toward the tarmac so that they could watch the detonation. Most of the Boeing 727 evaporated into a smoky fireball once the explosives were triggered. The tail section burned for hours on an isolated stretch of runway, filling the southern Beirut skies with a flickering orange glow concealed by an acrid plume of towering black smoke.

Before their release, the Jordanian sky marshals were restrained and beaten.[7] The hijacking—and the brutality—was more a dress rehearsal than a statement of political demand.

TWA Flight 847 went from Cairo, with connections in Athens and Rome, all the way west to San Diego International Airport, with stopovers in Boston and Los Angeles. The first legs of the flight, to be flown across the Mediterranean, were on a Boeing 727. The skies were sunny on June 14 and the trip from Cairo to Athens was quick and uneventful; the actual flight time was less than two hours. Athens International Airport was known to have less-than-top-notch security, but there was no intelligence about an impending attack and it was believed that terrorists would keep a low profile in the days following the Alia seizure.

In Athens a new TWA crew boarded, including Captain John Testrake, a thirty-year veteran of the airline and a Korean War veteran; Uli Derickson, the flight service manager; and several new passengers. Among them were two young Lebanese men, Mohammed Ali Hamadi and Hassan Izz-al-Din (also spelled Ezzadine), both Shiites from the southern slums. Hamadi was a distant cousin of one of the most prominent clans in the Hezbollah Order of Battle. The two, dressed in polyester suits, smuggled two hand grenades and a pistol on board the aircraft. A third hijacker, Ali Atwa, was bumped off the flight and later apprehended by Greek police.

At 10:40 a.m., twenty minutes after takeoff, while TWA 847 headed on a northwestern course toward Rome, the two Lebanese men produced their hardware and seized control of the aircraft and 150 passengers and crew. They identified themselves as members of the Islamic Jihad and threatened to blow up the aircraft if the hostages did not comply with their instructions. It wasn't clear who exactly was in charge. Some thought it was Hamadi. Hazel Hesp, one of the hostages, believed that Hamadi was taking orders from Izz-al-Din.[8]

The hijacker stood in the cockpit and barked orders madly, demanding that Captain Testrake fly to Beirut International Airport, but aviation authorities in the control tower wanted nothing to do with yet another hijacking. Testrake was resolute and unwilling to be daunted by Byzantine bureaucracy. Hamadi pulled the pin from the Soviet-produced F-1 antipersonnel grenade he waved around in murderous menace and threatened to blow up the cockpit. "He has pulled a hand-grenade pin and is ready to blow up the aircraft if he has to," Testrake radioed to the Beirut tower. "He is desperate. We must—I repeat—we must land at Beirut. We must land at Beirut. No alternative."[9] The terrorists reiterated their resolve. "We are suicide terrorists! If you don't let us land, we will crash the plane into your control tower, or fly it to Baabda and crash it into the Presidential Palace!"[10]

TWA 847 touched down at Beirut International Airport at 11:55 a.m. The Lebanese Armed Forces were nowhere to be found, but a full squadron of Hezbollah fighters had been anxiously awaiting the arrival of the Boeing 727 for several hours. The moment the aircraft's landing gear hit the sun-cooked tarmac, a motorcade of jeeps raced toward the aircraft at top speed. The jeeps sported heavy machine guns and 106-millimeter recoilless rifles, along with a complement of men toting AK-47 assault rifles. Several of the men climbed on board the aircraft to reinforce the two hijackers. The passengers were ordered to sit with their heads in their laps. Anyone who made eye contact with the men on board was promised a beating.

The two hijackers released the demands in the name of the Islamic Jihad. The hostages would be released unharmed only if Israel released seven hundred Shiite militants held in a prison facility in southern Lebanon and in a military stockade near Haifa. There was no mention, initially, of Badreddine and the other men languishing in their Kuwaiti prison cells; still, according to US intelligence, as leaked to the *New York Times*, Imad Mughniyeh was at the airport during the entire hijacking, alongside Iranian Revolutionary Guard officer Feirud Mehdi Nezhad.[11]

Captain Testrake pleaded with the control tower for the aircraft to be refueled, but Beirut International Airport administrators refused. The terrorists, to prove their intent, began to beat several of the hostages, including two US Navy divers who were on board the flight, returning from a construction mission in Egypt. But still the control tower refused to relent and dispatch a tanker truck. Once again Captain Testrake was forced to beg for the lives of the men and women in his charge. "They are threatening to kill the passengers. They are threatening to kill the passengers. We must get fuel. We must get fuel." Beirut tower stuttered a delayed response. "They are beating the passengers. They are beating the passengers. They are threatening to kill them now. They are threatening to kill them now. We want the fuel now, immediately!"[12]

At 13:30 TWA 847 was airborne once again. It flew a western path across the Mediterranean only to land in Algeria later that afternoon, at a remote section of runway at Houari Boumediene International Airport in Algiers. Algerian authorities were adamant that the aircraft not be allowed to land in Algiers, but the American pleaded with local authorities on "humanitarian grounds."[13] Once again hostages were removed from the aircraft and demands made that the aircraft be refueled. Once darkness fell, the aircraft was once again airborne—on a course back to Beirut. TWA 847 landed in Beirut in the middle of the night on June 15. It was just after 5:00 p.m. in the Beltway. The Reagan administration was slow in their response. The Israelis weren't about to be bullied by a ragtag Shiite militia. Not just yet.

Dozens of heavily armed men came on and off the aircraft that fateful night. Some were senior military men inside the organization; it is known that Imad Mughniyeh was one of them. They had collected the passports of all the passengers and crew seeking someone of value, someone to be made an example of. The men on board were looking for blood. They wanted to illustrate their rage and their violent intent and they focused the beatings specifically on the US Navy divers who were traveling with red military travel papers and not regular passports. One diver in particular received special treatment.

Master Chief Construction man and Second Class Diver Robert Dean Stethem joined the US Navy out of high school; he was a member of Underwater Construction Team ONE based in Little Creek, Virginia. The Connecticut native was kind and friendly. Stethem looked like a US Navy recruitment poster and he angered the Hezbollah muscle on board the aircraft. Stethem was restrained with a seat belt and then savagely beaten to within an inch of his life by the twelve to fifteen Hezbollah gunmen now on board. The young Shiite men took turns beating and mutilating Stethem, using their teeth and fingernails to tear the young diver apart. It is widely suspected that Imad Mughniyeh participated in the beatings.

As dawn neared, the front door to the fuselage was opened. Hamadi removed a nine-millimeter semiautomatic pistol from his waistband and fired a round into the back of Stethem's head. The diver's body was then thrown onto the tarmac below.

Seven Jewish hostages were ordered off the flight. Manhandled and blindfolded, they were walked down the mobile staircase bearing the logo of Lebanon's Middle East Airlines and then driven, with hoods over their heads, to Hezbollah safe houses in south Beirut. Lebanese authorities were powerless to stop the rapidly deteriorating situation. Hezbollah controlled the airport.

Hamadi then ordered Testrake to take off once again and chart a course for Algiers. "One zero eight passengers," Testrake relayed to the tower. "Eight crew. TWA 847, destination Algiers."[14]

By 7:45 a.m. on June 15, Ali Atwa had arrived in Algiers in Greek custody. The Greek government, eager to secure the release of its own citizens on the hijacked flight, released the Hezbollah gunman and transported him directly to his comrades secluded in a remote spot on the tarmac in the Algerian capital. All of the Greeks and more hostages were freed that day. Later that afternoon, the aircraft took off once again, once again to return to the Lebanese capital. ████

██

the USS *Nimitz*, a nuclear-powered multimission supercarrier headed toward the Lebanese coast.[15]

There was no military resolution to the crisis, of course. Amal militia commander Nabih Berri, acting as intermediary, negotiated his group's involvement in the ordeal. The hostages were removed from the aircraft and, in exchange, his group interceded to negotiate with the United States to see that the terrorists' demands were met. Berri was a moderate; his militia did not follow the fanatic frenzy of Khomeini's revolution, nor did it support the fundamentalist invasion of Lebanon. Berri was a local politician, the Minister for Southern Lebanon, and he used chaos to bolster his position; when TWA 847 was hijacked, after all, Berri's forces were engaged in bitter close-quarter combat in and around the Palestinian refugee camps of southern Beirut, in the attempt to vanquish the last vestiges of Arafat's army in Lebanon.

Negotiations for the release of the hostages continued for the next two weeks. Israeli prime minister Shimon Peres did not want to connect the fate of Shiite guerrillas to that of American hostages, but the veteran politician knew he had no choice. Israeli forces assembled 766 Shiite prisoners being held at the Atlit military detention facility in northern Israel and blindfolded them. The prisoners were issued brand-new Adidas tracksuits and were driven on buses with darkened windows north, toward the Lebanese frontier, and a return to their homes. The remaining hostages were assembled from their various holding cells and safe houses and transported, through Syrian lines in the Beka'a Valley, toward Damascus; and Druze militiamen, along with members of Rifaat Assad's Defense Companies, escorted the hostages on their high-speed overland journey away from Beirut. The remaining hostages met the press in the Syrian capital. They boarded flights home. The seventeen-day crisis was finally over.

As the last of the hostages were released from their Beirut dungeons and flown to Rhein Main Air Force Base near Frankfurt for a debriefing and a medical review, President Reagan, relieved that the crisis had ended without catastrophic loss of life, warned, "Terrorists, be on notice: we will fight back against you, in Lebanon and elsewhere."[16] But the terrorists had won again. Imad Mughniyeh had once again humbled the foreign forces that dared lay claim to a stake in the Lebanon land mine. The United States had been made to look weak. Israel had been forced into concessions, and the hijackers, victorious members of Imad Mughniyeh's growing underground army, disappeared into the shadows of Beirut's southern suburbs.

Reagan knew that the United States had been humiliated once again; CIA Director Casey knew it, as did the Chairman of the Joint Chiefs of Staff. Politically, though, a ceremony was called for to mark the end of the TWA crisis. The hostages were flown home and President and Mrs. Reagan met them on the tarmac at Andrews Air Force Base. A brilliant summer sun was shining. A military band played patriotic tunes as family members holding American flags and cardboard banners waved before the cameras. "Welcome home," Reagan offered the subdued crowd. But then he issued a warning, his anger visible even in the celebration of this moment: "None of you were held prisoner because of any personal wrong that any of you had done to anyone. You were held simply because you were Americans. A crime was committed against you. Hijacking is a crime. Kidnapping is a crime. Murder is a crime. And holding our people prisoner is a crime." Reagan continued, "Now you have returned to us and we have a deep-felt sigh of relief. But there are promises to be kept. The day your plane was hijacked the terrorists focused their brutality on a brave young man who was a member of the armed forces of the United States. They beat Robbie Stethem without mercy and shot him to death. We will not forget what was done to him. There will be no forgetting. His murderers must be brought to justice."*

The United States never raised William Buckley's name during the negotiations to free the TWA 847 captives. The fate of Buckley and the other hostages was old news.

As a rule, Soviet diplomats, KGB spies, and members of the Sovetskaya Armiya were protected from the kind of violence that had befallen Westerners in Lebanon. The Soviet Union maintained the largest embassy in the country and Soviet agents and military specialists were entrenched with the Syrian military and virtually all of the non-Christian militias in the country; operatives working out of the sprawling diplomatic compound were in many cases a weapons-and-

---

* Hamadi, Atwa, and Izz-al-Din were later indicted by the FBI for their role in planning and participating in the hijacking of TWA 847, resulting in the assault of multiple passengers and crew members, and the murder of one US citizen. Mohammed Ali Hamadi was arrested in 1987 in Frankfurt, Germany (then West Germany), while attempting to smuggle liquid explosives two years after the TWA Flight 847 attack. In addition to the West German charge of illegal importation of explosives, he was tried and convicted of Stethem's 1985 murder and was sentenced to life in prison. However, he was paroled and released by German officials on December 20, 2005, and returned to Lebanon. On February 24, 2006, his name returned to the FBI's Most Wanted Terrorists list.

cash lifeline to the commanders of the popular fronts and national liberation movements that had used Lebanon as both a safe haven and an international operational hub. The Soviets were, most importantly, Big Brother to the Syrian intelligence services that truly ran day-to-day life in much of Beirut and throughout much of Lebanon. There was no reason to attack any member of the Soviet delegation to the country, declared or covert: after all, they ran much of the show.

On September 30, 1985, Imad Mughniyeh crossed a line in the sand when his thugs kidnapped four Soviet diplomats traveling in vehicles with the telltale "171" on their consular plates.[17] Three of the four diplomats simply disappeared into the abyss of south Beirut and then, possibly, the Shiite villages south of the Beka'a and east of Israeli lines. A fourth diplomat was consular attaché Arkady Katkov. The thirty-two-year-old was shot and killed by the kidnappers two days after the abduction and his body dumped in a garbage pile in a parking lot near Beirut Stadium; his bullet-riddled corpse was discovered on October 2 by children foraging through the refuse, looking for scraps of metal.

The kidnapping was an attempt by Mughniyeh and Hezbollah to internationalize the plight of Hezbollah prisoners in Kuwait and to show that anyone in Lebanon could be used as barter. The thinking was that the seizure of the Soviet diplomats, and an accommodation to secure their release, would show Washington that negotiations were the only path to bring back the men snatched off the sidewalks of Beirut. Buckley's corpse was an issue, of course. His death—and the senseless murder of Katkov—weakened Mughniyeh's hand.*

---

* The three surviving Soviet diplomats were held captive for a little more than a month. According to the official Soviet and Syrian accounts, they were freed through both the tireless efforts of Syrian intelligence and the benevolence of

Early on the morning of October 1, 1985, the Israel Air Force launched what became known as Operation Wooden Leg, an air raid against the PLO headquarters in Hammam al-Shatt, near Tunis, Tunisia. The raid, launched in response to the murder of three Israeli tourists by Force 17 operatives in Cyprus on board a yacht days earlier, was carried out 1,280 miles from Israeli shores and was the longest-range sortie by the IAF since the Entebbe rescue nine years earlier. The raid had nothing to do with Imad Mughniyeh and William Buckley, of course, but the Hezbollah commander was savvy enough to manipulate opportunity toward his own political advantage. His Iranian bosses, conferring with him at the Islamic Republic's Embassy in Beirut, concurred.

The security guard working the midnight shift at the corporate headquarters for *An-Nahar* in West Beirut just off Martyrs' Square was startled by the man who suddenly appeared before him at 1:00 on the morning of October 4, 1985. The man wore a black leather jacket

---

their captors. The true story, however, is far more indicative of the Lebanese landscape. As explained in Matthew Levitt's *Hezbollah: The Global Footprint of Lebanon's Party of God*, the Soviet intelligence services and special operations forces were not at all interested in playing games with Imad Mughniyeh and his clannish objectives. Teams from the Alpha Group, the KGB counterterrorist and hostage-rescue unit, were flown to Lebanon with the orders to find the kidnappers and to deal with them decisively. According to Levitt, the Alpha commandos were able to identify relatives of the kidnappers by utilizing intelligence from Druze militiamen in their service. One account has the Alpha Group kidnapping a family member of the kidnappers and sending back his ear as a message; another account has the body parts returned being fingers. Another account, the one regarded as more accurate—if not the most pleasing—had the Soviet commandos kidnapping a male relative of the kidnapping squad and castrating him. The body, and the testicles, were left on the kidnapper's doorstep in southern Lebanon. The next day, October 30, 1985, the three Soviet diplomats were dropped off in front of the chancery in West Beirut.

and a motorcycle helmet; the visor was tinted a dark and concealing green. The man didn't say a word and he never removed his helmet. He simply tossed a tattered manila envelope on the security guard's desk and walked out the door. The guard, a pensioner who was trying to stay awake for his tour, called an editor upstairs and told him to come down immediately. The envelope contained a Polaroid of William Buckley sitting in front of a woolen blanket with a patchwork pattern of intersecting brown lines. He sported the same long-sleeved blouse he was wearing in the photograph of him distributed to the press five months earlier. This time, however, he was not wearing glasses. He had a month or two of beard growth, though his hair appeared combed. His nose was twisted, as if someone had taken a hammer to his face, and his eyes were bloodshot and tired. Buckley scowled directly at the camera—the stare on his face was one of helpless resignation.

A note accompanied the Polaroid. It was typewritten, on flimsy paper, and claimed to have come from the Islamic Jihad Organization. It stated, "We declare a revenge for the blood of the martyrs by announcing the execution of the death sentence for the American CIA agent in the Middle East and the head of its Lebanon station and the first political adviser at the American Embassy in Lebanon, the spy William Buckley, after publishing this statement."[18]

The next morning the photo appeared in *An-Nahar* underneath the headline ISLAMIC JIHAD: WE EXECUTED BUCKLEY. White House spokesman Larry Speakes could not confirm or deny the Lebanese reports. At the CIA, the sentiment was one of loss and anger. Previous reports from the Islamic Jihad Organization to *An-Nahar*, the veterans inside the Near East Division knew, had always proved to be accurate.

Friends of Buckley wanted revenge. They also wanted closure. They wanted to know how he had died and they wanted to bring his remains home to the United States. That particular insight, including details of Buckley's final days, would come from a hastily assembled multiagency, multi-jurisdictional intelligence and law enforcement hodgepodge known as the Hostage Location Task Force, or HLTF.

THE HLTF WAS formed in February 1985 by the National Security Council and the Joint Chiefs of Staff under the auspices of the CIA Counterterrorism Center (CTC) at headquarters in Langley. Its mission was simple: find William Buckley and the other American hostages. On paper, the task force was a multiagency and multi-jurisdictional force made up of CIA, FBI, and State Department agents; the State Department's security arm, remodeled following a congressional panel investigating the Beirut Embassy bombings, was expanded in size and scope, and renamed the Diplomatic Security Service, or DSS. In reality, the HLTF was one to two CIA officers, a junior DSS special agent straight out of FLETC (the Federal Law Enforcement Training Center), and a couple of Washington-based FBI agents not assigned to more pressing cases.

The HLTF was a Special Access Program, or SAP, housed on a blue-striped floor, inside the CTC located in the old headquarters building, outside where the statue of Nathan Hale stands. The HLTF chief was a gray-haired Cold War veteran named Tommy.* Cantankerous yet friendly to those in his inner circle, Tommy was a red-faced Irishman through and through who bore the scars from years fighting the Soviets and their satellites on battlefields around the world. Tommy worked directly for Duane "Dewey" Clarridge, the legendary

---

* Identity concealed for operational security.

CIA counterterrorist wizard. Clarridge gave his charge free rein to lead the task force as he saw fit, and Tommy made sure his group met weekly to discuss tips, leads, suspects, source reports, review maps, and overhead imagery of suspected hostage-holding sites.

The HLTF functioned simply, efficiently, and without much bureaucratic fuss. With no dedicated space of their own, task force members grabbed conference rooms, empty offices, and even hallways. HLTF went to the meetings with folders from their respective agencies, and background material, including library books on Lebanon. HLTF members took their breakfast or lunch to the meetings.

From time to time, an expert from the CIA would attend HLTF meetings for briefings on various topics, such as Iran or Hezbollah. "Hours were spent discussing the degree of Iranian control of the hostages, if any, with no firm conclusion one way or the other, but the general belief and working theory was that the Iranian intelligence services were behind the hostage takings, with the tactical command of their care and feeding by Hezbollah," Fred Burton, a young DSS agent assigned to the HLTF, recalled. One thing was clear, though: Hezbollah had control of the hostages; thus, it could be logically inferred that Iran was the puppet master.

The HLTF tried to find out the location of the hostages. Overhead satellite imagery was scrutinized and synced up with alleged hostage sightings. Rumor was the norm. Information peddlers, known as walk-ins, came forward to embassies throughout the Middle East and Europe offering information and looking for quick cash. An occasional foreign intelligence service would bring forth information. Academics and friendly journalists were visited and asked for help. Regardless of the credibility of the information, each hostage report was closely scrutinized and brought hope to the HLTF members, so that elements of the military could transform the data into actionable intelligence used in the planning of a rescue bid. Indeed, the Pentagon's covert forces were hard at work preparing for a raid to free the hostages in Beirut.

The building in south Beirut where the captives were warehoused was called "Basra Prison," a reflection of the neighborhood where they were being held. Converging in Miami's South Beach neighborhood on a row of buildings resembling those found in Beirut, ███████████ ██ ████████████████. The locals, uninformed about the live-fire training, assumed the shots came from shoot-outs between rival Colombian gangs.[19]

In south Beirut, US intelligence operatives covertly placed a video camera inside a building adjacent to the location where the hostages were held.[20] Additional intelligence was provided by Benjamin Weir, who was released in September 1985.

Mughniyeh's men had constructed a prison in the basement of an apartment building in a crowded Shiite neighborhood, complete with iron bars and heavy iron doors. There was room inside the ad hoc basement prison for as many as ten people. Armed men watched the prisoners at all times and stood guard outside the building. ██ ██

A short time before the raid was to be executed—days, perhaps weeks—Shiite boys playing soccer in an alleyway in southern Beirut kicked their ball inside a basement opening. When they went to look for their ball, they found Basra Prison. The hostages were removed to parts unknown later that evening. The return of the hostages would not be resolved militarily.

* * *

IMAD MUGHNIYEH WAS smart enough to know that he could never allow William Buckley to live to tell his tale of abduction and torture. And he knew that the longer Buckley remained alive, the greater the chances that Mustafa Badreddine would be freed from the sweltering hell of his cell in Kuwait's Central Prison. Buckley was his trump card, his ace in the hole. A living and breathing Buckley was an invaluable asset—one that grew in value exponentially as each day passed. But the moment Mughniyeh's men carried Buckley's lifeless body out of the south Beirut safe house that warm June morning, the entire endeavor began to lose its purpose as well as its chance of success. Tehran appreciated Mughniyeh's brutality and his penchant for operational success. He was a valuable tool in Tehran's export of revolution to the fractious and multiethnic Lebanese population. But he was nearsighted about the need for political flexibility. Shortly after a shallow grave was dug for William Buckley at the side of some nameless road in the Shiite suburbs, Mughniyeh's Iranian paymasters entered into secret talks with the United States government and Israeli intermediaries to exchange the lives of the hostages for American-manufactured weapons and military spare parts to keep the Iranian fighting machine functional in the war against Iraq. The hostage crisis had suddenly taken a dramatic pivot away from the plight of Mughniyeh's brother-in-law. Imad Mughniyeh, under relentless pressure from his Iranian paymasters, released Father Lawrence Martin Jenco on July 26, 1986. Jenco, a prisoner for nineteen months, was transported to Damascus; Syrian Foreign Minister Farouk al-Sharaa handed the Roman Catholic priest to the custody of William Eagleton, the United States ambassador to Syria.[21] A US Air Force transport plane then flew Jenco from Syria to the US Air Force military hospital in Wiesbaden, West Germany; the medical facility, an old Luftwaffe base with the emblem of Hermann Göring's air force still engraved in the brick-work, had become a mandatory stopover for all American hostages released from hostile regimes and terrorists. Jenco was welcomed to Wiesbaden by an army of doctors and psychiatrists, as well as thera-pists, nutritionists, and nurses. The facility was heavily protected by US Air Force Security Police teams armed with M16 assault rifles. The airmen wore navy blue berets smartly pressed over their right eyes and carried sidearms and handcuffs just in case. The press was kept far away.

The HLTF arrived in West Germany hours before Jenco's flight touched down. In November 1985 shipments of arms began to flow to Iran.[22] The debriefing team consisted of three men: Tommy, the CIA officer leading the HLTF; an FBI special agent named Edward;* and Fred Burton, a young State Department Diplomatic Security Service special agent. Jenco smiled as he entered. Dressed in casual clothes without his collar, his eyes ringed, his face pallid, he looked like a ghost. His beard, one part of his charm, had grown bushy and wild. Before the men could introduce themselves, Jenco said simply, "Wil-liam Buckley is dead." The four words, softly spoken, sucked the air out of the room.

Jenco was weak and tired. His hands were pale and shaky. But he continued. "He died of natural causes. I heard him calling out. He was hallucinating, ordering breakfast from the bathroom. I think he said, 'I'll have blueberry pancakes.' He coughed all the time and that got worse as he got weaker. Jacobsen and I pleaded with the guards to get him medical assistance. One night, they dragged him past me. The guards told me he was going to the hospital, but I knew he was dead." The HLTF members looked at one another in utter disbelief. Shoul-

---

* Identity withheld for security considerations.

ders slumped. "We knew that we had failed Bill," Burton recalled.[23] The three HLTF members sat in silence. Tommy watched intently, marking Jenco's every word and facial expression. Tommy knew many of Buckley's friends and he thought about the report he'd have to cable over once the debriefing of Father Jenco was complete.

The debriefing continued for most of the day. The story of Jenco's internment was one of torture and abuse, but also one of resilience. The HLTF report on Buckley's fate made it back to CIA Director Casey immediately. Buckley's next of kin would have to be notified.

Most at headquarters had long feared that if Buckley wasn't already dead, he would die in captivity from neglect and abuse. There was grief at the news, as well as anger. Some of the more religious men in the Near Eastern Division uttered a prayer in Buckley's memory.

ON SATURDAY, NOVEMBER 1, 1986, Imad Mughniyeh's gang released David Jacobsen. Jacobsen traveled from Beirut to Damascus; from the Syrian capital, he was flown to Wiesbaden and the US Air Force medical facility. Once again the HLTF was summoned. This time, the team consisted of representatives from the CIA, FBI, DIA, and ███; DSS Special Agent Fred Burton was also summoned. Jacobsen appeared in good health despite being frail and haggard. He had been viciously beaten with a rubber hose after Father Jenco's release. The debriefing was routine and matter-of-fact. Gathering information concerning Buckley's final days was a top priority for the HLTF contingent. "They took Buckley's body out of the room and outside the apartment," Jacobsen explained calmly. "There was a staircase outside where we were being held and the guards didn't even bother to carry Buckley away. They dragged him. And when they dragged him down the stairs you could hear the slow thud of his head banging on each and every step. It was horrific." To illustrate the point and the sheer barbarity, Jacobsen slapped his hands together and slammed them down on the conference table with as much force as his weakened frame could muster to mimic the sound of Buckley's head hitting the marble stairs. He clapped over and over again to illustrate how Buckley's head hit the marble staircase as he was dragged down toward a courtyard; he also crashed his open hand onto the table for effect.[24] The slow and terrible cadence of the reconstruction was horrifying to the men in the room. The spies, soldiers, and special agents sat in silence, aghast that even in death William Buckley's dignity had been so flagrantly violated.

Confirmation of William Buckley's death was kept from the media for months. In Langley, the concussive wave of despair and anger grew daily. Silence turned to anger, but the anger was directionless. The CIA still didn't know who Imad Mughniyeh was.

EMPTY ROOMS, EMPTY GRAVES

A SMALL TEAM OF analysts at CIA headquarters had spent the better part of two years trying to assemble a flowchart that could untangle the order of battle of the shadowy Shiite terrorist movement that had emerged in Lebanon. The chart was woefully incomplete. Names flowed in from Beirut Station, as did the names of prominent clans in the organization. But the names were all faceless. The men who planned and orchestrated the suicide bombings and the kidnappings remained largely anonymous. The Shiite army was a force of ghosts lurking invisibly in plain sight in the slums of the capital and in the villages of the south. The CIA—and the Pentagon—faced enormous challenges in battling this threat, because they didn't know who to target. The FBI, from a prosecutorial perspective, did not know whom to indict.

The CIA flowchart consisted of a series of interconnected boxes with notes and scribbles on a whiteboard. There was a box that covered the Iranian Embassy in Beirut and one for the Iranian Embassy in Damascus; a large box, with many connecting lines emanating from it, covered the Iranian Islamic Revolutionary Guard Corps's base at the Sheikh Abdullah Barracks. There were a few photographs on the chart, namely of Fadlallah and Abbas al-Musawi, considered the military head of the organization. But for over two years, a blank rectangular box stood in for the name of the head of the suicide-truck-bombing-and-kidnapping cell. The box was covered by the words "The Fox" and a question mark.

TWA 847 ended Mughniyeh's invisible reign as a faceless and nameless enigma. The FBI forensic and evidence-recovery teams that combed through the fuselage of the hijacked TWA Boeing 727 came across a set of bloody fingerprints that had been left in the first-class restroom of the aircraft. The prints were not in their database, though they knew that they had to belong to someone involved in the torture and murder of Robert Stethem. Another piece of the investigative puzzle came as a result of pure intelligence-gathering tenacity. Shortly after the hijacking, the name Imad Mughniyeh began to circulate in the rumor mills that produced raw intelligence in Beirut. Many of the intelligence peddlers who worked the back alleys of Beirut knew of someone who knew of someone who had heard of Hezbollah's master operative: the one who blew up the marines. Intelligence had value on the streets of Beirut; it was almost as valuable as gold or an American passport.

The name Mughniyeh also happened to spark the interest of one Arab intelligence agency* in particular.[1] The Arab spy service had

---

* To protect the source of the information, the name of the nation is not being revealed.

incredibly strong access inside the Lebanese bureaucracy and could run a license plate, find out the true owner of a piece of land, and obtain a telephone number faster than the Lebanese police. The intelligence service had high-value resources inside the Lebanese banking community and, most importantly, the Lebanese Ministry of Interior—the agency that issued birth certificates and passports. When Mughniyeh's name began to become prevalent in the intelligence chatter surrounding Shiite and Iranian operations in Beirut, the Arab intelligence service used its contacts to place a face next to the name. The spies sent in an asset to seize Mughniyeh's passport application, but by the time he arrived at the ministry, the paperwork and photo had disappeared, and all that remained was a poor photocopy. Hezbollah, too, had its intelligence sources well entrenched in the Ministry of Interior. Hezbollah was quick to pull Mughniyeh's application, leaving behind a tattered photocopy of the document with a poor-quality image. That image, soon circulated, would be the West's first glimpse of Mughniyeh. The photo was hazy but captured a young man with a chubby face and a small, narrow mustache. The CIA now had Mughniyeh's image. The information was shared with every intelligence service that maintained close operational and intelligence-sharing ties with Langley. Imad Mughniyeh would soon become the most wanted terrorist in the world. Only a handful of photographs of Mughniyeh would follow in those early years of his meteoric rise from PLO muscle to one of the most wanted terrorists in the world. Mughniyeh made it a point to be far from the cameras. He was smart enough to avoid the limelight. He realized that the CIA, the Mossad, and the other Western—and Arab—intelligence services whose citizens and interests had been obliterated by Hezbollah in Lebanon would be hunting him.

Following TWA 847, the US Department of Justice prepared a

sealed indictment against Imad Mughniyeh for Robert Stethem's murder. International arrest warrants were issued. There were many in the CIA, as well as the National Security Council, who urged President Reagan to be proactive in his approach to Hezbollah. When confirmation of Buckley's death reached Langley following the Jenco debriefing, there was a sense of urgency in dealing with the fissionable malignancy that had emerged in Lebanon.

IN THE SPRING of 1986, news that Mughniyeh had left Lebanon and was traveling in France reached ████████████. There was scant information concerning the tip, other than that it was from a high-level source that one nation's intelligence service had cultivated in Lebanon. The FBI also received the intelligence concerning Mughniyeh's travels to France. Many veterans of the CTC were puzzled by the intelligence, wondering why Mughniyeh would risk arrest or worse by leaving Lebanon. Many in the CTC wondered if Hezbollah was about to bring to the European continent the same carnage that they had inflicted in Lebanon.

The news of Mughniyeh's travel in Europe sparked great opportunity—and debate—in the Agency and the National Security Council. Director Casey wanted Mughniyeh abducted; President Reagan approved the recommendation from his trusted spymaster.[2] The NSC and the CIA wanted Mughniyeh dead or alive; the Justice Department and the Department of State worried about the legal and diplomatic ramifications. There were arguments in the White House Situation Room about notifying the French and whether they could be trusted with the intelligence. Casey and the NSC were certain that French president François Mitterrand wanted Mughniyeh's head on a platter—he had, after all, killed French soldiers in Beirut and he was holding French hostages. But, others objected, wouldn't Mitterrand place French interests in the Levant over the thirst for justice in putting Mughniyeh away? Both the Department of Justice and the Department of State warned of the ramifications of unilateral CIA action: operating on French soil without notifying the French could cause a major rift in US-French relations and affect cooperation on defense, intelligence sharing, and law enforcement.

By the time the debate ended in the White House, Mughniyeh had vanished. There was never absolute, concrete intelligence placing Mughniyeh in Paris; allegedly, he was traveling in France to negotiate terms for the release of French hostages, and the CIA had been alerted by the passport he would be using. An unconfirmed but widely circulated rumor in intelligence circles has always had it that Mughniyeh was, indeed, apprehended by French intelligence but released shortly thereafter because immediate threats were made to the lives of French hostages Mughniyeh's kidnapping cell was holding. In fact, according to these rumors, French intelligence agents met Mughniyeh several times over a six-day period and allowed him to leave the country in return for the release of a French hostage.[3] Still, an opportunity to apprehend a wanted man who had rewritten the rule book on terror had been lost.

There would be other false alarms. Several weeks following Mughniyeh's first Parisian sighting, reports that the Hezbollah commander had once again entered France reached the CIA. It also reached the French DGSE. French intelligence agents and secret service operatives suited up for a raid in a luxury hotel near the Place de la Concorde, a few steps from the sprawling US Embassy. When agents kicked down the door with their weapons drawn, they encountered a Spanish family on holiday.[4]

Imad Mughniyeh was promoted to Hezbollah's Majlis al-Shura in 1986. He became a commander in Hezbollah's terrorist arm and expanded the tactic of kidnapping foreigners in Lebanon; he was also named head of Hezbollah's overseas operations and one of the key commanders of special operations against Israeli forces in southern Lebanon. In three years of bloodshed and misery, Mughniyeh had killed scores of American spies and soldiers. He had decapitated the CIA, and befuddled its sense of security in a way that the Soviet Union at the height of the Cold War had never achieved. Mughniyeh was a ghost to the CIA—a lethal hornet whose intentions and capabilities were hard to predict.

CIA DIRECTOR WILLIAM Casey did not live to see William Buckley's return. The venerable OSS man who ran the Agency with a World War II ethos had tried to move heaven and earth to secure the release of the man he had dispatched to Beirut. But Casey couldn't even bring Buckley's remains back for proper burial. William Casey suffered two severe seizures on December 15, 1986—the day before he was to testify in front of a Senate committee concerning the Iran-Contra affair.[5] Days later, Casey underwent brain surgery to remove a malignant tumor; he also suffered from prostate cancer. Casey resigned from the CIA shortly thereafter. He died on May 6, 1987.

In August 1987 the Agency publicly acknowledged that William Buckley had died in captivity. The HLTF debriefings of the hostages freed in the course of the Iran-Contra affair provided what amounted to irrefutable proof that the CIA Chief of Station had, indeed, died on June 3, 1985. Chip Beck organized an impromptu private memorial to honor the friend he couldn't save. The ceremony was held in the rotunda adjoining the Tomb of the Unknowns at Arlington National Cemetery. Attending the unpublicized event were former CIA Director William Colby, the Reverend Jesse Jackson, Buckley's sister Maureen Moroney, his longtime companion Beverly Surette, and former hostages Jerry Levin, Father Martin Jenco, and Reverend Benjamin

Weir;[6] the press was kept away from the event. Chip Beck delivered the keynote speech and paid tribute to Buckley's remarkable résumé of service. Beck, looking over the vast, rolling plush of Arlington, home to so many brave souls, stated that Buckley was in his rightful place, even in absentia, among those honored in those hallowed grounds. The ceremony was merely a memorial, an opportunity to honor a man who deserved endless accolades. There was no formal marker and no headstone at the National Cemetery just yet.

On Friday, May 13, 1988, William Buckley was honored with a memorial service at a symbolic tombstone in Arlington National Cemetery. The procession was carried out with full military honors. Six white horses, three without riders, pulled a black artillery caisson carrying a flag-draped coffin. The ceremony is of sacred tradition. The riders were dressed in Army blue with riding breeches and boots with spurs, buffed to a mirror's shine. The section chief rode to the left front of the team. A caparisoned horse, for those of the rank of colonel or higher, was led behind the caisson wearing an empty saddle with rider's boots reversed in the stirrups, to indicate that the warrior would never ride again.[7]

Buckley's two sisters, Joyce Wing and Maureen Moroney, sat in the front row at Arlington. Beverly Surette stood silently in a black dress as the ceremony commenced; she wore a yellow ribbon over her heart. Sophia Casey, the widow of CIA Director William Casey, sat nearby, next to a US Army Special Forces brigadier general. Army Secretary John O. Marsh and the families of four hostages still held in Lebanon also attended. William Buckley would have blushed at the men and women who turned out in his honor.

CIA Director William Webster delivered the eulogy. "William F. Buckley was a man who did things that none of the rest would have done; he lived by example."[8] A letter from President Reagan was read aloud. Chip Beck helped to organize the ceremony. "Fate did not overcome Bill Buckley. He predicted what was to happen when I last saw him, and he met fate head-on. He endured, far longer than he had to. His body finally failed in captivity, but his spirit won," Beck said with defiant pride.

A US Army band played "The Star-Spangled Banner" and a bugler blew taps. Beverly Surette was handed the folded American flag. A lone cloud hovered over the tree line at Arlington. To Beck, the cloud was a reminder that his friend was dead. Beck knew that the saga would continue. His brother-in-arms still remained on a battlefield far from home. Many at the CIA, including Beck, longed for the day that their comrade and friend would be brought home for good.

William Buckley was the fifty-first CIA officer to die in the line of duty. A star with his name was carved into the wall of remembrance at CIA headquarters in Langley.

BOOK THREE

RECOIL AND RECOVERY

William Buckley, number 57 (*first row, far left*), boys' hockey, class of 1947 yearbook.

Major William Buckley's diorama that greets all visitors to the Lexington Visitor's Center, completed in 1962.

"Your diamond is OK but more nicks are appearing in the glass" were comments that William Buckley wrote to his girlfriend, Beverly Surette, on the back of a photo showing him clearing Viet Cong strongholds with his South Vietnamese troopers in January 1967.

COURTESY BEVERLY SURETTE

Above: William Buckley commanding a "junk" boat during Special Forces maritime operations in South Vietnam, February 1967.

COURTESY BEVERLY SURETTE

Right: Looking a bit tired after endless hours on an op, Lieutenant Colonel William Buckley (left) confers with a colleague while working with the Army of the Republic of Vietnam's 3/43 Infantry Battalion. Note the .45 caliber Thompson submachine gun carried by Buckley.

COURTESY BEVERLY SURETTE

Undated photo of US Army Special Forces (Airborne) Lieutenant Colonel William Buckley during his tours in Southeast Asia. COURTESY BEVERLY SURETTE

William Buckley's CIA comrade in arms—from Vietnam to Beirut—Chip Beck, seen here during a lull in the action in Laos. COURTESY CHIP BECK

ID badge photograph of William Buckley. CIA

June 6, 1982: Israeli forces pushing into southern Lebanon are greeted as liberators by Shiite villagers who endured years of abuse at the hands of Palestinian guerrillas.

YOEL KANTOR/IGPO

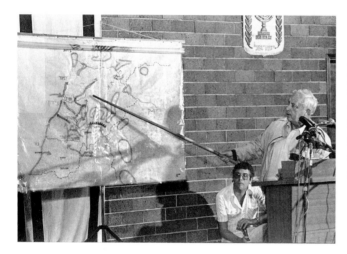

Israeli Defense Minister Ariel Sharon displays the limited scope of Israeli advances into southern Lebanon during a field press conference.

YA'AKOV SA'AR/IGPO

Israeli Prime Minister Menachem Begin addresses the press in the White House Rose Garden during urgent talks with President Ronald Reagan on June 21, 1982. Although elements in the Reagan White House, such as Secretary of State Alexander Haig, supported the Israeli invasion of Lebanon, the US president was wary of the possibility of Lebanon spiraling violently out of control.   YA'AKOV SA'AR/IGPO

An Israeli mechanized position overlooks the approaches to the Lebanese capital, July 1982. YA'AKOV SA'AR/IGPO

A new order in Lebanon: Israeli officers man a security checkpoint to the outskirts of Beirut alongside a Lebanese Forces officer. IGPO

An IAF F-4E flies a sortie over the Lebanese capital, August 1982. EITAN HABER/IGPO

Right: Israeli soldiers remove the bodies of men killed in the suicide bombing of the military headquarters in Tyre—the terrorist attack that weaponized martyrdom into the modern terrorism vernacular. MIKI SHUVITZ/IGPO

Below: The remains of the sprawling Israeli military and intelligence headquarters destroyed by a Shiite suicide bomber on November 11, 1982.

NATI HARNIK/IGPO

US Marines patrol the streets of downtown Beirut only two weeks before the bombing of the US Embassy in April 1983.

US DEPARTMENT OF DEFENSE

Above Left: US Marine Security Guards in full battle rattle move through the chaos in the aftermath of the April 18, 1983, Hezbollah suicide truck bombing of the US Embassy in West Beirut. US DEPARTMENT OF DEFENSE

Above Right: An MSG, nervously clutching his M60 light machine gun, stands guard in front of the collapsed façade of the US Embassy in Beirut hours after the blast.

US DEPARTMENT OF DEFENSE

The official agency portrait of William J. Casey, eleventh Director of Central Intelligence.

CIA

Above: President Ronald Reagan and his wife, Nancy, pay their respects to the dead returned home following the attack on the US Embassy in Beirut.   WHITE HOUSE

Right: A US marine stands guard outside the British Embassy in West Beirut, used by the State Department ███████████, as a temporary diplomatic ████ ████████ outpost in the city.

US DEPARTMENT OF DEFENSE

An undated photo of William Buckley looking out over the skyline of Beirut.

COURTESY BEVERLY SURETTE

The US Marine Corps barracks at Beirut International Airport, photographed in fall 1983.

US DEPARTMENT OF DEFENSE

October 23, 1983: Two thousand pounds of high explosives obliterates the US Marine Corps barracks in one of history's largest nonnuclear explosions.

US DEPARTMENT OF DEFENSE

Emergency crews search for survivors after the attack against US Marines in Beirut, October 23, 1983. Two hundred and forty-one marines and sailors were killed in the attack.

US DEPARTMENT OF DEFENSE, PHOTO BY 94TH AIRLIFT WING, II MARINE EXPEDITIONARY FORCE

The patch of the Moukafaha, the indigenous Lebanese military counter-terrorist force— ███████ ███████

The flag-draped casket containing the body of Steelworker 2nd Class (SW2) (DV) Robert D. Stethem is carried from a C-141B Starlifter aircraft by a Navy casket team upon the arrival from Beirut, Lebanon.

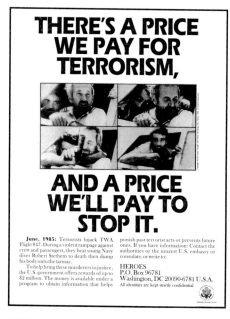

THERE'S A PRICE WE PAY FOR TERRORISM,

AND A PRICE WE'LL PAY TO STOP IT.

June, 1985: Terrorists hijack TWA Flight 847. During a violent rampage against crew and passengers, they beat young Navy diver Robert Stethem to death then dump his body onto the tarmac.

To help bring these murderers to justice, the U.S. government offers rewards of up to $2 million. The money is available under a program to obtain information that helps punish past terrorist acts or prevents future ones. If you have information: Contact the authorities or the nearest U.S. embassy or consulate, or write to:

HEROES
P.O. Box 96781
Washington, DC 20090-6781 U.S.A.
All identities are kept strictly confidential.

Messengers of Death

Imad Fayez Mugniyah	Ali Atwa	Hasan Izz-al-Din
Birth Date: 1962	Birth Date: 1960	Birth Date: 1963
Height: 5'7"	Height: 5'8"	Height: 5'9"-5'11"
Build: unknown	Build: medium	Build: slender
Hair/Eyes: dark	Hair/Eyes: brown	Hair/Eyes: black
Nationality: Lebanese	Nationality: Lebanese	Nationality: Lebanese
Aliases: Hajj	Aliases: Amar Mansour Bouslim, Hassan Roston Salim	Aliases: Ahmed Garbaya, Samir Salwwan, Sa-id

Wanted for Murder
Reward for Information

These men have been indicted by Argentina and the United States for murder, aircraft hijacking, placing explosives aboard aircraft, hostage taking and other crimes. The United States government is offering a reward for information that leads to the arrest or conviction of **Mugniyah, Atwa, Izz-al-Din** or any other individual for committing acts of international terrorism against U.S. persons or property.

Persons providing information may receive a reward of up to $5 million, protection of identity, and relocation with their family. If you have information, please contact the nearest U.S. embassy or consulate or write:

REWARDS FOR JUSTICE
Post Office Box 96781, Washington, D.C. 20522-0303 U.S.A.
www.rewardsforjustice.net • 1-800-877-3927

UP TO $5 MILLION REWARD
RESPONSES KEPT STRICTLY CONFIDENTIAL

US State Department wanted posters seeking information leading to the arrests of the men responsible for the hijacking of TWA Flight 847.

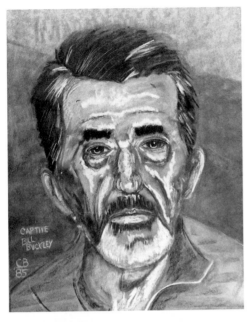

Above: The Hezbollah flag.

Left: A painting of William Buckley in captivity by his friend and comrade Chip Beck.   © CHIP BECK

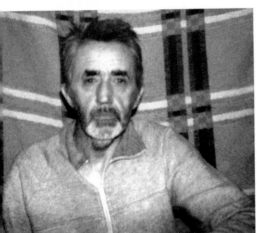

Above: Picture of—⬛ William Buckley distributed on October 4, 1985, by the Islamic Jihad to the press in Beirut, with a two-page typed communiqué announcing his execution.

GETTY IMAGES

Right: DSS special agent Fred Burton, somewhere over the North Atlantic, on a USAF military special air mission for the HLTF, with freed hostage David Jacobsen.   PRIVATE COLLECTION

US Marine Corps Lieutenant Colonel William R. Higgins, assigned to the United Nations peacekeepers in southern Lebanon.

A photo of Lieutenant Colonel William R. Higgins, wearing the distinctive blue beret of the United Nations peacekeeper, photographed in southern Lebanon.

Diplomatic Security Service special agent Scot Folensbee, one of the daring State Department operators who kept the besieged US Embassy in Beirut open during civil war and regional turmoil, seen here near the US Embassy in Christian East Beirut.

The "Nasty Boys" coat of arms.

Above: A Marine honor guard carries William R. Higgins' coffin to a hearse that will transport it to Quantico National Cemetery following the Return of Remains at Andrews Air Force Base together with William Buckley.

US DEPARTMENT OF DEFENSE/
LCPL CRAIG SHELL

Top Right: Beverly Surette is consoled by Chip Beck following the service for Buckley at Arlington, December 31, 1991.

COURTESY BEVERLY SURETTE

Bottom Right: US Marine Corps Commandant General Carl E. Mundy Jr. presents Major Robin Higgins with the flag that covered her husband's coffin during funeral services at Quantico National Cemetery.

US DEPARTMENT OF DEFENSE/
LCPL S. D. DOMMER

Above: The remains of the Khobar Towers barracks housing US Air Force personnel near Riyadh, destroyed by a "Saudi" Hezbollah tanker bomb, June 1996.

US DEPARTMENT OF DEFENSE

Right: Batya Arad, the mother of missing Israeli airman Ron Arad, addresses an assembly, pleading for political pressure to secure her son's release from captivity.

AVI OHAYON/IGPO

Israel Prime Minister Ariel Sharon (*right*) presides over the ceremony appointing his old friend and confidant Meir Dagan as the Mossad director on October 30, 2002.

YA'AKOV SA'AR/IGPO

Mustafa Dirani, seized in a daring Israeli commando strike, is released from custody in a prisoner exchange in 2004.

MOSHE MILNER/IGPO

US Army Brigadier General Kevin J. Bergner, spokesman for Multinational Force Iraq, conducts a news conference at the Combined Press Information Center in Baghdad, July 2, 2007, to update embedded media concerning the arrest of Hezbollah operative Ali Musa Daqduq in Basra.

US DEPARTMENT OF DEFENSE/SGT. SKY M. LARON, US ARMY

Hezbollah operatives file past the coffin and an image of assassinated Hezbollah commander Imad Mughniyeh.

RAMZI HAIDAR/AFP/ GETTY IMAGES

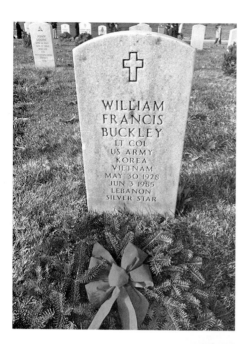

William F. Buckley's gravestone in Arlington National Cemetery.

ANYA ALFANO

Memorial at the US Embassy in Beirut honoring the two American embassies destroyed by Hezbollah suicide truck bombs.

COLLECTION OF
SAMUEL M. KATZ

14

CALL SIGN SUNRAY

T HE COMMUNICATIONS OFFICER at headquarters handled what
seemed like a tennis-match back-and-forth of cables and faxes
racing from New York City to southern Lebanon. The paperwork
was a nice break from the monotony of the day-to-day. UNIFIL,
the United Nations Interim Force in Lebanon, was celebrating its
tenth anniversary of failed peacekeeping, a dubious milestone of
checkpoints and patrols intended to separate Israeli forces from Palestinian fighters and, now, Shiite guerrillas. Any tenth anniversary
was worth celebrating, and an organization like the United Nations
spared little expense to make sure that such a noted accomplishment
would not be celebrated without a spit and polish and the obligatory
champagne, hors d'oeuvres, and photo opportunities. Commanders
issued orders to all UNIFIL personnel to prepare their gear—and
their vehicles—for the anniversary. The weather in February 1988 was

harsh. Cold winds and pounding rain had turned much of the countryside into a swamp of thick, cementlike mud and deep puddles. Boots were to be shined and the white armored vehicles were to be scrubbed clean to show their white scheme in a brilliant shine.

One of UNIFIL's mandates was to restore Lebanese authority to the hills of southern Lebanon that Palestinian guerrilla groups had claimed as a mini-state. UNIFIL could do little to stop Palestinian forces from returning to positions they had abandoned once Israel had invaded, and they could merely watch in 1982 as Israeli forces flooded into the country. UNIFIL at times consisted of more than ten thousand soldiers from a Tower of Babel of battalions from countries with no business having their troops in the shell-scarred no-man's-land of the Arab-Israeli dispute.* Nations that contributed units to UNIFIL included Austria, Bangladesh, Belgium, Brazil, Brunei, Cambodia, Fiji, Finland, Ghana, and Ireland. In February 1988, the Finnish Battalion, or FINNBATT, became the headquarters unit.

UNIFIL worked alongside the United Nations Truce Supervision Organization, or UNTSO. Set up in May 1948 during Israel's War of Independence, UNTSO was the first ever peacekeeping operation established by the United Nations. The force, headquartered in Jerusalem with offices in Beirut and Damascus, remained in the Middle East to monitor cease-fires, supervise armistice agreements, and prevent isolated exchanged shots between patrols from turning into full-fledged Middle Eastern conflicts. A Norwegian career soldier, Lieutenant General Martin O. Vadset, commanded UNTSO. A United States

---

* At the time of this book's writing, according to United Nations sources (https://peacekeeping.un.org/en/mission/unifil), 293 UNIFIL soldiers have been killed while carrying out their peacekeeping duties.

Marine Corps officer, Lieutenant Colonel William R. Higgins, was the force's chief military observer.

WILLIAM R. HIGGINS, known to his friends as Rich, was a native of Danville, Kentucky, and was commissioned a US Marine Corps officer in 1967, when he was twenty-two years old. A graduate of Marine Officer Basic Class 6-67, he went on to serve with the Third Marines as a rifle platoon commander, seeing extensive combat in 1968 in the Iron Triangle south of Con Thien in Vietnam. Higgins was a marine officer carved from the strongest human stone that the Corps could produce, and he was on a fast path up the chain of command. After returning to Vietnam to serve as an infantry adviser to the Vietnamese marine corps, he returned to Quantico and then fleet service, and excelled at all his billets. He became a headquarters mainstay, ultimately serving as the military assistant to the special assistant to Secretary of Defense Caspar Weinberger. Higgins graduated from the National War College in 1985 and returned to the Pentagon as the Secretary of Defense's military assistant. Higgins' colleagues and friends described him as a true southern gentleman.[1]

Higgins was still very much a combat officer out of Camp Lejeune—his white pickup truck and USMC decals were part of his day-to-day uniform. Although an indispensable aide to the most powerful man in the Department of Defense, Higgins would routinely place family first, rearranging his hectic schedule to babysit for his nephew. He served at the DoD for nearly two years until the posting with the United Nations emerged. Duty in Lebanon was considered a perk—a fast track to being promoted to a full-bird colonel. The deployment, slated to be a one-year hardship tour, meant separation from Higgins' wife, Robin, who was also a Marine Corps officer. The two had been married in 1977, but they were very much a Marine

Corps couple: their love was what fueled their lives, but the Corps was their career. Lebanon, however, presented Higgins with a unique threat potential. Robin was Jewish, and both Rich and Robin knew that her religion could never become public knowledge during his service in Lebanon. As frightening as the possibility was, the issue of Robin's faith never came up in any of the pre-assignment interviews that preceded his deployment to the treacherous fault lines of the Arab-Israeli dispute. Lieutenant Colonel William R. Higgins traded in his green garrison cap for a sky blue beret and joined the peacekeepers.

Higgins arrived in what United Nations commanders referred to as a peacekeeping theater of operations. It was a clinical Band-Aid to address a patchwork of real estate simmering with constant murder and teetering on full-scale conflagration. Both Amal and Hezbollah were engaged in open warfare to determine military dominance of the area. Israeli forces controlled the southern swath of the country, battling both Shiite militias and pockets controlled by Syrian-backed Palestinian terrorist factions, such as Ahmed Jibril's Popular Front for the Liberation of Palestine–General Command. The SLA, or South Lebanon Army, was a pro-Israeli Christian-led militia made up of Christians and Shiite residents of the south who feared the pro-Iranian fanaticism, Palestinian occupation, and Syrian domination of their ancestral areas. UNIFIL and the other blue-beret-wearing observers were in the middle of the fray. Outnumbered and outgunned, the peacekeepers were an ineffectual force. Soldiers manned checkpoints and occasionally exchanged gunfire with militiamen who did not recognize United Nations jurisdiction of the area.

Higgins was appointed the chief of the Observer Group Lebanon, or OGL, on January 8, 1988. He was in command of a multinational contingent of seventy-five men, including seven American soldiers, with several marines among them.² The OGL maintained six observation posts throughout the south, and Higgins' job was to monitor the forces in the area and to chart and mediate disputes before they could escalate. It was a very different type of staff job than supervising desks in the Beltway while working for Secretary of Defense Caspar Weinberger. In the Pentagon, Higgins worked with the most powerful people in Washington, DC, such as Lieutenant General Colin Powell, President Reagan's national security adviser, and Marine Corps Major General Al Gray, who were his personal friends.³ In UN service, though, Higgins' power and influence were less immediate; as an observer assigned to the wastelands of southern Lebanon, Higgins never knew who his friends actually were. The militia commanders Higgins met with regularly, local warlords who graciously invited him into their homes for tea and for lengthy conversations over stewed lamb and rice, were also men capable of savage acts of village-cleansing homicide. Loyalties in the precincts that Higgins traveled in were temporary; blood feuds lasted centuries.

Lieutenant Colonel Higgins displayed great grit, resolve, and determination in carrying out his duties. A marine through and through, Higgins proved to be an exceptional soldier, officer, and observer, serving the UNTSO in work that was always fraught with peril. Only four days after Higgins assumed command of the OGL, one of his officers was killed by an IED. Higgins had been briefed that he could be targeted because he was a US marine—a Canadian comrade offered to let him affix a Maple Leaf flag to his fatigues to masquerade as a Canadian officer when he traveled inside Lebanon—but Higgins was undaunted. There were no special security precautions for Higgins' travels throughout southern Lebanon. As a peacekeeper, Higgins wanted to avoid the trappings of firepower. He chose not to travel in armored convoys protected by platoons of riflemen; he did not have a permanent bodyguard assigned to him. Remarkably, Higgins traveled around southern Lebanon unarmed, as per UNTSO protocols. He never carried the ubiquitous .45 on his hip, the sidearm that would never have left his side during his tours in South Vietnam. Lebanon was a land where violence was the currency of day-to-day life—the warlords respected visitors who came to their tents with a phalanx of heavily armed bodyguards. But Higgins confided to those close to him that he felt he couldn't do his job as an observer and a peace broker by sitting down at a meeting and putting his sidearm on the table.[4]

Lieutenant Colonel Higgins traveled to and from his appointments in a Jeep Wagoneer painted in peacekeeping white and marked with two-foot-high decals of the letters "UN" emblazoned in black.[5] His days were long and frustrating. His Wagoneer was often crusted in thick cakes of mud from the many miles driven on the battle-scarred roadways of southern Lebanon. Flat tires were common for UN staffers. They were part of the maddening routine. Pressing the flesh was the only way he could talk to local commanders and assemble an accurate assessment of the military situation on the ground. Entering villages and sitting down to have a coffee with the men in camouflage fatigues who ruled by the business end of an AK-47 was risky; being known warranted exposure. Higgins often traveled with Mustafa,* his trusted translator. Mustafa, a local UN civilian employee from one of the nearby Shiite villages, knew the language, knew the local commanders, and knew which roads led to safe havens and which ones were rigged with IEDs meant for IDF patrols.

Midway through his tour, Higgins returned home for an emergency leave to visit his ailing father. It was a quick trip. Time with

---

* A pseudonym; Mustafa's real name has been concealed to protect his identity and the welfare of his family in Lebanon.

Robin was minimal. In the days before the Internet, text messaging, and WhatsApp, husband and wife separated by miles and duty maintained a consistent line of communication through telephone calls. During one of their conversations, Robin updated Rich with the news that his father's condition had worsened. "I don't think that I'll be able to make it home if anything happens," he reluctantly told his wife.[6]

"Rich was a man of unquestioned courage and leadership skills," Robin reflected. "He was the type of man to run towards danger and not from it."[7] There was an inaudible concern in Rich's voice when the two spoke a final time. Perhaps the reality of Lebanon had gotten to him; Robin remembers it as akin to an elephant in the room.

The last time Robin and Rich spoke on the phone was February 14, 1988. Robin remembers it vividly. It was Valentine's Day.

LIEUTENANT COLONEL HIGGINS was up early on the morning of February 17, 1988. The UNTSO off-duty living quarters were in Nahariya, a northern Israeli coastal town just four and a half miles from the Lebanese border. The city was home to some fifty thousand inhabitants, and although it had seen its fair share of terrorist attacks by sea, land, and air, Nahariya was considered a safer billet for UN officers than the frontline base at Naqoura. Higgins was already showered and had shaved and trimmed his graying mustache before dawn's first light. Personal effects were forbidden in Lebanon, and Higgins removed his wedding ring and made sure he wasn't carrying his wallet before leaving quarters. The drive to the border checkpoint at Rosh Hanikra was short, as was the travel time to Naqoura. Most officers based in Nahariya preferred having breakfast at headquarters in Naqoura, because ham and bacon were never on the menu in Israel.

Breakfast at UNIFIL's HQ in Naqoura came with its own soundtrack—the thumping cadence of rotor blades from an Italian

Bell 212 about to lift off for the morning's first patrol sortie. The ITALBATT (Italian Battalion) aerial component was a mainstay at the sprawling UNIFIL encampment that ran along the Mediterranean less than one and a half kilometers north of the Israeli frontier.

Men speaking a dozen different languages, sporting exotic camouflage patterns, and carrying different weapons moved around the facility. Everyone was wearing either a sky blue beret or a sky blue battle helmet.

The base, situated at the southwesternmost pocket of UNIFIL's area of responsibility, was not centrally located, but it was strategically situated in an area that would be easy to evacuate—either to awaiting ships offshore or south to Israel. February 17 was going to be a busy day for Higgins. There was a mountain of paperwork on his desk, and he had a late-morning meeting in Tyre with Abdel Majid Salah, Amal's top political officer for the southern portion of the country,[8] as well as, reportedly, with Daoud Daoud, a top Amal commander in southern Lebanon.[9] The meeting was important—skirmishes among all the factions in the south had become frequent and large-scale—but the meeting was routine. Still, there were security protocols that preceded the movement of UNTSO officers in southern Lebanon. All UN vehicles had to travel in pairs and check in at all UNIFIL checkpoints along the route. A lead vehicle would clear the path for Higgins' Jeep Wagoneer and provide protection should any threats be encountered. Higgins checked the comms before heading out to Tyre. The radios were receiving five-by-five, loud and clear. Higgins' call sign was Sunray.[10]

Higgins' meeting in Tyre was truly byzantine in the back-and-forth of opinions and demands. Every topic of conversation was preceded by a cup of piping hot Arab coffee laced with cardamom, every point made concluded with a mini-cup of scalding mint tea injected with loads of sugar. There were no clear agreements or arrangements made at the meeting—Middle Eastern volleys, be they words or 155-millimeter artillery shells.

No dates were confirmed for the next meeting. Higgins didn't speak Arabic, but he bid his hosts *salaam aleikum* at 14:00 hours. Twelve miles of coastal road connected Tyre and UNIFIL HQ at Naqoura.

The team of UN soldiers who drove the advance vehicle of Higgins' two-car convoy had been smoking with the Amal gunmen outside of Saleh's office. When Higgins emerged, they threw their cigarettes to the ground and shook hands with the Lebanese gunmen they had chatted with while Higgins and his hosts talked. The driver of the lead vehicle raced its engine and slunk out of town and onto the two-lane highway—the artery connecting the south with Tyre, Sidon, Damour, and Beirut—for the brief drive back to Naqoura. Higgins followed closely behind. The winter weather made the road conditions treacherous. Four miles south of Tyre, in a Shiite-controlled zone near the Rashidieh refugee camp, a brown Volvo took up a position behind Higgins' Wagoneer. At a bend in the road, where the driver of the advance UN vehicle lost sight of Higgins, the Volvo diverted the Wagoneer off the road.

There were no eyewitnesses and it isn't known whether Higgins had the opportunity to engage any of the assault squad with his personal sidearm. The kidnapping took less than a minute. In the blink of an eye the Volvo carrying Higgins disappeared, driven into one of the many citrus groves that dot the highway south of Rashidieh. By the time the driver of the UNIFIL advance car doubled back to see what was going on, Higgins had vanished. It was an astounding security failure and a monumental breach of protocols for safeguarding a protectee.

An alarm was sounded for all UN personnel in southern Lebanon. Search parties were mobilized. Salah cobbled together a sizable force of Amal militiamen to look for Higgins. But the effort was reactive and late. The abduction vehicles would have been changed several times, all under cover of olive groves or apple orchards, to deny the prying eyes of Israeli drones a bird's-eye view of the operations. Israel had pioneered the use of unmanned aerial vehicles, or UAVs, in 1982, when they were used as electronic warfare tools to trick Syrian antiaircraft radar during the opening days of Operation Peace for Galilee, and with great effectiveness as an aerial reconnaissance and intelligence-gathering platform, monitoring battlefield developments with real-time relays to command stations back in Israel. The Hezbollah squads in the south were several years into their guerrilla campaign against the IDF and were adept at avoiding the drones. Reportedly, brown Volvos were parked throughout the Shiite villages of the south to confuse UN and Amal forces searching for the Marine colonel.[11]

The US Embassy in Beirut was notified much later that evening by the UNIFIL duty officer. The Pentagon would have learned of the disturbing news of yet another American seized in Lebanon hours later through a blizzard of cable traffic to and from the Pentagon's 24-7 watch desk and the Defense Attaché's (DATT's) office. UNIFIL pressed its contacts in all the militias and popular fronts for any information or clues. A state of high alert was declared for all UNIFIL personnel. UNIFIL patrols were reinforced with additional personnel and they scoured the roadways in and around where Higgins was last seen. All searches yielded nothing.

On the morning of Friday, February 19, just after morning prayers in the small clan-centric mosques that dotted the small villages of southern Lebanon, the call many had dreaded came through to the wire services based in Beirut. A Hezbollah cell with the convenient front name Organization of the Oppressed on Earth, operating in the central section of southern Lebanon, claimed that it had abducted the spy William Higgins and that he would be executed unless Israel released Shiite prisoners it was holding. It was approximately 03:00 hours when the seismic news was received in the hallways of the Pentagon.

According to Joel Ross, Colonel Higgins' brother-in-law and a CIA officer at the time of the abduction, CIA headquarters alerted him to news reporting of a kidnapped US marine in Lebanon. Ross knew that his brother-in-law was the only US marine in Lebanon and immediately reached out to his sister Robin at the Pentagon. The CIA set up a special channel of alerts and information to ensure that Ross and his sister received any news and updates.[12]

At the US Embassy in Beirut, news of the abduction was first phoned into the State Department Operations Center on the seventh floor of Foggy Bottom, followed up by a FLASH precedence TER-REP (Terrorism Reporting) cable that notified several offices inside the State Department—including the CIA, FBI, DoD, NSC, FAA, and the Department of the Treasury. The FLASH precedence over-rode every other message in the State Department system, designed and reserved for real-time attacks and threats.

At FOGHORN, the DSS command center, the three special agents on duty behind a console of radios made coded open-line telephone notifications to the duty agents of offices such as the Counterterrorism Branch (now known as the Protective Intelligence Division), Intelligence and Threat Analysis, and Foreign Overseas Operations, and to the director. Similar watch offices scattered throughout the Beltway alerted agents and analysts of the new kidnapping.

As President Reagan and his staff pondered yet another hostage crisis, already deep into the mess of Buckley's murder and the human bazaar that led to the implementation of what would become known as Iran-Contra, Amal militiamen and UNIFIL troopers scoured the roadways and back alleys of southern Lebanon searching for the missing colonel.

MAJOR ROBIN HIGGINS was in a staff meeting when news of her husband's abduction was funneled to the Pentagon's office of public affairs, where she worked. "We'll have to stop what we're doing, and get on this right away," the public affairs official ordered. "A marine colonel was seized in Lebanon." All eyes turned to Robin. There was only one marine in Lebanon, they knew. "It was as if all the blood suddenly drained out of my head," Robin Higgins remembered. "My head began to spin. A chaplain was already on call. And then I snapped to attention. There were notifications to make to Rich's family. They couldn't hear about this on the news."[13]

Lieutenant Colonel William Higgins' father passed away later that night. Family members will never know if the dying man was conscious enough to hear his family talk about Rich's abduction.

A FEW DAYS following the abduction, a photo of Higgins' ID card was released to the wire services in Beirut. The HLTF took the lead in an effort to figure out who was behind Higgins' abduction and why he was seized. The HLTF sat inside the CIA's Counterterrorism Center and was formulated with one goal in mind: to find William Buckley. The group was soon overwhelmed with American and foreign hostages seized in Lebanon, and through their work they became expert in the religious-inspired blood feuds of Lebanon's internal strife and the bloody competition for power and vengeance. Higgins' abduction was a by-product of the schism between Amal and Hezbollah over dominance (Syria supported the more mainstream Amal while Iran supported Hezbollah). The fact that Hezbollah seized Higgins after he had met with Amal was a gesture meant, according to one former

Israeli intelligence official, "to stick a thumb into the eye of Amal and all they represented for stability of southern Lebanon."[14] Hezbollah had long charged that UNIFIL, and French peacekeepers in particular,[15] were nothing more than spies surveying Shiite territory in Lebanon's south; espionage under UN cover is formally forbidden under UN regulations. Higgins, according to this contention, was a spy and his abduction part of the rules of engagement that pitted Lebanon's Shiites against the rest of the world. There were reports, unconfirmed, that Higgins was working on a project focusing on Lebanon's Shiite militants.[16] There were a dozen theories as to why Hezbollah chose to kidnap Higgins—all of them were probably correct. The motives were irrelevant, of course. The Reagan administration and the US military and intelligence community began to grapple with the enormous ramifications.

There were many inside the Pentagon—and also inside the Counterterrorism Center at Langley—who knew that Higgins, like Buckley, was a prisoner Hezbollah would never release alive. The CIA and the DoD never considered Buckley and Higgins to be hostages, but rather prisoners of war.[17] Hezbollah—and, indeed, the Iranian Revolutionary Guard Corps—could never have permitted their interrogation techniques to become a matter of certifiable fact for American intelligence. But Higgins, like Buckley, was a target with a virtually unprecedented mental library of state secrets, and his deployment to Lebanon was, in hindsight, "a huge security lapse . . . absolutely, colossally stupid," a Department of Defense official claimed.[18] Higgins, because of his work as an aide-de-camp to Secretary of Defense Caspar Weinberger, was privy to the most sensitive of US military secrets, including, some reports indicated, US nuclear war fighting plans and the capabilities of spy satellites.[19]

There were other, extenuating concerns over Higgins' capture that the Department of Defense and the CIA were determined to keep out of the public eye. It was critical that any information about Robin Higgins' religion be kept out of the media. As a Marine Corps public affairs officer in the Pentagon, Robin knew many of the beat reporters assigned to cover defense matters. Her religion was never a secret, but to their credit the Pentagon press corps made it their business to keep the matter out of the papers and the many news reports that followed her husband's capture. Even more ominously, Robin's brother Joel was a CIA officer. This was information that Hezbollah could never discover.[20]

There is little doubt that he would have been savagely tortured for kicks, not to mention to obtain top secret information. It is unknown how many other hostile intelligence services offered to have a go at Lieutenant Colonel Higgins. According to a report in the *Philadelphia Inquirer*, "Soviet agents in Beirut 'are paying money and working hard to get their hands on him,' a U.S. government source who had worked in Beirut confided in the summer of 1988."[21]

On July 31, 1988, Sheikh Abbas al-Musawi, Hezbollah's secretary-general and military commander, gave a speech in the southern Lebanese town of Mashghara in which he admitted that the Party of God was, indeed, holding Higgins. "Higgins' presence in southern Lebanon constituted one of the most dangerous schemes against our [anti-Israeli guerrilla] struggle," Musawi preached to a gathering of Shiite elders. "We consider that abducting that agent as part of defending our nation. The 'Higgins affair' is linked to our struggle against the Israeli enemy, combating American bases and presence in the region."[22] Musawi and his lieutenant, Mughniyeh, were already expert in abducting individuals who possessed state secrets and who were symbols of the American presence around the world.

Hezbollah released one photo of Higgins while he was in captivity. The black sweater he wore only emphasized the pallor of a man locked away in darkness. A salt-and-pepper beard, looking as if it had taken half a year to grow, disguised the spit-and-polish Marine Corps recruiting poster good looks. He appeared to have been beaten. He looked gaunt and solemnly resigned to his fate.

Robin Higgins was relieved when the proof-of-life image came through the wire services. "It was disturbing to see him so thin and it was pretty clear that the treatment he was subjected to was very cruel," Robin said, "but it was something to cling to. He was still alive. It was very heartening for me to see the photo."[23]

THE KIDNAPPING OF Lieutenant Colonel William Higgins, just like the kidnapping of William Buckley, was a crime that was never supposed to have been perpetrated against a man of such rank and prominence. The power of the CIA and the sheer might of the Pentagon should have been enough to deter any group, especially one with a state sponsor, from even thinking of carrying out so provocative a move. But there was a sense in the ranks of the Iranian Islamic Revolutionary Guard and their Lebanese proxies that the United States was incapable of mounting a decisive retaliatory response. The assessment in Tehran and in the Shiite slums of south Beirut was that the United States would not—and could not—mount any serious effort to rescue either man. The Soviets were to be feared; the Americans, experience had taught, could be manipulated.

Israel couldn't be manipulated, though. And the Jewish State was inextricably entangled in the thickets of the Lebanese human bazaar.

OPERATION HANDSOME
YOUNG MAN

T HERE WERE STILL a few hours of darkness remaining very early on the morning of Friday, July 28, 1989, when residents of Jebchit were awoken from their slumber by the whooshing roar of IAF warplanes flying low passes overhead. Jebchit was a small hamlet in the hills near the south-central Lebanese town of Nabatiyah, just north of the Litani River and seven kilometers north of Israel's border. Jebchit was a Hezbollah stronghold, a place where Party of God flags were proudly flown alongside banners of the Ayatollah Khomeini. Many of the plush multistory homes in this sleepy village were inhabited by the families of Hezbollah commanders who controlled much of the area. Sheikh Abdel Karim Obeid was the regional Hezbollah commander and boasted the largest home in town. He had assumed command of Hezbollah forces in the area following the assassination of Sheikh Ragheb Harb, allegedly killed by Israeli intelligence on February 16, 1984,[1] and was involved in all area operations—including leading the abduction of Lieutenant Colonel Higgins. Obeid, thirty years old, usually slept with an AK-47 by his bed. The earsplitting roars of the sorties should have alarmed him, but the Israelis had been very active of late. Unconcerned, the guerrilla commander turned to his side and went back to sleep.

The Israeli flyover was a ruse—a sonic-boom diversion to mask the beating rotor blades of the two IAF CH-53 heavy transport helicopters that landed in the black of the wadi at the entrance to Jebchit. Twenty-five operators emerged from the choppers and raced into the darkness of the mountain road leading to the center of the hamlet; wearing night-vision gear and carrying suppressed weapons, the commandos moved silently as they raced forward. The commandos were from Sayeret Mat'kal, the most elite unit in the Israeli military, similar in mission and capability to Britain's legendary Special Air Service and the ███████████████████████. The raiding force, led by Major Amos Ben-Avraham,[2] himself a veteran of the epic Entebbe Airport hostage rescue in 1976, carefully avoided Hezbollah patrols as it moved through narrow alleys toward the operation's objective, the home of Sheikh Obeid, a three-story structure surrounded by a three-foot wall on the eastern side of the village. The Israeli commandos had trained on a model of this very location for over two months.

A force of operators assumed defensive positions around Obeid's home, while breachers popped open the building's large iron front door with little difficulty. The task force split into three and flowed to each of the floors. Operators armed with silenced pistols were to eliminate Sheikh Obeid's bodyguards, but the entry to the house was so swift that the assault force was able to subdue and gag them without having to fire a shot. Mona, Obeid's blue-eyed cherub-faced wife, emerged into a hallway and was quickly secured before she could make a sound. She directed the Israelis to her bedroom, where Obeid was fast asleep. Obeid tried to resist but a blow to the head expedited the inevitable submission. He was bound, gagged, and drugged.[3] He was carried out of the house and to the landing zone in the wadi down below. A neighbor who had come out to investigate some noise with his AK-47 in hand was shot and killed as he approached the Israeli perimeter.

Word of the Israeli operation soon spread in Jebchit. The local imam used the mosque's loudspeaker to summon the village's men to battle.[4] The sound of AK-47s being fired wildly into the night by men in their pajamas lasted until dawn, but the two IAF helicopters had long since vanished. By the time Hezbollah's Shura Council in Beirut learned of Obeid's abduction, he had already eaten his breakfast inside an Israeli cell. The Obeid mission, code-named Operation Handsome Young Man, had been a striking success.

Sheikh Abdel Karim Obeid played an instrumental role in the abduction and, in all likelihood, interrogation of William Higgins, but that's not why Israel seized him. Sheikh Obeid was known to have been one of the last men to see Ron Arad alive. Captain Ron Arad was an IAF Weapons Systems Officer on board an F-4E Phantom II from the elite Sixty-Ninth "Hammer" Squadron conducting a bombing sortie of a Palestinian target southeast of Sidon on the afternoon of October 16, 1986, when a malfunction caused one of the bombs connected to a pylon to detonate. The aircraft suffered catastrophic failure, and Arad and the aircraft's pilot, Yishai Aviram, were forced to eject. Both pilot and navigator came under thunderous ground fire as their parachutes floated them softly into Lebanese territory. "I thought I was dead," Aviram would confess, "and then I felt something tugging at my shoulders and I realized it was my chute. Ron Arad was maybe four hundred meters above me, to the north. I looked down and saw ambulances racing about on the main road and I saw pickup trucks with heavy machine guns on the back. Everyone was shooting at me. I steered my chute into a deep wadi, or dry river bed, south of the target and waited."[5]

The IAF dispatched an aerial armada of rescue helicopters to the area, including Bell 212s carrying operators from Unit 669, the elite aeromedical evacuation force, and CH-53 heavy transports. A tandem of Bell AH-1S Cobras, or Tzefas as they are known in Hebrew, flew overhead. The rescue attempt was chaotic. Local villagers, and Palestinian and Shiite forces in the area, threw unrelenting ground fire at the rescue aircraft. In the wadi where Aviram had sought shelter, heavily armed gunmen were closing fast on his position. *"Hada wachad,"* Aviram heard his pursuers scream to one another in Arabic, "Here's one!" With little time to spare, the two Cobras swooped into the opening to pull Aviram to safety. The lead Cobra, piloted by Ofer Nir, suffered small-arms damage and had to leave the scene. Aviram leaped onto the landing skids of the second Cobra gunship, piloted by Assaf Meitav. Meitav cut a path back to Israel, hoping to find a secluded and safe spot to have one of the airborne Bell 212s pick up the F-4E pilot, but a steady stream of fire followed their flight path south. Aviram remembers villagers staring at him as he held on precariously to the Cobra's skid; they fired their AK-47s from the terraces of their homes.[6]

A bright full moon illuminated the Cobra's path back to Israel. Rocket-propelled grenades and .50-caliber fire followed it for much of the journey.

The IDF had prepared a large-scale response to locate and rescue Arad. Sayeret Golani, the reconnaissance battalion of the First Golani Infantry Brigade, as well as other commando forces, had been mobilized and they were en route to the area where Arad had parachuted; Assaf Meitav and his number two knew the area the best, and they led the assault. But the destruction of the F-4E Phantom was a call to arms for thousands of gunmen in the area—each wanted to be the one to capture a souvenir from the destroyed Israeli warplane; each wanted a chance to take a shot at the Israeli aircraft flying overhead. It was deemed too risky to land a sizable Israeli contingent south of Sidon to search for Arad and then to bring him to safety. The risks were simply too great.[7]

Communications with Arad ceased the moment he ejected from the rear seat in the hardened cockpit of the F-4E Phantom. According to Yishai Aviram, he landed close to the coastal road and was seized seconds after his feet hit the ground. "We know that he was injured during the ejection," Yaakov Peri, a former head of the Shin Bet, explained in an Israeli television documentary. "He was seized by villagers and then handed off to Amal. He was then taken to one of the nearby villages where Amal had a detention and interrogation center and questioned by militiamen, and he was then taken to somewhere in the Syrian-controlled Beka'a Valley in order to distance him from the operational reach of Israeli forces."[8]

Amal demanded that the State of Israel pay it three million dollars to consider releasing Ron Arad, and that Israel release hundreds of terrorists, some of them Palestinian and others Lebanese, in exchange for the IAF navigator. But Israeli politicians, including Yitzhak Rabin, the defense minister, were still reeling from a prisoner exchange that had transpired three years earlier in which Ahmed Jibril's PFLP-GC succeeded in extorting the release of 1,150 Palestinian and international terror prisoners in exchange for three Israeli servicemen captured in Lebanon. Many of the men Jibril demanded be released were murderers, men with blood on their hands, and the Israeli public was outraged that killers were set free. Among those released was Kozo Okamoto, the surviving Japanese Red Army gunman responsible for the Lod Airport massacre on May 30, 1970, in which twenty-six people, primarily Puerto Rican pilgrims, were gunned down as they waited for their luggage.* Also released in the Jibril exchange was Ahmed Yassin, a quadriplegic fundamentalist Islamic cleric from Gaza who would leave his Israeli prison cell thanks to the prisoner exchange and return home to found a new terror group, Hamas, the following year.

By the time Israeli leaders could muster up the required support to pursue negotiations with Amal over Arad, Mustafa Dirani, Amal's head of security, defected to Hezbollah. He handed Arad over to Sheikh Obeid and his new paymasters. Obeid reportedly turned Arad over to an Iranian Revolutionary Guard unit operating in southern Lebanon.

Many people in American intelligence believe that Ron Arad and William Higgins were being held together in the same location.[9] Israeli intelligence believed that Obeid could provide critical information that would bring about Arad's release or at least some inkling as to his whereabouts and well-being. An impressive list of intelligence agencies around the world, from the Beltway to Wadi Sir in Amman, would have lined up to interview Obeid, and Israel was convinced that Hezbollah would do everything in its power to secure the release of such a high-ranking commander.

Obeid's interrogation, believed to have been held at Facility 1391, a top secret Israeli intelligence base and prison, yielded immediate results.[10] Although the Hezbollah commander was tight-lipped concerning Arad's fate, he was forthcoming about Higgins' abduction.

---

* In a bizarre twist of fate, Joel Ross, William Higgins' brother-in-law, was on the same flight as the three Red Army gunmen and survived the attack at the airport.

Obeid's Jebchit home was a station of the cross for all Hezbollah operations in the south—a conduit connecting Iranian interests in the country and Syrian meddling. Days following Obeid's capture, Israeli Defense Minister Yitzhak Rabin informed the Knesset that the Hezbollah sheikh had been directly involved in the Higgins kidnapping operation. The three Hezbollah operatives who had seized Lieutenant Colonel Higgins had slept in Obeid's home the night before the kidnapping, in preparation for the operation. One of the kidnappers returned to Obeid's home once Higgins had been seized in order to stash the vehicle involved; the car, according to initial Israeli interrogation, had been hidden in Jebchit for well over a month.[11] One of the commanders of the Higgins abduction operation was Mustafa Dirani. The instructions to seize Higgins came from Sheikh Musawi; the orders and operational logistics emanated from Imad Mughniyeh and Security Apparatus Chief Abdel Hadi Hamadi.[12] Sheik Obeid's men carried out the abduction.

On the morning of July 31, 1989, a messenger delivered two videotapes to the Beirut bureau of *An-Nahar*, Lebanon's leading newspaper. One VHS cassette contained brief, grisly footage of a lifeless Lieutenant Colonel William R. Higgins hanging from his neck in a dimly lit room. A blindfold covered his face and he was barefoot; he was wearing pressed fatigues. A note, in typewritten Arabic, accompanied the tape. It claimed that Higgins had been executed by the Organization of the Oppressed on Earth as a response to Israel—and the United States—not taking ultimatums to release Sheikh Obeid "seriously enough."[13]

"The American spy was hanged at 3:00 p.m. to make him a lesson," the note attached to the videocassette explained. "We reiterate our stand that the sheikh must be freed along with his two brothers because what will happen next will be worse. Let America and Israel shoulder the whole responsibility."[14]

Lieutenant Colonel William R. Higgins had been a prisoner of war for 529 days.

Some members of the Bush White House were furious with Israel, believing its unilateral operation seizing Obeid had resulted in Higgins' murder. According to the *New York Times*, US administration officials said that "Israel had privately told the United States that they assumed nothing would happen to the American hostages once Israeli commandos seized the sheikh because it was purely an Israeli operation."[15]

A copy of the Higgins cassette was carefully reviewed by agents and analysts from the HLTF, with forensic assessments of the tape made by the FBI laboratory and the CIA. There was much more footage on the second video. The full segment, filmed at some kind of tent encampment, showed Higgins' body being raised by the rope around his neck. Those who were hanging him chanted in celebration. Analysts pored over the imagery with magnifying glasses. Psycholinguistic analysis was conducted on every word used by the terrorists in an effort to make sense of the motive. The video was shot in daylight, probably, CIA analysts and medical experts assessed, in the Beka'a Valley or the mountains near the Nabatiyah region. Some Agency doctors and forensic specialists speculated that Higgins may have been drugged or already dead before being hanged.

A'man examined the Higgins video frame by frame and determined that the Marine colonel had been killed long before Operation Handsome Young Man. An analysis of the footage showed Higgins wearing winter fatigues, indicating that he had been executed during the cold-weather months.[16]

There was some speculation that Higgins had simply been beaten to death, tortured during what undoubtedly were brutally vicious interrogation sessions; the hanging was a convenient piece of theater to be used at a later date. Some intelligence sources have believed that Higgins was beaten to death in July 1988 as retribution for the accidental downing of Iran Air Flight 655 by the USS *Vincennes* in the Persian Gulf on July 3, 1988; 290 passengers and crew members were killed.* UNIFIL commanders said that Higgins had been tortured to death in December 1988 after attempting to escape his captors.[17]

THE KIDNAPPING AND murder of Lieutenant Colonel William Higgins was a nightmare for the United States. For the Department of Defense and the US intelligence community, the tragedy was William Buckley all over again. Once again a high-ranking US officer had been captured in Lebanon and once again there was nothing that the United States could do to secure his release.

Once again the United States had underestimated Hezbollah's capabilities, their ability to gather intelligence, and their murderous resolve.

---

* The downing of the Iran Air Airbus A300 was viewed as the precipitous spark that launched the eventual bombing of Pan Am 103 on December 21, 1988. Reportedly, the Iranian government paid Ahmed Jibril's Popular Front for the Liberation of Palestine–General Command (PFLP-GC) twenty million dollars to bring down an American airliner; a theory is that once PFLP-GC networks were infiltrated in Europe by the Israeli and German intelligence services, Jibril subcontracted the operation out to Libyan intelligence.

16

THE END OF THE ORDEAL

OFFICIALLY AT LEAST, Imad Mughniyeh had waged a seven-year campaign of abduction and murder in order to obtain the release of his brother-in-law Mustafa Badreddine from his cell inside the crumbling bowels of Kuwait City's Central Prison. The hostages that Mughniyeh's cells had seized had all been abducted to be used as barter for the release of Badreddine. Good men, like CIA Station Chief Buckley, were brutally murdered for the same goal. European governments did everything in their power to secure the release of their hostages, surrendering national pride and security concerns to bring their captives home. The United States, Mughniyeh's primary target, had secretly arranged arms sales to Iran in defiance of an arms embargo in exchange for that country's promise to help secure the hostages' release, a scandal that ultimately became known as the Iran-Contra affair. Such was the moral pressure on the Reagan White

House to free the captives. But after all the misery, after all the torture and murder, Badreddine was no closer to coming back to south Beirut.

Mustafa Badreddine was held in the main courtyard of Kuwait City's Central Prison. All inmates, upon entry into the facility, were forced to have their heads shaved—a humiliation that Badreddine, who wore an unkempt mane of wild dark brown hair like a badge of honor, would not have forgotten. Badreddine fancied himself a ladies' man, a Casanova among the willing and bored housewives of south Beirut, and he was always aware of his appearance.[1] Badreddine, known to his jailers simply by his nom de guerre of Elias al-Sa'ab,[2] had been a problematic prisoner since his pardon from death row, routinely picking the lock of his cell with plastic pen caps that he had melted together. Though handicapped with a wooden leg, Badreddine possessed boundless aggression. He slashed a captain of the guard with a razor, attempting to behead rather than simply kill the man. Even though he was one of the most guarded prisoners in all of Kuwait, he managed to oversee a Hezbollah plot to assassinate Kuwaiti emir Sheikh Jaber al-Ahmad al-Sabah in 1985.[3]

In the spring of 1988 Mughniyeh launched one final desperate gambit to secure Badreddine's release. On April 5, Kuwait Airways Flight 422 was hijacked over the Persian Gulf as the Boeing 747 made its preparation for landing in Kuwait City over the Gulf of Oman. The flight had originated in Bangkok with 112 passengers and crew members. Three members of the Kuwaiti royal family were on board the aircraft, as were six or seven Hezbollah operatives armed with handguns and grenades. One of the hijackers had done this before. Hassan Ezzadine was the most violent of the triumvirate who hijacked TWA Flight 847 in June 1985. He should have been dead or in prison, but he once again found himself commandeering an aircraft with a grenade in his hand. The hijackers demanded the release of seventeen men in Kuwaiti custody in exchange for the lives of the hostages.*

Flight 422 was diverted to the Iranian city of Mashhad; following several days on the tarmac, the aircraft was flown to Larnaca, Cyprus. The hijackers pistol-whipped many of the hostages; two Kuwaitis were shot in the back of the head and their bodies tossed onto the tarmac. The terrorists threatened to fly the aircraft into the Kuwaiti royal palace; they threatened to kill everyone on board. The aircraft was flown to a remote section of Houari Boumediene Airport in Algiers, Algeria. The entire ordeal lasted sixteen days before the terrorists surrendered to Algerian authorities. They were quickly released by the Algerians and flown on a private jet back to Beirut.

The US Department of Justice was incensed by the Algerian action, especially as there was an outstanding warrant for Ezzadine's arrest. So great was Algerian fear that Hezbollah would retaliate against its interests in Lebanon that political expediency trumped international justice.

Mughniyeh was also outraged over the incident. Mustafa Badreddine was still in prison.

Badreddine remained in Kuwait City's Central Prison for another sixteen months. According to Hezbollah folklore, when Iraq invaded neighboring Kuwait and its tanks rolled into Kuwait City on August 2, 1990, Badreddine built an explosive charge out of "chicken bones, salt, and cockroaches" in order to blow the door off his cell and es-

---

* Fred Burton led a team of DSS agents, in concert with the FBI, to debrief many of the hostages held captive on the flight. DSS agents in the New York field office also assisted, along with DSS CT and FBI agents dispatched to Kuwait and Germany.

cape.⁴ The truth was not quite so Ian Fleming. Iraqi Special Forces had assaulted the Central Prison and freed everyone inside. Badreddine had simply walked out of his cell. Before the Iraqi intelligence services could determine who was who, the wily Hezbollah commander had made his way to the Iranian Embassy on Isteghal Street, from where he was whisked away to Tehran before being repatriated to Beirut and the festive homecoming with his family, his comrades, and the Syrian and Iranian intelligence officers who financed and facilitated the Hezbollah empire.

The merchants who eked out an existence selling vegetables and fruit in the slums of West Beirut knew that something special was being planned as the first rain showers rolled into the city to usher in the autumn chill. The men in the black T-shirts and black leather jackets, the mufti of choice for Hezbollah muscle, had been buying extra-large quantities of dates and figs, as well as olives, tomatoes, and other telltale staples of a feast. Kilos of rice were obtained from the market. Rumor was that a dozen sheep were purchased and readied to be shipped for slaughter. There were no billboards alerting the citizens of the slums to an upcoming special event. There were no announcements in the paper of a speech by Party Secretary Nasrallah or even an inkling of a VIP visitor, perhaps an Iranian general. Just by the number of guns on the street and by the hissing of walkie-talkie chatter heard on every corner, the residents of the neighborhoods at the fault lines of Hezbollah's seat of power knew that whatever was happening was something of significance. The celebrations planned for Badreddine's return were low-key enough not to arouse interest from Israel and the other Western intelligence services that were interested in his whereabouts, but respectful enough—a feast, or *eiyd*, worthy of a warrior returning from battle.

There was less than a handful of individuals outside Hezbollah's ruling council who knew what Badreddine looked like and they all worked for an intelligence service. Only three or four known photographs existed of the enigmatic right-hand man and master bomb builder. He had never applied for a passport; the travel papers he carried were forged. He had never been issued a driver's license, he was not the registered owner of any property in Lebanon, and he didn't even possess a bank account.[5] Other than on the wanted posters that bore his likeness and name, he didn't officially exist. But by January 1991, Badreddine was Mughniyeh's head of internal security, a position that was designed for a ruthless soul who wouldn't flinch at the methods needed to extract a confession from a suspected traitor.

As Mughniyeh's shadow, Badreddine sat in on secret negotiations to end the hostage crisis once and for all. Nine live Western hostages were still being held by Mughniyeh's cells, along with the bodies of William Buckley and Lieutenant Colonel Higgins. The man responsible for trying to bring an end to Hezbollah's human bazaar was Giandomenico Picco, the United Nations envoy attempting to resolve the hostage crisis in Lebanon.[6] Fluent in English, Spanish, French, and Italian, the Italian-born diplomat was the United Nations' go-to guy for difficult negotiations with recalcitrant warlords, megalomaniac despots, and corrupt generals. He had stood his ground between Soviet generals and vengeance-seeking mullahs in ending the war in Afghanistan, and he was one of the architects of the cease-fire that ended the Iran-Iraq War in 1988. Picco now sat across the table from both Mughniyeh and Badreddine in what was the most daunting challenge of his career.

The call to Picco's hotel room usually came in the middle of the night. There were always strict instructions, and he couldn't bring a bodyguard even though Terry Waite, the previous negotiator seeking the hostages' release, had himself been abducted. A car would pull up in front of where Picco was ordered to wait, and he'd be blindfolded and driven to a location somewhere in Beirut where he was led to a cellar at gunpoint. The discussions were terse. The men who negotiated with Picco never introduced themselves, they didn't present their credentials when sitting across the dimly lit table, and they didn't wear uniforms. Picco didn't know if the men he spoke to were agents for the men who were in charge, or if they were the actual decision-makers. But from the number of bodyguards each man had, Picco assumed they were individuals who wielded great power. Israeli intelligence would later inform the United Nations negotiator that all along he had been negotiating with Mughniyeh and Badreddine.

It was apparent to Picco that Hezbollah was looking for a way out of what had become an unwinnable mess. The Iranians pressed Mughniyeh and Party Secretary Nasrallah to end the ordeal and Tehran knew Picco to be an honest broker with a moral compass. Mughniyeh did most of the talking during the back-and-forth, yet as the talks dragged on his tone changed from defiant to contrite. "He knew that seizing Westerners off the street in Beirut was wrong," Picco would write in an article; Mughniyeh "felt that such maneuvers [the abductions] were the only options at his disposal."[7]

On August 8, 1991, the first of several long-held American and British hostages were released by their Hezbollah captors. On December 4, Terry Anderson was freed by Hezbollah and driven to Damascus.[8] The AP bureau chief had been kidnapped exactly one year to the day after William Buckley, and Mughniyeh's muscle had held him captive in blindfolded darkness for a hellish 2,455 days.

The hostage ordeal was finally coming to an end. Many in the CIA and the Pentagon still yearned for justice. But first they wanted closure.

17

RECOVERY AND RETURN

THE BUNKER WAS a fitting name for the bar situated on the grounds of the heavily fortified eight-acre US Embassy compound in the northeastern Beirut suburb of Awkar. The scotch and bourbon flowed generously inside the Bunker, and the drinks were always accompanied by bar food favorites, such as spicy chicken wings, burgers, and large plates of fries. American diplomats and young marines drank at the Bunker, as did the security officers from the British, German, and French embassies; in the odd world of diplomats under siege, the imminent-threat reality of Beirut created strange bedfellows among the men stationed there. There were very strict State Department protocols prohibiting the mixing of firearms and alcohol, but long guns were conveniently positioned near the ice machine; the British, German, and French security officers were all allowed to enter the embassy—and the Bunker—armed.

Most of the six Diplomatic Security Service agents assigned to the embassy never went anywhere on the compound—even to the pool at the ambassador's residence—without their service weapons handy. The presence of so many firearms guaranteed that the fights were few and far between inside the Bunker—the patrons behaved, even those who had one too many. Anyway, it was the time of the year for peace and goodwill toward others. It was December 1991. Christmas decorations had already been hung up throughout the small watering hole. A faux mini–Christmas tree had already been propped up on the dark wood bar.

The Bunker's motto was, after all, "The safest place to get bombed." The Bunker, as important a fixture on the grounds of the US Embassy in Beirut as the chancery, was situated inside a small prefab building on a sprawling eight-acre compound along the Mediterranean coast, surrounded by rough hills covered with lush cedar trees. The US Embassy was in a little village, with the chancery in an old French-built colonial mansion. The perimeter of the US Embassy was heavily fortified. High walls surrounded much of the estate. The entire compound was surrounded by impenetrable rows of razor concertina; the blades, sharpened to a cruel edgé, constituted a seemingly impossible barrier to anyone intent on transgressing on the embassy grounds. Watchtowers—complete with guards and M60 7.62-millimeter light machine guns—covered every inch of the grounds.

The outer ring of defense was the responsibility of the Lebanese Armed Forces, the LAF. The LAF garrison positioned in a small camp near the embassy was carefully scrutinized by the Lebanese authorities to weed out possible Shiite troopers who might have blood or other ties to Hezbollah. The LAF security force was impressive, but it was nothing when compared to the "Nasty Boys," the local Lebanese bodyguard force that was employed by the Diplomatic Security

Service to provide muscle and firepower to embassy defense and virtually all moves by embassy personnel in and around Beirut and the remainder of the country. The Nasty Boys were just what their sobriquet implied: heavily armed muscle that wasn't to be messed with. The force was composed almost exclusively of Maronite Christians. The force drove heavily armored limousines and Suburbans in such a way that any vehicle in their path, from a sedan to an LAF tank, was wisely moved to the side of the road to get out of the way. Nasty Boy convoys included "top gun" positions: Suburbans with roof-mounted .50-caliber machine guns and RPGs. The Nasty Boys, one former assistant RSO remembered, weren't paid very well but they were reliable and loyal.[1]

Most embassy staffers didn't require a Nasty Boys convoy. Most travel on or off the embassy grounds was by air. US military choppers flew a risky though vital shuttle service between the landing pad on the embassy and the British Royal Air Force (RAF) Base in Akrotiri, near Limassol. Most vital cargo, including diplomatic pouches, flew on the military flights. Staffers were brought on and off the compound on these flights. Even the new US ambassador to Lebanon flew to Beirut in the belly of a UH-60 Black Hawk or carrier-based SH-60 Seahawk.

Ryan Clark Crocker presented his credentials to Lebanese president Elias Hrawi on November 29, 1990, confirming himself as President George H. W. Bush's personal representative to Lebanon.[2] Crocker, a career diplomat and native of Spokane, Washington, had come from a military family and was a veteran Middle East hand who understood the high stakes that were always on the line whenever the region went to war. Crocker launched his career at the US consulate in Khorramshahr, Iran, in 1972, and then was assigned to the newly opened US Embassy in Doha, Qatar. Schooled extensively in Arabic,

Crocker also served as the chief of the economic-commercial office at the US Interests Section in Baghdad, Iraq. In 1981, Crocker was assigned to Beirut, where he was the chief of the embassy's political section.

Nothing could have prepared Crocker for service in the war-ravaged hell of Lebanon. He was the primary American diplomat on the ground to witness the Sabra and Shatila massacre, and was present inside the embassy during the suicide bombing of 1983. A rising star in the State Department's Near Eastern Division, he was considered a fearless diplomat who would travel anywhere regardless of the threat.* Other diplomats would have taken the embassy bombing as an omen and opted for a safer assignment overseas or a desk position back in the Beltway. But Crocker had no intention of leaving Lebanon. He was one of many who remained behind in the rubble to try to start over, to recover and to rebuild.

Crocker was one of the few in the ad hoc embassy to get along with William Buckley, and the two men quickly became friends. When Crocker's tour in Beirut ended in January 1984 after three long and bloody years, he bade Buckley farewell. He learned of his friend's abduction several months later while he was in Washington.

When Crocker returned to Beirut as ambassador, his agenda was chock-full of political, military, economic, and cultural programs that he was to push in order to strengthen ties between the United States and Lebanon. Yet there was another, more pressing agenda. The bodies of William Buckley and William Higgins had yet to be recovered.

---

* Crocker would go on to serve as the US ambassador to Kuwait and Syria, as well as, following the September 11, 2001, terrorist attacks, Pakistan, Iraq, and Afghanistan.

Crocker vowed not to leave Lebanon until these Americans were returned home.

A month following Crocker's return, the US State Department ordered its embassy evacuated. The United States–led coalition in the Saudi desert was about to launch Operation Desert Storm and it was feared that Middle Eastern extremists would take advantage of this latest regional conflict as a pretext to target US embassies with terrorist attacks. The embassy did not reopen until the fallout from the conflict with Iraq had settled into an acceptable status quo. Diplomats were reassigned, while the loyal Foreign Service national workforce and the Nasty Boys held down the fort.

Before Ambassador Crocker could return to Lebanon, though, the embassy had to be reopened for business, which required that a small team of intrepid DSS agents make the compound and the surrounding terrain safe for American diplomatic personnel. DSS dispatched waves of TDYers—personnel on temporary assignment—to Beirut to make sure that the landscape around the embassy was safe enough for the diplomatic personnel who would live and work in the crosshairs. Ben Foster* was one of them. Ben started his DSS career later in life than many of the just-out-of-college recruits who flocked to the agency following 1985, but age didn't inhibit his energy or his skills. He spent five years in the DSS New York field office, conducting passport and visa fraud investigations and driving in a motorcade or standing at his post, earpiece fastened snugly to his Motorola radio. To advance his career—and to satisfy his sense of adventure—Ben bid on an open slot in Beirut to serve as an assistant RSO for a year of hardship duty. DSS was happy to have someone actually volunteer to work Beirut.

Beirut was unlike anything Ben had ever seen before. The city—

---

* A pseudonym.

the whole country—was a world upside down, chopped and scorched into two divergent universes. East Beirut, including Awkar where the embassy was, was pristine and very Mediterranean. The Green Zone, as it was defined by the DSS staff, was a series of grids on a map of Beirut—primarily the eastern section of the city, along with certain parts of western neighborhoods—where it was safe for Americans to travel with Nasty Boys protection. The Red Zone comprised the no-go areas—no-go under any circumstances—and they covered several of the Palestinian refugee camps and, of course, the Hezbollah-controlled bastion of southwestern Beirut. There was absolutely no travel off post—except, of course, for the ambassador, the DCM, and the political officer, and then only in eight- or nine-vehicle Nasty Boys motorcades.[3]

When Ben did travel into the city, through the Green Zone with the Nasty Boys, he was amazed by the magnitude of devastation that resulted from sixteen years of war. The scars were everywhere: destroyed buildings, shell craters in the centers of busy thoroughfares. Bullet and shrapnel holes adorned just about every structure and billboard. But still there was another Beirut. Along the Corniche, beautiful women strutted in tight jeans and carried Dior bags. Gulf Arabs, adorned in their desert garb, still rolled around town in their Porsches and Bentleys. Everyone in the city was always in one café or another; they were always eating out and partying. Beirut was, after all, Beirut. There were still nights when shooting could be heard throughout the city.

The threat quotient was exhausting to the diplomats and special agents who worked in Beirut. And Ben, like the others, let off some steam in the Bunker. The career foreign service officers, usually sitting at one of the few tables in the establishment, were easy to spot in their tan Wallabees and L.L.Bean cardigans. The military men ████

███████████████████████████████,

liked to sit at the bar and place their walkie-talkies on the heavily lacquered wood that was desperately in need of a new coat of varnish. A small, portable color television set was fixed above the bar, and it was usually tuned to Armed Forces TV or anything that had programming in English. The regulars sitting on their stools at the bar, including Ben, watched happily as a report came in from the US Army hospital in Rhein Main, an old Luftwaffe air force base near Wiesbaden, showing Terry Anderson being reunited with his family. Many of the men in the room, the regulars at the Bunker, had worked long hours and dealt with the most unsavory rogues and scoundrels to gather even the smallest morsels of data that could help locate the dungeon where Anderson was being held. Christmas was approaching. To many of the men watching the report of Anderson's release, the hostage's homecoming was a welcome gift.

EVERY ASPECT OF life at the Beirut Embassy was defined by security, a stringent list of slow-moving but necessary protocols set in place following the truck bombings of the two previous embassies. Most of the procedures were slow-moving and tedious. Heavy steel blast-mitigating doors had to be closed in order for the next doors to open. Gates had to be raised and lowered; anti-ram plates had to be manually opened or shut to impede or allow vehicles to enter. Every moment, every day, every move, was high threat. Every aspect of the high-threat reality was covered by a security protocol. This was the world of the RSO's office and the assistant RSOs assigned to the post. There was little glamour in working a high-threat post like Beirut— but the money was good.

Late on the night of Saturday, December 21, 1991, the Lebanese Gendarmerie received a tip that a body had been dumped by the side of the road on a remote stretch of gravel and blacktop leading to the airport from the slums of south Beirut. The police operator at the headquarters of the national Internal Security Force, or ISF, assessed from the anonymous caller's accent that he was a local.

Responding officers found a body, wrapped in a coarse gray blanket, dumped near a ditch along a fence. Once Terry Anderson was released, ISF commanders believed, the bodies of the two Americans killed in captivity would be returned as well. ISF investigators took photographs of the crime scene and had the body rushed to the American University Hospital in West Beirut. All movements were secret. One of the ISF commanders closed his office door and called a contact at the US Embassy.

███████████████ the RSO's office knew enough about the city to understand that nothing was ever what it appeared to be in Beirut. News that remains had been recovered in south Beirut was met by the convergence of overdue relief and apprehension. An urgent in-country meeting was called to assess the situation and to try to gather additional intelligence on the fluid events that were unfolding. There was a sincere sense in the embassy, one of the security staffers recalled, that news of a body, possibly that of either Buckley or Higgins, was a trap—either an ambush at the retrieval point of the body, or an IED placed in the remains.

One of the Nasty Boys was a Sunni who had married a Shiite woman from south Beirut and who had uncanny access to virtually all the factions at war with one another in the country; his name was Ra'ed,* and the former Lebanese soldier had displayed his courage and loyalty to the post on numerous occasions as one of the bodyguard force shift leaders. Ra'ed grabbed his .45 caliber semiautomatic and

---

*A pseudonym.

took one of the unmarked embassy cars and traveled to south Beirut. If he was lucky, a friend of a friend might know someone in Hezbollah who would confirm the identity of the body dumped near the airport. That was how information was confirmed in Lebanon: two men talking over a cup of diabetes-inducing sweet mint tea and a pack of cigarettes in the corner of a room where no one could overhear. Ra'ed's contacts confirmed that the body was that of a hostage. The RSO's office was immediately notified that the body sent to the American University Hospital was probably that of Lieutenant Colonel Higgins.

Ben, whose radio call sign was "Bandit," was one of the only members of the DSS contingent at the embassy who were what the agency referred to as shooters—more tactical than desk jockey. And even though he had only five years on the job, he was one of the senior men assigned to the post. Many of the agents were junior, fresh out of the Federal Law Enforcement Training Center in Glynco, Georgia, and had a small amount of time on the streets at one of the various DSS field offices throughout the United States.

Once Ra'ed's confirmation came in, the RSO asked Ben if "he wanted to take a ride." Ben knew exactly what that meant. He grabbed his weapons—a Colt Series 70 .45-caliber semiautomatic handgun and an unauthorized Benelli twelve-gauge shotgun—and met the Nasty Boys by their vehicles.

The drive to the American University Hospital took less than twenty minutes.

There was paranoia in the protocols for the security staffers at the embassy—a mental checklist of worry and mistrust that was forged in the everyday procedure by the lessons learned from two embassies being destroyed and William Buckley being kidnapped. "Everything was secretive," Ben explained; even the Nasty Boys were kept in the dark. The Nasty Boys advance team that checked out a route and made sure that the destination was safe would receive the motorcade's destination only thirty minutes before a move in order to minimize the chance of the detail being compromised.

Under heavy guard, Ben was ushered into the hospital's morgue where a body had been placed in a hastily assembled wooden box. "I remember in cables sent back and forth from post to Washington there was enormous interest in the question of whether there was any physical evidence of torture on the body."[4] Ben had seen his fair share of bodies while working as a detective in one of the largest cities in the United States, but he had only the most rudimentary forensic skills. Still, he had to examine the body. He wasn't about to allow an enclosed crate to enter the embassy grounds unless he knew exactly what was inside.

The only men allowed in the room with Higgins' body were Ben, several of the Nasty Boys, and the Lebanese doctor. A few of the Lebanese bodyguards removed their black baseball caps out of respect to the murdered Marine colonel. Ben asked the examining physician to take X-rays of the body as well as cranial imagery. The images would be critical in the preliminary identification of the body lying on the table, and it would rule out any fears that Ben had of explosives planted inside the cadaver. Security remained the primary concern every moment Americans were outside the embassy walls.

The makeshift coffin was placed inside one of the Nasty Boys' Suburbans and the motorcade raced back to the embassy. The DATT had made sure that a proper refrigerated location was set aside to store the body until both Higgins and Buckley could be flown out to Cyprus together. The air bridge was the link between the US Embassy in Beirut and a Sixth Fleet carrier in the Mediterranean and RAF

Base Akrotiri. The helicopters always flew in tandem coming into Beirut, and under cover of darkness. The possibility that one of the choppers would be shot down by ground fire limited the use of this air bridge to only the most critical circumstances.

DSS agents, officers in the DATT's office, and members of the Marine Security Guard contingent took turns watching over Higgins' body. There was ceremony to honor a fallen comrade. There was comfort in military protocol, a sense of reassurance. Higgins would have approved of the ceremony.

NEARLY A WEEK later the embassy was alerted once again. Just after dawn on December 27, 1991, an anonymous caller contacted Lebanese Security Service HQ instructing police to pick up a body near the Bourj el-Barajneh refugee camp cemetery along an airport access road. Bourj el-Barajneh was a predominantly Shiite municipality near the airport and also home to the Palestinian camp. It was a Hezbollah stronghold, though certain areas were administered by AK-47 edict courtesy of various factions of one Palestinian liberation front or another. The area was ground zero of the Red Zone no-go territories off-limits to all US personnel. The body had been thrown from a pickup truck at just after 1:00 on a cold, damp night. The cemetery was filled with weathered photos of Palestinian guerrillas killed in the fight against Israel. ███████████████ security specialists at the embassy would later conclude that Buckley had been buried there all along and hastily dug up to end once and for all Hezbollah's hostage-taking war against the United States.

By the time the Lebanese night commandant called the US Embassy at just before dawn, the responding police units had already brought the body to the American University Hospital. The notification to the embassy was brief, matter-of-fact. The duty agent quickly notified the RSO. The body had to be Buckley's.

Ra'ed confirmed it a few hours later following a quick trip to his contacts in the Shiite stretch of the capital. It was Friday, the Muslim Sabbath. Traffic in East Beirut was frenetically busy. Most of the journey, though, was through hostile territory, through areas controlled by militias and men carrying RPGs. The Nasty Boys motorcade never stopped for anything. The vehicles sliced through the divided city in record time.

The heavy wool blanket holding Buckley's remains was tattered and muddy. The body was decayed. It was clear that he had been dead for a very long time and buried in a grave that was in a location where there was poor drainage. Ben had been given a set of X-rays as a reference point to use when going to the hospital. The pathologist ordered X-rays so that the film could be used by the CIA to confirm the body's identity. Ben and the Nasty Boys were at the hospital all day. The X-rays were reviewed to match them with Buckley's dental records, which Ben had assembled in a file he had brought with him from the embassy. A broken right pelvis matched a skiing injury that Buckley had suffered years earlier.[5]

Ben looked at the bones and wondered what had happened to the Chief of Station nearly seven years earlier. What did the bastards do to him? How long did he survive? How did he survive at all? The bones didn't tell much of a story, Ben realized. The Green Beret deserved better. Call sign Bandit radioed back to the embassy that the body was, indeed, Buckley's. Ambassador Crocker had demanded to know immediately when the remains were positively identified.

Furious cable traffic burned up the wires between Beirut, Washington, DC, and Langley. The news feeds zigzagged across the city. The Beirut bureaus rushed B-roll footage with reporting from the hospital revealing word that Buckley's remains had been returned. An anonymous caller, speaking for Hezbollah's most ubiquitous calling card, the Islamic Jihad, told a Western news agency that it had "dumped Thursday night the body of American spy Buckley. We have, thus, fulfilled our pledge. The UN secretary general has to bring about the release of our brethren in Israel."[6]

The Nasty Boys motorcade raced back to the embassy, hoping to make it to the compound before the sun set into the Mediterranean. Like Higgins' casket earlier in the week, Buckley's coffin was draped in an American flag.[7]

THE AIR BRIDGE was summoned from RAF Base Akrotiri at dusk. Crocker had been friends with Buckley and he wasn't going to send his body back to United States territory without a hastily assembled honor guard to bring the two caskets to the landing pad to await the arrival of the Black Hawks. The ceremony was reserved and solemn. There were no bagpipes available; a bugler didn't blow taps. The procession consisted of marines in combat fatigues, army officers assigned to the DATT's office, and the security ███████████████ dressed in jeans and cowboy boots. Ambassador Crocker was stoic as he spoke of the sacrifices made by the two men who were about to embark on the final leg of their journey back home. The thumping cadence of rotor blades became louder as one Black Hawk came in for a landing while the other circled above.

Ben looked on as the marines and soldiers loaded the two caskets onto the army helicopter. The door gunner scanned nervously around the area, swinging his mounted M60D 7.62-by-51-millimeter machine gun to be ready to respond to any threat. The entourage that accompanied the bodies to the landing pad watched quietly as the Black Hawk lifted off and proceeded west. Storm clouds gathered to the west as the two choppers took off. A crack of thunder was heard in the distance.

18

FREE MEN

OVER AIR FORCE Base is home to the largest military mortuary in the Department of Defense, and has been used for processing military personnel killed in both war and peacetime; the remains of those killed overseas are traditionally brought to Dover so that remains can be identified before being transferred to their families and final resting places. The transfer of remains, according to the US Department of Defense definition, is not a ceremony but a process. And the process warranted that both William Buckley and William Higgins be transferred to the Charles C. Carson Center for Mortuary Affairs for a pathological examination and an autopsy. A senior Green Beret officer stood in front of the honor guard for Buckley. A senior Marine Corps officer presided over Higgins' casket. In the shadows and out of view, a small group of men from Langley closed their trench coats as they watched the proceedings in stone-cold silence.

Dental records reaffirmed the identity of Buckley's remains. Department of Defense pathologists attempted to determine the precise cause of death for William Buckley. They ran his bones through various forensic exams to search for evidence that could be used to reconstruct the final moments of the CIA Station Chief's life. The pathologists looked for any hints of gunshot wounds, punctures, blunt force trauma, and other signs of violence. Great care was taken to reconstruct the bones, but the pathologists were unable to agree on conclusive findings as to cause of death. The coroner's report was irrelevant to the men from Langley who stood by listening to the scientific step-by-step as it unfolded. The men knew that Buckley's death had been violent. He had been savagely murdered.

As with the autopsy of William Buckley, Air Force pathologists could not determine with any degree of certainty just what had killed Colonel Higgins. His body had been stored carefully for a while, they could determine, and then it had been held in a shallow, and somewhat damp, grave. There were physical signs that Colonel Higgins had been hanged, but that could have been postmortem. There were no gunshot wounds, no lacerations or punctures indicating a stabbing. But there were multiple signs of torture and abuse. The details were difficult to hear, horrific to comprehend. The men who had held Colonel Higgins had tortured him with a barbaric mania American prisoners of war had never been subjected to before. The news was infuriating and heartbreaking.*

---

*In April 2003, after lengthy and exhaustive efforts, Colonel Higgins was recognized as a prisoner of war, and posthumously awarded a Prisoner of War Medal.

* * *

ON THE MORNING of December 30, 1991, a week after their bodies had been returned, the United States government officially honored William Buckley and William Higgins. A select group of officials and journalists assembled at a hangar at Andrews Air Force Base, eight miles from the White House lawn; William Buckley's sisters, Maureen Moroney and Joyce Wing, along with Beverly Surette, were seated at the front of the gathering, as was Robin Higgins. The C-141 Starlifter that had flown the remains from Dover to Andrews parked behind them on the tarmac, providing a grand backdrop to the civilians who placed their hands over their hearts while the soldiers, sailors, airmen, and marines saluted. Marine pallbearers carried the two flag-draped coffins off the C-141. The Marine Corps band, bedecked in their scarlet full-dress coats, played "On Eagle's Wings"; the drum major, wearing the ornate sash known as a baldric across his chest, along with his bearskin headpiece and ornate mace, signaled the musicians with decisive precision. Higgins' coffin was taken from the plane to the accompaniment of Lee Greenwood's hit "God Bless the USA."[1] A Navy chaplain prayed for the two heroes of freedom while a Marine Corps honor guard in their dress blues lined up in two rows of twelve across a podium bearing the seal of the president of the United States. The skies were overcast and gray. General Carl E. Mundy Jr., the Marine Corps Commandant, presided.

CIA Director Robert Gates spoke first. Gates had been in the CIA since 1966 and he eulogized William Buckley; Gates was the Deputy Director of Intelligence when William Buckley was seized. Defense Secretary Richard Cheney spoke on behalf of the Department of Defense and for Lieutenant Colonel Higgins. Cheney was the only speaker who rendered a veiled threat toward the men responsible for

America's misery in Beirut. "An ugly chapter in terrorism is ending, and the lessons are clear," Cheney said as the winds on the tarmac blustered. "For its adherence, terrorism achieved nothing. For the people of Lebanon it only prolonged the violence that has destroyed their ancient land. For Americans, the hostage taking simply reaffirmed the importance of our resolve; and we will hold those who bear responsibility for these murders to account."[2]

Vice President Dan Quayle spoke last, and reminded everyone assembled that "all efforts should be invested to gain an accounting for all the missing, including Ron Arad."[3]

WILLIAM F. BUCKLEY was laid to rest later that afternoon at Arlington National Cemetery. A new headstone had been carved for the grave. It read: WILLIAM FRANCIS BUCKLEY; LT. COL.; U.S. ARMY; KOREA; VIETNAM; MAY 30, 1928; JUNE 3, 1985; LEBANON; SILVER STAR. The funeral was once again pure military, complete with a horse-drawn caisson, an Army honor guard, and a twenty-one-gun salute. Eight soldiers, in their Class A best, marched Buckley to Grave 346 in Section 59—the area in Arlington National Cemetery where twenty-two servicemen killed in Beirut in 1983 were also buried.[4] It is very likely that Buckley had come across many of these same young marines during his visit to the airport before the bombing that horrible October morning.

Colonel William R. Higgins was laid to rest in a separate ceremony, at the cemetery at the Marine Corps base in Quantico, Virginia. Marine Corps Commandant General Mundy presented Robin Higgins and their daughter Chrissy with the flag that had draped the coffin. He knelt before them to express his condolences and to show his respects to a family that embodied the internal iron of the Corps.[5]

There was a sense among some of those in attendance at the ceremonies that bone-chilling winter's day that the long and bloody ordeal of the American experience in Lebanon was over. As the last mourners left Arlington and Quantico, the ordeal was finally over. The twenty-one-gun salutes and the eulogies were over. The tombstones were a final punctuation mark giving closure to an America held at gunpoint by men it didn't understand, motives it couldn't comprehend, and tactics it couldn't imagine. A New Year was about to dawn, and for many—especially those in government—it was time to move on. It was an election year, after all.

But there were many in the hallways of CIA headquarters who seethed with the humiliating knowledge that one of their own, a station chief no less, had been captured and killed without anyone paying the price. Many old-timers at the CIA, men who played by the rigid rules set forth during the Cold War, knew that the spies didn't do enough to save William F. Buckley. Similar sentiments reverberated around the Pentagon. Friends of William Higgins wondered why the Joint Chiefs didn't simply authorize a raid to go into southern Lebanon and rescue him.

In Beirut and in southern Lebanon, the men responsible for America's nightmare asked these questions as well. Mughniyeh and his Iranian patrons wondered how much credence there actually was in Defense Secretary Cheney's warnings on the tarmac at Andrews, that "the United States [will] hold those who bear responsibility for these murders to account." They wondered when—if—the reckoning would happen. They knew that they were living on borrowed time. The desert proverb[6] that a bedouin who takes revenge after forty years has acted in haste was not lost on the men with blood on their hands.

SO KILL HIM . . .

THE STATE OF Israel did not get its captives back from Lebanon that cold and dreary December. Four Israeli soldiers were unaccounted for in Lebanon's murky human bazaar. Three soldiers—Staff Sergeant Zechariah Baumel, Staff Sergeant Zvi Feldman, and Staff Sergeant Yehuda Katz—went missing on June 11, 1982, during the tank battle against Syrian armored forces in the battle for Sultan Yakoub. There were many conflicting reports regarding the whereabouts and condition of the missing men, and the failure to recover them haunted Israeli intelligence.

Ron Arad's fate was just as agonizing and even more frustrating. Arad, already held captive for over five years, had been sold by villagers to Amal and then handed off as tribute to Hezbollah. The Israeli military maintains a sacrosanct contract with its soldiers that everything imaginable will be done to ensure that no one is ever left behind. This unwritten covenant is even more binding in terms of the pilots and aircrews that Israel dispatches far from its national frontiers on sorties against terrorist targets in Lebanon and against targets outside the envelope of regional range. Part of the reason the IAF is considered by many to be the best air force in the Middle East (some would say the world), able to achieve unchallenged aerial superiority and carry out spectacular operations like the Entebbe rescue and the bombing of Iraq's Osirak nuclear reactor, is that its airmen know that if they are shot down over enemy territory, Israel will bring medieval measures to secure their release. But airmen are also privy to state secrets of the highest order, so it was also a matter of state security that Arad be rescued.

Israel's predicament with Ron Arad mirrored America's—and its realization of the limits of its power. With the abductions of William Buckley and William Higgins, the United States at first tried covert measures, then covert arms trading, then downright bargaining to bring back its captives—dead and alive. Israel used military means to try to bring Arad home alive and not in a canvas satchel full of decaying bones. Sheikh Obeid's capture, it was hoped, would facilitate an expedient ending to Arad's third year as prisoner. But the effort failed.

The Mossad dedicated enormous resources in the attempt to locate Arad and it used Tevel, its international liaison division, to try to create some dialogue with Hezbollah to initiate a prisoner exchange. The German BND, in particular, had taken up the cause of negotiating through backdoor channels in Lebanon on behalf of Arad.[1] The Germans were deemed by Iran to be honest brokers. The clerics in Beirut proved uninterested in the outside overtures, and the Israelis were leery that Arad's fate would be decided by foreign spies. Israel's defense doctrine dictated that it deal with its challenges alone.

* * *

THE KIRYA, OR "Campus," is Israel's Pentagon. Situated in the heart of central Tel Aviv, the Kirya was once a series of British Army bungalows, a camp where German POWs were held during World War II, and developed into an enormous complex of high-rises, towers, office buildings, and underground operational nerve centers for the Israeli military. The Kirya abuts office buildings and tree-lined boulevards dotted with cafés filled with young conscripts wearing the olive and khaki uniforms of the IDF's branches of service and grabbing a quick lunch outside the base. The IDF General Staff is headquartered in the Kirya, as is the IAF and IDF/Navy, as is A'man. The Kirya was home to Major General Uri Saguy, a veteran reconnaissance officer and head of the military intelligence directorate. Ron Arad and Hezbollah topped his agenda.

Saguy, a seventh-generation Israeli with an endearing smile and a lanky frame, understood the military complexities of operations deep behind enemy lines. As the commander of Sayeret Golani during the War of Attrition, Saguy had led dozens of cross-border forays against entrenched Palestinian terror camps in Lebanon's south; he was severely wounded in 1971 as a battalion commander operating against Syrian commandos. Working the Ron Arad case consumed the analysts and operations commanders in A'man, and military intelligence was working on a brazen operation that, the IDF thought, would bring Hezbollah to its knees. They, along with the innovative planners in the IDF Operations Branch, and the commanders of Israel's top-tier special operations units, met regularly to concoct a feasible military solution to bring Ron Arad home at last.

Saguy and the other top commanders on the General Staff knew that Israel would have to be holding a winning hand to get Hezbollah to capitulate: either the IDF had to locate the safe house where Arad was being held so that a rescue raid could be organized, or the military had to seize something as important to Hezbollah as Arad was to Israel—something, or someone, they would trade for. All trails to Arad's whereabouts ran cold. It was deemed too risky to seize the organization's spiritual head, Sheikh Fadlallah, so three possible targets emerged: Hassan Nasrallah, Subhi al-Tufayli, and the organization's secretary-general, Abbas al-Musawi. The General Staff ultimately decided on Musawi and entrusted the mission to Israel's top two commando units: Sayeret Mat'kal, the elite General Staff Reconnaissance Unit; and Flotilla 13, the IDF/Navy's commando force. The operation was code-named *"Sha'at Ha'Layla,"* or "Operation Nighttime."

Planning an operation of this magnitude required intelligence and audacity. Musawi had to be snatched quietly and without collateral damage. His abduction was deemed a fitting dose of vengeance and deterrence to an organization that had made a name for itself by sacrificing young martyrs and grabbing innocent men off the streets. Work proceeded throughout the summer and autumn months of 1991 and intensified as winter neared, involving an all-out effort to monitor Musawi's movements. The return of the last American hostages in December 1991 convinced many in the hallways of the Kirya that time was fleeting if Arad was going to be brought home alive instead of in a coffin draped in the Star of David flag. RF-4E Phantom reconnaissance flights above Beirut and southern Lebanon increased. The high-altitude roar of the sorties became part of the soundtrack of the city. They could be heard at all times of the day and night. Patrons at the Bunker always knew something was in the works when the Israelis buzzed overhead.[2] No one heard the humming of the drones that constantly flew over Lebanon, especially when the cold winter winds whipped harshly.

* * *

SHEIKH ABBAS AL-MUSAWI was, perhaps, the most cautious of the top-tier of the Hezbollah hierarchy. Besides being a cleric, Musawi was a ruthless politician and a cunning military commander. Born in 1952, Musawi was old enough to be seen by many as a possible successor to Sheikh Fadlallah and young enough to take the reins of a growing military force whose lieutenants, men like Mughniyeh, defined an aggressive brand of diabolical that combined with highly skilled execution. Like many of the men who would emerge to lead Hezbollah, Musawi grew up in poverty in a small village in the eastern Beka'a Valley, where young men worked the land, became thugs and thieves, or entered the seminary. On his eighteenth birthday, Musawi traveled to the Shiite holy city of Najaf, Iraq, to begin an intensive eight-year education at the *hawza*, or seminary, belonging to Muhammad Baqir al-Sadr, an influential cleric who founded that country's religious Da'wa Party.[3] Students of al-Sadr like al-Musawi received a crash course in the harsh realities of counterintelligence tradecraft under the relentless menace of secret police scrutiny. Shiite clerics and their followers were always under surveillance by internal security agencies, always suspected of subversion and counterrevolutionary conspiracies. To remain alive yet keep their activities moving forward, these men learned how to do everything in a whisper, out of view, and within small and compartmentalized communities. Students, both innocent and guilty of subversive dialogue, were routinely rounded up and tortured; some were executed on even the slightest suspicion of religious-inspired sedition. Surviving this experience was as much an achievement as being ordained a cleric. Musawi returned to Lebanon in 1978, and emerged as one of the most influential founders of Hezbollah four years later. Musawi's teacher, Muhammad Baqir al-Sadr, was executed by Saddam Hussein's henchmen in 1980; reportedly, a spike was driven through his head.[4]

Men like Musawi were masters at secrecy. They didn't use telephones or move around much. Messengers, always blood relatives, carried messages back and forth. The bodyguards, and there were legions of them, were also connected by blood; the clans were impenetrable to ███████████████████████ intelligence services around the region that wanted men like Musawi dead. But Hezbollah's leaders were also politicians. They still had to press the flesh and show their constituents that they weren't afraid of assassins. They still had to be filmed attending the funerals of martyrs killed fighting the Israelis so that a soundtrack could be applied to the slickly edited clips that would air on Al-Manar Television, and then be proliferated throughout the mosques and markets on crudely copied VHS tapes. Musawi's day-to-day duties warranted that he occasionally leave his bunker. "Even terrorist commanders who live in the shadows must emerge for air sometime," a retired Israeli intelligence officer explained.[5]

One such event was the eighth anniversary of Ragheb Harb's assassination by Israeli forces. A small memorial ceremony had been hastily set up in the village of Jebchit in the Beka'a Valley by Hezbollah chieftains to commemorate the death of the man known as the "Sheikh of Martyrs."[6] The intelligence concerning this event came from an unlikely source. On Thursday, February 13, a translator in A'man's open-source intelligence-gathering unit came across a paid infomercial on the Voice of the People, the local Lebanese Communist Party station in Sidon: "Hezbollah will hold a rally on Sunday, February 16, at 0900, in Jebchit to honor the death of Sheikh Harb."[7]

News of the event ignited a series of rapid responses inside the Kirya.

Colonels from a myriad of units and commands began to accelerate the preparation for the envisioned snatch and grab. The intelligence required for such an operation, especially if the strike was to take place at the memorial service, was all-encompassing, from the basic A to Z of Shiite mourning to the specific ceremony involved in honoring the widow and the family[8] to the weather forecast for the day. The plan all along was for the kidnapping to take place south of the Litani River; operations closer to the Israeli frontier were deemed safer. But Operation Nighttime was still in its earliest planning stages and, as Brigadier General Danny Arditi, the head of special operations inside A'man, assessed, possibly a year away from being a viable reality that could be presented to the IDF Chief of Staff and the Minister of Defense for approval.[9] This, according to journalist Ronen Bergman, was the source of a serious miscommunication.[10] Brigadier General Arditi and the other high-ranking officers of the Research Department who met with General Saguy were convinced that the operational preparations being arranged to cover Musawi's attendance in Jebchit on February 16 were a dry run, a training model for the eventual abduction. The operation was an exercise, nothing more.

Major General Saguy understood the opportunity differently. According to his bureau, the dry run could easily become operational if the circumstances were right—not as a snatch and grab, but rather as an aerial assassination strike.[11] A flight of McDonnell Douglas AH-64 Apache helicopter gunships was ordered to be ready in Israel's north Sunday morning. The Apache pilots, along with many of the combat elements of Operation Nighttime, went home on Sabbath leave that Friday night. The analysts and Lebanon Desk specialists in A'man stayed at their desks. They would be there all weekend.

* * *

IT HAD BEEN a terrible Sabbath for the IDF. At 23:50 on February 14, three masked Israeli Arabs from the nascent Iranian-supported Palestinian Islamic Jihad killed three soldiers, new immigrants from the former Soviet Union, as they slept in their army tent in northern Israel. The fact that terrorists had infiltrated an IDF base was bad enough, but this attack was unique in its savagery—the terrorists had used knives, axes, and pitchforks to kill the three soldiers. The terrorists had also stolen four assault rifles before disappearing into the darkness.[12]

On Sunday, February 16, Major General Saguy arrived at the Kirya shortly after 7:00 a.m. He had worked the collateral fallout from the Night of the Pitchfork; the Islamic Jihad, financed by the Iranians to bring a Sunni version of Hezbollah to the West Bank and Gaza, was becoming a growing concern. A copy of *Yedioth Aharonoth*, Israel's leading newspaper, was waiting for him on his desk: the front page showed pictures of the three butchered soldiers under the headline THE MURDER AND THE DISGRACE. Saguy received an update from the team of Hezbollah specialists who had been sequestered over the weekend. The young soldiers, some of them still in their teens, looked exhausted. They had spent the day focused on the live feeds from Lebanon and making last-minute preparations for the monitoring exercise of Sheikh Harb's memorial in Jebchit. The weather was cool in Lebanon, but signs of an early spring were everywhere. Flight conditions were ideal for the drones cutting a path across the Lebanese skies.

The drone launched at 9:00 a.m. first hovered silently over the Hezbollah strongholds of south Beirut before being redirected south along the coastal highway, and then east across the Zahrani River and toward Jebchit. Word had come down through unnamed sources that

Musawi was already in Jebchit, but this could not be confirmed. At 10:30 the drone's operator shifted the unmanned aerial vehicle over a narrow dirt path and what appeared to be a four-vehicle motorcade: a white Range Rover lead car, two dark royal blue Mercedes sedans (the principal's vehicle and a decoy), followed by another white Range Rover follow car. Most of the officers watching the feed in real time in the Kirya felt in their bones that they had located Musawi. In Lebanon, warlords and drug kingpins were the only ones who traveled in such high-speed and heavily armed packages. The fact that the motorcade stopped in front of the local Husaniya, the Islamic community center in Jebchit, all but confirmed that Musawi had, indeed, been located.

At noon, IDF Chief of Staff Lieutenant General Ehud Barak returned to his office following a meeting with the defense cabinet in Jerusalem. Barak had grown up in Sayeret Mat'kal, the IDF's elite long-range intelligence-gathering and counterterrorist commando unit. Short and stocky with a devilish grin and striking dark hair, Barak was Israel's most experienced special operations officer; he was the most decorated soldier in Israeli history. Barak had been kept out of the loop about the ongoing A'man operation in Jebchit and he went about his business as scheduled. Major General Saguy requested that Barak join an exercise in progress in the "War Room" deep underneath the General Staff HQ building in the Kirya complex. When the IDF Chief of Staff entered the top secret command-and-control center, it looked as if Israel was going to war. Before he could ask, "What the hell is going on?" Saguy sounded off a bullet-point list detailing Musawi's itinerary for the day. Barak was angry, then intrigued. This was the first that he had heard about the "exercise" that was under way.[13]

The memorial service in Jebchit ended at precisely 13:00. A large procession of individuals could be seen emerging from the Husaniya and then dispersing into the village. Many made their way on foot to the village cemetery where Harb was buried. The size of the crowd, some visibly carrying weapons, only reinforced to many watching how difficult Operation Nighttime would be to pull off without there being significant civilian casualties. As the conscripts and officers gazed at the video screen, they could make out a figure, only a fuzzy outline on a screen, entering one of the Mercedes vehicles in the convoy parked out front. The convoy moved at top speed and cut across Jebchit, heading east, to join other mourners at the cemetery. Both Barak and Saguy were men of action, used to seeing an opportunity on the extended battlefield and then terminating it with innovative force. Both men began seriously to set the machinery in place to turn the exercise into a mission. Senior officers from A'man's Research Division were mortified by the developments. "Nighttime" was an exercise. Four AH-64 Apache crews were briefed at an airfield in northern Israel.[14] The thirty-millimeter rounds were counted and the AGM-114 Hellfire missiles brought to their launchers. Tel Aviv was notified that the four AH-64s were fueled and armed. The last Hellfires were loaded onto their pods and the fire control computers checked at 13:35—the same time that Musawi walked through the front door of Harb's home in order to pay his respects to the widow. One of the most closely guarded secrets of the day was that a flow of intelligence tracking Musawi emanated from an agent,[15] a deep-plant HUMINT source, who had had eyes on target.

The decision to move was up to the politicians, and both Barak and Saguy answered to Defense Minister Moshe Arens. Born in Lithuania in 1925, Arens and his parents emigrated to the United States in 1939; they settled in New York City and Arens served in the US Army during the Second World War. After moving to the newly formed Jewish

State in 1948, Arens returned to the United States and graduated from MIT. He worked in aeronautics before returning to Israel to teach and work in the country's fledgling aircraft industry. Arens was as tough-as-nails as they came, but he had a unique analytical mind in processing strategic opportunities and tactical realities.

Arens was fine with the idea of eliminating Musawi but expressed concern about the possible collateral damage. There was fear that passengers in the convoy included Lebanese politicians, possibly even Iranian emissaries, and that an air strike would have grave international political repercussions. Prime Minister Yitzhak Shamir's office was notified. The seventy-seven-year-old Israeli prime minister was hard-core and hard-line. The Belarus-born Shamir was one of the leaders of the notorious Lehi Group, responsible for (among other acts) the assassination of Lord Moyne, the British Secretary of State for the Colonies, in November 1944. He was also a veteran of Mossad's covert operations, eventually commanding Operation Damocles, the assassination campaign against German scientists helping Egypt develop an indigenous ballistic program.[16] Short and squat with Brillo-pad eyebrows, Shamir was no-nonsense and hawkish, yet very old-world European. When the IDF Chief of Staff called the prime minister's military secretary to seek authorization for the strike against Musawi, Shamir was midway through an afternoon nap.

Musawi's motorcade was set to depart Jebchit for the race back to the Lebanese capital. It was 15:30.[17] It would soon be dark, making the aerial sortie virtually impossible to carry out.

Sheikh Abbas Musawi's motorcade sprinted out of Jebchit just as it had arrived, leaving a cloud of debris in its high-speed wake. At 15:55 Prime Minister Shamir returned to his office and took a call on the secure line from the Kirya. The call from Chief of Staff Barak was the first that he had heard of the efforts against Musawi, but it took

Shamir only seconds to react. "So kill him," he ordered his military commander.[18]

The Apaches were airborne within minutes. Two Apaches raced toward the suspected path that Musawi's motorcade would take to Beirut, while a second pair flew out over the Mediterranean just in case the vehicles escaped the gauntlet. The plan called for the ambush to take place on a deserted stretch of road in order to minimize the chances of collateral damage. A drone connected the pilots and a small theater of officers in the War Room to the unfolding events in southern Lebanon. It took ten minutes for the Apache flight led by Lieutenant Colonel A. (an alias) to identify the convoy shooting west along the main road connecting Nabatiyah and the Zahrani Bridge on the coastal highway. The darkening skies of dusk loomed near.

Along the open road, the vehicles drove fast, without any regard for the traffic in the opposite lane. A 150-meter gap separated each vehicle in the high-speed convoy. Lieutenant Colonel A.'s Apache was five kilometers out when the first Hellfire was launched. The convoy neared the junction at the entrance to the village of Toufahta when the second Mercedes, the one carrying Musawi, erupted into a bright orange fireball. The follow car made a J-turn to escape the kill zone, but the white Range Rover was hit by a Hellfire. Several men inside managed to escape the blast and A.'s number two raked them with a dedicated burst of thirty-millimeter cannon fire. The decoy Mercedes immediately turned south along a dirt road to evade the Israeli attack helicopters, and managed to outmaneuver a Hellfire and hide near a structure, but a Hellfire fired by the Apache flight that was on call over the Mediterranean and had now joined the battle turned the sedan into glowing shards of metal and acrid black smoke. The driver of the lead Range Rover, trained to drive in dignitary-protection courses in Damascus and Tehran, raced toward the coastal highway at a speed in excess of 120 miles per hour. He had hoped to reach the bridge over the Zahrani River, but took a direct hit a kilometer from the coastal highway. The fires from the burning vehicles illuminated the darkening skies. The smoke billowing skyward was visible from the terraces belonging to the local Hezbollah commanders in Jebchit. It was 16:10.

IDF Chief of Staff Barak grabbed the shoulder of one of the officers in the War Room and smiled. He said, "Well done, job well done," as he left the underground command center to return to his office.[19]

Lieutenant Colonel A. and his flight of Apaches returned to base shortly before sunset. It was Israel's first-ever targeted assassination of a terrorist leader using an attack helicopter.

ISRAEL'S INTELLIGENCE HAD been spot-on. Sheikh Abbas Musawi had, indeed, been killed in the exercise turned hit. But Musawi's wife, Siham, and the couple's six-year-old son, Hussein, had also been killed in the missile strike—the two were sitting in the back seat of the blue Mercedes 280 when the Hellfire punched through the sedan. The collateral damage that had caused so much consternation and concern among senior IDF officers was worse than imagined. News broke in Tel Aviv and Beirut shortly after the attack. It also broke, like a bullet shattering the norm, in Langley and in Tehran.

No tears were shed at CIA headquarters for Abbas Musawi. He was an arch-terrorist, a man whose hands were soaked in the blood of a great many Americans: the CIA ████████ at the first embassy blast, the marines at the airport, William Buckley, and William Higgins. Musawi was one of the Iranian pillars in Hezbollah and he had been one of a handful of young men to lead the Party of God's bloody war against the United States and Israel. Before his death, Sheikh Musawi addressed a group of armed followers and stated, "Any notion of an American peace is submission to America's will."[20] ███████████ ███ heard of the assassination through his local contacts ███████████████████████████ ████████████████████████████████ were the first to hear of the Israeli Apache strike against the motorcade. Hezbollah radio stations began to play dirges and prayers. Men milled about the streets of south Beirut to play tag with tidbits of information and rumor that swelled among the Hezbollah faithful. Security precautions at the US Embassy were enhanced. ████████████████ the RSO, and the Marine Security Guards knew that there would be hell to pay. The Nasty Boys' shift leader phoned his wife to tell her he might not be coming home for a few days.

The CIA ████████████████████ was able to see Israeli radio and TV reports to learn details of the IAF strike. News broke quickly and proudly. This was not an operation that Israel could deny. To the contrary, Prime Minister Shamir was eager for the world to see how Israel dealt with terror chieftains; the IAF—and McDonnell Douglas—wanted word to get out about the all-powerful Apache in Israeli service. While the State Department drafted an ALDAC security notification of the hit, which went to every diplomat and consulate in the world, ████████████████████████████████, tens of thousands of copies of *Yedioth Aharonoth* were rolling off the printing presses with the morning edition. The front page featured a photo of the smoldering wreck of the Mercedes next to a photo of a bearded Musawi in his black cleric's garb. The headline read: THE HEAD OF HEZBOLLAH WAS TERMINATED next to a brief quote from IDF Chief of Staff Barak vowing that Israel would continue to pursue the heads of terror ██ ██

inside scoop was all over Israeli and Lebanese television.

The printing presses were busy in Beirut as well. Hezbollah intelligence officers scanned through the Musawi family albums to find photos of the sheikh, as well as of his wife and son, so that the propaganda posters could be printed and the photos broadcast in the Arab media.

Tens of thousands of mourners lined the procession from the mosque in south Beirut to the cemetery near the airport where the eight would be laid to rest. Hezbollah moral guidance officers had been busy distributing placards and banners bearing a black stenciled image of Musawi on a bloodred background. Many of the men in the crowd were armed; some, especially those walking point toward the graveyard, fired magazine-emptying bursts into the air. The stream of mourners walked with their fists raised behind the eight silver metal coffins. Many chanted, "Oh God, wipe Israel and America out of existence!"[21]

Many of the mourners had arrived in Beirut hours earlier on a special flight from Tehran. Musawi had been close to Iranian Supreme Leader Sayyed Ali Hosseini Khamenei, and Tehran had put together a large contingent of diplomats to mourn alongside their Lebanese brothers, spies, and special operations commander to plot the inevitable revenge. The assassination of Sheikh Abbas Musawi was a point of no return for Tehran and Hezbollah. Since the creation of the organization in 1982, Shiite blood in Lebanon was no longer spilled without cost, and Israel would pay a steep price for killing Musawi.

Before the last shovelful of dirt was poured over Musawi's grave, representatives from the Iranian Revolutionary Guard Corps and the Quds Force met with Imad Mughniyeh and his special operations commanders to discuss the Hezbollah response. The meeting was held in the Iranian Embassy, situated two kilometers north of the Beirut International Airport perimeter fence.

With so much devastation already on his CV, Mughniyeh's stock in the eyes of the Iranians was already high. Avenging Musawi's assassination would give him the ability to spread his reach. After all, in response to Musawi's death, Sheikh Fadlallah promised, "There would be much more violence and much more blood would flow."[22]

Hezbollah fired dozens of Katyusha rockets into northern Israel following Musawi's assassination. Israeli military commanders thought that the muted response was a welcome indication of how devastating Musawi's death was to Hezbollah's overall capabilities. The Katyushas were expected. After all, as the intelligence specialists liked to remind their non-Arabic-speaking counterparts, the old Arab saying "If you are going to play with a cat, then you should expect to be scratched" aptly applied to the Party of God.

THE ISRAELI EMBASSY in Argentina was located at 910 Arroyo Street in the Retiro section of Buenos Aires, one of the ritziest in the Argentinean capital. The chancery, a four-story building that looked like a colonial headquarters or the stately home of a duchess, was one of the landmarks that enhanced the area's European character. Small shops dotted the narrow tree-lined streets; the quaint area was a reminder of the country's Spanish heritage. The embassy did not have any bollards or concrete barriers providing setback or added protection. These measures would have interfered with the ambiance of the neighborhood. There was no parking in front of the building, of course. Embassy security officers patrolled the grounds to make sure that suspicious vehicles were nowhere near them.

At 14:45 on March 17, 1992, a red 1985 Ford F-100 pickup truck with a white fiberglass bed drove up on the curb with both of its passenger-side wheels and exploded after driving into a tree. The car was two meters away from the embassy wall at the time of the explosion. Much of the façade and the structure behind the main entrance disappeared into a fireball of devastation. The orange flames were soon covered by an acrid cloud of smoke, and rubble was strewn hundreds of yards away. The mushroom cloud of smoke and the fire could be seen throughout the city. The suicide bomber behind the wheel had parked at a nearby lot for well over an hour before setting out toward his target.

The F-100 had been crammed with between 225 and 345 kilograms of high explosives; the embassy had no center beams and crumbled like a sandcastle that had been smashed by a mighty kick.

Fire and medical crews who rushed to the kill zone seemed overwhelmed by the destruction. Twenty-nine people were killed in the explosion and the embassy's collapse, including four Israeli envoys and four local employees of the embassy. Approximately 250 people, including ten Israelis, were injured. It was, to that time, the worst terrorist attack in Argentinean history.

A week before the blast, Shin Bet Director Yaakov Peri had been in Buenos Aires meeting with his counterparts in the Argentinean intelligence agency,[23] the Secretaría de Inteligencia de Estado, known by its legendary acronym, SIDE. His trip had been a coincidence, a meet and greet to secure mutual cooperation. There had been no terrorist alerts before the blast; there were no warnings.

Hours after the blast the Islamic Jihad Organization in Beirut claimed credit for the bombing. "We hereby declare with all pride that the operation of the martyr infant Hussein is one of our continuing strikes against the criminal Israeli enemy in an open-ended war which will not cease until Israel is wiped out of existence," the statement read. "He [the bomber] pounded like a bolt of lightning on a terrorist Zionist base in Argentina, obliterating it in a split second."[24]

Just to hammer home their culpability, the group released a video-tape taken by the surveillance team that had gathered intelligence on the target.[25] Local police patrols were oblivious to their presence.

Iranian intelligence had a strong network of sleeper cells through-out South America. Hundreds of thousands of Lebanese and Syrian expatriates lived on the continent, a majority of them Shiites with sympathies to Hezbollah. Shiite communities thrived in Argentina and Brazil, in Venezuela and Colombia. The nuts-and-bolts planning for the operation occurred in the tri-border region where the Para-guayan city of Ciudad del Este, the Argentinean city of Puerto Iguazú, and the Brazilian town of Foz do Iguaçu all meet. The F-100 used in the bombing had been purchased just eight days after Musawi's assas-sination.[26]

Hezbollah—and Iran—had transmitted a sinister message with the rubble, debris, and death at 910 Arroyo Street. It had a global reach, one closing in on the same time zone as Washington, DC.

PURGATORY

WHEN A POWERFUL bomb hidden inside a Ford Econoline van exploded in the parking lot underneath the World Trade Center at 12:18 p.m. on February 23, 1993, suspicion was at first directed against Hezbollah. Such attacks, after all, were the Party of God's time-tested modus operandi. When investigators uncovered that the World Trade Center bombing was the handiwork of Sunni Muslims— Arab immigrants to the United States and members of the Afghan Arabs, a precursor to al-Qaeda, transnational holy warriors fighting a global jihad on behalf of a mysterious chieftain named Osama bin Laden—CIA focus shifted to new battlefields and far from Lebanon and the fight against Hezbollah.

Lebanon was still a major preoccupation for Israel, however. Israeli forces were fighting a lethal and often seemingly endless guerrilla war against fanaticism-fueled Hezbollah suicide squads. Reports of soldiers killed and wounded in suicide bombings and from IEDs became more frequent on the nightly news. The Israeli occupation of southern Lebanon was thick and muddled, like similar quagmires that other nations could not extricate themselves from. Lebanon had also come to Israel.

In the winter of 1992, Israeli prime minister Yitzhak Rabin ordered the deportation of 405 members of the Harakat al-Muqawamah al-Islamiyyah, or Islamic Resistance Movement, a Muslim Brotherhood offshoot known to the world as Hamas. Hamas terrorists had perpetrated a series of primitive but bloody attacks, including the kidnapping of soldiers hitchhiking home. In December 1992, following the kidnapping and murder of a Border Guard sergeant, Rabin deported the organization's leadership in the West Bank and Gaza Strip to the no-man's-land of southern Lebanon that was north of Israeli lines. The men, some of whom were engineers and doctors, others American green card holders, hunkered down in a desolate valley where they were educated by Hezbollah and Iranian Islamic Revolutionary Guard Corps officers about suicide tactics, explosives, and the ways and means to bring a guerrilla campaign of blood and destruction to Israel's cities. In an attempt to forward Middle East peace, US president Bill Clinton placed enormous political pressure on Prime Minister Rabin to return the 405 to their homes. Rabin relented. A little more than a year later, on April 6, 1994, a Hamas suicide bomber blew himself up near the central bus station in the northern Israeli city of Afula. Eight people died in the blast; scores more were wounded. Hezbollah had exported the explosive fabric of Shiite Beirut into the very heartland of the Jewish State.

THE SPYMASTERS WHO sat behind the fortified doors inside Mossad headquarters had spent many a sleepless night pondering the means and the method by which they could somehow bring Ron Arad home.

The same was true for the officers who worked for A'man, Israeli military intelligence. Ron Arad was a painful reminder that Iran and Hezbollah had humiliated Israel's vaunted intelligence and military capabilities. For eight years, Ron Arad's wife, Tammy, provided an eloquent and heartfelt reminder that business could not continue as usual while one of Israel's best and brightest remained a captive in the clutches of a ruthless enemy. The end of the Western hostage crisis in Lebanon only reinforced Israel's concern that Arad would soon be forgotten, chalked up as a tragic yet acceptable combat casualty.

But that fate was unacceptable to many in the Mossad and military hierarchy. When the remains of both William Buckley and William Higgins were finally returned to the United States, the sense was that the tragedy of Ron Arad was now solely an Israeli issue and no longer part of a more complex Middle Eastern reality of Iran's proxies holding men hostage and bartering them off. There was always the belief in the American and Israeli intelligence communities that Buckley had been transferred, even if for a brief time, to Iran for advanced interrogation. FBI reports, heavily redacted, suggested as much; one report claimed that "Buckley had been housed and interrogated in Lebanon, Syria and finally Tehran, Iran, during his captivity. Buckley is believed to have died of a heart attack in a Tehran hospital following prolonged torture."[2] Those same fears were held for Arad. The Israelis used the West German intelligence service, the BND, to enter into back-channel negotiations with the Iranians concerning Arad's release, but the covert communications led nowhere. Sayeret Mat'kal had already seized Sheikh Obeid; the IAF had assassinated Abbas Musawi. Still Arad was missing. Imad Mughniyeh was under deep cover, always watching his back, in the Shiite maze of south Beirut where he operated and was always protected; his only travels were to the safe precincts of Damascus or Tehran, where he was always afforded a protective detail and a motorcade that raced from airport to barracks at Le Mans speed. Israel's intelligence services searched for a key figure in the kidnapping apparatus who would know where Arad was and who might also be high enough up the ladder of command to be worth an exchange. Israeli officials were determined not to bring Arad back to Israel in a box, like Buckley and Higgins. In the spring of 1994, the name Mustafa Dirani emerged.

Mustafa Dirani had been one of the few Shiites allowed to serve in the Lebanese Armed Forces, eventually working as a military intelligence officer. When Israel invaded Lebanon in 1982, Dirani shed his uniform and fought alongside Sunni and Palestinian forces; he was critically wounded in the battles along the coastal highway and thereafter walked with a limp and the assistance of a cane.[3] Dirani served as head of security for the Amal Shiite militia, and took personal charge of Ron Arad when the IAF navigator was forced to parachute over southern Lebanon. Dirani, crippled and opportunistic, saw a more promising future as an operative in the pro-Iranian Hezbollah and he defected, taking Arad with him. Dirani sold Arad to the Iranian Islamic Revolutionary Guard for a king's ransom of three hundred thousand American dollars.[4]

Dirani's file in Israeli military intelligence was thick and extensive. He was an essential cog in Hezbollah's kidnapping machine and his network was composed of clan members who were veteran cutthroats involved in all sorts of illicit activity around southern Lebanon and the Beka'a. In December 1988, a force of Sayeret Mat'kal commandos was inserted into southern Lebanon to kidnap four members of Dirani's operation.[5] A'man chief Major General Uri Saguy and IDF Chief of Staff Lieutenant General Ehud Barak ordered the special operations components inside the IDF command to put a plan together. Over the course of months the idea of seizing Dirani went from an idea scribbled on a napkin, to a conceptual blueprint, to a full-blown operational model. The IDF computer that designates coded cover names for such cross-border raids dubbed the operation "Cobra Sting."

On the night of May 2, 1994, a Sayeret Mat'kal task force was flown by CH-53 heavy transport helicopters to Dirani's village of Qasr Naba, near the Beka'a Valley's provincial capital of Zahlé, some fifty miles from Israel's northern border. The commandos raced toward the village on foot. The homes were silent and darkened. Dirani's two-story house was one of the largest in Qasr Naba.

Abdel Karim Dirani, a relative living in the clan's bastion, told a Lebanese news crew that rushed to Qasr Naba the following morning that the Israeli commandos stormed the building at precisely 2:00 a.m. Several of Dirani's bodyguards were asleep on the sofas in the living room and they were quickly subdued by the assault force. Ali Dirani, Mustafa's young son, remembered the men silently entering his room and asking where his father was. The commandos knew the names of everyone in the house and where everyone slept. Dirani's children were brought to a central area where they could be guarded. Dirani's wife was also moved to where the operators could secure her; one of the Israeli commandos wrapped her in a blanket in order to protect her modesty.

Dirani was alone in his bed, fast asleep and wearing summer pajamas. Dirani slept with a nickel-plated semiautomatic pistol near his pillow, but as he reached for it the commandos quickly subdued him.[6] They gagged Dirani and bound his hands and feet. Some of the operators screamed at Dirani, their weapons aimed at his head, demanding to know where Ron Arad was.[7] They reportedly threatened to harm his family if he did not disclose the location of the Israeli airman. But Dirani, resigned to his fate, just looked back at the commandos with an arrogant glare of defiance.

The Mat'kal commandos grabbed computer disks, files, and note-books in the apartment. The commandos, Israeli television reported, searched the house for a specific videocassette that they knew existed.[8]

The entire operation took less than five minutes. The Israeli task force flew back to Israel over a circuitous low-altitude route mapped out to evade Syrian radars. The helicopters were met with intermittent antiaircraft fire as they flew over the Lebanese coast.

Arabic-speaking specialists sifted through the material seized from Dirani's home. Dirani himself, according to foreign reports, was held in a top secret Israeli prison called "Facility 1391"; according to these accounts, the location has been airbrushed from Israeli aerial imagery and deleted from maps.[9] Israeli interrogators introduced themselves to Dirani for what would be lengthy and often difficult question-and-answer sessions. The abduction of Dirani was viewed as a brilliant move in order to expedite Ron Arad's release. Even Benjamin Netanyahu, the head of the Likud opposition, praised Prime Minister Rabin for his decisiveness and resolve in trying to bring back the Israeli airman at any cost.

Mustafa Dirani was known in Hebrew as an *egoz kashe*, or a "tough nut." Israeli intelligence officers who interviewed him found him un-cooperative and defiant. Reportedly, the interrogators from Unit 504 used physical pressure on Dirani. One officer, known as Captain George, was alleged to have sodomized Dirani with a stick. The inter-rogations continued without letup. Dirani was suspected of having helped warehouse several of the hostages who had been seized by Mughniyeh's men and then shuffled from safe house to safe house, and American counterterrorist officials were very interested in interrogat-ing him. Dirani had long been a suspect in William Higgins' abduc-tion, torture, and murder, and he was also believed to have been one of the Hezbollah commanders who boarded the hijacked TWA 847 once it landed in Beirut,[10] so the FBI wanted to know about Dirani's role in the murder of Robert Dean Stethem.

MUSTAFA DIRANI WASN'T abducted solely as a bargaining chip. He was a ruthless thug and a psychopath, but his type were a dime a dozen in the villages of the Beka'a. Israel seized him because Ron Arad had passed through his hands alive, and the Israelis tried as hard as a nation could to piece together a path by which they could locate Arad and definitively deal with those who held him—or his corpse—captive. Dirani was, though, a symbol and a son of the clans of the south. Both the Mossad and A'man knew some sort of Shiite statement would follow. The Shin Bet ordered Israeli diplomatic posts around the world to be on high alert.[11]

At 9:53 on the morning of July 18, 1994, a suicide bomber driving a Renault Trafic van crammed with six hundred pounds of explosives crashed into the five-story Argentine Israelite Mutual Association headquarters in a commercial section of Buenos Aires. The AMIA was a center of community life for much of the Jewish population of the Argentinean capital. The van had been modified with new rear-axle shock absorbers and tires to be able to handle the extra weight of the explosive payload and still negotiate the stop-and-go rigors of Buenos Aires traffic.[12] The bomb had been carefully constructed as a shaped charge for maximum destructive yield. The bomb's explosively formed penetrator dispatched a glob of molten metal toward a specific kill zone. The air blast caused by the powerful explosion could topple almost any building, especially one of brick-and-masonry construction like the AMIA. The devastation was catastrophic: eighty-five people were killed in the bombing and another three hundred were critically wounded. The building collapsed in a cloud of fire and debris. The streets surrounding the AMIA building resembled the avenues of

Berlin at the height of the Allied air offensive during the Second World War. Rubble was strewn hundreds of feet away. Cars and people were on fire. The AMIA center was only twenty city blocks from the bombed-out crater that had once been the Israeli Embassy.

The Argentinean security services and the Policía Federal Argentina, the national federal police, embarked on an investigation of the bombing. The Mossad and the Shin Bet also sent investigators; the IDF sent a search-and-rescue team to sift through the smoldering rubble and twisted rebar for survivors. Two Diplomatic Security Service agents from the Protective Intelligence Division and a technician from the Bureau of Alcohol, Tobacco, and Firearms were dispatched by the US government to spearhead the investigation, along with representatives from the FBI.

A vast Iranian-financed and Lebanese-led Shiite terror network had facilitated the blast, through multiple terrorist cells, controlled by Iranian intelligence, the Islamic Revolutionary Guard, and criminal enterprises in the tri-border area connecting Paraguay, Argentina, and Brazil;* Hezbollah clerics had begun to dispatch emissaries to this lawless center of smuggling and narcotics as early as the 1980s, when Israeli forces were involved in operations in and around Beirut. The Shiite network in South America was vast and traveled from the halls of power in Venezuela to the beaches of Ipanema. Investigations would link several high-ranking Iranian intelligence officials to the

---

* According to "Terrorist and Organized Crime Groups in the Tri-Border Area (TBA) of South America: A Report Prepared by the Federal Research Division, Library of Congress under an Interagency Agreement with the Crime and Narcotics Center Director of Central Intelligence, July 2003," other criminal groups that were operational and influential in the tri-border area included the Russian Mafia, the Chinese Triads, and Colombian cocaine cartels.

bombing, along with one senior member of the Hezbollah special operations hierarchy: Imad Mughniyeh.[13]

The AMIA bombing was a clear and unequivocal statement by Iran that its reach—with Mughniyeh's trigger finger—was global.

IMAD MUGHNIYEH GREW bolder with each new attack. The bloodshed he orchestrated elevated his status. Each success made him more ambitious, and all the more cunning and ruthless. He was a spymaster's dream come true. Mughniyeh was rewarded by the Islamic Revolutionary Guard with rank and privilege. He became Iran's Lebanese ambassador of terror, though he limited his travels to locations where he knew he would be safe.

In April 1995, Mughniyeh traveled to Khartoum to attend the biannual Popular Arab Islamic Conference hosted by Sudanese president Hassan Abdallah al-Turabi. The Sudanese strongman was eager to use his impoverished African nation as a regional hub for Islamic terror and he allowed groups like Hamas, Hezbollah, the Palestine Islamic Jihad, and al-Qaeda to use his nation's resources at will. In hindsight, it is almost inconceivable to imagine a target-rich setting where men like Osama bin Laden and Imad Mughniyeh were together in the conference hall of a plush Western hotel. Convicted al-Qaeda member Ali Mohamed testified in court that he helped arrange a 1993 meeting between Mughniyeh and bin Laden in Khartoum, Sudan.[14] Clearly, the al-Qaeda leader was impressed by Mughniyeh's earlier tactics of simultaneous suicide truck bombings against sensitive targets.

The PAIC, as the conference was known, was not a closely guarded secret. The spies who worked out of the foreign embassies in the dusty city of five million inhabitants on the confluence of the White Nile, flowing north from Lake Victoria, and the Blue Nile, flowing west from Ethiopia, knew all about the gathering. President al-Turabi's state security men, sinister thugs hiding behind dark mirrored glasses, flooded the capital and the area near the Western hotels when the delegates arrived; al-Turabi's AK-47-toting commandos were everywhere to make sure nothing disrupted the proceedings.

▆▆▆▆▆▆▆▆▆▆ knew of Mughniyeh's presence in Khartoum, as did the FBI. The American intelligence community had details of the flight that he would take home to Beirut from Khartoum on April 7.[15] Some reports claimed that the flight was a regularly scheduled Lebanese Middle East Airlines flight on a Boeing 707 with a stop scheduled in Jeddah, others that the plan was to order the jet to land there under some pretext. What is known is that a team of FBI agents had coordinated with the Saudi Muchabarat and air traffic control supervisors at Jeddah's King Abdulaziz International Airport to arrest Mughniyeh once he was on Saudi soil and fly him to the United States on a waiting Bureau, or possibly military, jet. Anthony Lake, President Clinton's National Security Adviser, had arranged the operation with Prince Bandar bin Sultan, the kingdom's ambassador to the United States.[16]

But the Saudis reneged. According to an account broadcast on the Voice of Lebanon radio station, the control tower told the pilot there were security concerns and not to land, that the ticketed passengers waiting for their flight to Beirut in the Jeddah terminal would be picked up by a different aircraft.[17] According to some reports, the FBI agents were in place, though. The jet to take Mughniyeh to the United States was fueled and ready to go. Other accounts state that the FBI agents were in Europe on their way to the Kingdom of Saudi Arabia. A special FBI criminal-identification unit had been mobilized to positively identify Mughniyeh.[18]

According to some accounts rumbling inside the counterterrorist community, the Saudis' refusal to arrange for (or allow) Mughniyeh's aircraft to land outraged the FBI. Supervisory agents made frantic calls back to headquarters on satellite phones; calls went as high up the Department of Justice chain of command as they could. But there was nothing that the American agents could do. The Saudis wanted no role in apprehending Imad Mughniyeh. The kingdom's rulers and spy chiefs were terrified of making any move against the Lebanese Party of God. There were close to three million Shiites in Saudi Arabia; Saudi intelligence already knew that there were serious efforts by Iran's intelligence services to mirror the success of Lebanon in turning this neglected minority into a militant force. Saudi Shiites had already traveled to Lebanon to learn the tradecraft of terror from the world's best.

The US State Department was furious—cables flowed back and forth between State and the US Embassy in Riyadh. ▮▮▮▮▮▮▮ ▮▮▮▮▮▮▮▮▮▮▮▮▮▮▮▮▮▮▮▮▮▮▮▮▮▮ US Secretary of State Warren Christopher did not mount a formal request. He did, however, summon Rihab Massoud, the chargé d'affaires at the Saudi Embassy in Washington, DC, to the State Department for further clarification.[19] America's law enforcement and intelligence communities were poised to out the Saudi treachery to the media following the treachery in Jeddah, but days later, on April 19, 1995, Timothy McVeigh detonated a five-thousand-pound truck bomb outside the Murrah Federal Building in Oklahoma City, Oklahoma. The blast, the most devastating terrorist attack on US soil at the time, killed 168 men, women, and children; more than six hundred were seriously wounded. Suddenly the focus of America's war on terror was internal. Settling the scores of America's failed involvement in Middle Eastern mayhem would have to wait.

Still, the lost opportunity to bring Imad Mughniyeh to justice and to hold him accountable for the abduction and murder of William Buckley and other crimes too numerous to count did not sit well with the CIA and the FBI. It didn't sit well with President Bill Clinton either. On June 21, 1995, President Clinton signed Presidential Decision Directive 39 (PDD-39), enabling US law enforcement authorities to capture suspected terrorists by force from foreign countries that refuse to cooperate in their extradition.[20]

The Saudis believed that they had averted a catastrophic provocation of both Iran and Iran's Lebanese proxies. Had the kingdom acquiesced to demands from Washington and played any part in the apprehension—or execution—of Imad Mughniyeh in conjunction with the CIA and the FBI, the Saudi intelligence services believed, there would certainly have been some sort of Hezbollah terrorist response. The Saudis had seen Hezbollah in action in Lebanon; the GID, in particular, knew that Iran was providing scholarships for Saudi Shiites to travel to Lebanon to train in the Beka'a Valley and in south Beirut. The Saudi intelligence services, primarily from their spies in Beirut, knew all about Mughniyeh's ambitions and capabilities. Months had passed since the air traffic controllers at King Abdulaziz International Airport allowed Mughniyeh's chartered Airbus to fly over the kingdom without being forced to land. Saudi officials felt that they had made a prudent decision. They were concerned that if they allowed the US to move on Mughniyeh, there would be hell to pay in the kingdom. The November 13, 1995, suicide truck bombing of a joint US-Saudi military compound in Riyadh, the Saudi capital, killed six people, five of them American. The Saudis showed concern in public but privately expressed relief. Life in the kingdom continued.

At 21:45 on June 25, 1996, an oil truck erupted into a fireball in front of Building 131 in Khobar, a small city in the Kingdom of Saudi Arabia. Building 131, also known as Khobar Towers, was home to US Air Force personnel working at the nearby Dhahran Air Force Base; British and French servicemen and airmen, part of the enforcement of a no-fly zone against Saddam Hussein's Iraq, were also housed in the facility. Moments earlier, the fuel truck had entered the parking lot on the northwest comer of the building, along with a white passenger vehicle, US Air Force security policeman Alfredo Guerrero had noticed. Guerrero and two other Air Force security policemen were patrolling atop the roof of Building 131 when the two vehicles pulled up near the perimeter fence. When the driver ran from his truck, threw himself into the white vehicle, and sped away into the desert night, Guerrero and his team knew that an attack was under way.[21] Guerrero and his team raced down the emergency staircase of the building to evacuate those inside but they managed to make it down only two floors.[22] The blast killed nineteen American airmen and wounded over five hundred more. The bomb ripped the outer façade of the building clear off; the force of the blast dug an eighty-five-foot-wide and thirty-five-foot-deep crater at the point of detonation. The truck bomb had been built by Lebanon's Hezbollah;* the operation had been conducted by Saudi Shiites operating under the umbrella calling card of Hezbollah al-Hejaz, the Party of God in the Hejaz. The truck bomb had been built to be a weapon of mass destruction. Mughniyeh's Lebanon network successfully smuggled close to five thousand pounds of military-grade high explosives into the Kingdom of Saudi Arabia; the network, along with their Saudi agents, purchased a large oil-delivery

---

* On June 21, 2001, a federal grand jury returned a forty-six-count indictment charging thirteen Saudis with the truck bombing at the Khobar Towers. A fourteenth man, a Lebanese national and a member of Hezbollah, was also named in the indictment. Identified solely as John Doe, the individual was declared responsible for building the bomb and, in many ways, organizing the terror cell. John Doe was identified as a "Lebanese male, approximately 175cm tall, with fair skin, fair hair, and green eyes." There was always speculation in intelligence and law enforcement circles that John Doe was Mustafa Badreddine or, possibly, Mughniyeh himself.

tanker. The device took two weeks to prepare and was built, molded into a shaped charge, to deliver the effect of close to ten tons of TNT.

According to one of the Air Force officers posted at Khobar Towers, base officers had been briefed by OSI, the Office of Special Investigation, that Khobar Towers was considered to be the second most prized terrorist target in the world.[23] According to Michael Maness, a former Operations Officer with the Agency, "Khobar Towers was a textbook example of the dangers of focusing all of our security efforts against the day of the attack. The Downing Commission discovered that the surveillance teams preparing for the attack had cased the site on forty occasions and had actually been spotted by personnel at Khobar on at least ten occasions prior to the event. This information was never aggregated and analyzed, at least not until after the attack. Moreover, the security staff was rotated every forty-five days so there was no institutional memory, contributing to the failure to connect the dots prior to the attack. Additionally, it was discovered that the same terrorist surveillance team was observing a fish market where U.S. servicemen shopped, and the U.S. Consulate in Dhahran at the same time they were casing Khobar. All told, there were probably several dozen opportunities to identify the planning cell and thwart the attack. In the end, the VBIED driver parked the truck at the wrong angle, which ended up saving many lives. Had he parked it correctly, the death toll would have likely been significantly higher."[24]

It was the worst terrorist attack against the American military since the bombing of a Marine Corps barracks in Beirut in 1983.

THERE WAS A sense of frustration in the halls of the CIA and the Pentagon—the most powerful country in the world and the winner of the Cold War *should* be able to bring the world's most wanted terrorist to justice. Mughniyeh was one man, Hezbollah was an organization of just several thousand operatives, and Iran, its state sponsor, was still reeling from the devastation and cost of the war with Iraq. Once again coffins draped in the American flag were lined up in neat rows, reinforcing the sense of threat in America's counterterrorism community. The summer of 1996 was full of events in the United States that seemed like possible terror targets, including two presidential conventions and the Summer Olympics in Atlanta. When, on July 17, TWA Flight 800 crashed shortly after taking off from New York's John F. Kennedy International Airport, the fears of a major summer terrorist offensive intensified. The United States needed a counterterrorist victory.

A large-scale predeployment of US military assets was authorized to show the flag and have force ready in theater in the Middle East should a response to a terrorist attack against the United States or US interests around the world be needed. The shifting of forces was known as "Exercise Rugged Nautilus '96" and involved elements of a Navy Amphibious Ready Group, or ARG, carrying the Thirteenth Marine Expeditionary Unit Special Operations Capable with an attached SEAL platoon; the force was known as the Tarawa ARG after the flagship USS *Tarawa*, an amphibious assault ship, the lead ship of her class, and the second ship to be named for the World War II Battle of Tarawa. The addition of a second US Navy SEAL platoon and a Special Boat Squadron force increased the size of the rapid deployment response force to more than four thousand combat-ready and special-operations-capable troops. The marines and SEALs had been on countless missions like this before. The deployments usually concluded without incident.

But this would be no ordinary deployment. On July 21, 1996, the intelligence officers assigned to the Tarawa ARG received a tantalizing close-hold mission from the Commander Fifth Fleet. A rickety rust bucket of a merchant ship named the SS *Ibn Tufail* flying the Kuwaiti flag had just left the Qatari capital of Doha toward a destination in the Persian Gulf. It was ferrying a high-value target believed to be Imad Mughniyeh. The intelligence was sketchy; in the espionage world, this sort of data was sometimes called "hopefully concrete." Mughniyeh, the intelligence reported, was traveling with forged papers and a limited security contingent—reportedly only a half dozen shooters. His final destination was believed to be Abu Dhabi in the United Arab Emirates.

The Tarawa ARG was on liberty, in its home port of Manama, Bahrain, but ships were rushed out of port so fast and back to sea that several sailors were left behind. The warships would track the *Ibn Tufail* while the marines and the SEALs prepared to board the vessel and capture or kill Mughniyeh: the top secret mission was codenamed "Golden Ox Returns." ████████████████████ was the Marine Corps commander of Operation Golden Ox Returns; ██████ ████████████████████████████ was the SEAL platoon commander.[25] Both men had been given a copy of a faxed image of the target, the same image that a friendly Arab intelligence service had provided the CIA ██████ years earlier. An FBI contingent, including elements of its elite Hostage-Rescue Team, or HRT, was flown to the Middle East to escort Mughniyeh to the United States should he, indeed, be captured. Sixteen months earlier, HRT had been flown to Islamabad, Pakistan, to escort Ramzi Yousef, mastermind of the World Trade Center bombing, to the United States after he had been captured by two intrepid Diplomatic Security Service special agents working out of the US Embassy in the Pakistani capital.

The tactics of ship boarding and interception were nothing new to the marines and SEALs: VBSS (Visit, Board, Search, and Seizure) skills were second nature to the ARG and common to members of such agencies as the Coast Guard, the DEA, and even state and municipal law enforcement agencies. Marine and sniper teams were readied, as were the boarding parties. Additional US Navy warships were rushed to the area as well, to assist in the seizure. The plan was for US Marine Corps AV-8B Harrier jump jets to launch a diversionary low-level flyover of the *Ibn Tufail*, enabling the marines and the SEALs to launch their strike from small vessels; helicopters, some with snipers on board, were standing by. The Agency, US Naval intelligence, and other sources had been able to assemble intimate intelligence on the ship, named after a twelfth-century philosopher and novelist from the Islamic Golden Age; tactical planners knew the blueprints of the vessel and its internal layout, including details of its crew and cargo. "I'd never seen the kind of intelligence we had during this mission," SEAL Platoon Commander ███████████████ commented. "In less than forty-eight hours we had blueprints to the ship, the layout of the ship, pictures of the ship. Who was the crew, what they were carrying, what was their schedule? I mean, it was just amazing to me the amount of intelligence that we had."[26]

The only piece of the intelligence puzzle not firmly in place was definitive word of Mughniyeh's presence on the ship. And not having that piece of the puzzle, according to Clinton administration insiders, was troubling. On July 24, hours before the mission was set to launch, the Operation Golden Ox Returns commander received a dreaded one-word order from Washington, DC: "Abort!"[27] The reason remains sketchy. Several years later Nancy Soderberg, President Clinton's deputy assistant for national security affairs, said, "This is a man who President Clinton authorized numerous operations to get. This is not the only one we tried to do. And since we're still trying to get him, I think it's better not to get into too many details. It was just simply that when the final go/no-go decision comes you need to make sure that the information is there to justify moving. And in this case, unfortunately, it was not. No one wants to conduct an operation that you know in advance is going to be a failure if the target's not in your crosshairs. If there was even a remote possibility that Mughniyeh was on that vessel, President Clinton would have gone. No question about it. In this case, I think what it demonstrates is the commitment of President Clinton to do everything possible to get Mughniyeh."[28]

It is impossible to ascertain whether Mughniyeh was ever on board the SS *Ibn Tufail*. The Clinton administration's decision not to launch the marines and SEALs, especially in the context of a nation still grieving over the airmen killed at Khobar Towers, continued the malaise of the country under the Bush administration. Mughniyeh daunted America's decision-makers and spymasters. According to one Israeli intelligence official, "Mughniyeh and Hezbollah scared just about everyone."[29] The Iranians understood his value. A one-man terror spree had humbled the Israelis, the Americans, the French, the Saudis, and countless others. The Iranians couldn't have been happier at the spread of their regional influence at the hands of blood-soaked ambition.

21

CRIMES UNPUNISHED

*Anyone who doesn't display doubt cannot be an
intelligence professional.*

—Former Mossad Director Meir Dagan[1]

T HE SIXTY THOUSAND Israeli soldiers who crashed through the
northern fence and into Lebanon on June 6, 1982, rode personnel carriers and tanks boasting state-of-the-art armor. The soldiers
were a mixed lot. They were eighteen-year-old conscripts who had
just qualified as full-fledged riflemen and they were jaded reservists,
Israel's fabled citizen soldiers who left work and wives to fight in yet
another war. The Israeli soldiers viewed themselves as liberators,
freeing the citizens of northern Israel from the threat of Palestinian
terror and liberating the residents of southern Lebanon from living
under the tyrannical yoke of the Palestinian AK-47. The soldiers
entered Lebanon with exuberance. Lebanon was an adventure—a
sojourn with a true Middle Eastern character, one that required
body armor and a Galil assault rifle; many of the soldiers hoped to
bring home some souvenirs. No one expected to be in Lebanon for
very long.

Eighteen years later, the soldiers who had entered Lebanon as liberators were now leaving the neighbor to the north as weary-eyed reservists. The men, some balding and with middle-age spreads, had seen more than their share of bloodshed clearing paths and securing villages alongside strategic routes that were once the real estate of the Palestinian guerrillas but now belonged to the Shiite fighters. Israel's eighteen-year involvement in Lebanon had bloodied a generation of IDF conscripts who became expert in counterguerrilla operations, roadside IEDs, and suicide frontal assaults filmed for propaganda purposes on videocassette.[2] The Shiite army that men like Mughniyeh led was fanatic and hard. Israel's army, the strongest military in the region, learned the painful lesson of just how hard it was for a conventional fighting force to defeat a never-ending supply of men eager to die for God. Lebanon had become a bloody quagmire for Israel's military, just as it had been for earlier armies that had also tried with the sword and the olive branch to pacify the explosive hatreds that fueled everyday life.

Prime Minister Ehud Barak knew what Lebanon was—a quicksand trap of best intentions and blood—and he was determined to withdraw all Israeli forces from Lebanon by July 1, 2000.[3] IDF generals argued that Hezbollah would see the unilateral Israeli move as a retreat, a defeat under fire.[4] The generals were convinced that Hezbollah would use the Israeli withdrawal as a pretext to launch a series of bloody attacks to illustrate that Barak's move wasn't one of political courage but of an unequivocal military defeat. There was also the issue of the SLA, or South Lebanese Army, the hodgepodge force of Christians and Shiites who fought against the Palestinians—and Hezbollah—in southern Lebanon. The men and women who fought in this indigenous army would have to be looked after, as would their families. And there were logistical concerns about abandoning Israel's security zone, a buffer between its northernmost citizens and the madness of Hezbollah legions across the fortified frontier.

Israel's intelligence community learned that Hezbollah and the Syrians were taken completely by surprise by Barak's unilateral intentions. On May 22, IDF HQ prepared for the withdrawal, and Israeli intelligence came upon a shining jewel of opportunity: Hezbollah's top leaders would be reconnoitering areas in southern Lebanon to identify locations from where they could launch attacks against departing Israeli forces.[5] The list was impressive: Imad Mughniyeh; his deputy Talal Hamiyah, the commander of Unit 910, Hezbollah's special operations proxy force dispatched into action at the behest of the Iranian Islamic Revolutionary Guard Corps, and one of the masterminds of the Marine barracks bombing; and Mughniyeh's brother-in-law, Mustafa Badreddine.[6] In other words, there was a chance to eliminate Hezbollah's leadership, rendering the organization rudderless and in disarray for some time, as well as avenging the deaths of scores of Israelis, Americans, and Frenchmen. The source of the intelligence was so sensitive that even generals and lower-ranking Mossad agents were asked to step outside the conference room when Major General Amos Malka, the A'man chief, briefed Prime Minister Barak on details of a possible Israeli strike.[7]

As the Israeli prime minister and a few select generals planned Mughniyeh's termination, Malka informed Barak that Hezbollah was planning a series of devastating attacks against the departing Israeli forces and that the attacks would require a month or more to plan and coordinate. Barak faced a dilemma: pull out immediately, catching Hezbollah off guard and ensuring that the withdrawal be bloodless, or keep the schedule intact for a July pullout and risk a bloody end to a bloody run. Barak put the Mughniyeh hit on hold and ordered that the troops pull up stakes and withdraw from the last outposts in the security zone. The generals were flabbergasted.

For the next forty-eight hours columns of Israeli trucks, tanks, and armored personnel carriers streamed south toward the 1949 armistice lines that served as the international border between Lebanon and Israel. The many rows of heavy armor returning to Israel were joined by thousands of Christians and Shiites, the families of those who fought with Israel, who now ran for their lives; in some places, like the Christian Maronite village of Raymesh, home to twelve thousand, all the inhabitants fled to Israel.[8]

One of the last outposts abandoned was Beaufort Castle. Dating to 1139, during the Crusades, the fortification stood atop a sheer cliff, nearly three thousand feet above a valley overlooking the Litani River and much of southern Lebanon—and northern Israel. Beaufort Castle provided an eagle's-eye view to those who occupied its perch; the castle changed hands many times during the Crusades, the First World War, and then the Arab-Israeli conflict, when Arafat's legions used the castle to direct rocket fire against northern Israel. When Israel departed, Hezbollah's fist-and-AK-47 flag replaced the Star of David. History repeated itself in Lebanon once again.

Hezbollah fighters were quick to flood the abandoned Israeli and SLA positions, in some cases walking off with equipment that Israeli soldiers didn't have time to load onto their waiting transports. The Hezbollah fighters waved their Party of God banners and fired their AK-47s in joy. But Mughniyeh's men failed to exact a bloody toll on the Israel forces in retreat. When the last Israeli vehicle, a Merkava main battle tank, crossed the Good Fence near Metulla, the relieved soldiers waved the Israeli flag in a sense of joyous good riddance.

It was the day, though, that forever changed the way that Israel was perceived in the Arab world. Barak had stood by his word to extricate Israel from what he termed a "misguided eighteen-year tragedy."[9] But he couldn't extract Israel from the wrath of Imad Mughniyeh, a man Barak had come so close to killing.

At just after 14:00 hours on Saturday, October 7, 2000, an Israeli patrol driving near a fortification along the frontier near Mount Dov, a strategic hill northeast of the town of Kiryat Shmona along the Lebanese border, came under an intensive RPG-and-machine-gun fusillade, seriously damaging their unarmored jeep. Hezbollah sappers blew open a gate in the security fence. A Range Rover, which according to reports was painted to resemble a United Nations vehicle, crashed through the border. Men with AK-47s emerged from the all-terrain vehicle and dragged the three mortally wounded Israeli soldiers across the border. Separate vehicles were waiting on the other side of the border to whisk the soldiers' bodies to hiding locations prepared weeks in advance. By the time the IDF realized what had happened, the soldiers had disappeared into the labyrinth of Shiite villages in southern Lebanon. Days after the incident, Hezbollah Secretary General Hassan Nasrallah announced that a Hezbollah team had kidnapped an Israeli reservist, a colonel no less, after he had been lured to the Persian Gulf to partake in a narcotics deal.*

---

* It would take four years of brutal negotiations before a prisoner exchange was agreed to between Israel and Hezbollah; the talks were mediated by German intelligence. In order to secure the return of the bodies of the three soldiers killed in the abduction operation, along with the live reservist, the State of Israel released 435 prisoners, including both Sheikh Obeid and Mustafa Dirani, along with the bodies of fifty-nine Shiite terrorists killed by Israeli forces in battle. There was outrage in both Washington and Israel over the release of Obeid and Dirani—many in Israel feared that Israel no longer held any leverage in talks to bring Ron Arad home; many in US law enforcement knew that the two

Before Israel could deal with the situation up north, and the "I told you so" that many of Barak's generals had warned him about when he ordered the unilateral withdrawal, an intifada—a Palestinian uprising—erupted in the West Bank and the Gaza Strip. Ehud Barak's wish to become a peacemaker had ended in fire and fury. Barak's unilateral withdrawal had been seen as the first Arab military victory over Israel. The victorious Hezbollah legions, taunting Israeli forces across the frontier, emboldened combatants on the Arab-Israeli battlefield to realize a new reality: relentless violence waged through suicidal asymmetrical terror ultimately brought rewards.

The withdrawal from Lebanon and the subsequent intifada cost Ehud Barak his job. He was voted out of office in a landslide. The new Israeli premier was Ariel Sharon, a former general and the architect of Israel's Lebanon foray, known as a hard-liner against terror. Sharon, too, attempted to extinguish the Palestinian intifada but to little avail. In June 2001, Hamas launched its first suicide bombing of the uprising: twenty-one high school kids were killed in a discotheque. Two months later, on August 9, a Hamas suicide bomber blew himself up inside a pizzeria in Jerusalem, killing fifteen, including seven children. The death and destruction of the suicide mass murderer, the staple of the Shiite Party of God—the mass-murder fanaticism that Israel had left in Lebanon—was now tearing Israel's cities apart. A good deal of the bloodshed was financed and manipulated by Iran; those logistics were administered by Hezbollah and Imad Mughniyeh. Even the recruitment material that Hamas and the Islamic Jihad used to lure future martyrs to the bomb engineers and their personal fittings with explosive vests—posters that glorified martyrdom, that showed the

---

Shiite leaders would never have to pay the price for the abduction and murder of US citizens, specifically Buckley and Higgins.

dead in paradise surrounded by rivers and flowers and weeping willows—was pure Hezbollah.[10]

Mughniyeh, Americans had always said, was responsible for more American dead than any other terrorist in the world. Israeli intelligence and military commanders feared that Mughniyeh would soon become the terror chieftain with his hands dripping in more Israeli blood than Arafat or any of the other warlords who oversaw the popular fronts and the Islamic liberation armies. The Israelis saw no end in sight to the violence; there was no purely military option to end the bloodshed. ████████████████████
████████████████████

On the morning of September 11, 2001, the *New York Times* ran a front-page story discussing the unstoppable cycle of misery titled "Despite Plan for Talks, Mideast Violence Explodes."

IMAD MUGHNIYEH'S DEATH warrant should have been signed long before the September 11 attacks against the United States. He had been too ambitious, too lethal, and he had been too successful against too many nations and their respective intelligence services to live long enough to retire and enjoy his golden years with his grandchildren. The 9/11 attack against the United States created a global war on terror. There was a massive mobilization of manpower and resources against those responsible, with an unprecedented show of military might. The United States, through the CIA and the NSA, led an international terrorist intelligence onslaught to hunt down those responsible for previous attacks. The global war on terror did not differentiate between Sunni and Shiite terror. On January 29, 2002, President George W. Bush delivered the first State of the Union address after 9/11. Referring to Saddam Hussein's Iraq, North Korea, and the Islamic Republic of Iran, President Bush delivered an iconic classification of the world's enemies. "States like these, and their terrorist allies, constitute an axis of evil, arming to threaten the peace of the world. By seeking weapons of mass destruction, these regimes pose a grave and growing danger. They could provide these arms to terrorists, giving them the means to match their hatred. They could attack our allies or attempt to blackmail the United States. In any of these cases, the price of indifference would be catastrophic."[11]

Iran—and ultimately, Hezbollah—it appeared, would be held accountable for its past sins and current crimes.

A new—and very different—Central Intelligence Agency was created in the aftermath of 9/11. A dynamic, proactive, and paramilitary Central Intelligence Agency, one that shredded the restrictions imposed following the Church Committee, emerged in the aftermath of the al-Qaeda attack.

The CIA that existed when the duty officer received the call from Beirut that William Buckley had disappeared was very different from the Agency that would go to war on the morning of September 12, 2001. The CIA would lead the United States in that war, and a heavy emphasis was placed on HUMINT capabilities—the spies would be led by special-operations-capable officers who would hunt down Osama bin Laden and al-Qaeda's leadership in Afghanistan and Pakistan. A full-scale war was something new for Langley. The Counterterrorism Group at Langley, Buckley's final headquarters job before he shipped out to Beirut, had grown into the Counterterrorism Center, or CTC. The expansion was purely cosmetic. Officers assigned to the CTC had the reputation of being romantics and recluses, individuals with very narrow focuses and limited usefulness beyond their cubbyholes. Officers assigned to the CTC were often posted there because they had failed elsewhere. But, as *New York Times* correspondent Mark Mazzetti noted, "after the September 11 attacks the Counterterrorist

Center began the most dramatic expansion in its history, and over the course of a decade it would become the CIA's beating heart."[12]

██
██
██
██
██
██
██
██

The Israelis had a wealth of assets in Soviet-occupied Europe; Isser Harel,[13] one of the Mossad's founding fathers and one of its most legendary spymasters, wrote, "It quickly transpired that Israel had a vast potential for information and manpower in the strategic field. This was a surprise for us, but most for our American colleagues."[14] James Jesus Angleton, the CIA's legendary counterterrorism spymaster, held a special affinity for the fledgling Israeli intelligence service and became its most vocal proponent in CIA headquarters, the Pentagon, and Foggy Bottom. Angleton's relationship with the Mossad and the State of Israel was so close that after his death in November 1987 Jerusalem mayor Teddy Kollek, himself a former Mossad operative, and then–Defense Minister Yitzhak Rabin dedicated a memorial corner in a park near the King David Hotel with an inscription that read—in English, Hebrew, and Arabic—IN MEMORY OF A DEAR FRIEND, JAMES (JIM) ANGLETON.[15]

██
██
████████████████████████████████ But as America's interests, and involvement, in the Middle East intensified, conflicts and outright challenges to the relationship soon developed.

████████████████████████████████ ████████

████████████████████████████████ ████████

████████ Israel's invasion of Lebanon was another contentious trip wire. The close-knit relationship was almost permanently destroyed when, in November 1985, the FBI arrested Jonathan Jay Pollard, a Jewish-American analyst working for the US Navy's Intelligence Command; Pollard had passed the most classified of secrets to his handler, an IAF colonel studying for his master's degree at New York University. Pollard wasn't working for the Mossad but rather for an obscure contingent of the Israeli intelligence community known as La'ka'm, the Scientific Liaison Bureau run out of the Defense Ministry. La'ka'm's mission was the collection of industrial secrets to assist Israel's weapons industry. Rafi Eitan, a legendary Mossad veteran who had, among other exploits, helped capture Nazi fugitive Adolf Eichmann in Buenos Aires, was the director of La'ka'm and he should have known better: Pollard was an unstable agent to recruit and the entire episode highlighted what many in Israeli intelligence circles criticized as short-term stupidity that risked long-term necessity. The Pollard affair poisoned the Israeli-American ████████ relationship for many years; some inside ████████████████ ████████ claim the relationship suffered irreparable damage.

The relationship was reset on September 12, 2001. The United States suddenly found itself woefully unprepared to take the offensive in the Arab-speaking world. The Agency did not have enough Arabic speakers; the CIA did not know how to immerse its special operations personnel into a language, a religion, and a mind-set that had never been Agency priorities. The CIA was an intelligence-gathering behemoth, a government gargantua designed to collect information on foreign governments and not, as the mission became, man hunting.[16]

* * *

ONE OF THE reasons behind the renaissance in Israeli and American
███████ cooperation was Meir Dagan, appointed by Prime Minister Ariel Sharon in August 2002 to head the Mossad. The previous
director, British-born Efraim Halevy, had earned the nickname "Mr.
Cocktail" for preferring drinks with his Arab counterparts over getting down and dirty launching dangerous operations far from Israel's
shores.¹⁷ Sharon demanded that the Mossad redefine itself as a proactive, inventive, dynamic, and zealous force that would bring the war to
the doorstep of the enemy. Short and stocky, Dagan had anvil-like
forearms that told of enormous strength camouflaged by his diminutive
size. Dagan was no political insider and no ordinary spymaster. Dagan
was a dagger: part Rambo and part George Smiley. He understood that
fighting terrorists required tactics that were violent, relentless, and
highly complex and imaginative.

Meir Dagan was born on January 30, 1945, in Novosibirsk, in the
middle of the Siberian wasteland. His parents were survivors of Hitler's death camps and Dagan was raised on tales of suffering and resilience. Legend has it that Mossad agents about to embark on
dangerous missions behind enemy lines were escorted into Dagan's
office and directed to a photograph hanging on his wall of a bearded
Jew named Dov Ehrlich, wearing a talith, or prayer shawl, kneeling
on the ground with his arms raised in the air as two SS soldiers look
on. Ehrlich's stare is razor-sharp; his fists are clenched. The photo was
taken on October 5, 1942, in the town of Lukow in Nazi-occupied
Poland, and moments after the camera captured the image of Ehrlich,
he was murdered in cold blood. Dov Ehrlich was Meir Dagan's grandfather. Noted Israeli television reporter Ilana Dayan said of Dagan,
"He remains at heart a refugee." Dagan's life was chiseled by the Ho-

locaust and his career defined by decisive behavior that funneled into
the resolve that Jews like his grandfather would never again have to
beg for their lives. When, in 1970, Sharon tapped Dagan to create a
commando force to deal with a terrorist offensive in the newly seized
Gaza Strip, the result was outside-the-box decisiveness. Dagan used
every trick in the book to defeat Arafat's guerrilla underground. Dagan's commandos, many of whom were fluent Arabic speakers, infiltrated
both brothels and mosques, and they masqueraded as Palestinians to
gather intelligence and to tactically undermine the terrorists' sense of
safety in their own backyard. Dagan's commandos used violence zeal-
ously; some historians claim the unit was nothing more than a glorified hit squad. They never hesitated to pull the trigger to administer
point-blank justice in the field; in fact, they relished such opportunities. Force, Dagan learned as a commando-unit commander, was an
incredibly effective tool of deterrence.

Dagan's military career was meteoric: service in Lebanon, running
special operations in the West Bank, and, ultimately, upon retirement
from uniform, heading Prime Minister Benjamin Netanyahu's counterterrorism bureau. As both a soldier and a political appointee Dagan
was an open book whose outlook on the war on terror was well known.
In 1998, while serving as national counterterrorism adviser, Dagan told
Israeli television, "In my opinion, no terrorist should feel immune,
anywhere. I think that a person's life is forfeit the moment he decides
to adopt terrorist tactics."[18]

Dagan was someone who believed that the Mossad was not a
mythical spy organization, the fodder for espionage thrillers or Hollywood films, but rather an organization of incredibly accomplished
and—most importantly to him—straightforward people. In an interview with Israeli television, Dagan once quoted West Germany's leg-

endary first spymaster, Reinhard Gehlen, the first head of the BND, as saying that "the dirtiest work often involves the most trustworthy people."[19] Dagan demanded absolute loyalty and honesty from his people. When asked if he would fire an excellent agent over the matter of a missing thirty euros, Dagan did not hesitate. He said, "Without delay or without thinking twice. It's a question of if you lie or you don't lie." Dagan demanded absolute integrity from his agents and personnel. The agents knew that if they did their job to the boss's standards, he would fight for them against any and all foes.[20]

Shortly after Dagan assumed the duties as Mossad director, Hezbollah operatives and their contacts in al-Qaeda and the Palestinian terror groups began to die violently. In December 2002, Ramzi Nahara, a Hezbollah double agent, was killed by a car bomb in southern Lebanon; in March 2003, Farouq al-Masri, a senior al-Qaeda operative and Osama bin Laden's liaison to Hezbollah, was killed by a car bomb in the Ein el-Hilweh refugee camp near Sidon; in August 2003, Ali Hussein Saleh, Hezbollah's most experienced and talented explosives expert, was himself killed by a car bomb near his home in southwest Beirut; in July 2004, Ghaleb Awali, a Hezbollah liaison to Palestinian groups in the Gaza Strip, was killed by a car bomb in Beirut; in September 2004, Ezzeddine Sheikh Khalil was assassinated in Damascus in a car bombing; and, in May 2006, Mahmoud Majzoub, the Palestinian Islamic Jihad liaison to Hezbollah, was assassinated when a powerful explosive device was placed inside his vehicle in Lebanon.[21]

Israel denied involvement in any of the deaths. "We have no knowledge of this incident," a spokesman for the Israeli prime minister said of the Syria blast. But, he added, "Our longstanding policy has been that no terrorist will have any sanctuary and any immunity. They're in a very risky business, they live in a rough neighborhood, and they should not be surprised when what they plan for others befalls them."[22]

SINCE THE MID-1980S the CIA had viewed Mughniyeh as the most dangerous terrorist foe on the global battlefield—far more than Osama bin Laden. On October 10, 2001, Mughniyeh was placed on the FBI's first Most Wanted Terrorists list. A five-million-dollar price was placed on his head; ultimately, the bounty for information leading to his arrest was raised to twenty-five million dollars. Mughniyeh was featured on the most-wanted list in forty-two nations.

The mayhem continued unabated. On February 14, 2005, a suicide bomber detonated nearly one ton of high explosives inside a stolen truck as the motorcade belonging to former Lebanese prime minister Rafiq Hariri drove past the St. George Hotel in West Beirut. The blast was massive, and punched a twenty-meter hole across the fashionable tree-lined boulevard. Twenty-one people were evaporated by the blast, including Hariri, and some two hundred bystanders were critically wounded. Hariri was a bitter political opponent of Hezbollah's state within a state, and their Syrian protectors and Iranian backers; Syrian strongman Bashar al-Assad had threatened Hariri's life a short time earlier.[23]

A billionaire who had made his fortune serving as a contractor for the Saudi royal family, Hariri had donated much of his money to numerous charitable and educational foundations in Lebanon up until his entry into the fratricidal rumble that was Lebanese politics. Hariri was elected on a platform of national unity and prosperity as a path to Lebanese salvation; he preached that sectarian division and state-sponsored terrorism would forever prevent Lebanon from returning to its gloried past as a bastion of finance and pleasure in the Middle

East. The focus of his political life wasn't the Arab-Israeli dispute or the minutiae of religious strife, but rather a massive construction and rebuilding effort to restore the Lebanese economy. Rotund, jovial, and a darling of Western leaders, Hariri was a symbol of Lebanese hope and revival. He was, though, Riyadh's man in Beirut; he promoted Saudi efforts to return Sunni leadership to Beirut and to counter Iranian and Syrian influence in Lebanon. Iran was concerned that even though Hariri was out of office, he would be seen as a national warrior rallying troops in the trenches to stem the Shiite tide; the Syrians knew that he would use his political influence to enforce United Nations resolutions calling for the removal of all Syrian forces from Lebanon.

It is believed that the order to assassinate Hariri came from both Tehran and Damascus—Imad Mughniyeh would not have been able to act without authorization from both capitals. Imad Mughniyeh, the Hezbollah commander, ordered his men into action. Mustafa Badreddine led the operation. Eliminating Hariri would require the compartmentalized planning and logistics of Iranian and Syrian intelligence, and the executioner's brilliance of Mughniyeh and his team.

In the grand scheme of Iranian realpolitik, the assassination of Rafiq Hariri was identical in scope and operational prerequisite to the al-Qaeda assassination of Afghan Northern Alliance commander Ahmad Shah Massoud days before the 9/11 attacks. Iran and Hezbollah would never have been able to instigate a war with Israel with the political might of moderate Hariri in opposition. But by assassinating Hariri, Hezbollah reshaped the dynamics of Lebanese politics and the chemistry of its national identity. In the eyes of many Sunnis, Hezbollah ceased being Lebanese the moment it engineered the assassination of a beloved political figure; Hezbollah became nothing more than a powerful Persian pawn. In the summer of 2006, the Iranians unleashed Mughniyeh and Hezbollah once again.

THE FIRST TEAMS of US Secret Service and State Department DSS advance agents arrived in St. Petersburg on the morning of July 12, 2006. President George Bush and Secretary of State Condoleezza Rice would be coming several days later to attend the G8 Summit hosted by Russian president Vladimir Putin. This was Putin's acceptance into the G8 community, and the Russian president was preparing to impress his guests—the political leaders from the United States, France, Great Britain, Canada, Germany, Italy, and Japan—in the plush elegance of Konstantinovsky Palace in Strelna, Russia, in the Gulf of Finland off the coast of Saint Petersburg. The conference, scheduled to open on July 15, consisted of numerous meetings on energy, trade, and global security issues. One of the main topics was economic sanctions that would cripple Iran's nuclear-weapons ambitions. More sanctions were promised and the leaders in Tehran were outraged.

The US agents fetched their luggage from the carousel at Pulkovo International Airport. Protection specialists from the other nations collected their bags as well. The cleaning staff in Konstantinovsky Palace polished the crystal chandeliers and vacuumed the burgundy rugs. Preparations were also under way some 1,900 miles south of Konstantinovsky Palace, along the Israeli-Lebanese border. On the morning of July 12, 2006, a special strike force of Hezbollah commandos, wearing IDF uniforms and trained in Iranian intelligence schools to speak fluent Hebrew, crossed the border into Israel. The commando squad negotiated the terrain brilliantly, avoiding sensors and trip wires with Swiss-watchmaker precision. Their leader was Hassan Habib Merhi, commander of Hezbollah's special operations forces in Lebanon and one of the men in charge of the Hariri assassination.[24]

Once they reached their designated position, they readied their weapons and waited. The signal to attack would be unmistakable. At 09:00 hours, in a sophisticated command post deep inside a bunker in south Beirut, Imad Mughniyeh issued the order to his forces to launch a thousand ingeniously camouflaged Katyusha fire-and-forget rockets against the towns and villages of northern Israel; the rockets had been hidden in bunkers and in the basements and courtyards of civilian neighborhoods. Then the commandos struck. They fired RPG rockets at two IDF Humvees patrolling the fence and laced both with lethal fire. They killed three crew members in the first vehicle and abducted two IDF soldiers; both men were critically wounded in the attack. IDF units rushed to the scene of the attack to mount a pursuit of the Hezbollah abduction squad, but when they neared the fence to cross over into southern Lebanon, five more soldiers were killed as they were met by a lethal blanket of rocket and machine-gun fire from some one hundred Hezbollah special operations personnel who had been lying in ambush. The IDF attempted to initiate its controversial Hannibal Directive: a military protocol to use all force necessary to stop a soldier from being abducted, even if this placed the soldier at risk.[25]

Mughniyeh's kidnapping operation had been meticulously planned and brilliantly executed to coincide with the G8 Summit in Russia, where Iran's nuclear-weapons program was to be the primary topic of discussion. Instead, the world's premier economic forum had turned into a crisis group on Lebanon. But Mughniyeh had predicated his plan on the premise that Israel would do nothing.

Instead, Israel went to war. For the next thirty-four days, Israel and Hezbollah were locked in battle in a hard-fought campaign that took both sides by surprise. Israel waged largely an aerial campaign, using its overwhelming superiority to pound Hezbollah ground targets; the runway at Beirut International Airport was bombed out of service to prevent resupply by air. Israeli sorties focused on taking out Hezbollah missile-launching sites. Hezbollah fired nearly 4,000 rockets and advanced Iranian-supplied missiles into Israel's northern cities during the conflict, resulting in the first total war against a Western population since World War II. Nearly 50 Israelis were killed in the daily barrages of 100 or more missiles launched per day. The IAF flew more than 12,000 combat sorties over Lebanon during the conflict; naval and artillery forces fired 10,000 rounds against Hezbollah targets during the intensive fighting. It is believed between 1,000 and 1,500 Lebanese civilians were killed by the strikes.

On the ground, Hezbollah proved itself a capable foe. Israeli casualties were significant in alley-to-alley, house-to-house, and room-to-room fighting in the villages of southern Lebanon; it took the IDF nearly a month and a half to push twenty kilometers into southern Lebanon. Initially, the IDF encountered impassable walls of antitank rockets and missiles, and some of the most advanced IEDs ever encountered on the field of battle, including EFPs, whose molten lead and metal punched through inches of armor. There were 120 Israeli soldiers killed in the fighting; estimates range from 500 to 1,000 Hezbollah dead.

President Bush had hoped that Israel could—quickly and without too much collateral damage—forever silence Hezbollah. But the IDF found itself ill-prepared for the war and incapable of reclaiming territory it had captured in hours when it punched through Palestinian and Syrian defenses in 1982. From the onset, President Bush had supported the Israeli military option, calling the Hezbollah attack pathetic and claiming that Israel had every right to use force to defend itself.[26] The United States, of course, was having Hezbollah issues of its own once again. When the United States–led coalition invaded Iraq on March 19, 2003, the Islamic Republic of Iran first viewed the end of Saddam Hussein's regime as a golden opportunity for advancing its desired plan of domination in the Persian Gulf. Iranian intelligence and the Revolutionary Guard exhibited remarkable patience in waiting for the Ba'athist and al-Qaeda taking of Iraqi lives and normalcy to flow into gutters before acting on behalf of the interests of the Shiite majority. Iranian patience was legendary; as an intelligence chief from one of the emirates once commented, "How can you underestimate the waiting power of a people who can spend years making just one rug?" Iran, realizing that it, too, could find itself looking at the business end of an international coalition, proceeded cautiously, realizing that the Revolutionary Guard could not overtly engage US and coalition forces. Iran was determined to mirror in Iraq Hezbollah's success in Lebanon, but the planning had to be meticulous and the operations covert.

In the eyes of the Revolutionary Guard and the Ministry of Intelligence and Security (MOIS), Imad Mughniyeh was the perfect candidate to raise a Shiite underground army in Iraq from its embryonic state. Mughniyeh understood that a five-million-dollar bounty was on his head and that he would have to be careful operating in Iraq, which was under the occupation of the US military. But Mughniyeh's self-grandeur, elevated in the victory celebrations of the war in Lebanon, overcame his traditionally uncanny paranoia about his security. The Hezbollah commander soon found himself at high-level meetings in the Shiite marshlands near Basra, dangerously close to coalition forces. Mughniyeh's courage drew Shiite volunteers into the new Mahdi Army formed by cleric Muqtada al-Sadr, just as the sight of Iranian Revolutionary Guardsmen in Lebanon inspired a generation of Shiite volunteers from the slums of Beirut in the pressure-cooker months of 1982.

Mughniyeh traveled to Shiite Iraq with his best trainers, commanders, and bomb builders—men who had battled, baffled, and humbled the mighty IDF. As early as 2004, the Iranian Revolutionary Guard saw to it that the very best in the Mahdi Army were sent to Hezbollah's Harvard University of asymmetric warfare, the Sheikh Abdullah Barracks in Baalbek. Hundreds of these fighters received combat experience fighting the Israelis in the summer of 2006 before they were returned to Iraq for the campaign against American forces. Mughniyeh addressed these future martyrs at their graduation ceremonies, urging them to show no quarter in the holy struggle against the United States.

The Mahdi guerrillas were trained in how to assassinate rivals and to kidnap Americans, coalition soldiers, and international contractors. On January 20, 2007, Shiite gunmen trained by Hezbollah attacked the Karbala Provincial Joint Coordination Center, captured four American soldiers, and held them briefly before executing them. The kidnappers, all light skinned and speaking fluent English, drove armored GMC Suburbans identical to those driven by US diplomats and contractors, and they wore US military uniforms. The operation was a carbon copy of the attack that sparked the 2006 Second Lebanon War. It was classic Mughniyeh.

Mughniyeh's master bomb builders, considered among the finest in the world, taught the Mahdi Army the science and art of concealed IEDs and the deadlier EFPs, designed to penetrate thick layers of armored steel at longer distances. In Iraq, EFPs designed and crafted by Hezbollah sliced through US and coalition armored vehicles without difficulty. Hezbollah provided the Mahdi guerrillas with hundreds of Russian-built, Syrian-bought RPG-29 shaped-charge antitank missiles; the handheld rockets, considered the most lethal in the world, could penetrate thirty inches of armored steel. It is believed that Hezbollah's bomb and armor-penetrating technology helped the Shiite militia account for nearly one thousand coalition casualties in Iraq.

In March 2007, one of Mughniyeh's closest deputies, Ali Mousa "Daqduq" al-Musawi, was captured in Iraq by US Special Forces. Daqduq, who with Mughniyeh liaised between the Hezbollah command in Lebanon and the Revolutionary Guard Quds chiefs in Tehran, came from one of Hezbollah's founding families. He was a member of Unit 2300, a special operations force that Mughniyeh had created specifically to battle American and coalition forces on behalf of Iran in Iraq. Daqduq initially refused to talk to American interrogators, worried that his Lebanese accent would all but certify Hezbollah involvement in the Shiite war against American forces; his nickname, as a result, was "Hamid the Mute."[27]

Daqduq ultimately broke under questioning. He revealed intimate details of Hezbollah's support of the Iranian efforts against US and coalition forces in Iraq; he outlined an elaborate map of the regional military reach of Lebanon's Party of God. US Army general Kevin Bergner, the Deputy Commanding General for Multinational Forces in Mosul, Iraq, told a press conference that Daqduq had previously commanded a Hezbollah special operations unit and "coordinated protection" for Sheik Hassan Nasrallah, Hezbollah's leader. In 2005, Daqduq had been sent to Iran to train Iraqi terrorists.[28] General Bergner claimed that coalition forces were operating against secret cells and special groups of extremists funded, trained, and armed by external sources, specifically the Iranian Islamic Revolutionary Guard Corps Quds Forces and Hezbollah handlers and instructors. These operations were sanctioned by senior leadership in Iran.[29]

████████████████████████████████████
████████████████████████████████████
████████████████████████████████████
████████████████████████████████████
████████████████████████████████████
████████████████████████████████████
████████████████████████████████████
████████████████████████████████████
████████████████████████████████████
████████████████████████████████████
████████████████████████████████████
████████████████████████████████████

One of the program's biggest scores was—████████████

████████████████████████████████████

████████ [30] Asgari provided the ████████████

████████████████████████████████████
████████████████████████████████████
████████████████████████████████████

████████████████████ Asgari had, in the 1980s, been at the top of Iranian intelligence in Lebanon. He was one of the architects of Hezbollah and he had run Imad Mughniyeh while being the resident agent in charge of the MOIS desk at the Iranian Embassy in Beirut. In his book *The Good Spy: The Life and Death of Robert Ames*, author Kai Bird writes that Asgari quarterbacked the April 1983 bombing of the US Embassy that ultimately brought Buckley to Beirut. [31]

Asgari knew a great deal about Iran's quest for nuclear weapons and he knew many secrets about Imad Mughniyeh.

PERHAPS THE TELLTALE moment of this new era of close-knit cooperation between Israeli and American services came in September 2007:

"Operation Orchard," the Israeli air raid that destroyed a Syrian Al Kibar nuclear reactor under construction at Deir ez-Zor.[32] Great effort had been taken by the North Korean engineering team and the Syrian military to camouflage the building site.[33] ████████████

██
██
██
██
██
██
██
██
██
██
██
██
██
██
██
██

photos ████ confirming Syria's joint venture with North Korean nuclear scientists. It was reported that an Israeli special operations unit was flown to the site in order to gather soil samples.[34] The analysis was irrefutable. Israel wanted to attack.

The CIA had had a very unpleasant history with weapons of mass destruction in the Middle East—the bitter sting of the Iraq War and the failure even to notice Libya's progressing nuclear program was an embarrassment to both Langley and the White House. The Bush administration was adamant about not letting history repeat itself and it wanted diplomatic overtures to end the Syrian plans. According to US vice president Dick Cheney, Dagan traveled to Washington to make the case for an Israeli military option to take out the Syrian reactor.[35] On July 13, 2007, President Bush telephoned Israeli prime minister Ehud Olmert to discuss the Syrian reactor; Stephen Hadley, US Assistant to the President for National Security Affairs, and his deputy, Elliot Abrams, were also on the call. "The purpose of the call to Prime Minister Olmert," Abrams recounted to Israeli television, "was that we decided that there should be no bombing of the Syrian reactor and instead we would go the diplomatic route." Olmert, Abrams recalled, simply said in essence, "If you aren't going to bomb it, then we will."[36]

Ten IAF F-15Is from the Sixty-Ninth "Hammer" Squadron took off from Ramat David Air Force Base at 23:00 hours on the night of September 5, 2007. By 1:00 on the morning of September 6, the facility was completely destroyed. Once confirmation was received that the reactor was destroyed, Prime Minister Ehud Olmert reportedly asked Turkish prime minister Recep Tayyip Erdogan to convey a message to President Assad: no more military action was planned but Israel would never tolerate another nuclear plant.[37] The message was designed to calm Assad from even contemplating military retaliation against Israel. ██ ████████████████████████

The CIA had warned that military action would precipitate Syrian retaliation and plunge the Middle East into a full-scale conflict. Dagan argued the contrary. "I had long talks with [Meir] Dagan about what it was the Syrians would do if we or Israel did A, B, or C. I must admit that my end list was far less confident that the reactor could be destroyed without triggering a broader conflict in the Middle East," CIA Director Michael Hayden said in an interview about the Mossad. "But the head of Mossad [General Dagan], he had a view that it was possible to actually destroy the site and not trigger a broader war if one were careful about how one did. And he turned out to be correct. His judgment was the right one." Operation Orchard was a turning point. "This is a perfect example why small services and large services cooperate with one another," CIA Director Hayden added, "even when there are political issues between their political masters."[38]

There were more opportunities that warranted close-knit cooperation between the CIA and the Mossad in the target-rich Middle Eastern battlefield. Both sides pledged to work together even more closely.

THERE WAS NO single last straw that led to the decision to terminate Imad Mughniyeh. There was no crime worse than another that ultimately led someone, somewhere, to issue the edict that Mughniyeh had to die. Actionable intelligence and opportunity were all that was needed to give the intelligence services a green light. For the Israelis, Mughniyeh was a terrorist chieftain whose operations against Israel, and Jewish citizens in South America, warranted a preemptive end to his life. For the CIA and America's counterterrorism community, the issue of Mughniyeh was deeply personal.[39]

On January 21, 2008, the State of Israel launched the EL/M-2070 TecSar reconnaissance satellite into orbit. The TecSar, also known as the Ofek-8, was dispatched into space from the Satish Dhawan Space Centre in India. The satellite was fitted with advanced radar signal capabilities to counter darkness and foreboding weather. It was considered one of the world's most advanced space systems.[40] Foreign reports indicated that the satellite offered Israel's intelligence service an unprecedented view of what transpired in Iran and other locations throughout the Middle East.

22

A DEATH IN DAMASCUS

I T ISN'T KNOWN exactly when Imad Mughniyeh arrived in Damascus in early February 2008, or what he was doing there. Mughniyeh's travel plans were never broadcast to those outside his immediate
and trusted inner circle.

According to some reports, Mughniyeh was in Damascus to meet
with key officials of the Palestinian terrorist groups based in Damascus,
including Hamas and the Popular Front for the Liberation of Palestine–
General Command headed by Ahmed Jibril. The meetings were to be
held in the comfortable and anonymous apartment he maintained in
the Syrian capital.[1] According to another report, Mughniyeh met that
night with Ramadan Abdullah Mohammad Shalah, the head of
the Iranian-supported and Iranian-run Palestinian Islamic Jihad, or
PIJ.[2] Shalah had worked as a visiting professor at the University of
South Florida in Tampa. When his predecessor, Fathi Shiqaqi, was
assassinated—allegedly by the Mossad—in Malta in 1995, Shalah left

Florida and headed to Damascus to run the terrorist group. The PIJ perpetrated some of the most lethal suicide bombings in the 1990s and during the al-Aqsa Intifada of 2000; having run operations from the United States, Shalah had earned a spot on the FBI's Most Wanted Terrorist list. Mughniyeh had been promoted by Tehran to run all Iranian-led operations against Israel in the West Bank and Gaza and to coordinate operations with Hamas and the other Palestinian groups.[3] Shalah answered to Mughniyeh. Both men were known to be paranoid. Mughniyeh would frequently change his close circle of trusted associates and impulsively dismiss his bodyguards, sometimes the entire protective detail. Some of these bodyguards, the reports suggest, were killed to send a message, their bodies disposed of in the foundations of many of the new buildings that Iranian money was financing in the slums of south Beirut.[4]

Sometimes Mughniyeh abandoned his security force altogether. He felt anonymous without the security. There were stories that he sometimes hopped on a Vespa, a simple scooter, and would ride from Beirut to Hezbollah positions in the south near the Israeli frontier in order to inspect his men.[5]

Mughniyeh was a regular visitor to Damascus, traveling to the city fairly frequently for meetings with Syrian commanders and Iranian spy chiefs. Some reports claimed that Mughniyeh had traveled to the Syrian capital in early February specifically to have quiet and productive working dinners with General Qassem Suleimani, commander of the Iranian Quds Force. The two men, according to this account, ditched the telltale trappings of a security detail and enjoyed meeting on the quiet side streets of the Syrian capital, breaking bread together over a heaping bowl of hummus and falafel balls while chewing homemade pickled olives and sipping a bottle of orange soda. Like Mughniyeh, Suleimani was a living legend. Suleimani had been a division commander on the front lines of the Iran-Iraq War as a young man in his twenties. The Revolutionary Guard flag officer was known for his cunning brilliance and sheer brutality. After being given command of the Quds Force he quickly earned the sobriquet "the Ayatollah's Dagger." When Iran's interests required guile and a guillotine, he was the man who was summoned. When Suleimani needed a team of contract killers, he called Mughniyeh.

There were other possibilities for Mughniyeh's trip as well. Perhaps he had taken a mistress. Intelligence services around the world had long searched for such a morally compromising chink in Mughniyeh's armor that would provoke a momentary lapse in judgment or vigilance. His head of security and brother-in-law, Mustafa Badreddine, was known to be a playboy who dined in the finest restaurants wherever he traveled; Badreddine carried an assortment of mobile phones that he used to maintain contact with his various mistresses.[6] Mughniyeh struggled with his weight, and his face had ballooned to the point that he grew his beard long and scruffy in order to cover the unappealing appearance of a double chin. But now, reports indicated, he had taken a mistress, a Damascus beauty named Nihad Heidad.[7]

Little is known of Mughniyeh's mistress. There were some accounts that he had met her in Iran. There was, of course, no shortage of beautiful women in Damascus. Many spoiled Damascus damsels wore the hijab out of respect to the parents who financed their lifestyles, but the head covering was nothing more than an attempt to camouflage indiscretions for those who rarely bothered to cover their midriffs or thong-revealing, skintight designer jeans. Sexual promiscuity was not frowned upon in the swinging circles of Syria's capital, but it was not permitted by Hezbollah's ruling council, a body that preached a reign of virtue over their constituency. "The Shiites," noted Middle Eastern professor Fouad Ajami once wrote, "were frequently petty and nearly neurotic about the permissible and the impermissible."[8] Mughniyeh would have wanted to shield any dalliance from the eyes of his head of security. Part of Badreddine's mandate was to protect Mughniyeh from outside harm, and he was also sworn to protect the honor of his sister Sa'ada, Mughniyeh's wife.

It is not known just exactly how Mughniyeh managed to excuse himself from his security detail that night, but the Hezbollah commander was alone on February 12 as he drove a silver Mitsubishi Pajero SUV to the Iranian Cultural Center located in Kfar Suseh, one of the newer neighborhoods of Damascus. The vehicle was nondescript and ideally suited for weaving in and out of the frenetic Damascus traffic. Mughniyeh left his last meeting at his apartment—with Shalah or with his mistress—at around 8:30 p.m. The drive would have been a short one.

Situated in the southwest corner of the city, Kfar Suseh was an expansive afterthought to what was widely considered the true capital of the Arab world. Kfar Suseh did not boast any of the attractions that make the remarkable city of Damascus so legendary, such as the twisting spice-merchant-filled lanes of the ancient market, Saladin's mausoleum, the al-Azem Palace, or the bedazzling Umayyad Mosque. Kfar Suseh's attractions were those of privilege. Kfar Suseh housed many of Syria's state security and intelligence agencies, and was home to the top echelon of officers who facilitated state-sponsored terror, leading to the nickname "the Neighborhood of Spies." Many of Syria's top spymasters, their Iranian benefactors, and Lebanese, Iraqi, and Palestinian terrorist warlords who called Damascus home lived in Kfar Suseh. They dwelled alongside established families whose connections to the ruling Assad clan were ironclad; that is, of course, as long as they remembered at every turn to pay tribute to the Assads and their inner circle. The neighborhood was a bastion of government offices, luxurious flats, shops, and cafés for the powerful and the privileged.

Policemen, secret policemen, soldiers, and counterintelligence agents manned positions throughout the neighborhood—some in camouflage uniforms and others in plain clothes. The agents on patrol could challenge anyone at any time for their *bitaket hawiyeh*, or identification card. Fear on the street guaranteed the defense of the realm.

A SHARP, FRIGID wind sliced through the Neighborhood of Spies on the night of February 12, 2008. The face-numbing gusts blanketed the streets with a steady howl that was loud enough to muffle the steady percussion of honking horns that provided the nightly overture to the Syrian capital's frenetic evening soundtrack. The soldiers cradling AK-47s with shivering hands, who hoped that the numbing cold wouldn't penetrate their poorly lined field jackets, cursed the Prophet for pulling duty that frigid night. Hundreds of additional soldiers and policemen had pulled special assignment working protective security duties outside the Iranian Cultural Center. Their mission was to make sure that a reception celebrating the twenty-ninth anniversary of the Islamic revolution in Iran was not interrupted by Sunni jihadists, communists, or Zionist spies. Special occasions meant that extra officers would be wandering about, making sure no one was out of position or attempting to get in out of the cold. The counterintelligence spies could sit inside their Opel sedans to try to keep warm; the knuckle draggers walking a beat were out of luck.

The seemingly hermetic ring of Syrian security was augmented by a small legion of Iranian MOIS agents who worked at the embassy nearby. The Iranians, wearing their distinctive collarless orange polyester shirts and dark gray blazers, barked orders back and forth into their sleeves, which concealed their Siemens radio microphones; the

Farsi—the language of the Ajami, or non-Arab Persians—was arrogantly audible above the strong winter winds. The night's celebration was also a coming-out party to honor the appointment of Tehran's new ambassador to the Syrian Arab Republic, His Excellency Hojatoleslam Ahmad Mousavi.[9]

Damascus was one of the most important postings in the growing Iranian empire. Mousavi had been handpicked by the aging clerics in the Assembly of Experts to advance the close-knit intelligence, military, and revolutionary ties between Syria and the Islamic Republic. The minority Alawites who rule Syria constitute a sect of Shiite Islam, so an alliance with Iran was both logical and practical, especially since both nations were frontline combatants in the war against Israeli military hegemony in the Middle East. Yet Iran was widely feared and despised by the rest of the Arab world, and many—even those in the ruling Ba'ath Party and the Syrian military—viewed the relationship with Tehran as just another in a long line of arm-twisting foreign dominance that has plagued Damascus since independence. Syria had always been under the thumb of one great power or another, first the Ottoman Turks, then the French, and even after independence Syria was always trapped between Israeli military dominance and Soviet political dominance. Syria asserted its independence and relevance in the Middle East by supporting liberation movements and terrorist organizations throughout the world, as well as by allying itself with pariah states such as Iran and, to a lesser extent, North Korea and Venezuela. As the Middle East moved more into a Western orbit and the Soviet Union dissolved into an afterthought of history, Syria—resource barren and cash poor—was trapped by an adherence to the flickering embers of revolutionary violence that ultimately warranted interest and money from the Persian benefactor eager to forge an alliance with an Arab extremist government.

Ambassador Mousavi's reception was intended to be a gala event. Short of His Excellency President Bashar al-Assad or his top ministers and confidants, the guest list included everyone who mattered in Syria's political and security ruling class, as well as key officers in the numerous Palestinian resistance groups headquartered in Damascus, who were grateful for the invitation. The Iranian Embassy saw to it that the *ehtejhaj*, or ceremony, was lavish. Damascus was considered a Byzantine food paradise but the Iranians brought in caviar from the Caspian Sea, as well as succulent dates and pomegranates from desert plantations near Shiraz. The head chef at the Iranian Embassy even prepared a banquet-size portion of *kaleh pacheh*, a stew of sheep heads, brains, and hooves that was a childhood favorite of the new ambassador; sweet-and-sour chicken carrot *khoresh* was offered to those with more sensitive stomachs. Pitchers of freshly prepared pomegranate juice were iced to quench the guests' thirst. No alcohol was served at the event—that, of course, was haram. Ambassadors from the Gulf emirates, sticking out like swans in their flowing white and cream dishdasha robes and *ghutra* headdresses, knew that if they wanted a gin and tonic they would have to wait until later in the evening when they would hold court in one of the many gentlemen's clubs in the city featuring Moroccan hostesses and special escorts from the Palestinian Authority and Yemen.

Imad Mughniyeh was one of the VIP guests whom security agents at the door ushered in to pay his respects to the new Iranian ambassador. He viewed diplomatic functions with enormous disdain, but Sheikh Hassan Nasrallah had ordered him to offer congratulations to the new Iranian emissary in Damascus.[10] Conventional armies may have moved on their stomachs, but Hezbollah marched on Iranian cash. Mughniyeh did not disobey his boss.

Mughniyeh stayed at the reception for about an hour. It was just before 22:00 when he quietly embraced the new ambassador as he respectfully bid farewell, thanking his hosts for their hospitality and wishing them all of Allah's blessings in carrying out their duties on behalf of the liberation of Jerusalem. He then walked alone into the night. He had, as ordered, paid his respects. There was still work scheduled for the evening.

Mughniyeh's weeklong trip to Damascus was packed with meetings. One of the most pressing items on his packed agenda was to meet with Syrian intelligence officials to map out a series of catastrophic suicide terrorist attacks in retaliation for Israel's Operation Orchard six months earlier.[11] Mughniyeh's meeting was believed to have been with General Roustam Ghazali, the Syrian military intelligence station chief in Beirut, and his coconspirator in the February 14, 2005, car-bomb murder of Lebanese prime minister Rafiq Hariri.[12] General Ghazali, Mughniyeh's liaison in Lebanon with Syrian intelligence, would coordinate assets and move pieces along the global chessboard to execute Syrian revenge perpetrated by Hezbollah's hands.

Whatever his next destination was, Mughniyeh walked toward his car, passing dozens of heavily armed men in crimson berets walking a hurried patrol in the cold wind. He walked alone down Mahmoud al-Fakhani Road, toward the parking area that was full of Japanese and German sedans. Mughniyeh unlocked the driver's-side door of his Pajero and sat inside for a few moments as he fumbled with controls on the dashboard. A minute passed before he turned the key igniting the roar of the Pajero's 170-horsepower 3.2-liter diesel engine. He slid his head back into the headrest, ready to pull out into Damascus traffic. It was 10:15 p.m.

Witnesses recalled seeing a brief flash of pupil-contracting blue and white light, like a tungsten lightbulb blowing out, followed by what sounded like a muffled clap of thunder. It appeared as if a molten fist had punched through the windshield, deforming it into a shattered mess. The roof of the vehicle had been sliced wide open by the force of the blast and the driver smoldered inside.

There were some accounts that the device had been planted inside the rear spare-tire well. Other reports claim that the bomb was planted inside the vehicle. The bomb had been ingeniously designed by parties hoping to avoid any collateral damage to the surrounding buildings; there was a boarding school for girls located around the corner from where the Pajero was parked, and the building—as well as the students— sustained no damage.

The Syrian counterintelligence agents posted to the area proved to be amateurish first responders. The security gauntlet that assembled around the smoldering remains of Mughniyeh's car fumbled about confused, barking orders and setting up a series of perimeters. A flurry of radio and mobile phone chatter between headquarters and the boots on the ground sent soldiers and secret policemen to move attention away from the destroyed vehicle. The blast had aroused the concerned curiosity of guests attending the reception and those shuffling outside about to head home. The Pajero's interior, along with a body slumped over in the driver's side, smoldered ferociously. Not much had been left of Mughniyeh's torso. It is believed that several hundred grams of cyclotrimethylenetrinitramine, commonly known as RDX, a one-hundred-year-old explosive compound used to raze buildings, had been wrapped with nails and bolts and molded inside the headrest of Mughniyeh's Pajero. The blast vaporized much of the Hezbollah military commander's head and shoulders. Brain matter and pieces of Mughniyeh's face were found nearly fifty yards away.[13]

Frantic calls flooded the usually quiet 1-1-3 emergency phone exchange to summon the fire service. Neighborhood residents stared out shuttered windows, peeking through drapes, trying to catch a glimpse of firemen dousing the blaze with several hose lines. Responding police officers and soldiers stared nervously at the windows. Security service cars were rushed to Kfar Suseh from all around Damascus. Senior intelligence officers were summoned from home and ordered to respond as well; high-ranking counterintelligence commanders would not have been happy to leave the graces of a private dance at one of the city's discreet gentlemen's clubs that catered to the country's military and political elite in order to respond to the bombing. Calls were immediately made to Tehran and to Beirut. Mustafa Badreddine was one of the first to receive word of the attack. His job would be to inform the Hezbollah hierarchy of the loss of the organization's most senior military commander and to promise that the wheels were in motion to find and punish those responsible.

The professionals—Syrian Muchabarat, Hezbollah internal security apparatus, and Iranian MOIS and Revolutionary Guardsmen—who arrived in Kfar Suseh to examine the crime scene knew exactly what had happened when they came upon what was left of the Pajero. Many had responded to car bombings before; some had even built car bombs of their own. They knew that the pinpoint aim of the device and the ingenious placement of the charge and its shrapnel package were a pure tradecraft masterpiece. This was no ordinary explosion. Even the most rudimentary glance at the Pajero revealed the artistic and imaginative nature of the bomb's construction. If a criminal gang, or one of the other Arab intelligence services, had had the means, the access, and the luck to be in the right place at the right time to take out an enigmatic and difficult target such as Mughniyeh, they would have simply crammed five hundred kilograms of military-grade explosives into a van or a truck and set it off at a predetermined position.

If, in the process, one hundred innocent people were killed in the blast, the end results always justified any collateral damage.

As the minutes dragged on toward midnight, the crime scene became a typical finger-pointing and jurisdictional tug-of-war between the various security services. Duty commanders from each of the services asserted their importance by crouching near the Pajero and examining the damage with expressions of confidence indicating they knew exactly what they were looking for. But the territorial pissing contest was always one-sided in Syria, and on this cold night it ended quickly. Air Force Intelligence was king in all matters involving state security, and they quickly manhandled most of those representing the other security services away from the crime scene and assumed control of the area.

Suspicion, the currency of day-to-day life in any police state, was particularly rabid in Syria. Air Force Intelligence invariably suspected everyone in the country of one sort of treachery or another, and those suspicions were always amplified against anyone who wasn't from the ruling Alawite minority. The suspicions were legitimate. Investigators knew that any Mossad hit team—whether it had infiltrated the country on fake or legitimate foreign passports—would have had to have help from within to strike at a high-profile target like Mughniyeh. It appeared that Damascus was rife with traitors and security leaks. Those suspected of treachery would be dealt with harshly. The Syrians were embarrassed by the compromise of their hermetic state of national security. ██
██
██
██
██
██

Two of Syria's most powerful intelligence and security services would be at each other's throats in order to make sure that culpability wouldn't be directed at them.[14]

A tow truck was summoned and the Pajero quickly loaded onto the trailer bay. It was hurriedly driven to a basement garage in the bowels of the Syrian Ministry of Defense where local forensic experts, joined by Iranian and Hezbollah EOD experts, picked apart the mangled wreckage for clues. Under the watchful eyes of Shiite clerics, Mughniyeh's headless body was washed, and then transported by Syrian Air Force helicopter to Beirut. Hezbollah's military commander would be mourned in a state funeral the following day in Beirut's Martyrs' Square. As the Iranians said of their fallen in battle, "In the end, he drank the sweet syrup of martyrdom."[15]

Deep into that night in Kfar Suseh, and as the first rays of dawn appeared to the east, the intelligence agents in charge of the crime scene ordered the firemen to flush the blood and tissue debris, along with shards of splintered windshield, into the sewers. There were to be no remnants left behind of the explosion in Kfar Suseh, no evidence of the embarrassing security lapses that existed in Fortress Assad.

It was to be a quiet sunrise in the Neighborhood of Spies one way or another.

SYRIAN AND IRANIAN intelligence officers investigating the Mughniyeh murder felt strongly that the bomb was not the work of Arabs.* Those who planned, designed, and executed the assassination came

---

* In *The Triple Agent: The Al-Qaeda Mole Who Infiltrated the CIA* by Joby Warrick (Random House, 2012), the claim is made that Mughniyeh was killed by a Jordanian spy.

from the very top of the espionage and operational food chain. Improvised explosive devices designed to kill just the intended target were the specialty of one nation's intelligence services in particular: Israel. Israel's intelligence services, the Mossad in particular, were legendary for one-bomb/one-kill targeted assassinations. On December 8, 1972, in Israel's dedicated campaign of vengeance against those responsible for the Munich Olympics Massacre, the Mossad killed Dr. Mahmoud Hamshari, one of the key planners, by placing an explosive device inside the receiver of his home telephone; when Hamshari identified himself on a call, an electronic signal detonated the potent device. On April 11, 1973, an IED exploded under the hotel bed of Ziad Mokhsi, the Fatah representative agent in Cyprus. On June 28, 1973, Mohammed Boudia, the head of the Popular Front for the Liberation of Palestine (PFLP) operations in Europe, was killed when an IED placed under the driver's seat in his Mercedes sedan detonated in a Parisian side street; Boudia, realizing that he was being hunted for the Munich Olympics Massacre, had checked under his car and inside the engine for any signs of sabotage but never thought that simply sitting down in his car would activate the powerful device.[16] On January 6, 1996, Israel's Shin Bet internal security agency had an unwitting asset slip a Motorola cell phone crammed with fifty grams of RDX to Yahya Ayyash, the Hamas master bomb builder; the resulting blast peeled off most of Ayyash's face.[17]

The State of Israel has never confirmed or denied any involvement in Mughniyeh's assassination.

Adam Goldman of the *Washington Post* reported in 2015 that the assassination was, in fact, a joint operation conducted by both the Mossad and the CIA.[18] The Mossad had the intelligence that tracked Mughniyeh and followed him to Damascus; details of these intelligence assets and the sources of this information were not revealed[19]

██
██
██
██
██
██.

It is not known who was responsible for inserting the IED into the Pajero. The bomb, according to this report, was built at a "facility" somewhere in North Carolina and designed to send a burst of shrapnel across a tight radius ████████████████████████████

██
██
██
██
██.[20]

According to the *Washington Post* account of the operation, the assassination strike was designed in a peculiar but, for the United States at least, legally satisfying way. Agency assets on the ground could object to the operation—if there were civilians near Mughniyeh, for example—or even abort it, but they couldn't execute it. Detonation came from a radio signal emanating from Israel. Authorization for the Mughniyeh strike required the sign-off of the US Attorney General, the Director of National Intelligence, the National Security Adviser, and other legal counsels. President Bush also had to sign off on the assassination.

But the operation had gone off flawlessly. Perhaps Allen Dulles was right. Perhaps Israel [the Mossad] was the only nation that the CIA could continuously rely on.[21]

* * *

THOSE WITH A need to know received word of Imad Mughniyeh's death over encrypted communications networks and satellite feeds. Everyone else, even those at the higher rungs of American and Israeli intelligence, learned of the assassination through the true real-time intelligence in the Arab world: the twenty-four-hour-a-day Arab news networks. It was midnight when the newscasters broke into their regularly scheduled programming with breaking news from Damascus. Arabic speakers in the CIA and inside Israeli intelligence were watching when Al Jazeera from Doha, Qatar, interrupted its late-night programming with breaking news of a car bombing in Damascus. A Saudi satellite news station with a film crew that just happened to be nearby televised images of Mughniyeh's destroyed vehicle live from the crime scene. The raw intelligence of the operation's aftermath was vibrant. Hezbollah's own Al-Manar TV in Lebanon, the Party of God's global satellite media outlet to the rest of the Middle East, also broke into their regular programming with word that the holy warrior Imad Mughniyeh had joined the trail of martyrs assassinated by the enemy.

It was just after midnight in Tel Aviv; it was quitting time in the CIA, just after 5:00 p.m.

News of Mughniyeh's assassination traveled fast throughout the region and around the world—to Amman, Riyadh, Paris, London, and as far away as Buenos Aires. Spies everywhere were watching: Mughniyeh had made many enemies. The list of usual suspects who could have been responsible for the bomb in the Pajero was long. There was concern about Hezbollah retaliation. It was going to be a late night in many of the world's capitals.

THE CIA FINALLY had its eye for an eye. Biblical justice had been served to avenge and honor William Buckley and William Higgins.

And Robert Ames. And the hundreds of men and women—CIA agents, US marines, soldiers, and sailors—who, because of their vast numbers, had become statistics rather than individual tragedies. The man who conducted Hezbollah's homicidal attacks—and so much misery around the Middle East and around the world—had finally been silenced.

Who knows if a bottle of Johnnie Walker Blue was opened when the code words confirming a success in Damascus were received at the CTC? Those who would have lifted a glass to celebrate Mughniyeh's bloody death were sworn to secrecy. No word of any celebration at Mossad headquarters has been heard either. The American and Israeli governments have never admitted any role in Mughniyeh's death. CIA Director Michael Hayden said of Mughniyeh, "He had a reward on his head because he was a very bad man. Is the world better off with him removed from the battlefield? Absolutely." He then offered a smile and concluded, "I really don't have much more that I can add."[22] The Israelis, too, were tight-lipped, even tighter than usual. Israeli prime minister Ehud Olmert's office stated, "Israel rejects the attempt by terror groups to attribute to it any involvement in this incident. We have nothing further to add."[23] Meir Dagan did not admit any Israeli complicity in the assassination, though he revealed his own sentiment when he smiled as he told *60 Minutes*, "I am not sorry to see the fact that he has been perished from this world."[24]

The diplomats were less diplomatic. Department spokesman Sean McCormack captured the sentiment of the US government when he said, "The world is a better place without this man in it. He was a cold-blooded killer, a mass murderer, and a terrorist responsible for countless innocent lives lost. One way or the other, he was brought to justice."[25]

Ryan Crocker was the head of the political section at the US Embassy in Beirut on April 18, 1983; he barely survived the blast that killed ███████████████████████ and so many others. As ambassador to Lebanon, he stood in silent salute to both William Buckley and William Higgins before their flag-draped coffins were flown out of Lebanon one final time. And, as ambassador to Iraq at the height of the Hezbollah-fueled Shiite insurgency, Crocker was a witness to the lethal toll that Mughniyeh's men had taken on American and coalition forces. Crocker was a survivor of and witness to Mughniyeh's brand of brutality, and the ambassador did not pull his punches when reacting to the news that the Hezbollah commander had been killed. "All I can say is that as long as he drew breath, he was a threat, whether in Lebanon, Iraq, or anywhere else. He was a very intelligent, dedicated, effective operator on the black side. When I heard about it [Mughniyeh's death], I was one damn happy man."[26]

23

MARTYRS' CEMETERY

*Don't worry. This account will not be closed until
the killing of Hajj Imad is avenged.*
—A placard carried by a mourner at Imad
Mughniyeh's funeral in Beirut[1]

MOST SHIITE RESIDENTS of Beirut knew of Imad Mughniyeh, yet few knew what he looked like. His appearance was a state secret. Rumors spread that he stood six feet five inches, that his body was covered in scars from failed Mossad assassination attempts, that he had undergone extensive plastic surgery in Eastern Europe and Iran to hide his identity. When news of Mughniyeh's death was made public, Al-Manar news crews rushed to the family home in the Lebanese capital. Mughniyeh's mother wept, lamenting that she had no photographs to remember her son by.[2]

In fact there were thousands of photographs for Mrs. Mughniyeh to look at. Hezbollah had diligently kept a photographic and audiovisual library of Mughniyeh to be used for propaganda purposes if he were to be killed: there were photos of him dressed in a turtleneck and a leather jacket, photos of him sitting down addressing a conference, and, of course, scores of photos showing the middle-aged man wearing woodland-pattern camouflage fatigues. Mughniyeh always wore spectacles.

There were videos as well. Hezbollah made sure to release all the film clips of Mughniyeh that they had kept so secret in their archives. The videos were martial propaganda at its finest: war drums beating and men singing in the background as Mughniyeh inspected his suicidal soldiers, faces smeared in green and black camouflage grease, goose-stepping with their AK-47s slung tightly across their chests. The goose-stepping was shown in slow motion with cuts to Mughniyeh's approving face, against a soundtrack of a chorus of baritones singing a martial dirge. Other video clips superimposed Mughniyeh's face on a backdrop of Hezbollah fighters firing RPGs at fortified positions, then storming the bunkers in well-choreographed moves. The Moral Guidance Department of Hezbollah's military wing had worked overtime on the televised propaganda before the funeral. The production value wasn't quite Hollywood, but it wasn't Third World either.

By the fourteenth, when Hezbollah was ready to bid farewell to their martyred commander, nearly all of south Beirut was covered in banners and billboards. In some cases, the posters of Mughniyeh were gargantuan, large enough to cover the façade of an entire apartment block.[3] Less than forty-eight hours had passed since the molten chunks of shrapnel separated most of Mughniyeh's head from his torso.

Beirut was cold and wet that gray Thursday morning. Journalists who managed to get up close to the ceremony reported that there were some twenty thousand people in attendance; Hezbollah spokespeople claimed that a quarter of a million Lebanese and Syrians had made the trek to Beirut. The mourners included the young and the old: there were men past their prime, white whiskers on wrinkled faces, who clutched worry beads and a copy of the Koran, as well as young boys looking bewildered by the throngs of people standing outside in the rain. Scores of women covered from head to toe in the traditional Shiite chador stood outside as well; the women were of course kept separate from the men. But most of the mourners were young men in camouflage fatigues, a sea of crimson and green berets and strong chests produced by military drills and continual physical training.

Thousands packed into the funeral hall. Four men from Mughniyeh's special operations unit clad in black fatigues and berets stood a stoic watch over Mughniyeh's coffin. An honor guard wearing neatly pressed dress drill uniforms held regimental flags representing the forces that Mughniyeh had commanded throughout Beirut, the Beka'a Valley, and southern Lebanon. The men stood in rows twenty across, more than eight rows deep. The hastily assembled plywood stage trembled when they stood to attention.

Mughniyeh's coffin was draped in a yellow velour blanket emblazoned with the Hezbollah coat of arms. A large banner showing a photograph of Mughniyeh was placed behind his coffin. With all the trappings of a state funeral, the event was broadcast live on Al-Manar Television.

Shiite clerics were there in large numbers, as were Syrian and Iranian diplomats, politicians, security heads, and military officers. Iranian Foreign Minister Manouchehr Mottaki was one of the highest-ranking dignitaries to address the mourners. Mottaki read a letter from Iranian president Mahmoud Ahmadinejad: "These are operations that will shorten their corrupt and filthy life. Their smiles will not last long. The free people and the Lebanese people have lost one hero, but there are a million more Hajj Radwans ready to join the ranks of the resistance."[4] Mottaki left the podium after warranting deafening applause. He then embraced Mughniyeh's father and thanked him for the sacrifice of his son.

Hezbollah Secretary General Hassan Nasrallah was compelled to address the mourners on a video link; he was too fearful of an Israeli air strike in retaliation for launching the 2006 Second Lebanon War to emerge from his underground bunker or safe house. "You crossed the borders, Zionists." Nasrallah inflamed the crowd, prompting many to raise their fists in the air. "If you want an open war," Nasrallah warned Israel, "let it be an open war anywhere."[5] Others eulogized Mughniyeh as a warrior who had defended Lebanon from Israeli and American invaders.

Before Mughniyeh's coffin could be lowered into the moist earth, women threw candies and flowers at the procession. Some women threw rice. In the eyes of these devout Shiite women, wearing black chadors and raising their fists in anger, Mughniyeh was a new groom: he had died a martyr and was about to enter paradise to wed his seventy-two virgins.[6]

Ironically—or, perhaps, perfectly timed by fate—Mughniyeh's funeral procession coincided with another gathering in Beirut, this one two hundred thousand persons strong, to commemorate the third anniversary of Rafiq Hariri's assassination and to pray for the peaceful future of Lebanon. It rained at the Hariri rally as well. The gray of the day and the bluster of the winter's winds were offset by a sea of red, white, and green Lebanese flags representing the Muslim, Christian, and Druze ethnic factions that men like William Buckley and so many before and after had tried so diligently to meld together into the cohesive bond of one nation.

THE MIDDLE EAST has changed dramatically since Imad Mughniyeh sent a truck full of explosives into the entrance of the US Embassy in West Beirut one spring afternoon. Lebanon has changed. Syria has disintegrated into all-out civil war. Turmoil and barbarity define the present. Iran is no longer meddling in regional affairs by proxy; it has sent its own soldiers and generals to fight and die in Syria alongside its Hezbollah allies. A revolution built on suffering and sacrifice needs conflict in order to survive.

But, remarkably, the conflict between the United States and the Islamic Republic of Iran has changed as well, even as the flames of a Middle East at war burn brightly. On July 14, 2015, the P5+1 nations (the five permanent members of the United Nations Security Council plus Germany) reached a Joint Comprehensive Plan of Action agreement with Tehran to slow and possibly curtail Iranian nuclear ambitions. The JCPOA, as the resulting accords were known, were hailed by the United States as a diplomatic breakthrough to help end years of economic sanctions against Tehran and bring Iran back into the fold of nations and out of its leading spot in the axis of evil. Others considered it a capitulation, letting Iran off the hook for the bombing of two US embassies in Beirut and the murder of 241 marines and sailors. Iran, they argued, was not held accountable for William Buckley and William Higgins—or for the crimes, too multiple to list, that the Iranians had committed against the United States and its allies in the Middle East and around the world.

On October 11, 2015, Iranian state media broadcast the successful launch of a ballistic missile called the "Imad" capable of accurately striking targets up to one thousand miles away. The launch came on the same day that the Iranian parliament met to approve the JCPOA. It was no coincidence that the missile was named in honor of Imad Mughniyeh.[7] Symbols mean everything in the continuous Shiite war against the United States and Israel.

HEZBOLLAH STILL STOMPS on the American and Israeli flags after Friday prayers in south Beirut. There are still displays of suicidal vengeance in Shiite Beirut where young men, explosives strapped to their chests, pledge their willingness to die in battle. These parades and demonstrations are now done under oversize posters of Imad Mughniyeh.

The martyrs—from previous wars and from ongoing conflicts—are still buried in the Martyrs' Cemetery. Imad Mughniyeh's son Jihad is buried there. Jihad was killed along with high-ranking Iranian and Syrian officers as he toured lines near the Israeli frontier opposite the Golan Heights. Hezbollah claimed that Jihad was killed by an IAF helicopter strike; he had been touring the area with his Iranian and Syrian backers to set up an elite Hezbollah strike unit for attacks inside Israel when he was eviscerated by a large explosion. Israel denied any involvement in the incident.[8] Once again there was a state funeral in south Beirut. Once again Hassan Nasrallah addressed the tens of thousands of mourners on a video feed.

Mustafa Amine Badreddine was the next to go. Badreddine had been given command of the thousands of Hezbollah fighters battling Sunni forces, including those from ISIS, in Syria. Badreddine was cold-blooded and calculating. Most importantly, his Iranian and Syrian counterparts appreciated, he was capable and brutal. His skills had been fine-tuned and chiseled to perfection in the all-out conflagration of a Middle Eastern civil war fought along ethnic lines. But he had risen rapidly up the chain of Hezbollah's command structure following Imad Mughniyeh's assassination, though he lacked his brother-in-law's discretion. He was known as the "Pyromaniac Playboy";[9] according to noted Israeli journalist Ronen Bergman, Badreddine had more mistresses than bodyguards.[10] Badreddine was chairing a meeting of Hezbollah commanders in a fortified location adjacent to Damascus International Airport on May 10, 2016, when a large explosion consumed the structure. Scores were killed in the blast.

Badreddine was one of the final links to the crimes against the

United States and Israel in the early 1980s. It had been more than twenty years since William Buckley had been seized in order to secure Badreddine's release. Nation states did not forgive mass murderers. There was no statute of limitations for catastrophic destruction. There was no statute of limitations for kidnap, torture, and murder.

HONOR AND CEREMONY

EACH SPRING THE Director of Central Intelligence presides over the Agency's most solemn ritual: a memorial ceremony to honor those members of the Central Intelligence Agency who gave their lives in service of their country. The Memorial Ceremony is one of the largest annual events at the CIA. It is open to CIA employees and to the families of the fallen officers. The ceremony is held in the head-quarters, near the statue of Nathan Hale, always in the morning. A CIA honor guard presents the Agency's colors. There is the singing of "The Star-Spangled Banner" and an opening prayer. The Director's speech, usually brief, reaffirms the courage and sacrifice that the fallen displayed while operating far from home and at great risk. "We at CIA remember our heroes—the men and women commemorated by stars on our Memorial Wall," Director Leon E. Panetta said in June 2009. "Each of them, in their own way and own time, strengthened America and helped spread freedom across the globe."[1]

The names of the fallen are then read by four senior Agency officers, representing each of the CIA directorates. Following the roll call, a wreath is placed before the wall. The ceremony concludes with a benediction and the playing of taps. Great effort is made to allow the families to feel closer to their sons or daughters, brothers or sisters, fathers or mothers, who died on the front lines of wars declared and otherwise. "Ceremonies that honor the dead are, in truth, for the living. They remind us of our mortality but also celebrate the lives and memories of those we have loved, trusted, and respected," CIA Director Robert Gates explained at the inaugural ceremony held in May 1987. "Certainly, we mourn their loss—but we also glory in the knowledge of their extraordinary contribution to our service and to our country."[2]

When Director Gates presided over the first ceremony in front of the Agency's Memorial Wall, there were fifty gold stars carved into the white marble. To be honored with a star, according to official criteria, death must be of an inspirational or heroic character while in the performance of duty; or as the result of an act of terrorism while in the performance of duty; or as an act of premeditated violence targeted against an employee, motivated solely by that employee's Agency affiliation; or in the performance of duty while serving in areas of hostilities or other exceptionally hazardous conditions where the death is a direct result of such hostilities or hazards.[3]

William Francis Buckley's was the fifty-first gold star carved into the wall.*

RICHARD HOLM, THE head of the Agency's Counterterrorism Group, who recommended William Buckley for the open post of Chief of

---

* At the time of this book's writing, there are 133 gold stars carved into the wall at CIA headquarters.

Station in Beirut, officiated at many annual memorial ceremonies in the lobby of CIA headquarters during his long and illustrious career. To this day, even though he's retired, Holm still believes in ceremony and honor to those who died in service to their country while working in the shadows for the CIA. Each and every morning, Holm places an American flag on its bracket in honor of his friend Bill Buckley and another friend and colleague, Mike Deuel, who died in a helicopter crash while on assignment in South Asia. Both men are commemorated by stars on the CIA's Memorial Wall. Holm kept the flag that covered Buckley's casket from Lebanon back to the United States in 1991. The flag is now part of the permanent collection on display at the CIA Museum in Langley. William Buckley remains a permanent symbol of service, sacrifice, and honor to the men and women who worked at the Agency in the 1980s, and to those who currently work in the clandestine service of their country. All know the risk. The story of William Buckley is engraved in their minds and in their consciences in training.

When asked what he thinks about when remembering Buckley, Holm said, "He was a good friend. He was my Deputy of CTC. It was an ugly and nasty ending to his life."[4]

ACKNOWLEDGMENTS

As a young special agent in the 1980s, I was fortunate to be placed in a job I had no idea how to do. My boss and mentor, Steve Gleason, gave me a long leash to learn about the dark world of terror. Needless to say, it was a long way from a patrol car and the beat of a street cop, where life was much simpler.

The hunt for William F. Buckley and other Americans held hostage by Hezbollah was frustrating and heart-wrenching. Every day, I deeply regret failing to find Bill before he died at the hands of his captors. For that, I'm truly sorry. I hope the long arm of justice will hunt down his killers; rest assured, it would be my number one priority if I were back in the government and in a position to do so. Bill's killers can be found if someone makes it a priority.

Batman needs Robin and I need Sam Katz. I think the two of us are a pretty good team, but I'll let the reader be the judge. For the record, any faults or mistakes in this story are mine, not Sam's, and so are the redactions. Jim Hornfischer, our literary agent, was the first to believe in me and continues to watch my six. Tracy Bernstein, our editor at Penguin Random House, has shown the patience of Job inheriting a project that has taken way too long to finish.

No book is published without an army of backup and support. The old spooks who helped Sam and me put Bill's life puzzle together were amazing. Legends of the CIA pitched in, like Dr. Chip Beck, Richard Holm, Sam Wyman, Mike Maness, Larry Johnson, Bob Baer, and, before his death, Dewey Clarridge. Others from the CIA wanted total anonymity, but they never failed to lend a hand to help tell the story of their fallen colleague. A very special thanks to David Priess.

Bill's surviving family members were tremendously helpful. Bev Surette is a wonderful lady and helped immensely, as did Bill's sister, Maureen Moroney. John McDermott, the family lawyer, opened the door to both, who were rightfully very protective of Bill's memory. Both women shared personal observations of Bill that honored his memory with dignity and love. We hope they won't be disappointed.

Robin Higgins was extraordinarily helpful and candid, as only a marine can be, regarding her husband's kidnapping and subsequent murder. Joel Ross helped shape the chaos of a hostage family.

At the CIA, special thanks are owed to Toni Hiley, the CIA Museum Director; Kali Caldwell, Media Spokesperson; and Carolyn at the Publications Review Board. I've come to the conclusion that Toni must have the best job at the CIA. Former hostage Terry Anderson was also very generous in shedding light on his experience as a hostage.

Numerous former agents from SY, now the DSS, assisted with color and background of the era in Beirut, including Scott McHugh, Al Bigler, Pete Gallant, Jeremy Zeikel, and Steve Gleason. Steven C. Draper, Director of the US Army's 1st Cavalry Museum at Fort Hood,

Texas, was more than helpful regarding research into Bill's time in the Korean War. A special thanks is in order for Colin Riley at Boston University for his help piecing together Bill's college days. Tricia DiPietro, the librarian at Stoneham High School in Stoneham, Massachusetts, loaned us the library's one and only copy of the 1947 high school yearbook. Maureen Rynn of the Town of Lexington Visitors' Center in Lexington, Massachusetts, also brought to light Major Buckley's work with the diorama of the Battle of Lexington.

Special thanks are in order for my lawyer, Mark Zaid, Esq. Stratfor has always been extraordinarily supportive of my work and our talented Research Section uncovered buried nuggets about Beirut like nobody else. Amy Gamble and Chip Harmon of our executive team deserve special thanks. As with all of my projects, Anya Alfano, Rodger Baker, Korena Garcia, and Scott Stewart were always there to help. Joshua Cook, Stratfor's media guru, does more with less than anybody.

My love to Jimmy, Katie, and Maddie, and, of course, our aging Lab, Shadow. Finally, a special place in heaven waits for my dear wife, Sharon. She's been in my corner forever, from my days as a cop with Montgomery County, Maryland, to my life as an agent, when I was rarely home. She also gave up her career for the sake of mine when I couldn't take the world of counterterrorism anymore. God only knows what I would be without you.

Fred Burton
Austin, Texas
@fred_burton
August 2017

* * *

I WAS IN the Middle East in 1984 when I heard the news that yet another Westerner, this time an American named William F. Buckley, was kidnapped in Beirut. I read the story in a copy of the *International Herald Tribune*. Scant information was available about the abduction in the thin pages of the edition; fewer details were listed in the article, other than the fact that Mr. Buckley had worked out of the US Embassy in the Lebanese capital. I remember asking myself why anyone would be in a place like Beirut. Buckley must have been mad. The city was as close to hell on earth as one could find. The carnage of civil war and the endless factional massacres were followed by an Israeli invasion and more destruction, more massacres. A new superpower, Iran, had found an angry and, for so many years, beleaguered community eager for revenge and power. It was only later that it would be learned that William Buckley wasn't mad. He was a soldier and a spy, and one of the bravest American heroes the Special Forces and the CIA have ever produced.

There were no happy endings in the William Buckley spy story. The story is complex and involves the genesis of fundamentalist Islamic terror against the West; the United States, Israel, the Islamic Republic of Iran, Great Britain, Saudi Arabia, Jordan, the Soviet Union, and dozens of other nations were participants. William Buckley's story is also one that is still laced in secrecy. There are many elements of this one story of America and the West's war with Iran that, as the redactions illustrate, still cannot be told. As a result, the names of many of the individuals who were of great assistance in putting this book together cannot be revealed. These men and women in the shadows, veterans of their nations' security services, were remarkably open and candid in discussing William Buckley's life, his courageous service in Vietnam and later at the Agency, and in discussing the events that brought him to Lebanon and the ordeal he encountered at the hands of bloodthirsty terrorists. I would like to offer these men and women, who are located throughout the world, my gratitude. I am honored to have been included in their trust.

ACKNOWLEDGMENTS

I would like to thank Bruce Tully and Jeff Riner, two former special agents with the US Department of State's Diplomatic Security Service, for their kind and generous support. Both men have logged more miles in service of protecting this country than can be counted; both have a unique background in Lebanon and in America's war against terror. I am grateful for their kindness and support. I would like to thank Mohammed Najib, a noted Palestinian journalist, for his assistance with Arabic and his regional know-how. Political considerations—and safety concerns—prevent me from naming other journalists and experts who are based elsewhere in the Middle East.

In Israel, I would like to thank my collaborator and business partner on numerous military marketing ventures, the great Ziv Koren. Ziv is one of the world's top photographers; he is a person who knows no fear and who knows everyone worth knowing. I am very grateful to Dr. Ronen Bergman, probably the top expert on Israeli intelligence, for his time and insight. I would also like to thank Brigadier General Ariella Ben-Avraham and "Natan" for their critical assistance. I would like to thank Jim Hornfischer, our super agent, for finding this story a worthy home. Jim is a terrific guide and advocate and his guidance and patience made this project possible.

I also want to offer special thanks to my coauthor. I've known Fred for over twenty years—I met him during a United Nations General Assembly security detail when he was a special agent with DSS. Fred is a quiet professional, a patriot, and one of the most honorable men, whose moral compass was never dented despite all those years working in the Beltway. It has been a privilege working on this, our second book together. I hope for the chance to write many more with him.

I work at home, in the middle of the comings and goings of everyone here. I work strange hours and call a multitude of time zones at all hours; there are papers everywhere. As much of an inconvenience as this is, no one here ever complains. Quite to the contrary, my three terrific children are supportive and understanding and always looking out for me. I am truly blessed, and I thank them for making all of this worth it. The kids, of course, follow the example set by my wife, Sigi. A higher authority provided me with a winning lottery ticket when it came to my life's partner. I am truly a lucky man.

Samuel M. Katz
New York, NY
@samuel_ m_katz
August 2017

ENDNOTES

PROLOGUE

1. Interview with CIA officer to be known as "L.," February 29, 2016.
2. Interview, Jeremy Zeikel, June 1, 2015.

CHAPTER ONE: THE PREAMBLE TO DISASTER

1. Morteza Mutaharri, ed. and trans., *Jihad and Shahadat: Struggle and Martyrdom in Islam.*
2. Mehdi Abdei and Gary Legenhausen (Institute for Research and Islamic Studies, Houston, 1986), p. 126, as referenced by Captain Daniel Helmer (U.S. Army), "Hezbollah's Employment of Suicide Bombing During the 1980s: The Theological, Political, and Operational Development of a New Tactic," *Military Review*, July–August 2006.
3. Dubi Eichnold, *"Tzor 1982, Hayiti Kavur Be'Gehenom," Yediot Aharonot* YNET, October 26, 2012.
4. Martin Kramer, *Arab Awakening and Islamic Revival*, Transaction Publishers, New Brunswick, NJ, 1996, pp. 231–43.
5. Ibid.

6. Kevin Toolis, "When in Rome, Don't Forget the Bombs of 1983," *The Sunday Times* (UK), July 27, 2006.

7. Ibid., and as referenced in obituaries reproduced in *Al-Amaliyyat al-istishhadiyya: watha 'iq wa suwar: al-muqawama al-wataniyya al-lubnaniyya, 1982–1985, Al-Markaz al-arabi lil ma'lumat,* [Damascus, 1985], pp. 22–35.

8. Robert Baer, "The Cult of the Suicide Bomber: Ex–CIA Agent Robert Baer Uncovers the Mystery of This Weapon of Terror," produced by the Disinformation Company Limited, 2005.

9. http://www.lebaneseforces.com/blastfromthepast013.asp.

10. https://history.state.gov/milestones/1981-1988/lebanon.

11. Ronald Reagan, "Statement on the Assassination of President-elect Bashir Gemayel of Lebanon," September 14, 1982. Online by Gerhard Peters and John T. Woolley, the American Presidency Project, http://www.presidency.ucsb.edu /ws/?pid=42976.

12. Bob Woodward, "Alliance With a Lebanese Leader," *The Washington Post,* September 29, 1987.

13. Kai Bird, *The Good Spy: The Life and Death of Robert Ames,* Crown, New York, 2014, p. 177.

14. Ted Gup, *The Book of Honor: The Secret Lives and Deaths of CIA Operatives,* Anchor Books, New York, 2000, p. 262.

15. Martin Asser, "Analysis: Role of the SLA," BBC News, May 23, 2000.

16. Hugh Levinson, "South Lebanon: Israel's Vietnam?" BBC News, December 23, 1998.

17. Henry Kamm, "Israelis Find Little Unusual in the Case of Colonel Geva," *The New York Times,* August 1, 1982.

18. http://www.shabak.gov.il/english/heritage/affairs/pages/thetyrehqbombing.aspx.

19. Nicholas Blanford, *Warriors of God: Inside Hezbollah's Thirty-Year Struggle Against Israel,* Random House, New York, 2011, p. 44.

20. Ibid., p. 44.

21. Ibid., p. 47.

CHAPTER TWO: THE GHOST

1. James Feron, "Israel Puts Captured Arms on Display," *The New York Times,* October 12, 1982.

2. http://www.foia.cia.gov/sites/default/files/document conversions/1705143/GEHLEN %2C%20REINHARD%20%20%20VOL.%2070011.pdf

3. Judith Palmer Harik, *Hezbollah: The Changing Face of Terrorism,* I. B. Tauris and Company Ltd., London, 2004, p. 22.

4. Jillian Becker, *The PLO: The Rise and Fall of the Palestine Liberation Organization*, Author House, London, 2014, p. 96.

5. See Kai Bird, *The Good Spy: The Life and Times of Robert Ames*, p. 328.

6. Interview, Meir Dagan, Tel Aviv, September 8, 2015.

7. Ibid.

8. Fouad Ajami, *The Vanished Imam: Musa al Sadr and the Shia of Lebanon*, Cornell University Press, New York, 2012, p. 143.

9. See Judith Palmer Harik, *Hezbollah: The Changing Face of Terrorism*, p. 22.

10. Interview, December 4, 2015.

11. See Nicholas Blanford, *Warriors of God: Inside Hezbollah's Thirty-Year Struggle Against Israel*, p. 53.

12. Ibid., p. 54.

CHAPTER THREE: FLASH AND FIREBALL

1. http://www.state.gov/documents/organization/176699.pdf.

2. Interview, Al Golicinski, March 6, 2013.

3. Interview, Pete Gallant, October 30, 2014.

4. Interview, Bruce Tully, February 5, 2016.

5. Kai Bird, "Robert Ames and the CIA's History of Back-Channel Talks with 'the Bad Guys,'" *Los Angeles Times*, June 21, 2014.

6. Interview, Sam Wyman, March 9, 2016.

7. Robert Baer, *See No Evil: The True Story of a Ground Soldier in the CIA's War on Terrorism*, Crown, New York, 2002, p. 122.

8. Interview, "Mike," May 22, 2008, Paris, France.

9. Interview, Bruce Tully, February 5, 2016.

10. http://adst.org/2013/04/the-bombing-of-u-s-embassy-beirut-april-18-1983/re4z.

11. Thomas L. Friedman, "U.S. Beirut Embassy Bombed; 33 Reported Killed, 80 Hurt; Pro-Iran Sect Admits Action," *The New York Times*, April 19, 1983.

12. http://adst.org/the-stump/ptsd-in-the-foreign-service-a-study-of-the-1983-embassy-beirut-bombing/.

13. Interview, Nora Boustany, February 9, 2016.

14. https://www.youtube.com/watch?v=32uWMBmphM.

15. Ibid.

16. https://www.marines.mil/Portals/59/Publications/US%20Marines%20In%20Lebanon%201982-1984%20PCN%2019000309800_1.pdf.

17. Ken Dilanian, "CIA Discloses Names of 15 Killed In Line of Duty," *Los Angeles Times*, May 23, 2012.

18. See Robert Baer, *See No Evil: The True Story of a Ground Soldier in the CIA's War on Terrorism*, p. 67.

19. https://www.youtube.com/watch?v=1hnevAhSowY.

20. Maya Shwayder, "US Embassy Attacks and Bombings," *International Business Times*, September 11, 2012.

21. https://www.cia.gov/news-information/featured-story-archive/2011-featured -story-archive/heroes-richard-s-welch.html.

22. https://www.cia.gov/library/center-for-the-study-of-intelligence/kent-csi /vol43no3/pdf/v43i3a02p.pdf.

23. Richard L. Holm, *The Craft We Chose: My Life in the CIA*, Mountain Lake Press, Maryland, 2011, p. 422.

24. https://www.cia.gov/news-information/featured-story-archive/2015-featured -story-archive/william-buckley.html.

25. http://archives.nbclearn.com/portal/site/k-12/flatview?cuecard=1345.

CHAPTER FOUR: THE SOLDIER SPY

1. Dana Kennedy, "Sister Remembers Lebanon Hostage William Buckley," Associated Press, November 26, 1987.

2. Mary Battiata, "The Hostage Who Loved Her," *The Washington Post*, December 18, 1986.

3. Interview, March 23, 2015.

4. Interview, Colin Riley, Boston University Media Relations, March 6, 2015.

5. Interview, Maureen Moroney, March 3, 2015.

6. Ibid.

7. https://www.tourlexington.us/historic-sites-museums/pages/lexington-visitors -center.

8. www.sfob54.org/williambuckley!.html; or from the LTC William F. Buckley Memorial Chapter LIV, Special Forces Association, 58 Batterymatch Street, Suite 54, Boston, MA 02110.

9. Interview, Dick Nazzaro, February 11, 2016.

10. Interview, May 29, 2015.

11. General Orders Number 3549, Headquarters, United States Military Assistance Command, Vietnam, as relayed courtesy of William Buckley's sister Maureen Moroney, March 4, 2016.

12. Interview, March 18, 2015.

13. Interview, February 21, 2016.

14. http://www.arlingtoncemetery.net/tgougelmen.htm.

15. Interview, March 18, 2015.

16. Ibid.
17. Ibid.
18. Interview, March 9, 2016.
19. Ibid.
20. Ibid.

CHAPTER FIVE: A RACE TO BEDLAM

1. Interview, Pete Gallant, October 30, 2013.
2. Reuters, "President Honors Americans Killed by Explosion in Beirut," *The New York Times*, April 24, 1983.
3. Ibid.
4. Eric Pace, "William Casey, Ex–C.I.A. Head, Is Dead At 74," *The New York Times,* May 7, 1987.
5. Ibid.
6. Interview, Sam Wyman, March 9, 2016.
7. http://www.drcharlesgcogan.net/.
8. Ibid.
9. Richard L. Holm, *The Craft We Chose: My Life in the CIA*, p. 438.
10. See interview, Sam Wyman, March 9, 2016.
11. Interview, March 29, 2015.
12. Richard L. Holm, *The Craft We Chose: My Life in the CIA*, p. 422.

CHAPTER SIX: BRASS BALLS

1. Interview, U.S. intelligence veteran from Beirut, May 29, 2015.
2. Interview, "Glen," March 12, 2015.
3. Associated Press, "Lebanese Leader Fires 4 Colonels," *Los Angeles Times*, September 28, 1988.
4. See interview, U.S. intelligence veteran from Beirut, March 11, 2015.
5. Ibid.
6. Interview with officer to be known as "L," February 29, 2016.
7. Ibid.
8. See interview, U.S. intelligence veteran from Beirut, May 29, 2015.

CHAPTER SEVEN: MADNESS

1. Interview with CIA officer to be known as "L," February 29, 2016.
2. "Khomeini's Secret SAVAMA Is the Shah's SAVAK," *Executive Intelligence Review*, volume 6, number 44, November 13, 1979.

3. Interview, Tel Aviv, September 5, 2015.

4. Interview, Nora Boustany, February 9, 2016.

5. Ibid.

6. Ibid.

7. Interview, "Glen," March 12, 2015.

8. Benis M. Frank, *U.S. Marines in Lebanon 1982–1984*, History and Museums Division, Headquarters United States Marines, Washington D.C., 1987, p. 15.

9. Randy Gaddo, "They Came In Peace: Marines Remember Beirut Brothers, 20 Years Later," http://www.coldwar.org/articles/80s/beirut.asp.

10. See Benis M. Frank, *U.S. Marines in Lebanon 1982–1984*, p. 31.

11. See Randy Gaddo, "They Came in Peace: Marines Remember Beirut Brothers, 20 Years Later."

12. Ibid.

13. David C. Martin and John Walcott, *Best Laid Plans: The Inside Story of America's War Against Terrorism*, Harper and Row, New York, 1988, p. 147.

14. Interview, June 1, 2015.

15. James Phillips, "The 1983 Marine Barracks Bombing: Connecting the Dots," *The Daily Signal*, October 23, 2009.

16. Gordon Thomas, *Inside British Intelligence: 100 Years of MI5 and MI6*, J. R. Books Limited, London, 2009, p. 189.

17. See Benis M. Frank, *U.S. Marines in Lebanon 1982–1984*, p. 2.

18. https://www.youtube.com/watch?v=XBSEOJndWeo.

19. https://www.youtube.com/watch?v=H6glBalYCiM (*CBS Evening News*).

20. https://www.youtube.com/watch?v=DMv7HFkrvhI.

21. *ABC Close-up*, "War and Power: The Rise of Syria," June 14, 1984.

22. Ibid.

23. Interview, Scott McHugh, April 15, 2016.

24. Bernard E. Trainor, "'83 Strike on Lebanon: Hard Lessons for U.S.," *The New York Times*, August 6, 1989.

25. Thomas L. Friedman, "French Jets Raid Bases of Militia Linked to Attacks," *The New York Times*, November 18, 1983.

26. Mark Barabak, "Bob Hope Returns from Christmas in Beirut," UPI, December 28, 1983.

27. See interview, April 2, 2016.

28. Shane Harris, "How the Beirut Bombing Spawned the Modern Surveillance State," *Foreign Policy*, October 23, 2013.

29. Interview, March 13, 2015.

30. Steven O'Hern, *Iran's Revolutionary Guard: The Threat That Grows While America Sleeps*, Potomac Press, Washington, D.C., 2015, p. 60.

31. "Top Suspect in Hariri Murder Familiar Name in Kuwait Jail," Lebanon Wire, July 2, 2011.

CHAPTER EIGHT: BEIRUT RULES

1. Interview, "J," June 15, 2015.

2. Interview, June 2, 2015.

3. Interview, Luke, March 13, 2015.

4. Nora Boustany, "U.S. Marine Is Killed in Beirut Attack," *The Washington Post*, January 9, 1984.

5. Thomas L. Friedman, "University Head Killed in Beirut; Gunmen Escape," *The New York Times*, January 18, 1984.

6. Ibid.

7. Micah Zenko, "When Reagan Cut and Run," *Foreign Policy*, February 7, 2014.

8. http://www.thereaganfiles.com/84112-cia-analysis-of-terro.pdf.

9. Ibid.

10. Yoav Stem, "Lebanon: Hezbollah Prisoner Swap Marks 'Failure' for Israel," Reuters, July 1, 2008.

11. *Top Secret Missions of the CIA*, episode "Live Wire in Beirut," the History Channel, November 16, 1999.

12. Ibid.

13. Thomas L. Friedman, "Saudis' Consul General in Lebanon Is Kidnapped," *The New York Times*, January 18, 1984.

14. Interview, Bob Baer, May 27, 2015.

15. Interview, Chip Beck, July 4, 2016.

16. Ibid.

17. Ibid.

18. Interview, "Alan," February 29, 2016.

19. Ibid.

20. Interview, Jeremy Zeikel, June 1, 2015.

21. See interview, Chip Beck.

CHAPTER NINE: DAZED AND CONFUSED

1. Interview, Eliezer Tzafrir, September 5, 2015.

2. Interview, September 15, 2011.

3. See interview, Chip Beck.

4. Document IT, 90345.

5. Document declassified on June 8, 2007, System II ID 90371.

6. Ibid.

7. Ibid.

8. Ibid.

9. See interview, Chip Beck.

10. See interview, Bob Baer.

11. Interview, Sam Wyman, March 8, 2016.

12. Ibid.

13. Interview, May 8, 2016.

14. Ibid.

15. Kareem Shaheen, "Mustafa Badreddine: The Hezbollah Leader Who Left No Footprints," *The Guardian*, May 13, 2016.

16. Ronen Bergman, *The Secret War with Iran: The Thirty-Year Covert Struggle for Control of a "Rogue" State*, Simon and Schuster, New York, 2008, pp. 97–98.

17. Ibid.

18. See interview, Bob Baer.

CHAPTER TEN: ONE OF THE FAMILY JEWELS

1. Anthony Marro, "A Man of Intelligence," Book World, October 22, 1978.

2. See *Top Secret Missions of the CIA*, episode "Live Wire in Beirut."

3. Interview, April 4, 2016.

4. Bernard Gwertzman, "U.S. Aide, Abducted in Beirut, Seen on Videotape," *The New York Times*, January 29, 1985.

5. Matthew Levitt, "Why the CIA Killed Imad Mughniyeh," Politico, February 9, 2015.

6. Ibid.

7. Interview with Chip Beck.

8. Interview, February 27, 2015.

9. John Kifner, "Beirut Toll Apparently Curtailed by British Ambassador's Guards; They May Have Killed Terrorist Short of Goal—Toll Is Disputed," *The New York Times*, September 22, 1984.

10. Samuel M. Katz, *Relentless Pursuit: The DSS and the Hunt for the Al-Qaeda Terrorists*, Tor, New York, 2002, p. 58.

11. See John Kifner, "Beirut Toll Apparently Curtailed by British Ambassador's Guards," *The New York Times*, September 22, 1984.

12. David Crist, *The Twilight War: The Secret History of America's Thirty-Year Conflict with Iran*, Penguin, New York, 2012, pp. 151–52.

13. John Kifner, "23 Die, Including 2 Americans, In Terrorist Car Bomb Attack on the U.S. Embassy at Beirut; Blast Kills Driver," *The New York Times*, September 21, 1984.

CHAPTER ELEVEN: MELTDOWN AND MURDER

1. John Kifner, "Ex-Hostages on Kuwait Jet Tell of 6 Days of 'Sheer Hell,'" *The New York Times*, December 11, 1984.
2. Kathy Sawyer, "U.S. Hostage Urges 'Action'; Diplomat Kidnapped In Lebanon Appears on Videotape," *The Washington Post*, January 29, 1985.
3. Annika Henroth-Rothstein, "'We Don't Want to Forget': In Tehran, Revenge Is a National Ethos," *The Tower*, volume 39, June 2016.
4. The Honorable Lee H. Hamilton and the Honorable Daniel K. Inouye, Report of the Congressional Committees Investigating the Iran/Contra Affair.
5. Hala Jaber, *Hezbollah: Born with a Vengeance*, Columbia University Press, New York, 1997, p. 118.
6. John Kifner, "U.S. TV Reporter Free in Lebanon," *The New York Times*, February 15, 1985.
7. Trevor Mostyn, "Grand Ayatollah Mohammed Hussein Fadlallah Obituary," *The Guardian*, July 5, 2010.
8. Interview, May 27, 2015.
9. https://www.youtube.com/watch?v=R6EkyTRWb7Q.
10. Ibid.
11. Adam Goldman and Ellen Nakashima, "CIA and Mossad Killed Senior Hezbollah Figure in Car Bombing," *The Washington Post*, January 30, 2015.
12. See Hala Jaber, *Hezbollah: Born with a Vengeance*, Columbia University Press, New York, 1997, p. 70.
13. Mike Davis, "A History of the Car Bomb (Part 2), Car Bombs with Wings," Asia Times Online, April 18, 2006.
14. Interview, May 27, 2015.
15. Ibid.
16. Bob Woodward and Charles C. Babcock, "Anti-Terrorist Unit Blamed in Beirut Bombing," *The Washington Post*, May 12, 1985.
17. Ibid.
18. Gary C. Gambill, Bassam Endrawos, "The Assassination of Elie Hobeika," Middle East Intelligence Bulletin 4, January 2002.
19. http://www.telegraph.co.uk/news/obituaries/1382591/Elie-Hobeika.html.
20. Interview, Terry Anderson, March 27, 2015.

CHAPTER TWELVE: PROOF OF DEATH

1. "Lebanese Terrorists Say They Will Execute Kidnapped U.S. Official," *Los Angeles Times*, October 4, 1985.
2. See *Top Secret Missions of the CIA*, episode "Live Wire in Beirut."
3. Interview, Terry Anderson, March 27, 2015.
4. Ibid.
5. Ihsan A. Hijazi, "Beirut Hijackers Demand Departure of Palestinians," *The New York Times*, June 12, 1985.
6. Ibid.
7. Kenneth B. Noble, "Lebanese Suspect in Hijacking Arrested by the F.B.I. While at Sea," *The New York Times*, September 18, 1987.
8. George Boehmer, "Attendant on TWA Jet Says Stethem Was Brutally Beaten," Associated Press, September 28, 1988.
9. http://home.reaganfoundation.org/site/DocServer/ReaganMoments Essay/june_2015v3.pdf?docID=3365.
10. Ibid.
11. Matthew Levitt, *Hezbollah: The Global Footprint of Lebanon's Party of God*, Georgetown University Press, Washington, D.C., 2013, p. 55.
12. *ABC News*, Special Report, June 14, 1985 (https://www.youtube.com/watch?v =adBncB2FlOk).
13. Ibid.
14. ███
██████████████████████████████████████
15. Richard C. Gross, "Navy Official Says Rescue Mission All but Impossible," UPI, June 17, 1985.
16. http://home.reaganfoundation.org/site/DocServer/ReaganMomentsEssay /june_2015v3.pdf?doclo=3365.
17. Ihsan A. Hijazi, "4 Russian Men Taken Hostage in West Beirut," *The New York Times*, October 1, 1985.
18. "Threat to Kill Hostage in Lebanon Reported," Associated Press (through *The New York Times*), October 4, 1985.
19. Interview, ███ officer.
20. Ibid.
21. Ihsan A. Hijazi, "American Hostage Freed in Lebanon After 19 Months," *The New York Times*, July 27, 1986.
22. See Eric Pace, "William Casey, Ex–CIA Head, Is Dead at 74."

23. Ibid.

24. Fred Burton, *Ghost: Confessions of a Counterterrorism Agent*, Random House, New York, 2008, p. 94.

CHAPTER THIRTEEN: EMPTY ROOMS, EMPTY GRAVES

1. Interview, May 27, 2015.

2. http://adst.org/2015/02/the-failed-attempt-to-get-a-terrorist-mastermind/.

3. See Matthew Levitt, *Hezbollah: The Global Footprint of Lebanon's Party of God*, p. 30.

4. See http://adst.org/2015/02/the-failed-attempt-to-get-a-terrorist-mastermind/.

5. See Eric Pace, "William Casey, Ex–CIA Head, Is Dead at 74."

6. See interview, Chip Beck.

7. http://www.oldguard.mdw.army.mil/docs/default-source/pao-fact-sheets/old guardfacts.pdf?sfvrsn=6.

8. Joan Mower, "CIA Officer Slain in Lebanon Honored at Memorial Service," Associated Press, May 13, 1988.

CHAPTER FOURTEEN: CALL SIGN SUNRAY

1. Interview, Joel Ross, December 18, 2015.

2. Lieutenant-Colonel Robin Higgins, *Patriot Dreams: The Murder of Colonel Rich Higgins*, Marine Corps Association, Quantico, Virginia, 1999, p. 5.

3. Interview, Robin Higgins, December 22, 2015.

4. Interview, J.R., December 18, 2015.

5. See Nicholas Blanford, *Warriors of God: Inside Hezbollah's Thirty-Year Struggle Against Israel*, p. 88.

6. See interview, Robin Higgins.

7. Ibid.

8. Magnus Ranstorp, *Hizb'Allah in Lebanon: The Politics of the Western Hostage Crisis*, St. Martin's Press, New York, 1997, p. 100.

9. Ibid.

10. See Lietuenant-Colonel Robin Higgins, *Patriot Dreams: The Murder of Colonel Rich Higgins*, p. 5.

11. John K. Cooley, *Payback: America's Long War in the Middle East*, Brassey's US, Washington, D.C., 1991, p. 154.

12. See interview, Joel Ross, December 18, 2015.

13. See interview, Robin Higgins.

14. Interview, Tel Aviv, December 29, 2013.

15. See Magnus Ranstorp, *Hizb'Allah in Lebanon: The Politics of the Western Hostage Crisis*, p. 124.

16. Frank Greve and Marc Duvoisin, "He Knew Too Much, Say His Colleagues," *Philadelphia Inquirer*, August 1, 1989.

17. See interview, J.R.

18. Ibid.

19. Ibid.

20. Ibid.

21. Ibid.

22. Saeed Maalawi, "Hezbollah Leader Rejects U.N. Call for Higgins' Release," United Press International, July 31, 1988.

23. See interview with Robin Higgins, December 22, 2015.

CHAPTER FIFTEEN: OPERATION HANDSOME YOUNG MAN

1. Shimon Shapira, *Marbit Ha 'Meid'a A'd A'ta Laku 'ach Me'Hezbollah Bein Iran ve'Levanon*, Ha'Kibbutz Ha'Me'uchad, Tel Aviv, 2000, p. 121.

2. Moshe Zunder, *Sayeret Mat'kal: The Elite Unit of Israel*, Keter Publishing House, Tel Aviv, 2000, p. 255.

3. Ibid.

4. Ibid.

5. Israel Channel Ten News Documentary, *"Ron Arad: Sha 'ot Aharonof Shel Hofesh,"* 2011.

6. Ibid.

7. Ibid.

8. Ibid.

9. See interview with Robin Higgins, December 22, 2015.

10. Chris McGreal, "Facility 1391: Israel's Secret Prison," *The Guardian*, November 13, 2003.

11. See Moshe Zunder, *Sayeret Mat'kal: The Elite Unit of Israel*, p. 256.

12. See John K. Cooley, *Payback: America's Long War in the Middle East*, p. 154.

13. Ibid.

14. UPI release, "Col. Higgins Was Hanged, Shiites Say; Bush Outraged: Another Hostage Threatened," *Los Angeles Times*, July 31, 1989.

15. Bernard Weinraub, "U.S. Says C.I.A. Believes It Is Probable Higgins Was Killed Before Monday," *The New York Times*, August 3, 1989.

16. Ronen Bergman, *Medinat Yisrael Ta'ase Ha'col: Ha'Krav Ha'Hashai A'l Ha'Shvuim Ve'Ha 'Ne'darim*, Kinneret Zmora-Bitan Dvir Publishing House, Tel Aviv,

2009, p. 178. Also Dore Gold, *The Rise of Nuclear Iran: How Tehran Defies the West*, Regnery Publishing, New York, 2009, p. 107.

17. "Body Found in Beirut May Be Colonel's," *The New York Times*, December 22, 1991.

CHAPTER SIXTEEN: THE END OF THE ORDEAL

1. Alex Rowell, "Meet the Pyromaniac Playboy Leading Hezbollah's Fight in Syria," The Daily Beast, August 3, 2015.

2. "Top Suspect in Hariri Murder Familiar Name in Kuwait Jail," Lebanon Wire, July 2, 2011, http://www.lebanonwire.com/1107MLN/11070304ALRAI.asp.

3. "Hezbollah: Portrait of a Terrorist Organization," The Meir Amit Intelligence and Terrorism Information Center, Tel Aviv, December 18, 2012.

4. See "Top Suspect in Hariri Murder Familiar Name in Kuwait Jail," Lebanon Wire.

5. See Alex Rowell, "Meet the Pyromaniac Playboy Leading Hezbollah's Fight in Syria."

6. "Escaped Militant Has Role In Hostage Talks," *The New York Times*, October 16, 1991.

7. Giandomenico Picco, "Hostage Negotiator Reveals Secrets to Dealing with Iran," http://www.al-monitor.com/pulse/originals/2012/al-monitor/negotiating-with -iran-requires.html.

8. William Clairborne, "Anderson, Last U.S. Hostage, Is Freed," *The Washington Post*, December 5, 1991.

CHAPTER SEVENTEEN: RECOVERY AND RETURN

1. Interview, November 20, 2015.

2. https://history.state.gov/departmenthistory/people/crocker-ryan-clark.

3. Interview, March 27, 2015.

4. Ibid.

5. Ibid.

6. Marilyn Raschka, "Body Dumped in Beirut Identified as Buckley's: Hostage: Former Senior CIA Official, Kidnapped in 1984, Was Reported Slain in 1985," *Los Angeles Times*, December 28, 1991.

7. Ibid.

CHAPTER EIGHTEEN: FREE MEN

1. Brooke A. Masters and James Naughton, "2 Slain Hostages Buried as Heroes," *The Washington Post*, December 31, 1991.

2. Ibid.

3. "Return of Remains of American Hostages," C-SPAN, December 30, 1991.

4. Clifford Krauss, "2 Hostages, Slain in Beirut, Are Buried in U.S.," *The New York Times*, December 31, 1991.

5. Ibid.

6. Dr. Reuven Berka, "Revenge Was Served Cold," Israel Hayom, December 25, 2015.

CHAPTER NINETEEN: SO KILL HIM . . .

1. Christoph Shult and Holger Stark, "Missing for 23 Years: Secret Israeli Report Reveals Truth About Ron Arad's Fate," *Der Spiegel*, September 7, 2009.

2. Interview, "Ben," September 22, 2015.

3. Thomas R. Mockaitis, *The Iraq War Encyclopedia*, ABC-CLIO, Santa Barbara, California, 2013, p. 223.

4. Anthony Shadid, *Night Draws Near: Iraq's People in the Shadow of America's War*, Holt, New York, 2005, p. 164.

5. Interview, New York, October 15, 2015.

6. Dominique Avon, Anaïs-Trissa Khatchadourian, Jane Marie Todd, *Hezbollah: A History of the Party of God*, Harvard University Press, New York, 2013, p. 202.

7. Ronen Bergman, *Medinat Yisrael Ta'ase Ha'Col*, Kinneret Zmora-Bitan Dvir Publishing House, Ltd., Tel Aviv, 2009, p. 351.

8. Ibid.

9. Ibid.

10. Ibid.

11. Ibid.

12. Yaron Drukman, *"Ley! Ha'Kilshonim Ye'Ha'Mechablim Ha'Meumadim Le'Shihrur,"* Ynet Magazine, February 15, 2014.

13. See Ronen Bergman, *Medinat Yisrael Ta'ase Ha'Col*, p. 357.

14. Felix Frisch, *"Ha'Tayasim She'Ha'alu Le'Shilton Et Nasrallah,"* Ma'ariv, February 16, 2008.

15. Tal Tovi, *"Mesokim Neged Guerrilla ve'Terror,"* Military and Strategy: The Institute for National Security Studies, volume 7, issue 1, March 2009, p. 14.

16. Roger Howard, *Operation Damocles: Israel's Secret War Against Hitler's Scientists, 1951–1967*, Pegasus Books, New York, 2013, p. 1.

17. https://www.youtube.com/watch?v=V—CDKPl izM.

18. Ibid.

19. See Ronen Bergman, *Medinat Yisrael Ta'ase Ha'Col*, p. 366.

20. https://www.youtube.com/watch?v=RBt:rTJ gdSgg.

21. Clyde Haberman, "Israelis and Foes Trade Fire Near Border," *The New York Times*, February 18, 1992.

22. https://www.shabak.gov.il/English/Heritage/Affairs/Pages/TerroristEmbas syes1992.aspx.

23. Matthew Levitt, "Hezbollah's 1992 Attack in Argentina Is a Warning for Modern-Day Europe," *The Atlantic*, March 19, 2013.

24. William R. Long, "Islamic Jihad Says It Bombed Embassy; Toll 21," *Los Angeles Times*, March 19, 1992.

25. http://fas.org/irp/threat/terror_92/review.html.

26. See Matthew Levitt, "Hezbollah's 1992 Attack in Argentina Is a Warning for Modern-Day Europe."

CHAPTER TWENTY: PURGATORY

1. Clyde Haberman, "Israelis Abduct Guerrilla Chief from Lebanon," *The New York Times*, May 22, 1994.

2. FBI file #256A-WF-1, dated 02/29/1996.

3. Moshe Zunder, *Sayeret Mat'kal: The Elite Unit of Israel*, p. 286.

4. See Clyde Haberman, "Israelis Abduct Guerrilla Chief from Lebanon."

5. See Moshe Zunder, *Sayeret Mat'kal: The Elite Unit of Israel*, p. 287.

6. https://www.youtube.com/watch?v=twJa8l YffiM.

7. Amir Rappaport, *"Kach Nihtaf Dirani Me'Beito Be'Lebanon,"* *Israel Defense*, October 14, 2011.

8. See https://www.youtube.com/watch?v=wwFQsQQtqM8.

9. Chris McGreal, "Facility 1391: Israel's Secret Prison," *The Guardian*, November 16, 2003.

10. Jack Nelson, "FBI Has Reportedly Identified 4 or 5 Terrorists," *Los Angeles Times*, July 4, 1985.

11. See Clyde Haberman, "Israel Alerts Envoys and Border, Fearing Reprisals for Abduction," *The New York Times*, May 23, 1994.

12. See Matthew Levitt, *Hezbollah: The Global Footprint of Lebanon's Party of God*, p. 91.

13. http://www.interpol.int/News-and-media/News/2007/PR005.

14. Tim Naftali, *Blind Spot: The Secret History of American Counterterrorism*, Basic Books, New York, 2006, p. 255.

15. Jim Mann and Ronald J. Ostrow, "Saudis Derailed U.S. Plan to Seize Mideast Terror Suspect," *Los Angeles Times*, April 21, 1995.

16. Dore Gold, *Hatred's Kingdom: How Saudi Arabia Supports the New Global Terrorism*, Regnery Publishing Ltd., New York, 2004, p. 178.

17. See Jim Mann and Ronald J. Ostrow, "Saudis Derailed U.S. Plan to Seize Mideast Terror Suspect."

18. Ibid.

19. Ibid.

20. Kenneth Katzman, "Terrorism: Near Eastern Groups and State Sponsors, 2001," CRS Report for Congress, September 10, 2001, p. CRS-33.

21. http://www.airforcetimes.com/news/your-air-force/2016/06/26/khobar-towers -reflecting-20-years-after-the-attack/.

22. Steven Erlanger, "Bombing in Saudi Arabia: The Witnesses; Survivors of Saudi Explosion Knew At Once It Was a Bomb," *The New York Times*, June 27, 1996.

23. http://www.airforcetimes.com/news/your-air-force/2016/06/26/khobar-towers -reflecting-20-years-after-the-attack/.

24. Interview (via email), July 14, 2016.

25. http://www.cbsnews.com/news/shadow-warriors/.

26. http://www.leatherneck.com/forums/showthread.php?60891 -Bomb-kills-top-Hez bollah-leader.

27. See http://www.cbsnews.com/news/shadow-warriors/.

28. Ibid.

29. Interview, Kfar Saba, June 1, 2016.

CHAPTER TWENTY-ONE: CRIMES UNPUNISHED

1. Yarin Kimor, *"Sochnut Hayav Be'Meleyat 30 Le'Moto Shel Meir Dagan Z'l,"* Israel Channel 1, April 20, 2016.

2. Matti Friedman, *Pumpkin Flowers: A Soldier's Story*, Algonquin Books, New York, 2016, p. 34.

3. Major-General (Res.) Giora Eiland, *"So/ Ma 'ase Be'Machsheva Thila,"* Tzava Ve'Astrategia, volume 3, issue 3, December 2011, p. 64.

4. Ronen Bergman, "Secrets Behind Israel's Historic Withdrawal From Lebanon," *Ynet Magazine*, March 10, 2016.

5. Ibid.

6. Yossi Melman, *"Ha 'Hisool She'Lo Haya: Ha 'Hizdamnut She'Huhmatza Li'Gdo'a Et Rosho Shel Hezbollah,"* Ma'ariv, March 12, 2016.

7. Ibid.

8. Suzanne Goldenberg, "Chaos and Humiliation as Israel Pulls Out of Lebanon," *The Guardian*, May 23, 2000.

9. Deborah Sontag, "Retreat from Lebanon: The Triumphal Procession; Israelis Out of Lebanon After 22 Years," *The New York Times*, May 24, 2000.

10. Robert Fisk, "What Drives a Bomber to Kill the Innocent Child?" *The Independent*, August 10, 2001.

11. Jamie Fuller, "The 4th Best State of the Union Address: 'Axis of Evil,'" *The Washington Post*, January 25, 2014.

12. Mark Mazzetti, *The Way of the Knife: The CIA, A Secret Army, and a War at the Ends of the Earth*, St. Martin's Press, New York, 2012, p. 11.

13. Yossi Melman and Dan Raviv, *The Imperfect Spies: The History of Israeli Intelligence*, Sidgwick and Jackson, London, 1989, p. 72.

14. Ian Black and Benny Morris, *Israel's Secret Wars: The Untold Story of Israeli Intelligence*, Hamish Hamilton, London, 1991, p. 169.

15. Christopher Dickey, "My Lunch with 'The Spider' Who Nearly Wrecked the CIA," *The Daily Beast*, February 27, 2016.

16. See Mark Mazzetti, *The Way of the Knife: The CIA, A Secret Army, and a War at the Ends of the Earth*, p. 26.

17. Yaakov Katz and Yoaz Hendel, *Israel Versus Iran: The Shadow War*, Potomac Books, Washington, D.C., 2012, p. 94.

18. From a 1998 interview with Israeli Television's Channel 2 and Dan Baron, "Mossad Changes Courses," Jewish Telegraphic Agency, November 18, 2004.

19. https://www.youtube.com/watch?v=Ul42FYUop3Y.

20. Ibid.

21. Uzi Mahnaimi and Hala Jaber, "Israel Kills Terror Chief with Headrest Bomb," *The Sunday Times* (UK), February 17, 2008.

22. Joel Greenberg, "Palestinian Militant Slain in Damascus," *Chicago Tribune*, September 27, 2004.

23. Ronen Bergman, "The Hezbollah Connection," *The New York Times Sunday Magazine*, February 10, 2015.

24. Ibid.

25. http://glz.co.il/1087-84545-HE/Galatz.aspx.

26. Jim Rutenberg, "Bush Gives Qualified Support for Israel's Strikes," *The New York Times*, July 14, 2006.

27. Michael R. Gordon, "Hezbollah Trains Iraqis in Iran, Officials Say," *The New York Times*, May 5, 2008.

28. John F. Burns and Michael R. Gordon, "U.S. Says Iran Helped Iraqis Kill Five G.I.s," *The New York Times*, July 3, 2007.

29. https://www.youtube.com/watch?v=jQKQ44GM3Xc.

30. Ronen Bergman, "US Closer to Cracking Iran's Nuclear Secrets," Ynet News, July 8, 2007.

31. Jeff Stein, "Top Iran Terrorist Under CIA Protection in U.S., Book Says," *Newsweek*, May 19, 2014.

32. Erich Follath and Holger Stark, "The Story of 'Operation Orchard': How Israel Destroyed Syria's Al Kibar Nuclear Reactor," Der Spiegel International Online, November 2, 2009.

33. David Albright and Paul Brannan, "The Al Kibar Reactor: Extraordinary Camouflage, Troubling Implications," The Institute for Science and Security, May 12, 2008.

34. Eben Kaplan, "Nuclear Questions Aimed at Syria," Council on Foreign Relations, September 28, 2007.

35. Leslie Stahl, "The Spymaster Speaks," 60 Minutes, CBS Television, March 12, 2012.

36. https://www.youtube.com/watch?v=sayjLKb6D1Y.

37. See Erich Follath and Holger Stark, "The Story of 'Operation Orchard': How Israel Destroyed Syria's Al Kibar Nuclear Reactor."

38. Ibid.

39. Adam Goldman and Matthew Levitt, "Inside the Killing of Imad Mughniyah," The Washington Post, January 30, 2015.

40. Ninan Koshy (edited by John Feffer), "India and Israel Eye Iran," Foreign Policy in Focus, February 12, 2008.

CHAPTER TWENTY-TWO: A DEATH IN DAMASCUS

1. "Exclusive: The Final Hours of Imad Mughniyeh," al-Akhbar English, March 6, 2015.

2. Mark Perry, "The Driver," Foreign Policy, April 29, 2013.

3. Daniel Sobelman, "Iran Names International Fugitive as Terror Groups' Coordinator," The Jerusalem Post, September 12, 2000.

4. Ronen Bergman, The Secret War with Iran: The Thirty-Year Covert Struggle for Control of a "Rogue" State, One World Books, London, 2009, p. 96.

5. See Mark Perry, "The Driver."

6. Shane Harris, "Who Really Killed a Playboy Terrorist?" The Daily Beast, June 26, 2016.

7. Michael Bar-Zahar and Nissim Meshal, Ha'Mossad: Ha'Mivtza'im Ha'Gdolim, Yediot Books, Tel Aviv, 2010, p. 292.

8. Fouad Ajami, The Vanished Imam: Musa al Sadr and the Shia of Lebanon, Cornell University Press, Ithaca, 1986, p. 95.

9. Gordon Thomas, "Mossad's Most Wanted: A Deadly Vengeance," The Independent, February 22, 2010.

10. See Erich Follath and Holger Stark, "The Story of 'Operation Orchard': How Israel Destroyed Syria's Al Kibar Nuclear Reactor."

11. Uzi Mahnaimi and Hala Jaber, "Israel Kills Terror Chief with Headrest Bomb," The Sunday Times (UK), February 17, 2008.

12. Anne Barnard, "Syria Remains Silent on Intelligence Official's Death," *The New York Times*, April 24, 2015.

13. See Gordon Thomas, "Mossad's License to Kill," *Daily Telegraph*, February 17, 2008.

14. Ian Black, "WikiLeaks Cables: Syria Stunned by Hezbollah Assassination," *The Guardian*, December 7, 2010.

15. Dexter Filkins, "The Shadow Commander," *The New Yorker*, September 30, 2013.

16. Aaron J. Klein, *Striking Back*, Random House, New York, 2005, p. 179.

17. Dror Moreh, *The Gatekeepers* (documentary film), Sony Picture Classics, 2012.

18. Adam Goldman and Ellen Nakashima, "CIA and Mossad Killed Senior Hezbollah Figure in Car Bombing," *The Washington Post*, January 30, 2015.

19. Ibid.

20. See interview, Bob Baer.

21. See Ronen Bergman, *The Secret War with Iran: The Thirty-Year Covert Struggle for Control of a "Rogue" State*, p. 14.

22. See Yarin Kimor, *"Sochnut Hayav Be'Meleyat 30 Le'Moto Shel Meir Dagan Z'l."*

23. Sam F. Ghattas, "Hezbollah Militant Accused of Masterminding Killings of Americans in Lebanon Is Dead," *The San Diego Union Tribune*, February 13, 2008.

24. Leslie Stahl, "The Spymaster Speaks," *60 Minutes*, CBS Television, March 12, 2012.

25. Nada Bakri and Graham Bowley, "Top Hezbollah Commander Killed in Syria," *The New York Times*, February 13, 2008.

26. See Adam Goldman and Ellen Nakashima, "CIA and Mossad Killed Senior Hezbollah Figure in Car Bombing," *The Washington Post*, January 30, 2015.

CHAPTER TWENTY-THREE: MARTYRS' CEMETERY

1. Trish Schuh, "Inside Hezbollah Leader Imad Mughniyeh's Funeral," *Esquire*, February 21, 2008.

2. Gordon Thomas, "Mossad's License to Kill," *Daily Telegraph*, February 17, 2010.

3. See Trish Schuh, "Inside Hezbollah Leader Imad Mughniyeh's Funeral," *Esquire*, February 21, 2008.

4. Robert F. Worth and Nada Bakrifeb, "Hezbollah Threatens Attacks on Israeli Targets," *The New York Times*, February 15, 2008.

5. Kevin Peraino, "The Fox Is Hunted Down," *Newsweek*, February 25, 2008.

6. See Trish Schuh, "Inside Hezbollah Leader Imad Mughniyeh's Funeral."

7. Farzin Nadimi, "Iran Seeks to Strengthen Its Deterrence by Showing Off Its Missile Force," The Washington Institute for Near East Policy, Policy Watch 2512, October 28, 2015.

8. Yossi Melman and No'am Amir, *"Hisul Jihad Mughniyeh: Kach Sue/a 'Yechidat fLit' Shel Hezbollah,"* Ma'ariv, April, 2015.

9. See Alex Rowell, "Meet the Pyromaniac Playboy Leading Hezbollah's Fight in Syria."

10. Ronen Bergman, "Terrorist *Be'Yorn*, Playboy *Be'Layla*," *Yediot Aharonot*, May 15, 2016.

POSTSCRIPT: HONOR AND CEREMONY

1. https://www.cia.gov/library/publications/resources/cia-memorial-wall -publication/MemWall%20WebVrsn%20June2010b.pdf.

2. Ibid.

3. Ibid.

4. Interview, September 14, 2014.

INDEX

ABC, 51
Abrams, Elliot, 323
Abu Dhabi, United Arab Emirates, 297
Abu Nidal faction, 12
Action Service (France), 86
Advanced Armor Officer Course, Fort
    Knox, 57
Afghan Arabs, 282
Afghan Northern Alliance, 314
Afghanistan, 243, 307
Afula, Israel, 283
Agence France-Presse, 125, 162
AGM-114 Hellfire missiles, 273
AH-64 Apache helicopter gunships, 270,
    273, 275–77
Ahmadinejad, Mahmoud, 345
Ajami, Fouad, 328–29
AK-47s, 3, 25, 27, 94, 98, 101, 134, 184, 187,
    189, 232, 233, 304, 330
al-Amn al-'Aam (Lebanese intelligence), 41
al-Aqsa Intifada, 327
al-Assad, Bashar, 313, 323, 332
al-Assad, Hafez, 12, 17, 20, 148, 169, 170
al-Assad, Rifaat, 145, 148, 169, 170, 193
al-Dachia, Lebanon, 104
Al Jazeera, 340
al-Joura, Lebanon, 104
Al-Manar Television, 269, 340, 343, 345
al-Masri, Farouq, 312
al-Musawi, Ali Mousa "Daqduq," 320
al-Musawi, Hussein al-Sayed Yousef, 116
al-Qaeda, 282, 290, 307, 312, 318
al-Sabah, Sheikh Jaber al-Ahmad, 150, 240

al-Sadr, Imam Musa, 30–32, 175
al-Sadr, Muhammad Baqir, 268–69
al-Sadr, Muqtada, 318
al-Sharaa, Farouk, 201
al-Tufayli, Subhi, 267
al-Turabi, Hassan Abdallah, 290–91
al-Wazir, Khalil (Abu Jihad), 34
al-Yafi, 165, 166
Alawites, 24–25, 331, 336
Aley, Lebanon, 96
Aley–Beirut Highway, 105
Algeria, 86, 112, 174, 190, 191, 241
Ali the Iranian, 183
Alia bint Al-Hussein, Princess, 186n
Alia Flight 402, 186–87
A'man (Israeli military intelligence), 7–8,
    237, 266, 269, 270, 272, 273, 284, 288
American University Hospital, Beirut, 252,
    253, 255
American University of Beirut, 38, 43,
    124–25, 130
American University of Beirut Medical
    Center, 72–73
Ames, Robert, 43–44, 49–50, 78, 341
An-Nahar, 167, 196–97, 236
Anderson, Terry, 179, 181, 183–85, 244,
    251, 252
Andrews Air Force Base, 261
Angleton, James Jesus, 308
Arad, Ron, 232–35, 262, 264–67, 283–88, 304n
Arad, Tammy, 284
Arafat, Yasir, 8, 13, 25–29, 32, 36, 89, 192, 303,
    306, 311

Arditi, Danny, 270
Arens, Moshe, 273–74
Argentina, 279–81, 309
  Argentine Israelite Mutual Association
    (AMIA), Buenos Aires, 288–90
Argov, Shlomo, 12
Arlington National Cemetery, 185, 210–12
Armenians, 24–25
Armitage, Richard, 144
Army Intelligence Directorate
    (Muchabarat-al Jaish), 87
Army of the Republic of Vietnam, 62
Army Times, 103
Asgari, Ali Reza, 35–36, 44, 50, 107–8, 321
Associated Press, 182
Athens, Greece, 52
Athens International Airport, 188
Atwa, Ali, 188, 192, 194*n*
Australian Army Training Team Vietnam, 62
AV-8B Harrier jump jets, 298
Aviram, Yishai, 232–34
Awali, Ghaleb, 312
Awali River, 96
Awkar, East Beirut, 158, 245, 250
Awza'i, Beirut, 44
Ayn al-Dibah, Beirut, 32
Ayn Muraysah Mosque, Beirut, 45
Ayyash, Yahya, 338

Baabda Presidential Palace, 42, 189
Baader-Meinhof Gang, 23
Baaklini Office Building, East Beirut, 158–60
Ba'albek, Lebanon, 11, 101, 107, 151, 169–71, 319
Ba'ath Party, 318, 331
Badreddine, Mustafa (alias Elias al-Sa'ab),
    116–17, 128, 150, 158, 161, 166, 179, 186, 189,
    201, 239–44, 294*n*, 302, 314, 335, 348–49
Badreddine, Sa'ada, 117, 128, 329
Baer, Robert, 49–50, 151, 175, 177
Bailey, F. Lee, 61
Barak, Ehud, 272, 273, 276, 277, 285, 301, 302,
    304, 305
Bartholomew, Richard, 108, 109, 112–13, 132,
    144, 159, 160
Basra, Iraq, 318
Basra Prison, Beirut, 200
Bastinado, 184
Battalions of Lebanese Resistance (Amal), 31
Baumel, Zechariah, 264
Bay of Pigs invasion, 65

BBC World Service, 133
Beaufort Castle, Lebanon, 303
Beck, Chip, 64–65, 67, 68, 129–32, 137–38,
    143, 146–47, 157, 210–12
Bedouin army, 24
Begin, Menachem, 18, 95
Beheshte Zahra cemetery, Tehran, 171
Beirut–Damascus Highway, 95, 96, 136
Beirut International Airport, 30, 32, 73, 96,
    104–5, 106–8, 110–11, 113, 126, 127, 175,
    188–91, 317
Beka'a Valley, Lebanon, 14, 20, 31, 33, 34, 38,
    100, 107, 111, 115, 126, 128, 136, 152, 153,
    162, 169–71, 184, 193, 234, 237, 268, 269,
    285, 286, 293
Bell AH-1S Cobras (Tzefas), 233
Ben-Avraham, Amos, 231
Bergman, Ronen, 150, 270, 348
Bergner, Kevin, 320
Berri, Nabih, 192
Bigler, Al, 122, 135, 158–62
bin Laden, Osama, 282, 290, 307, 312, 313
bin Sultan, Bandar, 177, 291
Bir al-Abd, Beirut, 32, 174–75
Biralabin, Lebanon, 111
Bird, Kai, 25, 321
Black September Organization, 15, 26, 30
BND (West Germany), 143, 265, 284, 312
Border Guards, 7, 9
Boston University, 58
Boudia, Mohammed, 338
Bourj el-Barajneh refugee camp, 104, 175,
    186, 255
Boustany, Nora, 47–48
Brazil, 281, 289
Brinkley, David, 51
British Embassy, Beirut, 49, 74, 84, 112, 121,
    124, 127, 129
Buckley, Bob, 56
Buckley, Mrs. William H., 56
Buckley, Peg, 56
Buckley, William F. Jr., 59
Buckley, William Francis, 194, 226, 227, 238,
    239, 243, 244, 253, 276, 292, 305*n*, 307,
    321, 340, 346, 347, 349
  antiques, passion for, 67–68
  apartment in Beirut of, 1–2, 122–23, 135–36
  Beirut assignment (Chief of Station),
    78–80, 83–87, 90–94, 96, 106, 108, 109,
    112–15, 118, 120, 128–32, 155

birth of, 56
burial in Arlington National Cemetery, 262
in captivity, 152–56, 162, 167–68, 171,
    173–74, 182–85, 203–5
Casey, William and, 77–80, 142–43, 149,
    157, 210
CIA recruitment of, 58–59, 61
cigarette smoke and, 54–55
with CTG (Counterterrorist Group), 52–54
death of, 185–86, 195, 197, 201–4, 208, 210,
    260, 284
deputy, relations with, 91, 133
dress and appearance of, 1, 67, 79, 83, 113,
    131, 182
education of, 57, 58
enlistment in US Army by, 57
friendships of, 64–66, 68, 69, 131, 248, 352
gold star in Memorial Wall at CIA
    headquarters, 212, 351, 352
grave in Beirut of, 185, 201, 256
history, fascination with, 57, 59–60, 67–68
interrogations and torture of, 152–54, 162,
    171, 173, 179, 185, 284
kidnapping of, 3–4, 134–38, 141–45, 155,
    156, 158
in Korean War, 58
languages spoken by, 58
last morning of freedom of, 1–2, 132–33
as librarian, 59–60
Marine barracks bombing and, 113
medals awarded to, 58, 63
memorial services for, 210–12, 261–62
military career of, 1, 57–58, 61–64
moved in captivity, 173–74
office of, 84–85
personality of, 65, 67, 69
Phoenix Program and, 63
photographs of in captivity, 181–82, 197
physical appearance of, 70, 167–68,
    182–83, 197
private life of, 67
religion of, 59
remains returned to US, 255–60, 284, 342
search and rescue efforts for, 141, 144–47,
    149–51, 157, 265
sense of humor of, 67, 68, 120
with Special Activities Division, 62
as Special Forces combat commander, 62–64
Surette, Beverly and, 70, 129, 137, 162
threats to safety of, 130–32

vehicle of, 2, 92, 133–34
videotape of in captivity, 156–57, 167–68
in Vietnam War, 61–64
Buckley, William H., 56
Bundesnachrichtendienst (CASCOPE), 23
Bunker, the, 245–46, 250–51, 267
Bureau of Alcohol, Tobacco, and
    Firearms, 289
Burton, Fred, 199, 202–3, 241n
Bush, George H. W., 15, 54, 85, 114, 247
Bush, George W., 306–7, 315, 317, 323, 339

Camp David Accords, 28
Canada, 143
Carter, Jimmy, 155
Carton, Marcel, 181
Cary Memorial Library, Lexington,
    Massachusetts, 59
Casey, Sophia, 211
Casey, William, 54, 85, 137, 146, 183, 193, 203,
    208, 211
    Buckley, William Francis and, 77–80,
        142–43, 149, 157, 210
    as CIA director, 77–78
    death of, 210
    personality of, 76, 77
    in World War II, 76
Castro, Fidel, 65
CH-46 Sea Knight helicopters, 121
CH-53 heavy transport helicopters, 233,
    286, 287
Charles C. Carson Center for Mortuary
    Affairs, 259
Cheney, Richard, 261–62, 323
Chinese Triads, 289n
Chouf Mountains, 91–92, 133
Christians, 12, 17, 24–25, 27, 33, 50, 87, 88, 92,
    96, 99, 118, 140, 175, 178, 218, 247, 301, 303
Christopher, Warren, 292
Church, Frank, 142
Church Committee, 142, 177, 307
CIA (Central Intelligence Agency), 4, 23,
    244, 292, 293
    assets in Lebanon, 15–16
    Beirut Embassy bombing and, 49–50, 54,
        55, 75, 77–78
    Buckley as Chief of Beirut Station, 78–80,
        83–87, 90–94, 96, 102–3, 106, 108, 109,
        112–15, 118–20, 127, 128–32, 135–37, 155
    Buckley as paramilitary officer, 62, 64, 66–67

CIA (*cont.*)
  Buckley kidnapping and, 142–46, 150–51, 156, 168–69, 182–83, 204, 263
  Church Committee and, 142, 307
  Counterterrorism Center (CTC), 198, 208, 226, 227, 307–8, 341, 351, 352
  CTG (Counterterrorist Group), 52–54
  Fadlallah car-bomb strike and, 177–78
  flowchart of Shiite terrorist movement, 205–6
  Higgins kidnapping and, 225, 227–28, 237
  Iraq War and, 323
  Levin escape and, 174
  Memorial Wall of, 212, 350–52
  Mossad and, 308, 324
  Mughniyeh, Imad and, 207–10, 313
  Mughniyeh assassination and, 338–41
  Near East Division, 43, 93, 146, 147, 174, 183, 203
  9/11 terrorist attacks and, 306–9
  Office of Technical Services, 84
  Phoenix Program, 62–63
  President's Commission on CIA Activities within the United States and, 142
  recruitment of Buckley, William Francis, 58–59, 61
  return of Buckley's body and, 259, 260
  rotation of officers in Beirut, 89–90
  with Special Activities Division, 62
  Special Operations Group, 53
  Wyman, Sam and, 69
Civil War, 57
Clarridge, Duane "Dewey," 198–99
Clemenceau (aircraft carrier), 114
Clinton, Bill, 283, 292–93, 298–99
Cobra Sting, 285–87
Cogan, Chuck, 78, 79, 90, 146
Colby, William, 210
Cold War, 14, 52, 53, 118, 143, 210, 263, 295
Colombia, 281, 289*n*
Columbia University, 59
Commodore Hotel, West Beirut, 101
Compressed-butane gas canisters, 111
Concord and Lexington, Battles of, 60
Corniche, Beirut, 38, 39, 43, 72, 74, 84, 112, 120, 121, 130, 159, 250
Country Club Junction Massacre, 28
Crocker, Ryan Clark, 47, 247–49, 256, 257, 341–42

Crusades, 303
CSIS (Canada), 143
Cuba, 65
Cyprus, 131, 196

Dagan, Meir, 29, 300, 310–12, 323–24, 341
Damascus, Syria, 326–31
Damour, Lebanon, 178
Daoud, Daoud, 222
Da'wa Party, 268
Day of Martyrs, 11
Dayan, Ilana, 310
Defense, US Department of, 42, 84, 106, 145, 217, 225, 227–28, 238, 259, 260, 261
Deir ez-Zor nuclear reactor, 322–24
Derickson, Uli, 188
Deuel, Mike, 352
Deuxième Bureau (Second Bureau), 41, 87, 178
DGSE (France), 209
Dhahran Air Force Base, 293
DIA (Defense Intelligence Agency), 161, 203
DiFranco, Eddie, 109
Dillon, Robert Sherwood, 41, 43, 46, 49, 73
Diplomatic Security Service (DSS), 198, 203, 225, 241*n*, 246–47, 249, 250, 253, 289, 297, 315
Dir Qanoun an-Nahr, Lebanon, 10
Dirani, Abdel Karim, 286
Dirani, Ali, 286
Dirani, Mustafa, 235, 236, 285–88, 304*n*
Doha, Qatar, 297
Dover Air Force Base, 259
Downing Commission, 295
Draper, Morris, 157
Dromi, Uri, 282
Druze, 17, 24–25, 88, 92, 96, 105, 119, 129, 175
Druze mountains, 38
Dubs, Adolph, 158
Dulles, Allen, 339
Dur, Philip, 144

Eagleburger, Lawrence, 144
Eagleton, William L., 170, 201
East Germany, 86
Egypt, 140
  Camp David Accords, 28
Ehrlich, Dov, 310, 311
Eichmann, Adolf, 309
Eichnold, Dubi, 8
Ein el-Hilweh refugee camp, 312
Eitan, Rafi, 309

EL/M-2070 TecSar (Ofek-8) reconnaissance satellite, 324–25
Engineer Officer Course, Fort Belvoir, 57
Entebbe Airport hostage rescue, 196, 231, 265
Erdogan, Recep Tayyip, 323
Executive Order 11905, 177
Executive Order 12333, 177
Exercise Rugged Nautilus '96, 296

FAA, 225
F-4E Phantom II, 232–34
Facility 1391, 287
Fadlallah, Sheikh Muhammad Hussein, 31–34, 175–78, 206, 267, 268, 279
Faraci, Phylis Nancy, 49
Farash, Hussein, 130
Farsi language, 33, 98, 101, 331
Fatah guerrilla army, 25–30
FBI (Federal Bureau of Investigation), 198, 203, 205, 206, 208, 225, 237, 241n, 284, 288, 289, 291–93, 297, 313
Feldman, Zvi, 264
FINNBATT (Finnish Battalion), 216
First Parachute Chasseur Regiment (France), 112
FLETC (Federal Law Enforcement Training Center), 198
Flotilla 13 (Israel), 267
Fontaine, Marcel, 181
Force 17 (Fatah), 28–30, 36, 196
Ford, Gerald, 142
Foreign Internal Defense (FID) missions, 157
Foreign Legion, 45
Foreign Service, 38, 41, 249
Fort Belvoir, Virginia, 57
Fort Knox, Kentucky, 57
Fortier, Donald, 144
Foster, Ben (pseudonym), 249–51, 253–54, 256, 257
France, 86, 103, 209
Francis, Ghadi, 33
Frangieh, Suleiman, 40
French barracks (Beirut), 112–14
French Embassy, Kuwait, 116
French peacekeepers, 45, 227
Friedman, Thomas L., 50–51

G8 Summit (2006), 315, 316
Galilee, 12
Gallant, Pete, 73, 74

Gannon, Matthew, 39n
Gannon, Rich, 38–41, 43, 46, 158
Gargano, Edward J., 121
Gates, Robert, 261, 351
Gaza Strip, 7, 271, 283, 305, 311, 312, 327
Geagea, Samir, 33
Gehlen, Reinhard, 312
Gemayel, Amine, 16, 42, 51, 114
Gemayel, Bashir, 13–16, 41
General Staff Reconnaissance Unit (Israel), 267
Geraghty, Colonel, 113
German Red Army Faction, 168
Geva, Eli, 18
Ghazali, Roustam, 333
Going All the Way: Christian Warlords, Israeli Adventurers, and the War in Lebanon (Randal), 123
Golan Heights, 348
Goldman, Adam, 338
The Good Spy: The Life and Death of Robert Ames (Bird), 25, 321
Göring, Hermann, 202
Gougelmann, Tucker Pierre Edward, 65, 132
Gray, Al, 219
Great Britain, 23, 49, 103
Great War, 57
Guadalcanal, 65

Haas, Kenneth Eugene, 16, 43, 45, 49, 50, 78, 79
Habib, Philip, 14, 42, 49, 157
Hadley, Stephen, 323
Haig, Alexander, 14, 76, 120
Haiga, Israel, 28
Hale, Nathan, 198, 350
Hamadi, Abdel Hadi, 236
Hamadi, Mohammed Ali, 188, 189, 191, 194n
Hamas, 235, 283, 290, 305, 326, 327
Hamiyah, Talal, 302
Hammam al-Shatt, Tunisia, 196
Hamshari, Mahmoud, 338
Hannibal Directive, 316
Harakat al-Muqawamah al-Islamiyyah (Islamic Resistance Movement) (see Hamas)
Harb, Sheikh Ragheb, 230, 269, 271, 273
Harel, Isser, 308
Hariri, Rafiq, 313–14, 316, 333, 346
Harvard University, 59
Hassuna, Muhammed, 44–46

INDEX

Hay es Salaam, Lebanon, 104
Hayden, Michael, 324, 341
Hegan, Charles, 165–66
Heidad, Nihad, 328
Hesp, Hazel, 188
Hezbollah: The Global Footprint of Lebanon's Party of God (Levitt), 196n
Hezbollah (Party of God), 19n, 33, 50, 107, 108, 112, 116, 124, 128, 130, 131, 150, 161, 175, 191, 195, 199, 207, 226–27, 283, 307, 312–13, 314–15, 320, 327, 332, 333, 345, 347, 348
  Amal, schism with, 226–27
  Badreddine and, 242–43
  Buckley kidnapping and, 152
  establishment of, 20–21
  flag of, 20, 303
  Higgins kidnapping and, 224–28
  hijacking by, 165–66
  in Iraq, 19n, 33, 50, 107, 108, 112, 116, 128, 130, 131, 150, 161, 175, 191, 195, 199, 207, 283, 307, 318–20
  Israeli captives of, 264–67, 284–86
  Majlis al-Shura, 209
  Mughniyeh as commander in, 209–10
  Mughniyeh's assassination and, 335, 343–45
  Musawi and, 267–69, 272–79
  Obeid interrogation and, 235–36
  Organization of the Oppressed on Earth, 224
  Saudi Arabia and, 292–94
  Sudan and, 290
  training of volunteers, 101
  TWA Flight 847 hijacking and, 287–88
  Weir kidnapping and, 155
Higgins, Chrissy, 262
Higgins, Robin, 217–18, 221, 225, 226, 228, 229, 261, 276
Higgins, William R. (Rich), 243, 248, 265, 287, 305n, 340, 347
  burial in Quantico, Virginia, 262
  death of, 236–38, 260
  kidnapping of, 223–28, 231, 235, 236, 263
  memorial service for, 261–62
  military career of, 217–19
  with OGL (Observer Group Lebanon), 218–22
  photograph in captivity, 228–29
  return of remains of, 253–55, 257–60, 284, 342
  security for, 219–20

Hijabs, 99, 102, 328
Hitler, Adolf, 77
Hixon, Deborah M., 49
Hobeika, Elie, 178–79, 179n
Holm, Richard L., 51–53, 77, 79, 351–52
Holocaust, 310–11
Hope, Bob, 114
Hostage (Miron), 168–69
Hostage Location Task Force (HLTF), 198–200, 202, 203, 210, 226, 237
Hostage-Rescue Team (HRT), 297
Houari Boumediene International Airport, Algiers, 190, 241
Hussein, Imam, 11
Hussein, King of Jordan, 24, 186n
Hussein, Saddam, 97, 102, 116, 139, 171, 269, 293, 306, 318
HYPNOSIS, 150

Ignatius, David, 50
Imam Musa Sadr Brigades, 187
Imam Rida Mosque, Beirut, 32
Incident Response Team (IRT), 77, 146
Internal Security Force (ISF), 252
International Herald Tribune, 133
International peacekeepers, 13, 14, 19, 32, 45, 103, 104, 215–17, 219, 227
Iran, 31–34, 50, 75, 97–103, 106–7, 115, 116, 126–28, 130, 151–53, 155, 156, 170, 171–74, 178, 284, 289, 290, 299, 306, 307, 315, 316, 321, 347
Iran Air Flight 655, 238
Iran-Contra affair, 210, 225, 239
Iran-Iraq War, 11, 20, 97, 98, 100, 102, 116, 171, 172, 201, 243, 296, 328
Iranian Cultural Center, Damascus, 329, 330
Iranian Embassy, Beirut, 127, 152n, 186, 206, 279
Iranian Embassy, Damascus, 171, 206, 330, 332
Iranian Revolution, 18, 20, 51
Iranian Revolutionary Guard, 20, 32–36, 97, 100, 113, 127, 128, 153, 161, 172–74, 185, 206, 227, 229, 235, 278, 283, 285, 289, 302, 318
Iraq, 18, 241–42, 265, 268, 293, 306, 318–20
Iraq War, 322
Iraqi embassy, Beirut, 40, 41
Irgun, 18
ISA, 161
ISIS, 348
Islamic Amal, 107, 116, 129, 218, 222–26, 234, 235, 264, 285

Islamic Jihad Organization, 51, 130, 181, 188, 189, 197, 257, 271, 280–81, 290, 305, 312
Islamic Republic Embassy, Beirut, 196
Islamic Republic Iranian Air Force (IRIAF), 172
Israel, 116, 118, 127, 229, 244, 333
    Buckley kidnapping and, 150–51
    Camp David Accords, 28
    captured Palestinian documents and, 23
    captured soldiers and airmen of, 234, 262, 264–67, 283–84
    Cobra Sting, 285–87
    Country Club Junction Massacre, 28
    EL/M-2070 TecSar (Ofek-8) reconnaissance satellite, 324–25
    First Golani Infantry Brigade, 233
    Hezbollah and, 282, 301–5, 312–13, 315–17
    invasion of Lebanon (1982), 11–18, 22, 30, 41, 76, 216, 285, 300–1, 309, 317, 318
    Mossad, 29, 34n, 86, 97, 139–41, 177, 265, 274, 283, 284, 288, 289, 302, 308–12, 324, 326, 336, 338–39, 341, 343
    Mughniyeh assassination and, 338–39, 341
    Operation Handsome Young Man, 231–32, 237
    Operation Litani, 28–29
    Operation Millstone, 95, 101
    Operation Nighttime (Sha'at Ha'Layla), 267–77
    Operation Orchard, 321–24, 333
    Operation Peace for Galilee, 12, 17, 224
    Sixty-Ninth "Hammer" Squadron, 232, 323
    TWA Flight 847 and, 189, 190, 192, 193
    Tyre military headquarters bombing (First Tyre Disaster), 7–11, 18, 34–35
    UAVs (unmanned aerial vehicles) and, 224
    war for independence (1948), 18, 24–25, 216
    withdrawal from Lebanon, 301–3, 305
Israel Air Force (IAF), 170, 174, 196, 230, 232–34, 265, 266, 277, 284, 296, 309, 317, 323, 348
Israel Defense Forces (IDF), 7–9, 12–13, 17, 18, 28, 30, 35, 95–96, 140, 178, 220, 224, 233, 266–67, 271, 272, 285–86, 289, 301, 302, 304, 315–17, 319
Israeli Embassy, Buenos Aires, 279–81, 289
ITALBATT (Italian Battalion), 222
Italy, 86, 103, 147, 168, 315
Iwo Jima, 49, 111

Iyad, Abu (Salah Khalaf), 29–30
Izz-al-Din (Ezzadine), Hassan, 188, 194n, 240–41

Jackson, Jesse, 210
Jacobsen, David, 180, 202–4
Japanese Red Army, 23, 234–35
Jebchit, Lebanon, 230–32, 236, 269–73, 276
Jenco, Lawrence Martin, 167, 181, 201–3, 210
Jennings, Peter, 51
Jerusalem, 26, 216, 272, 305, 308, 333
Jibril, Ahmed, 218, 234, 235, 238n, 326
Johnson, Luke (pseudonym), 111, 115, 135
Johnston, Frank J., 49
Joint Chiefs of Staff, 125, 144, 146, 193, 198, 263
Joint Comprehensive Plan of Action, 347
Jones, Alan (pseudonym), 96–97, 137
Jordan, 24–26, 186, 337n
Jounieh, Lebanon, 140
Jumblatt, Walid, 124
Justice, US Department of, 207–9, 241, 292

Karantina, Beirut, 127
Kassis, Louis, 88, 129, 133
Kassis, Simon, 88–89
Katkov, Arkady, 195
Katyusha rockets, 22, 279, 316
Katz, Yehuda, 264
Kelley, Paul X., 110, 114
Kennedy, John F., 53
Kerr, Malcolm, 124–25, 127
Kfar Suseh, Damascus, 329–30, 335, 337
KGB, 22, 29, 53, 66, 74, 86, 122, 194, 196n
Khalde, Lebanon, 96
Khalil, Ezzeddine Sheikh, 312
Khamenei, Sayyed Ali Hosseini, 278
Kharg Island, 172
Khobar Towers bombing, 293–95, 299
Khomeini, Ayatollah, 10, 21, 31–33, 97–100, 102, 107, 134, 139, 171, 175, 192, 230
Kilburn, Peter, 162–63
King Abdulaziz International Airport, Jeddah, 291, 293
Kirya, Tel Aviv, 266, 267, 269, 271, 272
Kissinger, Henry, 40
Kollek, Teddy, 308
Konstantinovsky Palace, Strelna, Russia, 315
Korean War, 41, 58, 65
Kurd rebels, 139
Kuwait, 116, 117, 128, 150, 189, 195, 239–42

INDEX

Kuwait Airway Airbus A310 jetliner, 164–66
Kuwait Airways Flight 422, 240–41
Kuwait International Airport, 116
Kuwait National Petroleum Company,
    Raytheon, 116
Kuwait Seventeen, 166

La'ka'm (Scientific Liaison Bureau), 309
Lake, Anthony, 291
Laos, 53
Lebanese Armed Forces (LAF), 17, 19, 42,
    87, 92, 96, 104, 105, 114, 118, 124, 126, 127,
    129, 140, 157, 178, 189, 246, 285
Lebanese Ministry of Interior, 207
Lebanese National Covenant of 1943, 16
Lehi Group, 274
Levin, Jerry, 130, 156, 168, 170–71, 174, 210
Levin, Lucille, 170
Levitt, Matthew, 196n
Lewis, James F., 49
Lewis, Monique N., 49
Libya, 28, 30–31, 74n, 175, 238n, 322
Litani River, 24, 28, 29, 230, 270, 303
Lod Airport massacre, 235
Long Hai Mountains, Vietnam, 63
Losey, George, 105
Luang Prabang Province, Laos, 62, 64
Lukow, Poland, 310

Maameltein, Lebanon, 140
MacArthur, Douglas, 58
Mahdi Army, 318
Majzoub, Mahmoud, 312
Malka, Amos, 302
Maness, Michael, 295
Marine Corps barracks bombing (1983),
    109–15, 126, 158, 172, 295, 302, 347
Maronite Christians, 12, 87, 88, 96, 140, 247, 303
Marsh, John O., 211
Mashghara, Lebanon, 228
Mashhad, Iran, 241
Massoud, Ahmad Shah, 314
Massoud, Rihab, 292
Mazzetti, Mark, 307–8
McCormack, Sean, 341
McFarlane, Robert, 144
McVeigh, Timothy, 292
Medford, Massachusetts, 56, 57, 59n
Mehrabad International Airport, Tehran, 165
Meitav, Assaf, 233

Meloy, Francis E. Jr., 40
Merhi, Hassan Habib, 315
MI5, 23
MI6, 23, 86, 143
Middle East Airlines, 191, 291
Miers, David, 160
Military Assistance Command Vietnam
    (MACV), 61–62
Miron, Murray S., 168–69
Mitterand, François, 208
MNF (Multinational Force), 103, 104, 126
Mohamed, Ali, 290
Mohtashamipur, Ali Akbar, 106–7
Mokhsi, Ziad, 338
Moreau, Arthur S., 144
Moro, Aldo, 168
Moroney, Maureen, 56–57, 59, 210, 211, 261
Mosler safes, 85
Mossad, 29, 34n, 86, 97, 139–41, 177, 207, 265,
    274, 283, 284, 288, 289, 302, 308–12, 324,
    326, 336, 338–39, 341, 343
Mottaki, Manouchehr, 345
Mount Dov, 304
Mousavi, Hojatoleslam Ahmad, 331–33
Moyne, Lord, 274
Moynihan, Daniel Patrick, 77
MR-I Guerrilla Battalions (BGs), 64
Mughniyeh, Amina, 24, 343
Mughniyeh, Imad Fayez, 165, 167, 172, 176,
    179, 181, 184, 195, 196, 196n, 200, 204,
    206, 228, 236, 268, 287, 301, 305, 306, 316
    Asgari, Ali Reza and, 35–36, 44, 321
    assassination of, 333–42
    attempts to capture or kill, 208–9, 291–93,
        297–99, 302, 324, 326
    birth of, 23–24
    brother-in-law's release and, 117, 128, 186,
        239–41
    Buckley kidnapping and, 150, 151, 153, 154,
        173, 174, 182, 185–86, 201
    childhood of, 25
    Fadlallah security detail and, 32–34, 177
    Fatah and, 25–30
    on FBI most-wanted list, 313
    funeral of, 337, 343–46
    Hariri assassination and, 314
    in Iraq, 318–19
    Marine barracks bombing and, 107, 112
    meetings in Damascus, 326–28, 333
    missile named in honor of, 347

mistress of, 328, 329
negotiations with, 243–44
photographs and videos of, 207, 343–44
physical appearance of, 26, 328, 343
religion and, 33
response to Musawi assassination, 278–79
Saudi Arabia and, 294, 294n
security and, 284–85, 327
status of, 290
Stethem murder and, 208
in Sudan, 290, 291
travel in Europe by, 208–9
TWA Flight 847 hijacking and, 189–91,
    193, 206
Tyre military headquarters bombing and,
    34–35
US Embassy bombings and, 44, 45, 50, 161
wife of, 117, 128, 329
Mughniyeh, Jihad, 176–77, 179, 348
Mughniyeh, Mahmoud Jawad, 24, 345
Mughniyeh clan, 23–25, 27, 29, 32
Muhammad, 100
Mundy, Carl E. Jr., 261, 262
Munich Olympics Massacre (1972), 15, 26, 30,
    43, 338
Murrah Federal Building, Oklahoma City,
    Oklahoma, 292
Musawi, Sheikh Hussein Abbas, 31–32, 107,
    108, 112, 114, 116, 128, 206, 228, 236,
    267–69, 272–80, 284
Musawi, Siham, 276, 278
Muslim Brotherhood, 283
Mustafa (pseudonym), 220
Mutaharri, Ayatollah Morteza, 7

Nabatiyah, Lebanon, 230, 237, 275
Nahara, Ramzi, 312
Nahariya, Israel, 221
Najaf, Iraq, 32, 107, 175, 268
Naqoura, Lebanon, 221, 223
Nasrallah, Sheikh Hassan, 108, 242, 244, 267,
    304, 320, 332, 346, 348
Nasty Boys, 246–47, 249, 250, 252–54, 256,
    257, 277
National Security Agency (NSA), 153, 161,
    186, 306
National Security Council (NSC), 125, 144,
    198, 208, 225
NBC News, 54
Netanyahu, Benjamin, 287, 311

New Georgia, 65
New York Times, 75, 167, 189, 237, 306–8
Newsweek, 133, 136
Nezhad, Feirud Mehdi, 190
Night of the Pitchfork, 271
9/11 terrorist attacks, 306–9, 314
Nine-millimeter pistols, 93, 184
Ninth Parachute Chasseur Regiment
    (France), 112
Nir, Ofer, 233
North, Oliver, 144–46
North Korea, 306, 322, 331
North Vietnamese Army, 62

Obeid, Mona, 231
Obeid, Sheikh Abdel Karim, 230–32, 235–37,
    265, 284, 304n
Oberammergau, West Germany, 58
Office of Islamic Liberation Movements, 20
Office of Strategic Services (OSS), 76,
    142, 210
Officer Candidate School, 57
OGL (Observer Group Lebanon), 218–22
Okamoto, Kozo, 234
Olmert, Ehud, 323, 341
Operation Damocles, 274
Operation Desert Storm, 64n, 249
Operation Golden Ox Returns, 297–98
Operation Handsome Young Man, 230–32, 237
Operation Litani, 28–29
Operation Millstone, 95
Operation Nighttime (Sha'at Ha'Layla),
    267–77
Operation Orchard, 321–24, 333
Operation Peace for Galilee, 12, 17, 224
Operation Wooden Leg, 196
Organization of the Oppressed on Earth,
    224, 236
Orient-Le Jour, L', 168
Ortega, Alexander, 105
Osirak nuclear reactor, Iraq, 18, 265
Ottoman Turks, 92, 331
Ouzai, Lebanon, 103, 104

Paganelli, Robert, 147–48, 149
Pakistan, 39, 43, 68, 248n, 297, 307
Palestinian Islamic Jihad (PIJ), 271, 312, 326–27
Palestinians, 10–17, 22–34, 39, 40, 89, 96, 103,
    104, 140, 186, 192, 216, 218, 232, 233, 255,
    266, 271, 285, 300–1, 311, 312

INDEX

Pan Am Flight 103, 39n, 238n

Panetta, Leon E., 350

Paraguay, 289

Patrice Lumumba University, Moscow, 53

Patton, George, 62

Pearl Harbor, Japanese bombing of, 57

Peres, Shimon, 192

Peri, Yaakov, 234, 280

Peterson v. Islamic Republic of Iran, 109n

PETN (pentaerythritol tetranitrate), 46, 111

Phalange Party (Lebanon), 13

Philadelphia Inquirer, 228

Philippines, 57

Phoenix Program, 62–63

Phuoc Tuy Province, Vietnam, 63

Picco, Giandomenico, 243–44

PLO (Palestine Liberation Organization), 22, 26, 29, 101, 103, 167, 196, 207

Poindexter, John M., 145

Pollard, Jonathan Jay, 309

Popular Arab Islamic Conference (PAIC), 290–91

Popular Front for the Liberation of Palestine (PFLP), 40, 338

Popular Front for the Liberation of Palestine–General Command (PFLP–GC), 218, 234, 238n, 326

Powell, Colin, 219

Presidential Decision Directive 39 (PDD-39), 293

President's Commission on CIA Activities within the United States, 142

Princeton University, 59

Prisoner of War Medal, 260n

Provincial Reconnaissance Units (PRUs), 62–63

Provisional Irish Republican Army, 23

Psycholinguistic analysis, 168, 237

Pugh, Bonnie, 74

Pugh, David, 74

Pugh, Robert, 137

Purple Heart, 58

Putin, Vladimir, 315

Qasir, Ahmed, 10–11, 18, 34

Qasr Naba, Lebanon, 286

Qom, Iran, 31

Quayle, Dan, 262

Quds Force, 97–98, 100, 101, 107, 278, 320, 327–28

Rabin, Yitzhak, 234, 236, 283, 287, 308

Ra'ed (pseudonym), 252–53, 256

Ramat David Air Force Base, Israel, 323

Ramlet al-Baida, Lebanon, 40, 112

Randal, Jonathan C., 50, 123

Ras Beirut, 122–23, 135

Rashidieh refugee camp, 223

Raymesh, Lebanon, 303

RDX (cyclotrimethylenetrinitramine), 334, 338

Reagan, Nancy, 75, 193

Reagan, Ronald, 15, 41, 42, 49, 54, 74–76, 85, 104, 105, 113, 125, 127, 143, 144, 147, 155, 156, 172–73, 177, 193–94, 208, 211, 225

Red Brigades, 168

Regier, Frank, 130

Republic of Congo, 53

Reservists, Israeli, 8, 23, 95, 300, 301

Reuters, 182

Revell, Oliver "Buck," 154

Revere, Paul, 60

Revolutionary Organization 17 November, 52

Revolutionary War, 60

RF-4E Phantom reconnaissance flights, 267

Rhein Main Air Force Base, Germany, 193

Rice, Condoleezza, 315

Rice, Major General, 144

Riyadh military compound bombing, 293

Roberts, Sir David, 49

Rockefeller, Nelson, 142

Ross, Joel, 225, 228, 235n

Royal Air Force (RAF), 247, 254–55, 257

Royal Jordanian Airline, 186n

Russell, Stephen E., 110

Russian Mafia, 289n

Sabra refugee camp massacre, 14, 18, 33, 41, 103, 104, 179, 248

Saguy, Uri, 266, 270–73, 285

Saint-George Yacht Club and Marina, Beirut, 38

Salah, Abdel Majid, 222, 223

Salameh, Ali Hassan "the Red Prince," 15, 16, 25–26, 29–30, 43

Saleh, Ali Hussein, 312

Salibi, Kamal, 125

Satish Dhawan Space Centre, India, 324

Saudi Arabia, 30, 38, 177, 291–95, 313, 314

Saudi Embassy, Beirut, 130

SAVAK, 35, 97, 108

SAVAMA (National Information and Security Organization of Iran), 97

Sayara al-Difa (Defense Companies), 148, 193

Sayeret Golani, 233, 266

Sayeret Mat'kal, 231, 267, 272, 284–86

Sayeret Mat'kal General Staff Reconnaissance Unit, 34n

Scheid, John F., 60

Schleyer, Hanns Martin, 168

Schultz, George P., 76, 120, 144, 172

Second Lebanon War, 319, 346

Secretaría de Informaciones de Estado (SIDE), 280

Sécurité Militaire (Algeria), 86

Semtex, 18

Senate Select Committee to Study Governmental Operations with Respect to Intelligence Activities, 142

Servizio per le Informazioni e la Sicurezza Militare (Italy), 86

Shah of Iran, 35, 97

Shalah, Ramadan Abdullah Mohammad, 326

Shamir, Yitzhak, 274–75, 277

Sharif, Omar, 38

Sharon, Ariel, 11, 305, 310, 311

Shatila refugee camp massacre, 14, 18, 33, 41, 103, 104, 179, 248

Sheikh Abdullah Barracks, Lebanon, 20, 35–36, 113, 128, 151, 152–53, 161–62, 164, 170–71, 173, 174, 206, 319

Shiites, 10, 17, 19–21, 24–34, 40, 44, 50, 88, 97–101, 103, 104, 107, 114, 115, 126–28, 137, 162, 163, 172, 174–75, 179, 184, 186, 189, 190, 192–93, 195, 205, 207, 215, 218, 225, 227, 233, 281, 285, 288, 289, 292–94, 301, 303, 304n, 305n, 306, 314, 318, 319, 328 347, 348

Shin Bet, 8, 9, 19, 139, 234, 280, 288, 289, 338

Shiqaqi, Fathi, 326

Sigheh, practice of, 99–100

Silva, Peer de, 152

Silver Star, 53, 58, 63, 262

Skull and Bones secret society, 59

SLA (South Lebanese Army), 17, 218, 301, 303

Smith, Glen (pseudonym), 102

Soderberg, Nancy, 298–99

Solomon Islands, 65

South Vietnamese Special Forces, 62

Soviet Embassy, Beirut, 74

Soviet Union, 12, 14, 22, 29, 52–53, 66, 74, 75, 86, 140, 143, 194–95, 196n, 210, 228, 229, 271, 331

Spanish American War, 57

Spartan camps, 22, 23, 26

Speakes, Larry, 197

Special Access Program (SAP), 198

Special Air Service (Britain), 177, 231

Special Forces Officers Course, 61

SS Ibn Tufail, 297–99

Stanford, William, 166

State, US Department of, 38–39, 41, 49, 74, 76, 84, 125, 145, 147, 156, 159, 172, 198, 208, 209, 225, 245, 248, 249, 277, 292, 315

Stethem, Robert Dean, 191, 194, 194n, 206, 208, 288

Stoneham, Massachusetts, 56

Strelna, Russia, 315

Sudan, 13, 77, 155, 290–91

Suleimani, Qassem, 327–28

Sunnis, 15, 17, 24–25, 27, 50, 87, 88, 99, 175, 282, 285, 306, 314, 330, 348

Suq al-Gharb, Lebanon, 105

Surette, Beverly, 70, 129, 137, 162, 210–12, 261

Syria, 12, 14, 75, 105, 126, 140, 144–45, 147–50, 169–70, 226–27, 264, 284, 314, 322–24, 327–31, 334–38, 348

Syrian Air Force Intelligence Directorate, 17

Syrian Military Intelligence Directorate, 17, 86

Tarawa ARG, 296, 297

Tayr Dibba, Lebanon, 23–24, 25, 27, 35

Tel Aviv, Israel, 266, 273, 276, 340

Temporary marriage, 99–100

Terrorist Incident Work Group (TIWG), 144, 145

Testrake, John, 188–91

Tevel, 265

Toufahta, Lebanon, 275

Treasury, US Department of the, 225

The Triple Agent: The Al-Qaeda Mole Who Infiltrated the CIA (Warrick), 337n

TWA Flight 800, 296

TWA Flight 847, 188–94, 206, 207, 240, 287

Tyre, Lebanon, 7, 9–11, 18, 19, 23, 31, 32, 101, 222–23

Tzafrir, Eliezer, 139–41

INDEX

UAVs (unmanned aerial vehicles), 224
UNIFIL (United Nations Interim Force in
    Lebanon), 215–18, 221–25, 227, 238
Unit 504 (Israeli military intelligence), 8,
    139, 287
US Air Force military hospital, Wiesbaden,
    West Germany, 201-2, 203
US Air Force Security Police, 202
US Embassy, Beirut, 37–43, 84, 120, 127, 134–35,
    224, 225, 245–47, 249–52, 254, 255, 277
    Acoustic Conference Room, 44, 73–74
    bombings of, 44–51, 54, 72, 73, 75, 86, 105,
        161, 171, 172, 248, 321, 346, 347
    relocation to British Embassy, 74
US Embassy, Damascus, 170
US Embassy, Doha, 247
US Embassy, Islamabad, 39, 297
US Embassy, Kuwait, 116
US Embassy, Riyadh, 292
US Embassy, Tehran, 39
US Embassy Annex, East Beirut, 158–62,
    171, 172
US forces
    Army Reserves, 61
    Battalion Landing Team, 104
    Eleventh Special Forces Group
        (Airborne), 61
    First Cavalry Division, 58
    Marine Corps, 32, 64, 103–4, 107, 109–15,
        125, 127, 128
    Marine Corps Security Guard (MSG),
        39–40, 46–47
    Marine Raiders, 65
    Navy Amphibious Ready Group (ARG), 296
    Navy SEALs, 73, 296
    Sixth Fleet, 114, 120, 254
    Special Boat Squadron, 296
    Special Forces, 19, 42, 320
    Special Forces Fifth Group (Airborne), 157
    Third Marines, 217
    Thirteenth Marine Expeditionary Unit
        Special Operations Capable, 296
    Thirty-Second Marine Amphibious
        Unit, 104
    320th Special Forces Detachment, 61
    Twenty-Fourth Marine Amphibious Unit,
        104, 109–11, 127
    Twenty-Second Marine Expeditionary
        Unit, 49
US Secret Service, 158, 315

USS Guadalcanal, 46–47
USS New Jersey, 105, 114, 119, 129
USS Nimitz, 192
USS Tarawa, 296
USS Vincennes, 238
UNTSO (United Nations Truce Supervision
    Organization), 216, 219–22
UTA Flight 772, 74n
Uzis, 98

Vadset, Martin O., 216
VBIED (vehicle-borne improvised explosive
    device), 41, 46, 176, 295
VBSS (Visit, Board, Search, and Seizure), 297
Veil (Woodward), 177
Venezuela, 281, 289, 331
Vietcong, 62
Vietnam War, 53, 61–64, 142, 217
Visnews, 167
Voice of Lebanon, 291
Voice of the People, 269
Votaw, Albert, 75n

Waite, Terry, 243
Waring, Robert O., 40
Warrick, Joby, 337n
Warsaw Pact, 14, 30, 52
Washington, George, 62, 68
Washington Post, 47, 178, 338, 339
Webster, William, 211
Weinberger, Caspar, 15, 76, 114, 217, 219, 227
Weir, Benjamin, 154–56, 168, 181, 200, 210–11
Welch, Richard Skeffington, 52
West Bank, 7, 271, 283, 305, 311, 327
West Germany, 23, 58, 194n, 201-2, 311
Wing, Joyce, 211, 261
Woodward, Bob, 177
World Trade Center bombing (1993), 282, 297
Wyman, Laurie, 69, 148
Wyman, Sam, 68–69, 78, 79, 147–50

Yale University, 59
Yassin, Ahmed, 235
Yedioth Aharonoth, 271, 277
Yousef, Ramzi, 297

Zahlé, Lebanon, 286
Zahrani Bridge, 275, 276
Zahrani River, 271, 276
Zeikel, Jeremy, 4, 120–21, 135–37